D0758646

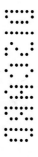

*Modern Drama
from
Communist China*

MODERN DRAMA from COMMUNIST CHINA

edited by WALTER J. MESERVE,
Indiana University
and RUTH I. MESERVE

1970

NEW YORK: New York University Press
LONDON: University of London Press Ltd.

Copyright © 1970 by New York University
Library of Congress Catalog Card Number: 77-92524

SBN: 8147-0302-x (cloth)
SBN: 8147-0491-3 (paper)

Manufactured in the United States of America

Preface

The constantly changing party line of Communist China demands a chronological analysis of the dramas in this volume. In this arrangement the plays, with the Introduction, suggest the development or the change in dramatic literature, theater, and politics in Communist China from 1919 to the current "cultural revolution." All of the plays included here have been either performed on the Chinese Communist stage and/or published by the Communist press — which means that they have been at one time, and in some instances still are, acceptable to the Communist Party leaders. Propaganda, then, or art as a weapon for propagandistic purposes, must remain the primary objective in these plays. Our purpose in the Introduction has been to provide a commentary on developing Communist attitudes toward drama which make the plays understandable in the social, political, and theater milieu. We have included comments by Chinese critics who may or may not delight in the truth, but their appraisals are a valid part of Communist China's party-controlled dramatic criticism. We have also suggested an assessment of the plays from our own critical position with the hopeful result that the reader may enjoy the plays for whatever they bring to him.

RIM

WJM

Contents

*Modern Drama
from
Communist China*

INTRODUCTION

The drama of any culture or country vividly and sometimes violently reflects the ideas and ideals, the conflicts and complacencies, the struggles as well as the sterility of that society. Theater presents a mirror image, as one might, at one time, have shown quite clearly in the drama of China. When political power struggles occur, however, and censorship becomes a miasma enveloping the artist, the mirror image is frequently shattered. All that remains are a few slivers of that truthful reflection, and these are quickly removed when it is discovered that they scratch or cut the picture image of society that the controlling power demands. The new Communist drama is not a mirror of society but an intriguing picture of society—a picture of red banners waving everywhere, of heroic deeds by workers, peasants, and soldiers (especially women), all of whom are armed with Mao Tse-tung's thoughts on art and literature. This is the new Communist drama, and the picture is frequently artless and sterile, without depth, without truth, and without reality. But it is, nevertheless, an extremely powerful drama because it is being used as a dominant force in the creation of a new Communist society.

Modern China begins with the May 4, 1919, Movement and the creation of the Communist Party in 1921. Immediately, there emerged a revolutionary movement in Chinese literature. In contrast to the past, the vernacular style of writing was emphasized, literature was popularized, new literary societies were established, and the number of literary publications was increased. At the same time, all literary and artistic activity, while serving the masses, was emphasized as a weapon in the political struggle to oppose feudalism, imperialism, and the bourgeoisie. In the terms of the Communist writers, the objectives of this new literature must be to free the masses from oppression and to help agitate as well as organize the masses in their struggle, while presenting a clear understanding of life from the proletarian view. Such objectives obviously meant that new literature was necessary, since any attempt to raise the level of the masses to appreciate true and great art would be interpreted as a refusal to serve the masses.

1

By the early 1930's Mao Tse-tung was giving practical advice to the Workers' and Peasants' Red Army on art and literature. From that time on, and particularly after Mao took undisputed leadership of the Communist Party (at a meeting of the Political Bureau of the Central Committee of the Party in Tsunyi, Kweichow Province, January, 1935), art and literature became an integral part of the Red Army's political work. The following year (August 1, 1936) writers and artists in China agreed to use their pens in a united front against Japanese aggression. On March 27, 1938, the All-China Resist-the-Enemy Federation was formed in Hankow and immediately called upon writers to join the army or to go to the countryside in order to carry out intensive propaganda for resistance. The effect of the writers' activities through this Federation (which joined with other literary organizations to become the All-China Federation of Writers in July of 1949 on the "eve of the Communist takeover") is not difficult to determine. The role of literature in war was recognized, and "ideological remolding" became a byword in the Chinese Communist Party.

In declaring their purpose to remold man, ideologically, the Chinese Communists meant that all "backward" ideas should be overcome and replaced with "the advanced ideas of the working class."[1] Long before the Communists came to power in 1949, however, drama and theater had played a vital role in the rise of Chinese Communism. During the eighteen years before 1949, when China had been pillaged in turn by numerous warlords, the Kuomintang troops of Chiang Kai-shek, the invasion by the Japanese, and the Civil War action after 1945, agitation-propaganda plays were written and frequently produced in the villages and army camps. These plays graphically depicted the cruelties of the Japanese (*Lay Down Your Whip*) or exposed the abuses of the Kuomintang (*Victory at All Costs*). It was during this time, too, that Mao Tse-tung delivered his *Talks at the Yenan Forum on Art and Literature* (1942). A basic text for writers and artists in Communist China, the *Talks* demanded that art and literature (1) serve the workers, peasants, and soldiers, and (2) expose evil while extolling good. "In the fighting years the drama played an active part with the people's forces at the front in mobilizing the people to support the resistance."[2]

In spite of the success of these plays—in terms of both effective propaganda and popular participation among the peasants—there is evidence that by the end of the 1940's the masses were beginning to tire of the numerous and similar war plays. Previously, they had been accustomed to the rich subject matter of the traditional operas and dramas which were, of course, part of the "feudal" past and therefore condemned by the Communists as containing evil elements or "feudal dregs." Difficulties arose when some people wanted a return to the classical repertory while others demanded that all such dramas be discarded. Mao, however, in the tradition of the Communist Party, solved the problem with a new slogan: "Weed through the old to let the new emerge." This idea proved effective. The slogan became the dictum for reform in all literature and art and was officially used to determine whether or not a play was of "benefit to audiences today."[3] Realistically, then, the main criterion for selection of a play was the political or ideological one; but Communist writers have also claimed that they stressed "the artist criteria, including those technical points of stagecraft which are useful to us," while admitting that some ideas in traditional plays are "relatively harmless and easy to modify."

In selecting and modifying traditional opera and drama, the Chinese Communists have shown considerable talent, although one must accept the fact that before a literary work can be published it must follow the current party line. As the party line changes, so does the literature that is published. A play may be acceptable one year and not the next; hence a playwright or literary man must be ideologically agile to keep his work before the public. Representative of those traditional or classical dramas which were acceptable during the years of communism before and immediately after the takeover is *Snow in Midsummer* from the Yuan Dynasty (1260–1368, also called the Mongol Dynasty).

Snow in Midsummer by Kuan Han-ching is a typical Yuan Dynasty drama with four acts, a single main character who sings, and secondary speakers who are reminiscent of the individual performers of the ballad form that was then popular. Kuan Han-ching, author of more than sixty plays, was one of the more prolific playwrights during the last half of the thirteenth century and is generally acknowledged as the Father of Chinese Drama. For the Communists he has been considered sufficiently important to be the subject of a play by Tien Han, *Kuan Han-ching*. This play, published in 1961, was said to have inspired those who saw it to feel strong opposition to imperialism and political persecution.

Considered an indignant playwright by historians who see the Yuan drama as based upon and growing out of the indignation of a people, Kuan Han-ching was eulogized as a "militant playwright" by the Communists. Yet not even he was above criticism. Although Kuan Han-ching's original version, *Tou Ngo*, was performed in China as late as 1958, it is *Snow in Midsummer*, a revision of the original, that Peking Foreign Languages Press published, presumably with the necessary party line modifications. Originally, the heroine, Tou Ngo, was more powerful than she is in *Snow in Midsummer* although here she represents the defiant will of man, resisting the corruption of local politics and social chaos. In style the play has a simplicity of action and a folk naïveté in the presentation of characters and ideas, although much of the charm of the unsophisticated Yuan Dynasty drama is destroyed by the straight forward emphasis of Communist thought. Essentially, the play dramatizes the theme of justice which, though denied a deserving person, at last prevails. To the Communists, however, it is the story of a common heroine who overcomes corruption. Speaking to a poor scholar who becomes an official and brings her final justice, the spirit of the heroine says:

> With sharp sword of authority and tally of gold
> You will kill all evil and corrupt officials,
> To serve your sovereign and relieve the people!

Throughout this modern period—from the May 4, 1919, Movement, which is recognized as the beginning of modern drama in China, until the Communist takeover in 1949—selected and modified traditional operas and dramas remained a staple of the Chinese theater. There were also the numerous war plays during the "fighting years," but theater activity during this period was much more varied and "modern" than these two kinds of drama suggest. Two major reasons prompted this activity: demands by the Chinese Communist Party for more dramas, and a tremendously increased interest by workers and peasants in amateur dramatic companies which by 1954 numbered about one hundred thousand.[4]

As might be expected, plays on contemporary themes began to appear, and playwrights such as Lu Hsun, Tsao Yu, Lao Sheh, Kuo Mo-jo, Tien Han, Hung Shen, and Ouyang Yu-chien became important in the Chinese theater. Their plays generally showed a social unrest and were built around the evils of the old family system, including feudal marriage practices and oppression by the wealthy. The position of women in society was a dominant theme, and the number of heroines rather than heroes in these plays is quite overwhelming. Of interest, too, is the influence of Western culture on both the structure and content of these plays. Ibsen and O'Neill, among moderns, are respected, and the principles of Aristotle are occasionally discernible—yet one must quickly note that the Communist Party line had to be clear in any produced or published work.

Writing under the pen name of Lu Hsun, Chou Shu-jen (1881–1936) is frequently regarded as the greatest modern Chinese writer, particularly in fiction (*The True Story of Ah-Q, Diary of a Madman*) and in the essay. From the very beginning of the literary revolution he submitted literary theories that were acceptable to the Communists: that literature must be subordinate to revolutionary politics, and that it must play an active role in the struggle against feudalism. Later, Lu Hsun was highly praised by Mao Tse-tung and made a national hero for his work as a popularizer of literature that served workers and peasants. His prose-poem in dramatic style, *The Passer-by* (1925), would seem to be a rather philosophical play about Everyman searching for truth. The characters are common people aware of beauty and truth who recognize that for the undaunted individual neither fate nor death is a deterrent to understanding. In only one instance is the propaganda blatant—when the Passer-by craves a place without landlords, expulsion, cages, or artificial smiles. In this play there is a universal charm in both style and content.

In *Theatre in the East: A Survey of Asian Dance and Drama*, Faubion Bowers called Tsao Yu (1910–   ) the greatest playwright of modern theater in China. In Communist China, however, he is an excellent example of the persecuted playwright. Dramatists such as Tien Han, Hsia Yen, and Chou Hsin-fang have fallen out of favor with the party and have been purged. Tsao You has seemingly slipped away into obscurity. Graduating from Tsing Hua University in 1934, he showed his interest in Western drama by studying not only the Greek dramatists and Shakespeare but the plays of Chekhov, Ibsen, and O'Neill. A man of the theater as well as of dramatic literature, he acted, not only in Chinese plays, but in Ibsen's *A Doll's House* and *An Enemy of the People*. Between 1934, when he wrote *Thunderstorm*, and 1941, he produced his greatest works. Throughout the 1940's (with the exception of the little mentioned *The Bridge*) and until the mid-1950's, Tsao Yu was quiet. Then, with *Bright Skies* (1954), he produced a potent Communist drama about the ideological remolding of the intellectuals in China shortly before and during the Korean War. This play, filled with propaganda and slogans, showed little of his previous talent. Later, during the early 1960's, he was reported to be writing historical dramas, which might have been one way to avoid some of the strict Communist censorship. Since 1963, however, with the increasing influence of Chiang Ching (Mao Tse-tung's wife) culminating in her present position of authority in the "Great Proletarian Cultural Revolution," that type of writing has been discouraged. The present Communist emphasis in art and literature is on the contemporary man and his conversion to Communism. For the sensitive artist in Communist China there seems to be little hope, and Tsao Yu, although he was honored in his country as head of the Peking People's Art Theater, well illustrates the subsequent loss to a culture that strict censorship makes inevitable.

One who has remained ideologically agile in his playwriting is Lao Sheh (1898–1966), the only modern dramatist of major distinction who comes from North China. Probably best known in America for his novel, *Rickshaw Boy*, Lao Sheh (the pen name of Sha Ch'ing-ch'ien) has been honored with the title of "People's Artist" for his realistic plays on social conditions. Communist critics extol him for his activity in organizing writers and artists during the revolutionary movement and for his "understanding" of the anti-Japanese democratic movement and the traitorous atrocities of Chiang Kai-shek's forces. Although he lived in America from 1946 until 1949, he returned to China after the "Liberation" and demonstrated an adaptability to Communist demands upon the writer that opens to question his artistic integrity. Until his alleged suicide he wrote popular plays of which *Dragon Beard Ditch* (1950) is a good example.

It is clear from both his preface to *Dragon Beard Ditch* and the play itself that Lao Sheh knew the Peking situation well. Impressed by the feelings of the people who lived near the Peking ditch that served as his model, and standing in great admiration of the Communist government, Lao Sheh created a propaganda play which emphasized a stage realism reminiscent of Sidney Kingsley's play about slum conditions in New York—*Dead End* (1935). Particularly interesting are the long stage directions in *Dragon Beard Ditch* in which the scenes, sounds, and odors are described. The first act of the play is excellent melodrama: the good people versus bad officials and gangsters; a generally good place to live, marred by a foul ditch. Then, the Liberation—and the remainder of the play is talky propaganda. By the end of Act II everyone is converted to Communism. Unfortunately, the conflict ended and the complications were re-

6

solved at the end of Act I, and as most dramatists know, Hell is more interesting to dramatize that Heaven.

Consistent with the demands of the Communist government that drama should serve the masses by reflecting Mao Tse-tung's ideas, and yet using the style of the traditional operas, are the new revolutionary operas on contemporary themes. Of these operas none has achieved wider acclaim than *The White-haired Girl*, a collective work of the Lu Hsun Academy of Art and Literature and written by Ho Ching-chih and Ting Yi. It all started from a story being circulated around the northwest Hopei Province in 1940 about a "white-haired goddess." Reported widely during the next few years, the story was first produced as an opera in 1945 and given major revisions in 1947 and in 1949. It was this final version that shared with *The Hurricane* (a novel by Chou Li-po) the Stalin Prize in 1951, the date of its popular acceptance. Ma Ho, in "China's Modern Opera," *People's China*, describes the opera:[5]

> It was the first Chinese opera to tackle a theme worthy of grand opera and a theme drawn from significant happenings in our times—something absolutely new in the history of modern Chinese opera. The music, however, is not in the style of the Western grand opera, nor much like Western operetta, but follows the pattern of traditional Chinese opera with its fusion of singing, dialogue, and dancing. It draws on the wealth of Chinese folk song, opera, revolutionary songs, and also draws on the modern Western music for certain technical devices like the *leit-motif*, for harmonization and counterpoint. The band to which the original orchestration was necessarily limited also used some Western instruments.

As a drama, *The White-haired Girl* is first-rate melodrama with nearly all the traditional devices. Only the main character develops; the rest are stereotypes, easily identified as good or evil. Clearly, the objective of the opera is to arouse emotion, and there is a great deal of suspenseful action. There are also a drunk scene, an opium scene, and a ghost scene. Various devices such as broken bowls are used, and spectacle abounds in the scene preparing for the wedding, in the contrast of poverty and wealth, and in the crowd scene. True to time-honored practice, everyone worth saving is "Saved!" in the final act with the arrival of the Red Army. The ending of the play, however, is extremely weak—abrupt, anticlimactic, and without action. The crowd has been built up to a feverish pitch—and nothing hap-

7

pens. For the American audience the extremely trite phrases in the English translation detract from the effect of the play, but its popularity in China is understandable.

For the Communist audience *The White-haired Girl* "deals with the class struggle between landlords and peasants as reflected in the life of a sweet and beautiful peasant girl."[6] Early in Act I the actions of the landlord's steward provide evidence of the evils of the feudalistic landowners. Almost immediately the suicide of the heroine's father further dramatizes the torment of the people and their need for help. Throughout the play the feudalistic belief in fate is thoroughly condemned, while political propaganda slogans appear frequently: "Resist Japan and Reduce Rents"; "the poor are going to be masters"; "the Eighth Route Army, led by the Communist Party, is like one family with the common people"; "Magistrates, rich men —you tigers and wolves!"

In spite of this seemingly appropriate propaganda, this opera, *The White-haired Girl*, has not been performed during the past few years. In its place there is a new revolutionary ballet of *The White-haired Girl*.[7] In this work there is an epilogue in which the heroine joins the Red Army to show her determination to carry out the revolution. Her father, on the other hand, does not commit suicide, but in the "positive" spirit of revolt fights back and is beaten to death. (During the years between the opera version and the ballet, the party stressed the idea that art and literature should express "positive" rather than "negative" actions and characters. This policy has been strictly enforced by Mao's wife, and numerous nonadherents have fallen into ill repute as a result.) There are also more slogans in the ballet, such as this one when the heroine is rescued:

> The sun has risen to shine far and wide. . . .
> Chairman Mao is the sun—
> The sun is the Communist Party.

There was no mention of Mao Tse-tung in the opera-drama. All of these changes, however, uphold Communist theories on art and literature: it must serve the people and the changing dictates of the Party. In whatever form it appears, the story of the "white-haired goddess" has the potential to entertain as well as educate the people. Doubtless it will be revised and revised again. Writing on "The Dialectics of Theatrical Reform" for *Wen Hui Pao*, a Shanghai newspaper, July 13, 1965, Ting Chai stated: "When one play is produced, it will be a very important problem to make continuous revision to enhance its quality with the spirit of uninterrupted revolution."

The now defunct Ministry of Culture in Communist China included a Bureau of Drama Reformation and a Central Drama College. Recognizing theater as the only form of mass culture that enjoys wide participation by peasants in China's rural areas, the Communist government has encouraged theater until almost every village has a space where performances are given by local or traveling drama troupes. Drama as persuasion, as propaganda, and as a means to agitate is of extreme importance to the Communists. As a major teaching device for a complex country, short, well-written, one-act plays that can be produced with limited facilities and under almost any conditions are in continuing demand. Generally, however, this demand has been met by amateur playwrights whom one might also call political hacks. Their agit-prop (agitation-propaganda) plays are similar to those written in America during the 1930's, and they also use the technique of the "living newspaper" developed by the Federal Theater group in America during this same period. The plays are invariably poor drama and monotonously Communistic; yet the Communists claim great popularity for them.

One example of this agit-prop drama is *The Women's Representative* by Sun Yu, a first-place prize-winner in the 1953 competition. (Actually, it is not strictly agit-prop because it does not urge a particular action at the climax, but it does dramatize a necessity for conversion to Communism.) Farcical, with stereotyped characters who are moved to action through the convenience of the plot and the demands of the Communist censor, the play emphasizes youth, women, and a breaking up of the old feudal family system. The abundance of plays on similar themes is almost overwhelming. One might list *The Day the New Director Came* (1957), *On the Farm Front* (1960), and *Taking Goods to the Countryside* (1966).

Short comedies and comic dialogues comprise another type of drama used by the Communists for propaganda effects. *Yesterday* (1961 edition), a comic dialogue by Chao Chung, Chang Pao-hua, and Chung Yi-ping, simply compares life before the Liberation with life afterwards. Such subjects as the place of intellectuals, employment, money, landlords, the Kuomintang, and medicine become a part of a vaudeville dialogue between a comedian and his straight man. Much of this humor is based on the unexpected or the ridiculous, but the Communists would see the contrast of the wonderful present with the ridiculous past as an aspect of Communist advancement.

The emphasis on youth in Communist plays since 1949 has been dominant, but the very recent drama reflects the interest of the newly educated young people in becoming "socialist minded." The activity of youth or children in the theater, however, is not a recent development in China. In *One Fifth of Mankind* (1938), Anna Louise Strong tells of a Children's Dramatic Club, a group of twenty-four Shanghai children, aged nine to nineteen, who toured the country during the war years reciting and performing plays. Youth or children *in* plays and plays *for* children are two distinctly different things, however, and it is interesting that the Communists have worked both angles. Chou Yang observes that "children's literature and plays for children which have the task of educating the rising generation in the spirit of communism have received special attention."[8] Illustrating his point is Jen Teh-yao's *Magic Aster*, a three-act drama for children published in 1963. The thesis of this play may be explained as "we have to create our own happiness," a theme consistent with the party line. There are also comments on the feudal marriage system and capitalistic greed. Mainly, however, the play strikes the Western reader as an exciting fantasy with a delightful pantomime of "animals," a clever and simple plot of good versus evil, imaginative characters, and spectacular scenes—everything that would fascinate the young.

Presumably all of the plays of Communist China serve the workers, peasants, and soldiers, but it is a long step from the fantasy of *Magic Aster* to the realism of *Letters from the South* (Vietnam), *War Drums on the Equator* (Congo), and *Storm over the Andes* (South America). These plays, however, illustrate the propaganda play of international interest, which must always remain both a real and a potential objective for the Party leaders. Combining realism with melodrama, spectacles, and propaganda, the plays on the war in Vietnam show still another view of Communist drama. One such play, a four-act song-and-dance drama called *Flames of Anger in the Coconut Groves*, was written by members of the armed forces and produced in a theater plastered with slogans, posters, and bulletins on the Vietnamese people's latest victories. *Letters from the South* (1964), written jointly by Sha Seh, Fu To, Ma Yung, and Li Chi-huang, is described in *China Pictorial*: "It vividly describes the struggle of the people of South Viet Nam in heroically resisting the invaders and exposes the heinous crimes of the U.S. imperialists."[9] It

10

is true that cruel tortures and atrocities are quite graphically portrayed in this play, but the Americans are mainly pictured as stupid, cowardly, and misguided. The bitterest attacks are reserved for the cruelties and traitorous actions of the Vietnamese "puppets." The play itself is fine melodrama with intrigue, secret police, passwords, and good scenes of tension and action. The use of time as a controlling agent, a characteristic of melodrama, is evident throughout. Only toward the end of the play does the preaching and propaganda seem to be more important than melodramatic action; then, as with a number of Communist plays, the drama becomes simply dull.

Since coming to power in 1949, the Communist Party has constantly reconsidered and renewed its position relative to the staging of different types of drama. Until the late 1950's, however, there was a Party policy of general tolerance—of "letting a hundred flowers blossom and a hundred schools of thought contend." Designed to allow the arts to flourish and to unite the people while strengthening the dictatorship of the proletariat and the leadership of the Communist Party, this policy also allowed a freedom of criticism which the government began to curb in June, 1957, before initiating purges in conjunction with the "great socialist cultural revolution" during the early 1960's.

One form of traditional Chinese drama that has recently all but disappeared from the Chinese stage is the Peking opera. With its distinctive style and a history of more than a hundred years, this opera was started in the Ch'ing Dynasty (also called the Manchu Dynasty, 1644–1911) in Peking where the best Peking opera companies have always been found. Its comprehensive conventions included little or no scenery or properties, elaborate costumes of the Ming Dynasty (1368–1644), stylized gestures, emphasis on the actor (whose face and beard, for example, may be traditionally colored to indicate his character), and a combination or singing, acting, dancing, and acrobatics. As time went on, particularly during the mid-1950's, the value of individual classical operas was carefully analyzed for "positive" or "negative" political content with the result that some Peking operas were rejected and others modernized. New operas were introduced, and Peking opera adopted revolutionary modern themes with a sacrifice of the traditional conventions. Although even in 1961 and 1962 articles appeared that reaffirmed the value of the traditional operas, the supporting critics have since been made to confess their ideological mistakes, and the "feudal morality" of the

11

traditional dramas, even the very popular plays, has very nearly pushed them from the stage.

The objective of the current cultural revolution is clearly to destroy all old ideology and culture as well as old customs and habits. In "A New Year Message to Compatriots Abroad," Chang Chun-ch'iu, a Peking opera actor, noted the rapid progress of the Peking opera since it became concerned with the contemporary scene:[10]

> The "emperors, kings, generals, ministers, scholars and beauties" who dominated the Peking opera for over two centuries have been replaced by new masters as if the whole world has been changed. The central characters on the stage today are the advanced persons in all lines of trade and heroes among the laboring people, who are building our socialist motherland; in other words, they are simple, common but great people, who have consciousness and accomplishments, and are living around us.

The latest development with regard to Peking opera occurred at the November 28, 1966, rally of literary and art workers, held in Peking to support the "Great Proletarian Cultural Revolution." Since 1964, the Peking opera stage has abandoned all traditional opera for presentation to its people, and only five revolutionary Peking operas are permitted on the opera stage: *Taking the Bandit's Stronghold*,[11] *On the Docks, Raid on the White Tiger Regiment, Shachaipang,* and *The Red Lantern.* (Some traditional opera scenes were performed for visiting delegations on major holidays as late as 1965.) At this November rally, interestingly enough, it was revealed that all five new Peking operas were selected and produced under the direction of Chiang Ching, wife of Mao Tse-tung, who, having once been a poorly paid actress before her marriage in 1938, became a professor of drama at the Lu Hsun Art College in Yenan and in August of 1966 was given the title of "first deputy head of the central cultural revolution team." Her direction of the five Peking operas is considered a "struggle" against certain "persons in authority" who were later expelled from the Party—the former Chinese Communist Party Peking Municipal Committee, former playwrights of the CCP Central Committee, and former Ministry of Culture leaders—and these operas, which have been carefully revised and frequently performed, are currently praised by the Communist leaders for their success in "revolutionizing the Peking opera theater."

The Red Lantern (1964) is one of the currently acceptable Peking operas, adapted by Wong Ou-hung and Ah Chia. In its original version as a Shanghai opera it showed blood ties with three generations, an aspect eliminated in later versions that promoted the "revolutionary sentiment of the proletariat." Its success for the Communist Party is explained by Tan Man-ni:[12]

> Audiences called the opera itself a 'red lantern' in the sense that it has lighted a way in today's revolution in culture by successfully dramatizing themes of present-day significance through a traditional method. And it has done this while at the same time maintaining a high artistic level and making creative developments in the old art form.

As a play, *The Red Lantern* is excellent melodrama with exciting action and an unbelievably heroic central figure who is never daunted. Like all Communist melodramas, this play emphasizes the party line with less subtlety as it progresses, and it ends with a spectacular scene praising Red Communism. As a whole, however, and in spite of the Communist propaganda, the play, from its central device and symbol—the red lantern—through its exciting crises, is one of the more effective Chinese Communist stage presentations.

The current period of the "Great Proletarian Cultural Revolution" has not only brought more intense censorship of the drama and therefore less selectivity in the plays that are permitted productions; it has also instigated a reassessment of various theories of art and literature. This means outlawing of theories shown to be bourgeois, capitalistic, or reactionary and suppression of their advocates. Of the several theories attacked, two were related to particular dramatists. The theory of "truthful writing," for example, seemed to expose some bad aspects of socialist society while pointing out certain elements called "feudal dregs" by the Communist censors: Fen Hsueh-feng, a dramatist, stood accused. Commenting on another theory, that of opposition to "subject matter as the decisive factor," the Party accused dramatists Tien Han and Hsia Yen of wanting to discard revolutionary classics, of feeling that too much was written about war, and of becoming interested in humanism and the love of man. According to the Communist Party, the only correct theory is that of the Party as stated by Mao Tse-tung: "Life as reflected in the works of art and literature ought to be on a high plane, more intense, more concentrated, more typical, nearer the ideal, and therefore more universal than actual everyday life."[13]

With Mao Tse-tung's constant prodding, the Chinese Communist theater remains active. One might list first the "eight model

13

theatrical works": the five previously mentioned revolutionary Peking operas, a revolutionary symphony entitled *Shachaipang*, and two revolutionary ballets, *The White-haired Girl* and *The Red Detachment of Women*. Current Communist critics also praise two song-and-dance dramas about proletarian revolutionaries—*The January Tempest* and *Spring Thunder in the Southwest*. To celebrate the fortieth anniversary of the founding of the Chinese People's Liberation Army (PLA), a four-act drama entitled *The Night Battle at Sea* was produced. This play took the occasion of a sea battle on August 6, 1965, in which two of Chiang Kai-shek's warships were presumably sunk, to praise Mao Tse-tung's military thinking.

The drama in Communist China is also used to publicly condemn deviates from Mao's philosophy. Liu Shao-chi, former Chairman of the People's Republic of China, was recently accused of eight specific crimes against the people.[14] Almost immediately "the first modern drama denouncing China's Khrushchov," *Locust Tree Village*, was presented by the "proletarian revolutionary artists" of the PLA in Peking. "It reviews the key political struggles in the countryside between the two classes—proletariat and bourgeoisie, the two roads —socialist and capitalist, and between the proletarian revolutionary line and the counter-revolutionary line from the time of the land reform in the late 1940's up to the events in 1962. These struggles focus on the question: whither China—to socialism or to capitalism?"[15]

The dramatist in modern Communist China has a very precarious career. As the party line changes, so must the thoughts in his plays and even the techniques that he uses to express himself in the theater. No critic can tell what will be an acceptable play in the very near future. He can only suggest what at the present moment are the characteristics of an acceptable play. Invariably, as Li Lun writes, plays show that the writers, directors, actors, and musicians have studied Mao Tse-tung's writings, have lived among the "workers, peasants and soldiers" whom they represent in plays, and have kept at the task of acquiring the Communist world outlook. Heroes must have "boundless loyalty to the Communist Party, the motherland, the people, and the Socialist cause." Generally, plays deal with the younger generation who are dramatized as becoming the "first generation of cultured, socialist-minded peasants"—to which one might add workers and soldiers, for it is all three whom the Communist drama serve.[16] Wang Chi-ning praises a military theatrical troupe known as the Sea-going Cultural Work Troupe, stationed in Can-

14

ton. Calling the troupe "a political work team, a propaganda team, a service team," he noted that "first and foremost among the troupe's task is to disseminate the thought of Mao Tse-tung by every means."[17] Obviously the dramatist, although extremely important, is no longer an artist expressing his feelings and ideas. In the main, he is a professional propagandist and an amateur dramatist, for this is the era of Mao Tse-tung—an era in which the men of the Red army and the disseminators of Mao's thoughts have replaced those "scholars," "specialists," and "professors" who oppose Communism and the Party. The theater, that mirror of society, reflects only the "great red banner of Mao Tse-tung's thought" which guides life in modern Communist China.

NOTES

1. Ting Yi, A Short History of Modern Chinese Literature (Peking, 1959), p. 84.
2. Hsiao Wen, "Drama for a great Cause," Chinese Literature, No. 11 (November, 1965), p. 104.
3. Kuo Han-cheng, "New Developments in the Traditional Chinese Theatre," Chinese Literature, No. 1 (January, 1960), pp. 127–139.
4. Li Ko, "One-Act Plays in New China," People's China (December 16, 1954), p. 24.
5. People's China, (September 1, 1957), pp. 26–31.
6. MaKo, "China's Modern Opera," People's China (September 1, 1957), p .28.
7. See Chinese Literature, (August, 1966).
9. (April, 1965), pp. 18–19.
8. The Path of Socialist Literature and Art (Peking, 1960), p. 25.
10. China News Release, No. 4274 (December 16, 1965), as reported in "The Revolutionization of the Chinese Theatre in 1965," Union Research Service, XLII, No. 9 (February 1, 1966), 124–138.
11. In Peking Review, December 26, 1969, a revision of this play appeared under the title, Taking Tiger Mountain By Strategy (October, 1969, script), emphasizing, among other things, the Communist hero as a thinking man.
12. " 'The Red Lantern,' An Example for New Peking Opera," China Reconstructs, (December, 1965), pp. 35–38.
13. The Great Socialist Cultural Revolution I, (Peking, 1966), p. 9.
14. Wan Ta-hsing, "The Mao-Lin Group's Anti-Liu Offensive," Chinese Communist Affairs, Vol. IV, No. 4 (August, 1967), 19–20.
15. "Modern Drama–'Locust Tree Village'—a New Play on Rural Class Struggle," Peking Review, No. 1 (January 3, 1968), p. 46.
16. "Socialist Times, Socialist Heroes, Socialist Drama," China Reconstructs (August, 1965), pp. 27–30.
17. "A Shining Example in Carrying Out Mao Tse-tung's Thought on Literature and Art," China Reconstructs (October, 1966), pp. 27–32.

SNOW IN MIDSUMMER*

By Kuan Han-ching

Translated by Yang Hsien-yi and Gladys Yang

CHARACTERS

MISTRESS TSAI, a widow.
TOU TIEN-CHANG, a poor scholar, later a government inspector.
TOU NGO, TOU TIEN-CHANG's daughter TUAN-YUN.
DOCTOR LU.
OLD CHANG.
DONKEY, his son.
PREFECT.
ATTENDANT.
THE OFFICER IN CHARGE OF EXECUTIONS.
EXECUTIONER.

ACT I

[*Enter* MISTRESS TSAI.]
MRS. TSAI:

> A flower may blossom again,
> But youth never returns.

I am Mistress Tsai of Chuchow. There were three of us in my family; but unluckily my husband died, leaving me just one son who is eight years old. We live together, mother and son, and are quite well off. A scholar named Tou of Shanyang Prefecture borrowed five taels of silver from me last year. Now the interest and capital come to ten taels, and I've asked several times for the money; but Mr. Tou cannot pay it. He has a daughter, and I've a good mind to make her my daughter-in-law; then he won't have to pay back the ten taels. Mr. Tou chose today as a lucky day and

---

*Reprinted from *Selected Plays of Kuan Han-ching* (Peking: Foreign Languages Press, 1958), pp. 21–47.

16

is bringing the girl to me, so I won't ask him to pay me back, but wait for him at home. He should be here soon.

[*Enter* Tou Tien-chang, *leading his daughter* Tuan-yun.]

Tou:

> I am master of all the learning in the world,
>
> But my fate is worse than that of other men.

My name is Tou Tien-chang, and the home of my ancestors is Changan. I have studied the classics since I was a child and read a good deal; but I haven't yet taken the examinations. Unfortunately my wife has died, leaving me this only daughter, Tuan-yun. She lost her mother when she was three, and now she is seven. Living from hand to mouth, I moved to Shanyang Prefecture in Chuchow and took lodgings here. There is a widow in this town named Tsai, who lives alone with her son and is fairly well off, and as I had no money for travelling I borrowed five taels from her. Now, with the interest, I owe her ten taels; but though she has asked several times for the money, I haven't been able to pay her. And recently she has sent to say she would like my daughter to marry her son. Since the spring examinations will soon be starting, I should be going to the capital; but I have no money for the road. So I am forced to take Tuan-yun to Widow Tsai as her future daughter-in-law. I'm not marrying my daughter but selling her! For this means the widow will cancel my debt and give me some cash for my journey. This is all I can hope for. Ah, child, your father does this against his will! While talking to myself I've reached her door. Mistress Tsai! Are you at home?

[*Enter* Mistress Tsai.]

Mrs. Tsai: So it's Mr. Tou! Come in, please. I've been waiting for you.

[*They greet each other.*]

Tou: I've brought you my daughter, ma'am, not to be your daughter-in-law—that would be asking too much—but to serve you day and night. I must be going to take the examination. I hope you will look after her.

Mrs. Tsai: Well, you owed me ten taels including interest. Here is your promissory note back and another two taels for your journey. I hope you don't think it too little.

Tou: Thank you, ma'am! Instead of asking for what I owe you, you have given me money for the road. Some day I shall repay your kindness in full. My daughter is a foolish child. Please take care of her, ma'am, for my sake.

MRS. TSAI: Don't worry, Mr. Tou. I shall look after your daughter
as if she were my own.

TOU [*kneeling to her*]: If the child deserves a beating, ma'am, for
my sake just scold her! And if she deserves a scolding, for my
sake speak gently to her! As for you, Tuan-yun, this isn't like at home,
where your father used to put up with your whims. If you're
naughty here, you'll be beaten and cursed. When shall I see you
again, child? [*He sighs.*]

> I drum sadly on my sheath;
> I have studied the Confucian classics;
> My unhappy wife died young,
> And now I am parted from my only daughter. [*Exit.*]

MRS. TSAI: Now Mr. Tou has left me his daughter, and gone to the
capital for the examination. I must see to the house.
[*Exeunt.*]
[*Enter* DOCTOR LU.]

DOCTOR:

> I diagnose all diseases with care,
> And prescribe as the Herbal dictates;
> But I cannot bring dead men back to life,
> And the live ones I treat often die.

I am Doctor Lu. I own a drug shop here. I've borrowed ten taels
of silver from Mistress Tsai of this town, and with interest now
owe her twenty taels. She keeps coming for the money; but I
haven't got it. If she doesn't come back, so much the better. If
she does, I have a plan. I'll sit in my shop now, and wait to see
who turns up.

[*Enter* MISTRESS TSAI.]

MRS. TSAI: I am Mistress Tsai. Thirteen years ago Mr. Tou Tien-
chang left his daughter Tuan-yun with me to marry my son, and
I changed her name to Tou Ngo. But after their marriage my son
died, so now she's a widow. That was nearly three years ago, and
she'll soon be out of mourning. I've told her that I'm going to
town to collect a debt from Doctor Lu. Now I've reached his
house. Is Doctor Lu in?

DOCTOR: Yes, ma'am, come in.

MRS. TSAI: You've kept my money for a long time, doctor. You must
pay me back.

DOCTOR: I've no money at home, ma'am. If you'll come with me
to the village, I'll get money for you.

18

MRS. TSAI: Very well. I'll go with you.

[*They start walking.*]

DOCTOR: Now we are outside the city. Here's a good spot, with no one about. Why not do it here? I've got the rope ready. Who's that calling you, ma'am?

MRS. TSAI: Where?

[*The* DOCTOR *strangles the widow with the rope. Enter* OLD CHANG *and his son* DONKEY. *As they rush forward, the* DOCTOR *takes to his heels.* OLD CHANG *revives* MISTRESS TSAI.]

DONKEY: It's an old woman, Dad, nearly strangled to death.

CHANG: Hey, you! Who are you? What's your name? Why did that fellow try to strangle you?

MRS. TSAI: My name is Tsai, and I live in town with my widowed daughter-in-law. Doctor Lu owes me twenty taels so he lured me here and tried to strangle me. If not for you and this young man, it would have been all up with me!

DONKEY: Did you hear that, Dad? She has a daughter-in-law at home! Suppose you take her as your wife and I take the daughter-in-law? Propose it to her, Dad!

CHANG: Hey, widow! You've no husband and I've no wife. How about the two of us getting married?

MRS. TSAI: What an idea! I shall give you a handsome sum of money to thank you.

DONKEY: So you refuse! I'd better strangle you after all.

MRS. TSAI: Wait! Let me think a moment, brother!

DONKEY: What do you need to think for? You take my dad, and I'll take your daughter-in-law.

MRS. TSAI [*aside*]: If I don't agree, he'll strangle me! [*To them.*] Very well. Come home with me, both of you.

DONKEY: Let's go.

[*Exeunt.*]

[*Enter* TOU NGO.]

TOU NGO: I am Tuan-yan, and my home was in Chuchow. When I was three I lost my mother; and when I was seven I had to leave my father, for he sent me to Mistress Tsai as her son's child-bride, and she changed my name to Tou Ngo. At seventeen I married; but unluckily my husband died three years ago. Now I am twenty.[1] There is a Doctor Lu in town who owes my mother-in-law twenty taels including interest; and though she has asked him several times for the money, he hasn't paid her back. She's gone today to try to collect the debt. Ah, when shall I escape from my misery?

> My heart is full of grief,
> I have suffered for so many years!
> Morning or evening it is all the same:
> From dawn to dusk I can neither eat nor sleep,
> Racked by sad dreams at night, sad thoughts by day,
> Unending sorrow which I cannot banish,
> Unceasing reasons for fresh misery.
> Wretchedness makes me weep, grief makes me frown;

Will this never come to an end?

> Is it my fate to be wretched all my life?
> Who else knows grief like mine?
> For my sorrow, like flowing water, never ceases.
> At three I lost my mother, at seven was torn from my father;
> Then the life of the husband I married was cut short;
> So my mother-in-law and I are left as widows,
> With no one to care for us or see to our needs.
> Did I burn too little incense in my last life
> That my marriage was unlucky?
> We should all do good betimes;
> So I mourn for my husband and serve my mother-in-law,
> Obedient to all her bidding.

My mother-in-law has been gone a long time to collect that debt. What can be keeping her?

[*Enter* Mistress Tsai *with* Old Chang *and* Donkey.]

Mrs. Tsai: Wait here at the door while I go in.

Donkey: All right, mother. Go in and tell her her husband is at the door.

[Mistress Tsai *sees* Tou Ngo.]

Tou Ngo: So you're back, mother. Have you had a meal?

Mrs. Tsai [crying]: Ah, poor child! How am I going to break this to you?

Tou Ngo:

> I see her in floods of tears,
> Hiding some grief in her heart;
> Greeting her quickly, I beg her to tell me the reason.

Mrs. Tsai: How can I say this?

20

TOU NGO:

She's shilly-shallying and looks ashamed.

What has upset you, mother? Why are you crying?

MRS. TSAI: When I asked Doctor Lu for the silver, he lured me outside the town, then tried to strangle me; but an old man called Chang and his son Donkey saved my life. Now Old Chang is going to marry me; that's why I'm upset.

TOU NGO: That would never do, mother! Please think again! We're not short of money. Besides, you are growing old—how can you take another husband?

MRS. TSAI: Child, I couldn't do anything else!

TOU NGO: Mother, listen to me!

What will become of you
If you choose a day and solemnize a wedding?
Now your hair is as white as snow,
How can you wear the bright silk veil of a bride?
No wonder they say it is hard to keep women at home,
If at sixty, when all thought of love should be over,
You've forgotten your former husband,
And taken a fancy to another man!
This will make others split their sides with laughter!
Yes, split their sides with laughter!
Like the widow who fanned her husband's tomb,
You're no tender bamboo shoot, no tender shoot.
How can you paint your eyebrows and remarry?
Your husband left you his property,
Made provision for the future,
For daily food and a good livelihood,
So that you and your son could remain beholden to no one,
And live to a ripe old age.
Did he go to such trouble for nothing?

MRS. TSAI: Since it has come to this, I think you'd better take a husband too, and today can be the wedding day.

TOU NGO: You take a husband if you must. I won't!

MRS. TSAI: The date is fixed, and they are already here.

DONKEY: Now we shall marry into their family. Our hats are brushed as good as new, and have narrow brims like bridegrooms'! Good! Fine!

TOU NGO: Stand back, you fellows!

Women should not believe all men say;

Such a marriage could not last.
Where did she find this old yokel,
And this other ruffian here?
Have you no feeling left for the dead?
You must think this over again.
Your husband worked in different cities and counties
To amass a well-earned fortune, and lack nothing.
How can you let his estate go to Donkey Chang?
He tilled the land, but others are reaping the harvest. [*Exit.*]

CHANG [*to* MRS. TSAI]: Let us go and drink, ma'am. [*Exeunt.*]

DONKEY: Tou Ngo refuses to have me, but I shan't let her get away: she will be my wife. Now I'll drink with my old man! [*Exit.*]

ACT II

[*Enter* DOCTOR LU.]

DOCTOR: I am Doctor Lu. I lured Mistress Tsai outside the town and was just going to strangle her when two men rescued her. Today I am opening shop. I wonder who will turn up.
[*Enter* DONKEY.]

DONKEY: I am Donkey Chang. Tou Ngo still refuses to marry me. Now the old woman is ill, I'm going to poison her; for once the old one is dead, the young one will have to be my wife. Ah, here is a drug shop. Doctor! I want a drug!

DOCTOR: What drug do you want?

DONKEY: I want some poison.

DOCTOR: Who dares sell you poison? How can you ask such a thing?

DONKEY: You won't let me have it then?

DOCTOR: I won't. What are you going to do about it?

DONKEY [*seizing him*]: Fine! Fine! Aren't you the man who tried to murder Mistress Tsai? Do you think I don't recognize you? I'll take you to court.

DOCTOR [*in panic*]: Let me go, brother! I've got it! I've got it. [*Gives him the poison.*]

DONKEY: Now that I've got the poison, I'm going home. [*Exit.*]

DOCTOR: So that man who came to buy poison was one of the men who rescued the widow. Since I've given him poison, he may get me into further trouble later. I'd better close my shop and go to Chuchow to sell drugs. [*Exit.*]

[*Enter* MISTRESS TSAI, *supported by* OLD CHANG *and* DONKEY.]

22

CHANG: I came to Mistress Tsai's house hoping to be her second husband. Who would have thought that the widow would fall ill? I am really too unlucky. If there's anything you fancy to eat, ma'am, just let me know.

MRS. TSAI: I'd like some mutton tripe soup.

CHANG: Son, go and tell Tou Ngo to make some mutton tripe soup for her mother-in-law.

DONKEY: Tou Ngo! Your mother-in-law wants some mutton tripe soup. Look sharp about it!

[Enter Tou Ngo.]

TOU NGO: I am Tou Ngo. My mother-in-law is unwell and wants some mutton tripe soup, so I've made her some. When you think of it, some women are too fickle!

> She wants to lie with a husband all her life,
> Unwilling to sleep alone;
> First she married one, and now she has picked another.
> Some women never speak of household matters,
> But pick up all the gossip,
> Describe their husbands' adventures,
> And are always up to some low tricks themselves.
> Is there one like Lady Cho,[2] who stooped to serve in a tavern?
> Or like Meng Kuang,[3] who showed such respect to her husband?
> The women today are different:
> You can neither tell their character from their speech,
> Nor judge them by their actions.
> They're all of them faithless, all run after new lovers;
> And before their husbands' graves are dry
> They set aside their mourning for new clothes.
> Where is the woman whose tears for her husband
> Caused the Great Wall to crumble?[4]
> Where is she who left her washing
> And drowned herself in the stream?[5]
> Where is she who changed into stone
> Through longing for her husband?[6]
> How shameful that women today are so unfaithful,
> So few of them are chaste, so many wanton!
> All, all are gone, those virtuous women of old;
> For wives will not cleave to their husbands!

Now the soup is ready. I had better take it in.

DONKEY: Let me take it to her. [*He takes the bowl.*] This hasn't much flavor. Bring some salt and vinegar.

[*Tou Ngo goes out. Donkey puts poison in the soup. Tou Ngo comes back.*]

TOU NGO: Here are the salt and vinegar.

DONKEY: Put some in.

TOU NGO:

> You say that it lacks salt and vinegar,
> Adding these will improve the flavor.
> I hope my mother will be better soon,
> And the soup will serve as a cordial.
> Then the three of you can live happily together.

CHANG: Son, is the soup ready?

DONKEY: Here it is. Take it.

CHANG [*taking the soup*]: Have some soup, ma'am.

MRS. TSAI: I am sorry to give you so much trouble. You have some first.

CHANG: Won't you try it?

MRS. TSAI: No, I want you to drink it first.

[*Old Chang drinks the soup.*]

TOU NGO:

> One says: "Won't you try it?"
> The other says: "You have it!"
> What a shameful way to talk!
> How can I help being angry?
> The new couple is in transports;
> Forgetting her first husband,
> She listens to this new man's lightest word.
> Now her heart is like a willow seed in the breeze,
> Not steadfast as a rock.
> Old love is nothing to new love:
> She wants to live with this new man forever,
> Without a thought for the other man far away.

CHANG: Why has this soup made me dizzy? [*He falls to the ground.*]

MRS. TSAI: Why should you feel unwell after that soup. [*Panic-stricken.*] Take a grip on yourself, old man! Don't give up so easily! [*Wails.*]

TOU NGO:

> It's no use grieving for him;
> All mortal men must die when their time is up.

> Some fall ill, some meet with accidents;
> Some catch a chill, some are struck down by heat;
> Some die of hunger, surfeit or overwork;
> But every death has its cause.
> Human life is ruled by fate,
> And no man can control it,
> For our span of life is predestined.
> He has been here a few days only;
> He is not of your family,
> And he never sent you wedding gifts:
> Sheep, wine, silk or money.
> For a time you stayed together,
> But now he is dead and gone!
> I am not an unfilial daughter,
> But I fear what the neighbors may say;
> So stop your moaning and wailing;
> He is not the man you married as a girl.

[OLD CHANG dies.]

MRS. TSAI: What shall we do? He's dead!

TOU NGO:

> He's no relation—I have no tears for him.
> There's no need to be so overcome with grief,
> Or to cry so bitterly and lose your head!

DONKEY: Fine! You've poisoned my father! What are you going to do about it?

MRS. TSAI: Child, you had better marry him now.

TOU NGO: How can you say such a thing, mother?

> This fellow forced my mother-in-law to keep him;
> Now he's poisoned his father,
> But whom does he think he can frighten?

MRS. TSAI: You'd better marry him, child.

TOU NGO:

> A horse can't have two saddles;
> I was your son's wife when he was alive,
> Yet now you are urging me to marry again.
> This is unthinkable!

DONKEY: Tou Ngo, you murdered my old man. Do you want to settle this in private or settle it in public?

TOU NGO: What do you mean?

25

DONKEY: If you want it settled in public, I'll drag you to the court, and you'll have to confess to the murder of my father! If you want it settled in private, agree to be my wife. Then I'll let you off.

TOU NGO: I am innocent. I'll go with you to the prefect.

[DONKEY *drags* TOU NGO *and* MISTRESS TSAI *out.*]

ACT III

[*Enter the* PREFECT *with an* ATTENDANT.]

PREFECT:

I am a hard-working official;
I make money out of my lawsuits;
But when my superiors come to investigate,
I pretend to be ill and stay at home in bed.

I am prefect of Chuchow. This morning I am holding court. Attendant, summon the court!

[*The* ATTENDANT *gives a shout.*]

[*Enter* DONKEY, *dragging in* TOU NGO *and* MISTRESS TSAI.]

DONKEY: I want to lodge a charge.

ATTENDANT: Come over here.

[DONKEY *and* TOU NGO *kneel to the* PREFECT, *who kneels to them.*]

PREFECT [*kneeling*]: Please rise.

ATTENDANT: Your Honor, this is a citizen who's come to ask for justice. Why should you kneel to him?

PREFECT: Why? Because such citizens are food and clothes to me! [*The* ATTENDANT *assents.*]

PREFECT: Which of you is the plaintiff, which the defendant? Out with the truth now!

DONKEY: I am the plaintiff. I accuse this young woman, Tou Ngo, of poisoning my father with soup. Let justice be done, Your Honor!

PREFECT: Who poisoned the soup?

TOU NGO: Not I!

MRS. TSAI: Not I!

DONKEY: Not I!

PREFECT: If none of you did it, I wonder if I could have done it?

Tou Ngo:

> Your Honor is as discerning as a mirror,
> And can see my innermost thoughts.
> There was nothing wrong with the soup,
> I know nothing about the poison;
> He made a pretence of tasting it,
> Then his father drank it and fell down dead.
> It is not that I want to deny my guilt in court;
> But I cannot confess to a crime I have not committed!

PREFECT: Low characters are like that; they'll only confess when put to torture. Attendant! Bring the bastinado to beat her.
[The ATTENDANT beats TOU NGO. Three times she faints, and he has to sprinkle her with water to bring her around.]

Tou Ngo:

> This terrible beating is more than I can bear.
> You brought this on yourself, mother. Why complain?
> May all women in the world who marry again
> Be warned by me!
> Why are they shouting so fiercely?
> I groan with pain;
> I come to myself, then faint away again.
> A thousand strokes: I am streaming with blood!
> At each blow from the bastinado
> By blood spurts out and my skin is torn from my flesh;
> My spirit takes flight in fear,
> Approaching the nether regions.
> Who knows the bitterness in my heart?
> It was not I who poisoned the old man;
> I beg Your Honor to find out the truth!

PREFECT: Will you confess now?

Tou Ngo: I swear it was not I who put in the poison.

PREFECT: In that case, beat the old woman.

Tou Ngo [hastily]: Stop, stop! Don't beat my mother-in-law! Rather than that, I'll say I poisoned the old man.

PREFECT: Fasten her in the cangue and throw her into the jail for the condemned. Tomorrow she shall be taken to the marketplace to be executed.

MRS. TSAI [weeping]: Tou Ngo, my child! It's because of me you are losing your life. Oh, this will be the death of me!

27

Tou Ngo:

> When I am a headless ghost, unjustly killed,
> Do you think I will spare that scoundrel?
> Men cannot be deceived forever,
> And Heaven will see this injustice.
> I struggled as hard as I could, but now I am helpless,
> I was forced to confess that I poisoned the old man;
> How could I let you be beaten, mother?
> How could I save you except by dying myself?

[She is led off.]

DONKEY: If she's to be killed tomorrow, I'll hang around. [Exit.]

MRS. TSAI: Poor child! Tomorrow, she will be killed in the marketplace. This will be the death of me! [Exit.]

PREFECT: Tomorrow Tou Ngo will be executed. Today's work is done. Bring me my horse; I am going home to drink.

[Exeunt.]

[Enter the OFFICER in charge.]

OFFICER: I am the officer in charge of executions. Today we are putting a criminal to death. We must stand guard at the end of the road, to see that no one comes through.

[Enter the ATTENDANTS. They beat the drum and the gong three times; then the Executioner enters, sharpens his sword and waves a flag. TOU NGO is led on in a cangue. The gongs and drums are beaten.]

EXECUTIONER: Get a move on! Let no one pass this way.

Tou Ngo:

> Through no fault of mine I am called a criminal,
> And condemned to be beheaded—
> I cry out to Heaven and Earth of this injustice!
> I reproach both Earth and Heaven
> For they would not save me.
> The sun and moon give light by day and by night,
> Mountains and rivers watch over the world of men;
> Yet Heaven cannot tell the innocent from the guilty,
> And confuses the wicked with the good!
> The good are poor, and die before their time;
> The wicked are rich, and live to a great old age.
> The gods are afraid of the mighty and bully the weak;
> They let evil take its course.
> Ah, Earth! you will not distinguish good from bad,

> And, Heaven! you let me suffer this injustice!
> Tears pour down my cheeks in vain!

EXECUTIONER: Get a move on! We are late.

TOU NGO:

> The cangue round my neck makes me stagger this way and
> that,
> And I'm jostled backward and forward by the crowd.
> Will you do me a favor, brother?

EXECUTIONER: What do you want?

TOU NGO:

> If you take me the front way, I shall bear you a grudge;
> If you take me the back way, I shall die content.
> Please do not think me wilful!

EXECUTIONER: Now that you're going to the execution ground, are there any relatives you want to see?

TOU NGO: I am going to die. What relatives do I need?

EXECUTIONER: Why did you ask me just now to take you the back way?

TOU NGO:

> Please don't go by the front street, brother,
> But take me by the back street.
> The other way my mother-in-law might see me.

EXECUTIONER: You can't escape death, so why worry if she sees you?

TOU NGO: If my mother-in-law were to see me in chains being led to the execution ground—

> She would burst with indignation!
> She would burst with indignation!
> Please grant me this comfort, brother, before I die!

[Enter MISTRESS TSAI.]

MRS. TSAI: Ah, Heaven! Isn't that my daughter-in-law? This will be the death of me!

EXECUTIONER: Stand back, old woman!

TOU NGO: Let her come closer so that I can say a few words to her.

EXECUTIONER: Hey, old woman! Come here. Your daughter-in-law wants to speak to you.

MRS. TSAI: Poor child! This will be the death of me!

TOU NGO: Mother, when you were unwell and asked for mutton tripe soup, I prepared some for you. Donkey Chang made me fetch more salt and vinegar so that he could poison the soup, and then told me to give it to you. He didn't know his old man would drink it. Donkey Chang poisoned the soup to kill you, so that he could force me to be his wife. He never thought his father would die instead. To take revenge, he dragged me to court. Because I didn't want you to suffer, I had to confess to murder, and now I am going to be killed. In future, mother, if you have gruel to spare, give me half a bowl; and if you have paper money to spare, burn some for me, for the sake of your dead son!

> *Take pity on one who is dying an unjust death;*
> *Take pity on one whose head will be struck from her body;*
> *Take pity on one who has worked with you in your home;*
> *Take pity on one who has neither mother nor father;*
> *Take pity on one who has served you all these years;*
> *And at festivals offer my spirit a bowl of cold gruel.*

MRS. TSAI [*weeping*]: Don't worry. Ah, this will be the death of me!

TOU NGO:

> *Burn some paper coins to my headless corpse,*
> *For the sake of your dead son.*
> *We wail and complain to Heaven:*
> *There is no justice! Tou Ngo is wrongly slain!*

EXECUTIONER: Now then, old woman, stand back! The time has come.

[Tou Ngo *kneels, and the* EXECUTIONER *removes the cangue from her neck.*]

TOU NGO: I want to say three things, officer. If you will let me, I shall die content. I want a clean mat and a white silk streamer twelve feet long to hang on the flagpole. When the sword strikes off my head, not a drop of my warm blood will stain the ground. It will all fly up instead to the white silk streamer. This is the hottest time of summer, sir. If injustice has indeed been done, three feet of snow will cover my dead body. Then this district will suffer from drought for three whole years.

EXECUTIONER: Be quiet! What a thing to say!

[*The* EXECUTIONER *waves his flag.*]

TOU NGO:

> *A dumb woman was blamed for poisoning herself;*
> *A buffalo is whipped while it toils for its master.*

EXECUTIONER: Why is it suddenly so overcast? It is snowing! [*He prays to Heaven.*]

30

Tou Ngo:

> Once Tsou Yen caused frost to appear:[7]
> Now snow will show the injustice done to me!

[The EXECUTIONER beheads her, and the ATTENDANT sees to her body.]

EXECUTIONER: A fine stroke! Now let us go and have a drink.

[The ATTENDANTS assent, and carry the body off.]

ACT IV

[Enter Tou TIEN-CHANG.]

TOU: I am Tou Tien-chang. It is thirteen years since I left my child Tuan-yun. I went to the capital, passed the examination, and was made a counselor. And because I am able, just, and upright, the Emperor appointed me Inspector of the Huai River Area. I have traveled from place to place investigating cases, and I have the sword of authority and golden tally so that I can punish corrupt officials without first reporting to the throne. My heart is torn between grief and happiness. I am glad because I am a high official responsible for seeing that justice is done. I am sad, though, because when Tuan-yun was seven I gave her to Mistress Tsai; and after I became an official and sent for news of the widow to Chuchow, the neighbors said she had moved away—to what place they did not know—and there has been no word since. I have wept for my child till my eyes are dim and my hair is white. Now I have come south of the Huai River and am wondering why this district has had no rain for three years. I shall rest in the district office, boy. Tell the local officers they need not call today. I shall see them early tomorrow.

SERVANT [calling out]: The officers and secretaries are not to call on His Excellency today. He will see them early tomorrow.

TOU: Tell the secretaries of the different departments to send all their cases here for my inspection. I shall study some under the lamp.

[The SERVANT brings him the files.]

TOU: Light the lamp for me. You have been working hard, and you may rest now. But come when I call you.

[The SERVANT lights the lamp and leaves.]

TOU: I shall go through a few cases. Here is one concerning Tou Ngo, who poisoned her father-in-law.[8] Curious that the first culprit's surname should be the same as mine! To murder one's father-in-law is one of the unpardonable crimes; so it seems there are lawless elements among my clan. Since this case has been dealt with, I need not read it. I'll put it at the bottom of the pile and look at another. Wait, I suddenly feel drowsy. I suppose I am growing old, and am tired after traveling. I will take a short nap on the desk. [*He sleeps.*]

[*Enter Tou Ngo's ghost.*]

Tou Ngo:

> Day after day I weep in the underworld,
> Waiting impatiently for my revenge.
> I pace on slowly in darkness,
> Then am borne along by the whirlwind;
> Enveloped by mist I come swiftly in ghostly form.

[*She looks about her.*] Now the door-gods will not let me pass. I am the daughter of Inspector Tou. Though I died unjustly, my father does not know it; so I have come to visit him in his dreams. [*She enters the room and weeps.*]

Tou [*shedding tears*]: Tuan-yun, my child! Where have you been? [*Tou Ngo's spirit leaves, and Tou wakes up.*]

How odd! I fell asleep and dreamed that I saw my daughter coming towards me; but where is she now? Let me go on with these cases.

[*Tou Ngo's spirit enters and makes the lamp burn low.*] Strange! I was just going to read a case when the light flickered and dimmed. My servant is asleep; I must trim the wick myself. [*As he trims the lamp, Tou Ngo's spirit rearranges the file.*] Now the light is brighter, I can read again. "This concerns the criminal Tou Ngo, who poisoned her father-in-law." Strange! I read this case first, and put it under the others. How has it come to the top? Since this case has already been dealt with, let me put it at the bottom again and study a different one. [*Once more Tou Ngo's spirit makes the lamp burn low.*] Strange! Why is the light flickering again? I must trim it once more.

[*As Tou trims the light, Tou Ngo's spirit once more turns over the file.*] Now the lamp is brighter, I can read another case. "This concerns the criminal Tou Ngo, who poisoned her father-in-law." How extraordinary! I definitely put this at the bottom of the pile just before I trimmed the lamp. How has it come to the top again? Can there be ghosts in this office? Well, ghost or no ghost, an injustice must have been done. Let me put this underneath and read another. [TOU NGO's *spirit makes the lamp burn low again.*] Strange! The lamp is flickering again. Can there actually be a ghost here tampering with it? I'll trim it once more. [*As he trims the wick,* TOU NGO's *spirit comes up to him and he sees her. He strikes his sword on the desk.*] Ah, there's the ghost! I warn you, I am the Emperor's inspector of justice. If you come near, I'll cut you in two. Hey, boy! How can you sleep so soundly? Get up at once! Ghosts! Ghosts! This is terrifying!

TOU NGO:

> *Fear is making him lose his head;*
> *The sound of my weeping has frightened him more than ever.*
> *Here, Tou Tien-chang, my old father,*
> *Will you let your daughter Tou Ngo bow to you?*

TOU: You say I am your father, ghost, and offer to bow to me as my daughter. Aren't you mistaken? My daughter's name is Tuan-yun. When she was seven she was given to Mistress Tsai as a child-bride. You call yourself by a different name, Tou Ngo. How can you be my child?

TOU NGO: After you gave me to Mistress Tsai, Father, she changed my name to Tou Ngo.

TOU: So you say you are my child, Tuan-yun. Let me ask you this: are you the woman accused of murdering her father-in-law and executed?

TOU NGO: I am.

TOU: Hush, girl! I've wept for you till my eyes grew dim, and worried for you till my hair turned white. How did you come to be condemned for this most heinous of crimes? I am a high official now, whose duty it is to see that justice is done. I have come here to investigate cases and discover corrupt officials. You are my child, but you are guilty of the worst crime of all. If I could not control you, how can I control others? When I married you to the widow's son, I expected you to observe the Three Duties and Four Virtues. The Three Duties are obedience to your father before marriage, obedience to your husband after marriage, and obedience to your son after your husband's death. The Four Virtues are to serve your parents-in-law, to show respect to your husband, to remain on good terms with your sisters-in-law, and to live in peace with your neighbors. But regardless of your duties, you have committed the gravest crime of all! The proverb says: "Look before you leap,

or you may be sorry too late." For three generations no son of our
clan has broken the law; for five generations no daughter has married again. As a married woman, you should have studied propriety
and morality; but instead you perpetrated the most terrible crime.
You have disgraced our ancestors and injured my good name. Tell
me the whole truth at once, and nothing but the truth! If you
utter one false word, I shall send you to the tutelary god; then
your spirit will never re-enter human form, but remain a hungry
ghost for ever in the shades.

Tou Ngo: Don't be so angry, Father. Don't threaten me like an
angry wolf or tiger! Let me explain this to you. At three, I lost
my mother; at seven, I was parted from my father, when you sent
me to Mistress Tsai as her future daughter-in-law, and my name
was changed to Tou Ngo. At seventeen, I married; but unhappily
two years later my husband died, and I stayed as a widow with my
mother-in-law.[9] In Chuchow there lived a certain Doctor Lu, who
owed my mother-in-law twenty taels of silver. One day when she
went to ask him for the money, he lured her outside the town and
tried to strangle her; but Donkey Chang and his father came by
and saved her life. Old Chang asked: "Whom do you have in your
family, ma'am?" My mother-in-law said: "No one but a widowed
daughter-in-law." Old Chang said: "In that case, I will marry you.
What do you say?" When my mother-in-law refused, the two men
said: "If you don't agree, we shall strangle you again!" So she was
frightened into marrying him. Donkey tried to seduce me several
times, but I always resisted him. One day my mother-in-law was
unwell and wanted some mutton tripe soup. When I prepared it,
Donkey told me to let him taste it. "It's good," he said. "But
there's not enough salt and vinegar." When I went to fetch more,
he secretly poisoned the soup and told me to take it to her. But
my mother-in-law gave it to Old Chang. Then blood spurted from
the old man's mouth, nose, ears, and eyes, and he died. At that
Donkey said, "Tou Ngo, you poisoned my father. Do you want to
settle this in public or in private?" "What do you mean?" I asked.
"If you want it settled in public," he said, "I shall take the case
to court, and you will pay for my father's death with your life. If
you want it settled in private, then be my wife." "A good horse
won't have two saddles," I told him. "A good woman won't remarry. For three generations no son of our clan has broken the
law; for five generations no daughter has married again. I'd rather
die than be your wife. I am innocent. I'll go to court with you."

Then he dragged me before the prefect. I was tried again and again, stripped and tortured; but I would rather have died than make a false confession. When the Prefect saw that I wouldn't confess, he threatened to have my mother-in-law tortured; and because she was too old to stand the torture, I made a false confession. Then they took me to the execution ground to kill me. I made three vows before my death. First, I asked for a twelve-foot white silk streamer and swore that, if I was innocent, when the sword struck off my head no drop of my blood would stain the ground— it would all fly up to the streamer. Next I vowed that, though it was midsummer, Heaven would send down three feet of snow to cover my body. Last, I vowed that this district would suffer three years' drought. All these vows have come true, because of the crime against me.

> I complained not to any official but to Heaven,
> For I could not express the injustice that was done me;
> And to save my mother from torture
> I confessed to a crime of which I was innocent,
> And remained true to my dead husband.
> Three feet of snow fell on my corpse;
> My hot blood gushed to the white silk streamer;
> Tsou Yen called down frost,
> And snow showed the injustice done me.
> Your child committed no crime,
> But suffered a great wrong!
> For resisting seduction I was executed!
> I would not disgrace my clan, so I lost my life!
> Day after day in the shades
> My spirit mourns alone.
> You are sent by the Emperor with authority;
> Consider this case and this man's wickedness;
> Cut him in pieces and avenge my wrong!

Tou [weeping]: Ah, my wrongly slain daughter, how this wrings my heart! Let me ask you this: is it because of you that this district has suffered for three years from drought?

Tou Ngo: It is.

Tou: So! This reminds me of a story. In the Han dynasty there was a virtuous widow whose mother-in-law hanged herself, and whose sister-in-law accused her of murdering the old woman. The governor of Tungngo had her executed, but because of her unjust

death there was no rain in that district for three years. When Lord
Yu came to investigate, he saw the dead woman's ghost carrying
a plea and weeping before the hall; and after he changed the verdict, killed a bull and sacrificed at her grave, there was a great
downpour of rain. This case is rather similar to that. Tomorrow
I shall right this wrong for you.

> I bow my white head in sorrow
> Over the innocent girl who was wrongly slain.
> Now dawn is breaking, you had better leave me;
> Tomorrow I shall set right this miscarriage of justice.

Tou Ngo [bowing]:

> With sharp sword of authority and tally of gold,
> You will kill all evil and corrupt officials,
> To serve your sovereign and relieve the people!

[She turns back.] There's one thing I nearly forgot, Father. My
mother-in-law is old now, and has no one to look after her.

Tou: This is dutiful, my child.

Tou Ngo:

> I ask my father to care for my mother-in-law,
> For she is growing old. My father now
> Will reopen my case and change the unjust verdict.

[Exit.]

Tou: Dawn is breaking. Call the local officers, and all those concerned in the case of Tou Ngo.

Servant: Yes, Your Excellency.

[The Prefect, Mistress Tsai, Donkey Chang, and Doctor Lu
are sent in. They kneel before Tou.]

Tou: Mistress Tsai, do you recognize me?

Mrs. Tsai: No, Your Excellency.

Tou: I am Tou Tien-chang. Listen, all of you, to the verdict!
Donkey Chang murdered his father and blackmailed good citizens.
He shall be executed in public. Let him be taken to the marketplace to be killed. The prefect passed a wrong sentence. He shall
be given one hundred strokes and have his name struck off the
official list. Doctor Lu is guilty of selling poison. Let him be be-
headed in the marketplace. Mistress Tsai shall be lodged in my
house. The wrong sentence passed on Tou Ngo shall be recinded.

> Let the Donkey be killed in public,
> The prefect dismissed from office;
> Then let us offer a great sacrifice
> So that my daughter's spirit may go to heaven.

                          Curtain

NOTES

1. There is some confusion regarding her age and the year of her husband's death.

2. Cho Wen-chun, the daughter of a rich man, who eloped with Ssuma Hsiang-ju, a famous Han Dynasty scholar. Since they were poor, they kept a small tavern in Chengtu where she served as barmaid.

3. Wife of Liang Hung of the Later Han Dynasty.

4. Thousands of the men conscripted by the First Emperor of Chin to build the Great Wall died. According to a legend, Meng Chiang-nu, the wife of one of these conscripts, wept so bitterly at the wall that part of it crumbled.

5. During the Spring and Autumn Period (770–475 B.C.), Wu Tzu-hsu fled from the state of Chu to Wu. A woman washing by a river took pity on him and fed him. Upon leaving, he asked her not to tell his pursuers which way he had gone. To set his mind at rest she drowned herself.

6. This legendary woman, whose husband left home, climbed a hill every day to watch for his return, till at last she was transformed into a boulder.

7. Tsou Yen of the Warring States Period (475–221 B.C.) was a loyal subject of the Prince of Yen, but because an enemy slandered him he was imprisoned. Since such great injustice had been done, frost appeared in summer.

8. This indicated relationship is incorrect; Tou Ngo did not marry Donkey.

9. See note 1.

THE PASSER-BY*

By Lu Hsun

Translated by Yang Hsien-yi and Gladys Yang

Time: Some evening.

Place: Somewhere.

CHARACTERS

THE OLD MAN, aged seventy, has a white beard and hair and wears a black gown.

THE GIRL, about ten, has auburn hair and black eyes, and is wearing a gown with black squares on a white background.

THE PASSER-BY, aged between thirty and forty, looks tired and crabbed, with a smoldering gaze. He has a black moustache and tousled hair. Dressed in a short black jacket and trousers that are tattered and torn, he has shabby shoes on his stockingless feet. A sack is hanging from his arm, and he leans on a bamboo pole as tall as he is.

To the east are a few trees and ruins; to the west a forlorn-looking graveyard, and a faint track can be made out. A little mud hut has its door open facing this track. Beside the door is a dead tree stump.

THE GIRL is about to help the old man up from the stump on which he is sitting.

OLD MAN: Hey, child! Why have you stopped?

GIRL [*looking eastward*]: There is someone coming. Look!

OLD MAN: Never mind him. Help me inside. The sun is setting.

GIRL: Oh, let me have a look.

---

*Reprinted from *Selected Works of Lu Hsun*, I (Peking: Foreign Languages Press, 1956), pp. 332–38.

OLD MAN: What a child you are! You can see heaven, earth, and the wind every day; isn't that enough for you? There is nothing else worth looking at. Yet you still want to look at some person. Creatures which appear at sunset can't do you any good. . . . We'd better go in.

GIRL: But he's already quite close. Ah, it's a beggar.

OLD MAN: A beggar? That isn't likely.

[THE PASSER-BY limps out from the bushes on the east, and after a moment's hesitation walks slowly up to the old man.]

PASSER-BY: Good evening, sir.

OLD MAN: Thank you. Good evening.

PASSER-BY: Sir, may I make so bold as to ask for a cup of water? I am parched after walking, and there's not a pool or waterhole to be found.

OLD MAN: Yes, that's all right. Please sit down. [To THE GIRL.] Child, fetch some water. See that the cup is clean.

[THE GIRL walks silently into the hut.]

OLD MAN: Please sit down, stranger. What is your name?

PASSER-BY: My name? That I don't know. Ever since I can remember, I've been on my own; so I don't know what my name was. As I go my own way, people call me by this name or that as the fancy takes them. But I can't remember them, and I have never been called the same name twice.

OLD MAN: I see. Well, where are you from?

PASSER-BY [hesitating]: I don't know. Ever since I can remember, I have been walking like this.

OLD MAN: All right. Then may I ask you where you are going?

PASSER-BY: Of course you may. The thing is, I don't know. Ever since I can remember, I have been walking like this, on my way to some place ahead. All I can remember is that I have walked a long way, and now I have arrived here. I shall push on that way [he points to the west] ahead!

[THE GIRL carefully carries out a wooden cup of water and gives it to him.]

PASSER-BY [taking the cup]: Thank you very much, lass. [He drinks the water in two gulps, and returns the cup.] Thank you very much, lass. This was very kind, indeed. I really don't know how to thank you.

OLD MAN: There is no need to be so grateful. It won't do you any good.

PASSER-BY: No, it won't do me any good. But I feel much better now. I shall push on. You must have been here for quite a long time, sir. Do you know what kind of place that is ahead?

OLD MAN: Ahead? Ahead are graves.

PASSER-BY [startled]: Graves?

GIRL: No, no, no! There are ever so many wild roses and lilies there. I often go there to play, to look at them.

PASSER-BY [looking west, and appearing to smile]: Yes, there are many wild roses and lilies there. I have often enjoyed myself there too watching them. But those are graves. [To THE OLD MAN.] Sir, what comes after the graveyard?

OLD MAN: After the graveyard? That I don't know. I have never been beyond.

PASSER-BY: You don't know!

GIRL: I don't know either.

OLD MAN: All I know is the south, the north, and the east where you come from. Those are the places I am most familiar with, and they may be the best places for such as you. Don't take offence at what I say, but you are already so tired I think you would do better to go back; for if you keep on going, you may not come to an end.

PASSER-BY: I may not come to an end? . . . [He thinks this over, then starts up.] No, that won't do! I must go on. If I go back, there's not a place without troubles, not a place without landlords, not a place without expulsion and cages, not a place without artificial smiles on the face, not a place without tears outside the eyes. I hate them. I am not going back.

OLD MAN: It may not be like that. You may come across some tears that spring from the heart, some sorrow for your sake.

PASSER-BY: No, I don't want to see the tears that spring from their hearts. I don't want them to sorrow for my sake.

OLD MAN: In that case, you . . . [He shakes his head.] you will just have to go on.

PASSER-BY: Yes, I'll just have to go on. Besides, there is a voice ahead urging me on and calling me so that I cannot rest. The trouble is my feet are bruised through walking; I have cut them so many times and lost so much blood. [He raises one foot to show THE OLD MAN.] I haven't got enough blood; I need to drink some blood. But where can I get it? Besides, I don't want to drink just anyone's blood. So I have to drink water instead to make up for it. There is always water on the way; I have never found any lack of it. But my strength is failing fast, no doubt because there is too much water in my blood. Today not even one small waterhole did I find. That must be why I did not walk so far.

OLD MAN: That may not be why. The sun has set; I think you had better rest for a time, like me.

PASSER-BY: But the voice ahead is telling me to push on.

OLD MAN: I know.

PASSER-BY: You know? You know that voice?

OLD MAN: Yes. It seems to have called to me before as well.

PASSER-BY: Is it the same voice that is calling me now?

OLD MAN: That I can't say. It called me several times but I ignored it; so then it stopped, and I can't remember it clearly.

PASSER-BY: Ah, you ignored it . . . [He thinks this over, gives a start, and listens.] No! I must still go on. I cannot rest. What a nuisance that my feet are torn and bleeding. [He prepares to leave.]

GIRL: Here! [She gives him a length of cloth.] Bandage your feet.

PASSER-BY: Thank you very much, lass. [He takes the cloth.] This is really . . . This is really very, very kind of you. With this I can walk much further. [He sits down on some rubble to bind the cloth around his ankle.] No, this won't do. [He tries to stand up.] I had better give it back to you, lass. It is not enough for a bandage. Besides, this is too kind of you, and I have no way of showing my gratitude.

OLD MAN: There is no need to be so grateful; it won't do you any good.

PASSER-BY: No, it won't do me any good. But to me this is the finest gift of all. Look, can you see anything so fine on me?

OLD MAN: You need not take it so seriously.

PASSER-BY: I know. But I can't help it. I'm afraid that I behave like this: if I receive a gift, I am like a vulture catching sight of a corpse; I hover around longing for her death, hoping to see it myself. Or I curse all other people but her and pray that they may perish, including myself, for I deserve to be cursed. But I am not yet strong enough for that. Even if I were, I wouldn't want her to come to such an end, because usually they don't like to come to such ends. So I think this way is best. [To THE GIRL.] This cloth is very good, but a little too small. So I'll give it back to you.

GIRL [falling back, frightened]: I don't want it! Take it with you.

PASSER-BY [with something like a smile]: Ah. . . . Because I have held it?

41

GIRL [nods and points at his sack]: Put it in there, and keep it for fun.

PASSER-BY [stepping back despondently]: But how am I to walk with this on my back?

OLD MAN: Because you won't rest, you have no strength to carry it. After a rest you will be all right.

PASSER-BY: That's right, a rest . . . . [He reflects, but suddenly gives a start and listens.] No, I cannot! I must go.

OLD MAN: Don't you even want to rest?

PASSER-BY: I do.

OLD MAN: Well then, rest here for a while.

PASSER-BY: But I cannot. . . .

OLD MAN: You still think you had better go on?

PASSER-BY: Yes, I had better go on.

OLD MAN: Very well, you must go then.

PASSER-BY [stretching himself]: Good, I'll say goodbye then. I am very grateful to you. [To THE GIRL.] I'll give this back to you, lass. Please take it back.

[Frightened, THE GIRL draws back her hand and hides herself in the hut.]

OLD MAN: Take it along. If it is too heavy, you can throw it in the graveyard any time.

GIRL [coming forward]: Oh no, that won't do!

PASSER-BY: No, that won't do.

OLD MAN: Well then, you can hang it on the wild roses and lilies.

GIRL [clapping her hands and laughing]: Good!

PASSER-BY: Ah . . . .

[For a second there is silence.]

OLD MAN: Goodbye then. I wish you luck. [He stands up and turns to THE GIRL.] Child, help me inside. Look, the sun has already set. [He turns to the door.]

PASSER-BY: Thank you both. I wish you luck. [He hesitates thoughtfully, then starts.] But I cannot! I have to go on. I had better go. . . . [Raising his head, he walks resolutely towards the west.]

[THE GIRL helps THE OLD MAN into the hut, then shuts the door. THE PASSER-BY limps on toward the wilderness, and night falls behind him.]

(March 2, 1925)

DRAGON BEARD DITCH*
(A Play in Three Acts)

By Lao Sheh

Translated by Liao Hung-ying

CHARACTERS

THE WANG FAMILY:

MOTHER WANG, *a widow of about fifty. Her elder daughter is married. Earns her living together with her second daughter, by soldering mirror-frames and sewing.*

ERH-CHUN, MOTHER WANG's *second daughter, aged nineteen. Can read a few characters.*

THE CHENG FAMILY:

MAD CHENG, *in his early forties. Formerly a popular entertainer,[1] and a good singer of ballads, especially "shu-lai-pao."[2] Because he got into trouble with gangsters in the theater world, he could not get engagements, and so moved to live in the slums of Dragon Beard Ditch. Wears a long gown as if still in his former profession. Is a little queer, and so is called "MAD CHENG."*

NIANG-TSE, *wife of* MAD CHENG, *who always calls her "NIANG-TSE," though it is not really her name; everyone else does the same. In her middle thirties. Supports her husband and herself by sewing, and by doing a little business in the market.*

("Niang" *means "mother" or simply "woman"; "tse" is a common suffix in personal names, indicating affection or familiarity.*)

THE TING FAMILY:

TING SZE, *about thirty; a pedicab[3] driver.*

("Sze" *means "four"; he must have been the fourth child in his family.*)

SZE-SAO, TING SZE's *wife. About thirty. Helps to support the family by sewing.*

(*As her husband is fourth in his family, she is addressed as "SZE-*

---

*Reprinted from Foreign Languages Press, Peking, 1956.

sao," meaning "fourth elder sister-in-law." The styles "elder
brother" and "elder sister-in-law" are used by relatives and friends
on the husband's side who are younger, or for courtesy's sake
regard themselves as younger.)

KA-TSE, the TINGS' son, aged twelve, but not at school. Goes out
every day to pick cinders off the rubbish heaps for fuel, or just to
play about.

LITTLE NIU, the TINGS' daughter, aged nine, also not at school; follows her brother around everywhere.

("Niu" is a northern Chinese word for "girl.")

OLD CHAO, a bricklayer, aged sixty; no family.

POLICE SERGEANT LIU, over forty.

DOG FENG, aged twenty-five. The local gangster boss, BLACK WHIRL-
WIND (who does not appear), uses him to do his dirty work. Hence
his nickname "DOG," a term commonly used for someone who
does dishonest work for others.

PROPRIETOR LIU, over sixty; proprietor of a small teashop.

A YOUNG MAN.

TWO POLICEMEN.

A NUMBER OF LOCAL RESIDENTS.

A LOCAL BAD-HAT (only appears at side stage, and does not speak).

ACT I

Time: 1948, the year before the liberation of Peking. A morning in
early summer; it has rained during the night.

Place: Dragon Beard Ditch, a notorious ditch, east of the Bridge
of Heaven.[4] The Ditch is full of muddy, slimy water, mixed with
rubbish, rags, dead rats, dead cats, dead dogs, and now and
then dead children. The waste water from the nearby tan-
nery and dyeworks flows into it and accumulations of night-soil collect there to putrefy. The water in the Ditch is of various shades
of red and green, and its stench makes people feel sick quite
far away. Hence the district has earned the name of "Stinking
Ditch Bank." On the two banks, closely packed together, there
live laborers, handicraft workers—the multifarious toiling poor.
Day in and day out, all the year round and all their lives, they
struggle in this filthy environment. Their houses may tumble
down at any moment; most of their yards have no lavatories, let
alone kitchens. There is no running water; they drink bitter and

rank-tasting well water. Everywhere there are swarms of fleas, clouds of mosquitoes, countless bedbugs and black sheets of flies, all spreading disease. Whenever it rains, not only do the streets become pools of mud, but water from the Ditch overflows into the yards and houses, which are lower than the street level, and thus floods everything.

Setting: A typical small "courtyard" of the district; it contains only four tumbledown mud huts. Doors and windows are fixed anyhow; one is an old and broken lattice window, one is altered from "foreign-style" window, another was probably originally a Japanese sliding door. Some have old and mouldy newspaper pasted on; others just have broken wooden boards or pieces of old and tattered matting nailed on. Even if there is a small piece of glass anywhere, it is so covered with grime, soot, and dust that it hardly lets any light through.

On the north side (i.e., the left hand side of the audience) is the WANG family's house. A large earthenware water-butt stands in front of the door, together with a few broken wooden boxes. There is an oblong table placed so that the sun, which is just breaking through the dark clouds, shines on it; a piece of cotton cloth used as a wrapper is spread out on the table to dry. MOTHER WANG is lighting the stove, which burns coal balls and is used both for soldering mirror-frames and for cooking.

On the east side there are two families, the TINGS and the CHENGS, occupying one room each. The room on the left is the TINGS' house; the roof leaks and half a piece of tattered rush matting is tied on top of it, with a few broken bricks to keep it down; an old tire hangs under the eaves. A torn red curtain, covered with patches, hangs in the doorway. In front of the door there is hardly anything except a stove and a few broken pedicab parts. The room on the right is the CHENGS' house; an old bamboo curtain with the lower part half torn off hangs in the doorway. There are many cigarette cards pasted on the window. A stunted date tree grows near the door; a small trellis is supported by the tree and on the trellis climbs a morning glory. Under the trellis, at the top right hand corner, is the wood-burning stove, built of mud and fixed to the ground. CHENG NIANGE-TSE is lighting a fire with sticks which she has gathered. She is going to steam "wo-wo-tou"[5] for her husband's breakfast. (Most of the people in this district have only two meals a day.) The corner of the wall behind the

45

stove has fallen down, and through this gap can be seen distant houses, a few electric supply poles, and the lowering sky.

On the south side is the main gate of this courtyard, very low and narrow, so that one has to bend down when passing through. Outside the gate is a narrow lane, on the opposite side of which stands a large dilapidated house, with a board lettered in gold "Pawnshop" hanging from its top corner. On the west side of the main gate there is a broken-down wall, at the end of which stands OLD CHAO's house, consisting of a single room. The door is shut. In front of it lie a few of the bigger tools used by bricklayers. There are also a bench and a broken water-butt upside down. Some rubbish and brickbats are piled up behind the water-butt, and on these NIANG-TSE is drying her cigarette tray, tea, and other odds and ends of wares.

Lines are strung across here and there on which the families have hung out their old and tattered clothes and bedding to dry. All is mud underfoot except for patches where ashes, cinders, broken bricks or wooden boards have been laid down. The corners and the foot of the walls are mildewed and green with lichens. Overhead, dark clouds move slowly. The sun comes out one moment and goes in the next.

Curtain Rises: Outside the main gate are heard the cries of peddlers selling vegetables, pigs' blood, donkey meat and beancurd, the cries of barbers and of rag-and-bone men, and the voices of housewives arguing over prices. Nearby, there are also the sounds of the blacksmith's hammering, of handlooms, and of tin kettles and pans being beaten by the tinsmith. CHENG NIANG-TSE is sitting on a small bench in front of the stove and putting more sticks on the fire. LITTLE NIU is moving broken bricks from the foot of the wall by the gate, so as to make a path in the courtyard. TING SZE-SAO is using a broken basin to bail out the water which has flooded their room. The sun has just risen and WANG ERH-CHUN comes out of their room with wet clothes in her arms, looks at the sky, and hangs them on the line. MOTHER WANG, having lit the stove, looks up at the sky, and carefully gathers up the large cotton wrapper from the table and is going to take it into their room. ERH-CHUN, on her way back into the room, takes it from her mother and goes in. MOTHER WANG picks up the kettle, and walks toward the water-butt, but, feeling uneasy about the wrapper having been taken by her daughter, turns round and looks at her. Then

46

*she ladles water into the kettle and puts it on the stove; she sits
down and begins to work.*

SZE-SAO [*handing a basin of dirty water to* LITTLE NIU]: Mind you
look where you're going; if you drop the basin, see if I don't smack
you!

LITTLE NIU: Why always me? Why don't you mind brother? He
slips out early in the morning and doesn't do a thing!

SZE-SAO: Him? You wait and see; I'll give him such a hiding when
he gets back!

LITTLE NIU: How about Daddy? He doesn't come home at all!

SZE-SAO: Don't talk to me about him! If I don't settle with him
when he comes back. . . .

MAD CHENG [*inside the room, singing*]:

> My dear Sze-sao, you shouldn't rebuff him,
> The day you wed him you promised to love him.

NIANG-TSE [*putting the remains of last night's wo-wo-tou on the
stove to warm up*]: Get up! The room is soaking wet; how can
you go on lying there?

MAD CHENG:

> You tell me to get up, so up I get,
> Respected Niang-tse, please don't fret.

LITTLE NIU: Mad Uncle, get up quick and come and play with me!

SZE-SAO: You dare go and play! Empty that basin quickly! I want
to get on with my sewing; we've got nothing for our meal yet!

MAD CHENG [*in a worn gown of coarse linen, holding a palm-leaf
fan, fanning energetically as if to drive away the stench, walks out
of their room, bows to everyone*]: Good morning, Mother Wang!
Good morning, Niang-tse! Good morning, young ladies!

LITTLE NIU [*still not going to empty the basin*]: Please sing, Uncle!
I'll beat time for you!

SZE-SAO [*walking over*]: You empty the water first!

[LITTLE NIU *goes out.*]

NIANG-TSE: A grown man like you! Little Niu is more use. She helps.
But you . . . !

MAD CHENG: Niang-tse, you are mistaken.

[*Sings.*]

> I keep thinking, when I was on the stage,
> Singing ballads and earning a wage,
> Every day was happy as New Year's Day

Until they cheated me and took away my pay.
So now Ditch, people and all, stink till I choke,
And my breath comes out black, as foul as smoke.

[He fetches water to wash his face with.]

NIANG-TSE: You! My whole life's been a mess because of you!

SZE-SAO: Don't talk like that. At least he's better than my old man. After all, he's not quite right here [pointing to her head]. There's nothing wrong with mine; he just won't work. When he can't get a fare, he loafs around; if he does earn anything, he spends it on drink.

MAD CHENG [wiping his face]:

I've nothing wrong in my head, you know,
It's the stink of the Ditch that has brought me low.

[The call of a beancurd peddler is heard outside.]

There'll come a day when the Ditch won't stink, and the water will be sweet,
Then our land will be great, the people happy, and the world at peace.

[Sits down to eat wo-wo-tou.]

LITTLE NIU [enters, imitating the sound of bamboo castanets in the shu-lai-pao rhythm]: Kua-chi, kua-chi, kua-chi kua.

NIANG-TSE [picking up her cigarette basket]: Mother Wang, Sze-sao, please look after him for me. I'm going to market.

MOTHER WANG: The streets are all mud. How can you put up the stall?

NIANG-TSE: I'm going to have a look. If I don't try and get some money in, how shall we get anything to eat? This is a hellish place. Whenever the sky is overcast, I feel as if I had a pain in my heart. If July is going to be wet every day like this, we can only look on and go hungry. [Walks towards gate, then stops.] Look! It's getting dark again.

LITTLE NIU: Ma! I want to go out with Auntie Niang-tse.

SZE-SAO: Now be a good girl and stay here; you're not going anywhere! [She starts to sweep the courtyard.]

LITTLE NIU: I want to go! I want to go!

NIANG-TSE [at the gate]: Little Niu, you stay here. I'm going to make some money and I'll bring you back something to eat. Be good! It's all muddy and slippery outside. You might fall into the Ditch! What should we do then?

48

MAD CHENG:

>*Niang-tse, my dear, won't you be nice,*
>*And bring me back a girdle-cake[6] about this size?*

[*He makes a gesture indicating the size of a rice bowl.*]

NIANG-TSE: You? Pooh! A girdle-cake! I won't even buy you a peanut! [*Exit.*]

LITTLE NIU: Mad Uncle, whenever Niang-tse scolds you, she always brings you back something nice to eat!

SZE-SAO: Oh! Niang-tse is really wonderful!

MAD CHENG: Of course she is. It isn't that I don't want to help, but I can't. I feel so bad seeing her do everything, outside as well as at home. But . . . there's nothing I can say.

OLD CHAO [*coming out of his room, groaning*]: Give me a little water, someone!

MAD CHENG: Oh! You're up, Uncle Chao!

ERH-CHUN
LITTLE NIU } [*run over to him*]: How are you? How do you feel?

MOTHER WANG: We've been so busy, we've forgotten the old man. Erh-chun, put some water on.

ERH-CHUN [*running back*]: I'll get the can. [*Enters their room.*]

SZE-SAO [*sitting down on a stool and starting to sew*]: Uncle Chao, do you want anything?

MAD CHENG:

>*Ting Sze-sao, you've no time,*
>*And caring for the sick is just my line!*

ERH-CHUN [*bringing out the can, fills it from the kettle, puts it on the stove and then goes to look in the water-butt*]: Ma! There's not much water left!

LITTLE NIU: I'll go and get some!

SZE-SAO: No, not you! It's too far and too muddy. Not you!

MAD CHENG: I'll go and get it.

[*Sings.*]

>*You don't have to tell me I'm not very bright,*
>*Brewing tea and pouring water I'm all right.*
>*For helping people I'm just the man,*
>*At that sort of work I'll do all I can.*

MOTHER WANG [*standing up*]: Is it malaria then, Uncle Chao?

OLD CHAO [*nodding*]: Oh! Just now I was freezing, and now I'm all hot again!

MAD CHENG: Mother Wang, let me have the bucket.

49

MOTHER WANG: Sze-sao, let little Niu help. Mad Cheng is so clumsy. Supposing he fell in the Ditch!

SZE-SAO [*hesitates and then nods*]: All right, Little Niu, you may go. But take care and don't go too fast!

LITTLE NIU: Mad Uncle, we'll carry a bucket between us; it's three-quarters of a mile there and back. We shan't be able to carry more than that. [*Finds the pole.*] You take the bucket.

ERH-CHUN [*hands bucket to* MAD CHENG]: Aren't you going to take off your gown? It'll get muddy.

MAD CHENG [*taking the bucket*]:

> Under this gown I've nothing to wear,
> I can't go about with my back all bare!

LITTLE NIU: Kua-chi, kua-chi, kua-chi kua. [*Exit with* MAD CHENG.]

MOTHER WANG: Uncle Chao, shall we get a doctor to look at you?

OLD CHAO: A doctor? Even if I had the money, I wouldn't spend it on getting a doctor. Huh! I have this every year, and always about this time; after the rains when houses tumble down; just the time when I should have plenty of work, I always go and get this malaria! After a few goes, I feel like a wet rag. Terrible! Give me a drop of water, I'm thirsty!

MOTHER WANG: Erh-chun, fan the fire up!

OLD CHAO: Yes, do, there's a kind girl!

SZE-SAO: Uncle Chao, you should go and burn incense to the god of medicine, and then the malaria devil might leave you alone!

ERH-CHUN: Sze-sao, malaria is due to mosquito bites. Look what swarms of mosquitoes we've got here!

MOTHER WANG: Young girls shouldn't talk so much. As if she didn't know better than you! [*Sits down again.*]

ERH-CHUN [*pours boiling water into a coarse yellow bowl and brings it to the patient*]: Drink it, Uncle Chao.

OLD CHAO: Oh! Good girl; good girl! This'll save my life! [*Drinks.*]

ERH-CHUN [*seeing* OLD CHAO *driving flies away with his hand, borrows* SZE-SAO's *palm-leaf fan and gives it to him*]: Now I understand why my sister's never been back!

MOTHER WANG: Don't talk about her. That heartless girl. After all I've done for her, she's not been back to see me once since she got married! Don't you be like that and leave your mother with no one to look after her!

ERH-CHUN: You can't blame her, Ma; it's so filthy here, it drives you mad!

MOTHER WANG: It's dirty here, but there is work. You'll never find another place like this in Peking for getting a living. All round here, so many people, and only Mad Cheng out of a job. What use would a clean place be with nothing to eat? We'd starve.

ERH-CHUN: Yes, money's easy to get here, but it's easy to lose, too. Whenever it rains, the stalls can't be put up, you can't get out to work—you starve then too! Our rooms are flooded with stinking water; our things are soaked; they all cost money, don't they?

SZE-SAO: That's right! Last night the bed⁷ was soaked; I had to squat all night and hold these waistcoats on my head with an umbrella over them. It's bad enough to have our own things getting wet, but if our work gets spoilt, how can we pay for that?

ERH-CHUN: And because it's filthy, people get ill; when you're ill, you can't work—and you even have to pay out for medicine!

MOTHER WANG: Don't talk like that. A little dirt won't kill you, as they say. I've lived here thirty years and I've put up with it!

ERH-CHUN: What do you say, Uncle Chao? You get malaria every year, don't you?

MOTHER WANG: Let Uncle rest. He's ill. I know what's going on in your little head!

ERH-CHUN: What is it? Tell us!

MOTHER WANG: H'm! You're always running around to your sister's. I suppose she goes on about Dragon Beard Ditch; it's filthy, it stinks! She never stops to think this is where she was born and brought up! She's only been gone a few months and now she won't come near us; she says she'll be sick the moment she gets here! Don't you look at me like that! I'm not going to be caught again; I won't marry you to anyone outside!

ERH-CHUN: Then am I to be stuck here the rest of my life? And always have to go outside because there isn't a lavatory anywhere?

MOTHER WANG: Male or female, you can always get enough to eat here as long as you're willing to work. That's the most important thing; nothing else matters. This is a lucky place; if it isn't, why do more and more people come to live here?

ERH-CHUN: I've never seen a lucky place like this! There isn't one solid house here. Whenever there's a downpour, someone gets buried alive. Lucky place, indeed!

OLD CHAO: Erh-chun, is there a little more water?

ERH-CHUN [*takes the bowl from him*]: You have what there is, Uncle.

OLD CHAO: Oh, thank you!

MOTHER WANG: Won't you eat something?

OLD CHAO: I'm not hungry; only thirsty.

SZE-SAO: Malaria pulls you down: you ought to eat something, Uncle Chao.

ERH-CHUN [*handing water to him*]: Here it is.

OLD CHAO: Sorry to give you so much trouble.

ERH-CHUN: Don't mention it, Uncle.

OLD CHAO: Erh-chun, I'll tell you something.

ERH-CHUN: Go on!

OLD CHAO: Dragon Beard Ditch is not a bad place.

MOTHER WANG: Didn't I say so? Isn't that just what I said?

OLD CHAO: The place is good. The people are good, too. But there are two bad things about it.

ERH-CHUN: What?

SZE-SAO [*coming over with her sewing to join in*]: Tell us!

OLD CHAO: The officials are bad and the gangsters are bad!

MOTHER WANG: Uncle, we can be heard outside; be careful what you say!

[*The sky darkens as the sun is hidden behind clouds.*]

OLD CHAO: I know, but I don't care. I'm over sixty and I might have been dead before now. What have I got to be afraid of?

MOTHER WANG: Don't talk like that! Better alive than dead, no matter how you live!

OLD CHAO: Officials are bad. . . .

[POLICE SERGEANT LIU, *belt in hand, as if going on duty, passes the gate.*]

MOTHER WANG [*interrupting CHAO*]: Uncle Chao, there's someone. . . . [ERH-CHUN *runs to the gate and looks out.*] Erh-chun, come here!

ERH-CHUN [*at the gate*]: Oh, it's you, Sergeant!

SZE-SAO: [*running to the gate*]: Please come in and sit down!

SERGEANT: I'm due on soon, you know.

SZE-SAO: Come in and sit down. I want to ask you something.

SERGEANT [*enters*]: What is it, Sze-sao?

SZE-SAO: Ka-tse. You were going to look out for . . .

MOTHER WANG: Oh, Sergeant Liu, aren't you on duty, then?

SERGEANT: I was just going on when Sze-sao stopped me. [*Turning towards* OLD CHAO.] How are you, Uncle Chao?

MOTHER WANG: Poor man, he's got malaria again.

SERGEANT: Bad luck. Are you taking anything for it?

OLD CHAO: I never take medicine!

SERGEANT: You ought to take a good dose. If you're always ill like this, Mother Wang and Sze-sao have to look after you. . . .

ERH-CHUN: Never mind. I can look after him.

SERGEANT: But you've got work to do. In this courtyard no one has anything to fall back on. Take Sze-sao, now; her husband hardly ever comes home. . . .

SZE-SAO: That's just it. I asked you to come in because I wanted to ask you about that apprentice's job for Ka-tse that you were going to look out for. Have you found anything?

SERGEANT: I haven't forgotten. But these days, when prices jump half a dozen times a day, nearly all the regular businesses have shut up shop. It isn't easy.

MOTHER WANG: Yes, that's quite true.

SZE-SAO: Ka-tse's really willing and he's not afraid of hard work. Please do your best, Sergeant.

SERGEANT: Right, I'll keep it in mind. And by the way, Sze-sao, ask your husband to be careful and not to talk so much when he's had one or two. [Lowering his voice.] The night before last during the house-to-house search, five were taken off. They said they were . . . [Looking around, makes a figure of 8 with his hand.[8]] this! They've probably been . . . . Why must it be like this? We're all Chinese. I can't play this game.

OLD CHAO: You're right!

SZE-SAO: We heard two got away last time; was that your doing?

SERGEANT: My dear woman! For pity's sake keep your mouth shut, unless you want to see my head off!

SZE-SAO: Don't worry, none of us would talk outside.

ERH-CHUN: Sergeant, can't you get Ka-tse into a factory? I'd like to go, too!

SZE-SAO: Yes, that would be fine!

MOTHER WANG: Erh-chun, you're mad, a girl working in a factory!

SERGEANT: All the proper factories are closed, too. Don't worry; I'll think of something.

SZE-SAO: Thank you very much. Do sit down for a while.

SERGEANT: No, I can't.

SZE-SAO: Just a little while. Why not? [Brings MAD CHENG's bench across. SERGEANT has to sit down.]

OLD CHAO: You see, it's just as I was saying, the officials are bad. When the officials are bad, people simply can't live. It isn't only the factories; the traders too, big and small, have been forced out of business. Only the officials themselves seem to get fat on it.

ERH-CHUN: That's why there are more and more poor people!

MOTHER WANG: Erh-chun, don't talk so much!

OLD CHAO: Never mind the rest. Just take this stinking Ditch of ours. When the Japanese were here, we paid taxes for it to be dug out. Was it ever done?

ERH-CHUN: Never. And the money collected just vanished!

MOTHER WANG: Erh-chun, come here. [ERH-CHUN comes back.] Be careful what you say!

OLD CHAO: After the Japanese went, the government said the Ditch would be filled in. Well then, when it rained the place would have become a lake. So money was collected again; it mustn't be filled in, it must be dug out. But was anything done?

SZE-SAO: Damn them! The money went into their pockets again!

MOTHER WANG: Don't swear like that in front of an unmarried girl, Sze-sao!

ERH-CHUN: Damn them!

MOTHER WANG: Erh-chun!

OLD CHAO: Mad Cheng is always saying something about:

> The Ditch won't stink, and the water will be sweet,
> Our land will be great, the people happy, and the world at peace.

He's right; he's not mad. We must have clean officials before we can have clean water. I'm a bricklayer: I know that wherever the big officials live there are tarred roads. When somebody becomes an official, he always builds a large mansion. As for us poor devils, who cares about us?

SERGEANT: That's right enough!

SZE-SAO: Money collected from us goes straight into their pockets!

OLD CHAO: As long as we have these officials, we shall live by the stinking Ditch for ever and ever! Why, everywhere else in the city there's running water, but we don't get it!

MOTHER WANG: Don't grumble. We've got the well water; shouldn't we say a prayer to the Buddha for that?

SZE-SAO: The water's bitter, Mother Wang!

MOTHER WANG: Not too bitter. Don't be so fussy!

ERH-CHUN: Oh Ma, why must you always be so *patient*?

MOTHER WANG: And why won't you put up with things? You want to be like your sister, I know—marry and go away, and never give another thought to home. Have you no respect for parents at all?

OLD CHAO: Sergeant Liu, both times the money collected was handled by you. I ask you, where has it gone to?

54

SERGEANT: You ask me, do you? And who can I ask? My conscience is clear all right. [*Standing up and walking towards* CHAO.] If I made one cent out of that money, may I be struck by lightning from those clouds overhead! Others take the money; I get the abuse. Is it fair, I ask you?

OLD CHAO: Everyone in this neighborhood knows you; they all say you're all right!

SERGEANT: What can I do, Uncle Chao? I've got five mouths to feed; otherwise, I'd have got out of it long ago, instead of putting up with this life!

OLD CHAO: I understand. To come back to what we were saying. Besides the officials, we have the gangsters. They steal, they rob, they swindle; no one dare get across them. Some time ago, Inspector Chang tried to interfere and got three stab wounds in his stomach for his pains. What a world!

SERGEANT: They've got powerful backing. They can even kill people and get away with it!

MOTHER WANG: Don't! It makes me shiver!

OD CHAO: If they come my way, I'll settle with them once for all!

MOTHER WANG: Mind how you go, Uncle Chao. Do be careful how you talk when you're having a drink outside!

OLD CHAO: You wait and see! If they try anything on with me, I'll send them away with their tails between their legs!

SERGEANT: I really must go. Who can tell what trouble there may be today! [*Starts to walk out.*]

SZE-SAO [*following him out*]: Please don't forget about the job for Ka-tse, Sergeant!

SERGEANT: I'll remember. [*Exit.*]

SZE-SAO: Thank you very much.

MOTHER WANG: Sergeant Liu really is a decent man.

OLD CHAO: There aren't many like him. But you see, he can't do anything.

SZE-SAO: Even if he wanted to do something, he couldn't do it by himself. [TING SZE, *dispirited, enters.*] So you've come back!

TING SZE: You think I like coming back?

SZE-SAO: If you don't like coming back, you can go out again! We don't need a lout like you here!

[TING SZE *says nothing, yawns, and walks toward their room.*]

SZE-SAO [*stopping him*]: Give me the money.

TING SZE: You want money the moment I come back?

SZE-SAO: What do you think? There's nothing to eat in the house!

TING SZE: Nothing to eat? Would you care if I died on the street?

SZE-SAO: And would you care if the children and I died? Oh, don't talk so much, give me the money.

TING SZE: I haven't got any.

SZE-SAO: Where's it gone?

TING SZE: To pay the pedicab hire.

SZE-SAO: None of those tales! You think I don't know? You've been drinking!

TING SZE: That's none of your business. I'm the master and I can spend what I earn. What are you going to do about it? Let's hear!

SZE-SAO: What am I going to do about it? This broken-down home is yours as well as mine! All right then, we'll neither of us bother about it! [*Throws down her sewing.*]

TING SZE: You won't bother about it! Go ahead, don't bother!

SZE-SAO: You're out the whole day and you come back without a copper? You drink the money away, that's what it is.

TING SZE: Mind your own business. I tell you!

SZE-SAO: What? Mind my own business? When there's nothing for the pot? You're a fine one, aren't you!

TING SZE: I made a mistake; I shouldn't have come back. I'll go.
[SZE-SAO *stops him; he lifts the gate bar to strike her.* ERH-CHUN *rushes over and snatches it away from him.*]

OLD CHAO [*shouting*]: Ting Sze!
[TING SZE *is startled by* CHAO'S *angry call, bows his head and walks toward their room, without speaking.* SZE-SAO *sits down and cries.* ERH-CHUN *squats down and tries to comfort her.*]

OLD CHAO: This is your family affair. I really shouldn't butt in, but we've lived here together a long time. After all, I watched you grow up. So now I'm going to say something you won't like.

TING SZE [*dropping down on the seat*]: Let's have it.

OLD CHAO: Stop crying, Sister, and listen to me. [SZE-SAO *stops crying.*] [*To* TING SZE] What were you doing last night? Didn't you know there were three mouths waiting to be fed? The children are yours; don't you think of them?

TING SZE [*with tears in his eyes*]: It's not like that, Uncle Chao. It isn't that I don't think of them. It was drizzling the whole day yesterday; I had very few fares. In the evening I sat by a stall, and what do you think?—A loaf[9] which cost sixty thousand in the morning had jumped to a hundred and twenty thousand by the evening. After I paid the pedicab hire, there was nothing left. Prices double in a day! You know it's like that!

56

OLD CHAO: That's true. These prices will finish us. But, money or no money, you should have come back. It isn't right not to come home at all. Even for your own sake, it's dangerous to be out at night. Nowadays they inspect houses in the middle of the night, and if there is anything the slightest bit wrong, they take you away for the army, that is, if you're lucky. If you're unlucky, they say you're a Communist, give you the water torture, and load you up with the heavy beams; even if you were ground to powder no one would know how you died!

TING SZE: I know all that. Damn them! They're always going for us drivers, that goes without saying. Why, only yesterday, I thought I was in luck; I got a fare. But I took another look; I was in luck all right! A soldier! Still, I had to take him. From Yungting Gate to Tehsheng Gate, ploughing through muddy roads, in pouring rain, and me sweating like a pig from head to foot. Of course he didn't pay, and on top of that he nearly beat me up. Damn him! Riding in my cab and not paying! What sort of a bastard is that! After I'd turned in the cab, it started to rain again. I ran towards home . . . after a few steps I came a cropper. If you don't believe me, look at my bruises. So I thought, I couldn't possibly get along this stretch of road without slipping into the Ditch. So I sat up half the night in the Lius' teashop. I hardly slept, for fear of being taken off for a soldier. I tell you, as long as we have this stinking Ditch, no one can live a decent life.
[*The sounds of iron being hammered, bellows blowing, and looms weaving are heard more loudly.*]

SZE-SAO: Don't blame the lavatory because you're constipated! The Legation Quarter and the Forbidden City don't stink and aren't filthy; why don't you condescend to work there? Everyone round here's working. You're the only one without a regular job.

TING SZE: I drive the cab, don't I? I'm not on vacation every day!

SZE-SAO: What a job! There isn't another one like it! Everyone in the Ditch has a regular trade . . . the ironsmith, the weaver, the tanner . . . . They're all proper trades. But what sort of a trade is yours?

TING SZE: H'm! Trade or no trade, once on my cab, I'm away from this sinking Ditch. I was born under the sign of the ox, not under the sign of the housefly, and I hate this stinking place!

OLD CHAO: That's enough, both of you! [SERGEANT LIU *enters.*] Anything wrong, Sergeant?

SERGEANT: Didn't I say there'd be trouble today!

57

SZE-SAO: What is it, Sergeant?

SERGEANT: Oh—I can't help it. They've sent me to collect tax again!

ALL: What? Tax again!

SERGEANT: Yes, you see how hard it is for me.

TING SZE: We haven't even got any bread; how can we pay any dammed tax?

SERGEANT: True enough. But what can I do when they give me the order?

OLD CHAO: Well, let's hear, what's the tax for this time?

SERGEANT: Whatever it's for, it's tax; you'd better look after yourself and get better. Don't ask a lot of questions. Tax is tax. Give me the money and I'll hand it over to them. Then we'll all feel easier in our minds!

OLD CHAO: Come on, tell us, I'm listening!

SERGEANT: If you must know, Old Uncle, I'll tell you. This time it's Sanitation Tax.

OLD CHAO: What tax?

SERGEANT: Sanitation Tax.

OLD CHAO [laughing wildly]: Sanitation Tax! Sanitation Tax! [Again laughing wildly.] Ting Sze, where is our sanitation? Sergeant Liu, whose idea was this? May eight generations of his ancestors be damned!

[TING SZE supports him into his room.]

SERGEANT: Oh dear! What can I do?

MOTHER WANG: Don't blame the old man, Sergeant. If he hadn't got the fever, he would never swear at people like that.

ERH-CHUN: Ma, why are you always so afraid of trouble? Look at this place of ours. Is there a clean lavatory or a clean path? No one ever bothers about us. What should we pay Sanitation Tax for?

MOTHER WANG: My young lady, don't talk so much! Sergeant Liu, don't mind her. She's a child, she doesn't understand!

SERGEANT: Mother Wang, I belong here, too. What you have to put up with I have to put up with, too. Don't say any more. [Turns to go.]

MOTHER WANG: Won't you have a cup of tea? Yours is official business; it's not easy.

SERGEANT: Official business, that's right! Official business, ha-ha!

SZE-SAO: About how much will each family have to find?

TING SZE [coming out of CHAO's room]: Of course you must find out exactly; you're itching to pay!

SZE-SAO: And you're not, are you? Brave words! If you don't pay up, you go to jail!

TING SZE: Sergeant, tell them, if they make the roads up and clean out the Ditch, I'll pay. If they don't, I can't drive my cab, and I haven't any money to pay. If they want my life, all right, but I haven't any money!

SERGEANT: My good sir, who are you, who am I, to argue with the authorities?

MOTHER WANG: Ting Sze, don't make it more difficult for the sergeant. Being in his position isn't easy.

[Enter MAD CHENG and LITTLE NIU carrying the bucket of water between them.]

MAD CHENG: Kindly look out! Here comes the water! How do you do, Sergeant?

SERGEANT: How are you, Mad Brother?

[MOTHER WANG moves the water-butt cover and kitchen knife on to the small bench she is sitting on. ERH-CHUN takes the bucket and, with her mother's help, pours the water into the butt. MAD CHENG wants to help, too.]

TING SZE: What! Two of you and only half a bucketful!

LITTLE NIU: Mad Uncle sways about so! He kept on stumbling and all the water spilled out!

ERH-CHUN: No running water, and they demand sanitation tax!

SERGEANT: I'm not the water company either, my girl! Good bye!
[Exit.]

TING SZE [to CHENG]: Look at your gown; the bottom is caked with mud!

MAD CHENG:

> Black mud spots on a long white gown,
> Doesn't it look just like a picture!

[Sits down to scrape the mud off.]

TING SZE: For this we must also pay Sanitation Tax!

SZE-SAO: Pay or not, you ought to go and try to get something. We've got nothing to eat today yet.

TING SZE: I was sitting half the night under the eaves of a little teashop. Can't I sleep for a bit?

SZE-SAO: Then I ask you, what shall we eat?

TING SZE: You ask me; who am I to ask?

MOTHER WANG: Don't worry, Heaven won't let even a blind sparrow starve. Take some mixed flour of mine for today and let Ting Sze

59

rest. You can let me have it back tomorrow when he gets some money.

TING SZE: Is it really all right, Mother Wang?

MOTHER WANG: Of course! You'll return it. Go along now and get some sleep. [*She gives him a push.*]

[*TING SZE, head down, enters the room. ERH-CHUN has already gone inside and now brings out a small basin of flour which she takes to the TINGS' room. SZE-SAO follows her.*]

ERH-CHUN: Where shall I put it, Sze-sao?

SZE-SAO [*gratefully*]: My dear—give it to me. [*Takes it in.*]

[*KA-TSE comes in the gate, running, holding a glass bowl.*]

KA-TSE: Little Niu! Little Niu! Come and look at this!

LITTLE NIU [*running over*]: Ooh! Two little goldfish! Give them to me! Give them to me!

KA-TSE: They are for you. Haven't you been asking for goldfish ever since New Year?

LITTLE NIU [*holding the bowl*]: Lovely! Oh, Brother, you are nice! Mad Uncle, come and look, two of them, two of them!

MAD CHENG [*squatting down like a child to look at the goldfish, imitates the Peking goldfish peddlers*]:

> Goldfish, big and small
> Who'll buy my goldfish—o!

SZE-SAO: Ka-tse, you've been out since early morning. What've you been doing? Tell me!

KA-TSE: I . . . .

SZE-SAO: Where did you get the goldfish?

KA-TSE: Peddler Hsu Liu gave me them.

SZE-SAO: Why is he so kind to you? He's given you the bowl as well as the fish! Why is everyone so nice to you? You'd better tell me the truth. We may be poor, we may be dirty, but we don't steal! Tell me the truth, or I'll give you a good thrashing!

TING SZE [*inside the room*]: Has Ka-tse stolen something? I'll give it to him!

SZE-SAO: Don't you bother. I'll do it. Ka-tse, go and return the fish. If you don't, your father will give you the beating of your life! Now get on with you!

LITTLE NIU [*about to cry*]: Ma, I've wanted two little fish like these for ever so long.

ERH-CHUN: Sze-sao, we've only got flies and mosquitoes in this place of ours. Now Little Niu's got two goldfish, let her keep them!

60

SZE-SAO: I can't let the child be a thief!

MAD CHENG [*unbuttoning his gown*]:

> Ka-tse my boy, the truth you must tell,
> I'll bear your strokes and the scolding as well.

KA-TSE: Hsu Liu asked me to look after his fishtubs. I took two for Little Niu. She's got nothing to play with!

MAD CHENG [*taking off his gown*]: Give Hsu Liu my gown!

SZE-SAO: Of course not, that would never do! Two little fish aren't worth so much, anyway!

MAD CHENG:

> If only Little Niu will dry her eyes,
> What do we care about the price!

ERH-CHUN [*rushing over*]: Mad Brother, put on your gown. [*Gives two notes to* KA-TSE.] Run and take these to Hsu Liu!

[KA-TSE *takes the money and darts out.*]

SZE-SAO: Come back straight away! [*The sky gradually darkens.*] You shouldn't have done it, Erh-chun! Little Niu, aren't you going to thank Granny Wang and Auntie?

LITTLE NIU [*going across, the bowl in her hands*]: Thank you, Granny! Thank you, Auntie!

MOTHER WANG: Look after them carefully; don't let some stray cat eat them!

LITTLE NIU [*handing the bowl to* MAD CHANG]: Mad Uncle, look after them for me. I'm going to get some water-weed from the goldfish pond. Red fish and green weeds, won't they look lovely!

SZE-SAO: You mustn't go alone, you may fall in the Ditch!

[*By the time* SZE-SAO *has run after her to the gate,* LITTLE NIU *has run off.* DOG FENG *comes along, guided by another* LOCAL BAD-HAT; *the latter points out the gate and* DOG *enters, swaggering. The other goes away again.*]

SZE-SAO: Hallo, who are you looking for?

DOG: What's your name?

SZE-SAO: My name's Ting. Who are you looking for? Say something! You can't lounge around all over our courtyard like that!

DOG: Where do the Chengs live?

ERH-CHUN: What do you want them for?

MOTHER WANG: Keep quiet! [*Tries to push* ERH-CHUN *into the room.*]

DOG: You little slave, don't ask questions!

ERH-CHUN: Why shouldn't I?

MOTHER WANG: My young lady, do as I say and go in!

ERH-CHUN: Why should I go in? What can he do to me?

[*By this time* MOTHER WANG *has pushed her inside and shut the door, which she holds tightly closed.*]

DOG [*turning round, sees* MAD CHENG]: Isn't that Cheng?

SZE-SAO: He's mad. What do you want him for?

MOTHER WANG: Yes, he's mad.

DOG [*speaking at the same time as* MOTHER WANG]: Damn you women! Mind your own business! [*To* MAD CHENG.] You, my son, come over here!

ERH-CHUN [*from inside the room*]: Don't you come here and bully people!

MOTHER WANG [*to* ERH-CHUN *inside the room*]: Please don't make trouble for me!

SZE-SAO: He's quite mad. You can tell me what you've got to say.

DOG [*to* SZE-SAO]: Woman, if you interfere any more, I'll give you a hiding.

SZE-SAO [*walking away upset*]: You're doing fine, aren't you!

MAD CHENG [*coming over to divert the threat from* SZE-SAO]: I am Cheng. You sir, whatever you have got to say, say it to me!

DOG: Listen, you! On behalf of my lord and master, Black Whirlwind, I'm going to teach you a lesson. Never mind whether it's you or your woman or any of your neighbors, you've all got to remember: when you go to do business in the secondhand market, if one of Lord Black Whirlwind's men takes something from you, it gives you face, see? I, Feng, gave your woman face today by taking two packets of cigarettes from her, and she went and called the police! She should know her place! I won't have any dealings with her; she's a woman and not worth hitting, so I'm going to teach you a lesson!

NIANG-TSE [*comes in, carrying the cigarette basket, which has been kicked and broken by* DOG, *angry and fighting back her tears, her head bowed. As she enters, she sees* DOG FENG *throwing his weight about*]: Do you want to finish us all off? You rob and loot; you kick over my basket and now you even come to our own front door to bully us!

[SZE-SAO *takes the broken basket from* NIANG-TSE, *who runs at* DOG FENG.]

DOG [*leaving* MAD CHENG *and slowly but threateningly advancing on* NIANG-TSE]: Kicking your basket was nothing; if you really get me angry, I shan't let you go out at all!

62

NIANG-TSE [*bravely, but forced to retreat*]: Will you be reasonable or not? How can you come and act the bully like this? Let's go; we'd better go to the police after all.

DOG [*threatening*]: A gentleman doesn't fight women. [*Turning to* MAD CHENG] You, my son, this'll teach you. [*He brutally slaps* MAD CHENG's *face several times, so that his mouth bleeds.*]

[MAD CHENG *doesn't resist, but sheds tears.* NIANG-TSE *in a rage rushes fearlessly at* DOG, *but he grabs hold of her.* ERH-CHUN *bursts out of the room and tries to hit at* DOG; MOTHER WANG, *terrified, pulls her back;* SZE-SAO *wants to help* NIANG-TSE *but doesn't dare come near.*]

OLD CHAO [*comes out of his room trembling with anger*]: Get out of the way, Niang-tse and Sze-sao; I'm going to deal with him. Beating people up like that! Hitting someone who wouldn't even hurt a fly! Do you want a row? [*Snatches up* MOTHER WANG's *kitchen knife.*]

DOG: Old man, why the devil do you meddle in other people's business? Do you want to get hit, too?

MOTHER WANG [*seeing* OLD CHAO *holding her knife*]: Sze-sao, Niang-tse! Stop Uncle Chao, he's got a knife!

OLD CHAO: I'll kill the swine!

NIANG-TSE: Kill him! Kill him!

ERH-CHUN: Kill him! Kill him!

SZE-SAO [*holding* NIANG-TSE, *blocks* OLD CHAO's *way*]: Ting Sze, come out quick! He's going to use a knife!

MOTHER WANG [*to* DOG]: Are you still not going? He's really got a knife!

DOG [*seeing that things look ugly*]: I'll leave you be for now, and you can leave me alone. But we'll see what happens next time we meet! [*Exit.*]

ERH-CHUN: You dare come back again!

TING SZE [*comes out of the room rubbing his eyes*]: What's the matter? What's the matter?

SZE-SAO: Take the knife away from him!

TING SZE [*goes across and takes the knife away from* CHAO]: Uncle Chao, don't use a knife!

MOTHER WANG [*anxiously*]: Uncle Chao, Uncle Chao, what have you done! How can you offend one of Black Whirlwind's men? Even the police are afraid of them. How can we afford to offend them? Oh dear! No good will come of this!

OLD CHAO: They even bully Mad Cheng! I can't stand it any longer!
I've been wanting to deal with them for a long time; they can't
lord it over Dragon Beard Ditch forever!

MOTHER WANG: Niang-tse, wipe the blood off Mad Cheng's face and
change his clothes; get him away quick and hide him. If Dog
brings some of his gang here, whatever shall we do? Ting Sze, take
Uncle Chao away and hide, too. There's going to be real trouble!

NIANG-TSE: It's all right for me to scold Mad Cheng, but I won't
stand for other people bullying him. I'm going to wait for Dog.

MOTHER WANG: Don't talk; you'd better get away quickly.

OLD CHAO: I'm not going away. I'm going to wait for them with a
knife! We're too meek and mild; that's why they get like that! If
we're not afraid to stand up to them with force, they'll run away
with their tails between their legs! I'm not feverish any more, I
mean what I say!

MOTHER WANG: Go away for my sake. I'm terrified of fights. There
are too many in their gang, and we can't afford to offend them.
Once you start fighting, someone's bound to be killed!

OLD CHAO: If I stay here, they won't come. But if I go, they'll certainly come.

TING SZE: You're right. I'm going back to bed. [Enters room.]

NIANG-TSE: Mad Cheng, if we're going to die, let's die together. I'm
not going away.

MOTHER WANG: Oh dear, or dear, this is terrible! Whatever's going
to happen!

ERH-CHUN: Ma, why are you so timid!

MOTHER WANG: You're very brave! You don't know how terrible
they are!

MAD CHENG [in a sad voice]:

> Mother Wang, Ting Sze-sao,
> However you look at it, I caused the row.

[Sits down dejectedly.] In the old days, when I worked in the city
as an entertainer, I wouldn't toady to the officials, so I got beaten
up; I couldn't go on the stage there any more. Then I came here
to the Bridge of Heaven; again I refused to pay bribes and again
I was beaten up and left lying half dead at the foot of the Temple
of Heaven wall.[10] Since I came to again, I've never left the Ditch
here!

NIANG-TSE: Don't feel so sorry for yourself!

64

ERH-CHUN: Let him talk: he'll feel better when he gets it off his chest.

MAD CHENG: I'm a good man, Erh-chun. But if good men have no strength in their bodies, then they are terrorized. It is wrong to beat people, but it is also wrong to suffer beating. Yet I can't do anything but suffer it. Why, I want to work too, don't I? I don't want to see Niang-tse going and wearing herself out for me.

NIANG-TSE [moved]: Oh, don't say any more, please!

MAD CHENG: But I have no strength; I can't do any work. I'm only a half-mad man. [Distracted.] That's it! I must go away! I'll go. I can hide myself somewhere.

KA-TSE [runs in and obstructs him.]

KA-TSE: Ma, I gave the money to Hsu Liu. He didn't say anything. Ma, there's lightening again in the distance. It's going to rain again!

NIANG-TSE [holding MAD CHENG]: Don't give me any more trouble please.

SZE-SAO [looking at the darkening sky]: Oh! Heaven, have pity on us poor people. Don't rain. Everything's soaking—filthy water everywhere. Where can we hide? If there is lightening, let it strike the gangsters; if there is rain, let it fall on the fields. Don't grind us poor devils down for ever!

[Distant thunder.]

MAD CHENG [stands stiffly looking at the sky]: Where can I go? Is there a place for me in the whole world?

[Thunder.]

NIANG-TSE: Quick, take the things inside!

[All rush into their rooms with their belongings; rain falls in torrents, POLICE SERGEANT rushes in.]

SERGEANT: Something terrible has happened! Little Niu has fallen into the Ditch!

ALL: Little Niu . . . . [They rush out pushing.]

SZE-SAO [crying wildly]: Little Niu! [Runs out of the gate.]

[Fierce wind and pelting rain.]

Slow Curtain

ACT II

SCENE 1

Time: *After the liberation of Peking. The first anniversary of* LITTLE
NIU's *death.*

Place: *Same as Act I.*

Setting: *Before dawn. All dark in the courtyard, but windows and
doors in the various houses are just visible. Outside the gate, the
former pawnshop has been transformed into a "Workers' Coopera-
tive"; its signboard is now brightly lit by the street light. Gradually
the sky gets lighter, showing up the courtyard as somewhat tidier
than in Act I. Some windows and doors have been repaired. There
is less rubbish. The torn matting on the* TINGS' *roof has gone.*

Curtain Rises: OLD CHAO *is the first to get up. He comes out of his
room, looks at the dawn, smiles, opens the gate, picks up a broom
and sweeps out the courtyard. There are various noises in the distance: cocks crowing, carts creaking, etc.*

[DOG FENG, *pulling his hat down, enters quietly, and stands by
the gate.* OLD CHAO, *sweeping, raises his head.*]

OLD CHAO: Who is it?

DOG [*pushing up his hat and showing his face*]: It's me. I've something to say to you. Let's go to the Temple of Heaven and talk
outside the wall there.

OLD CHAO: If you've something to say, you can say it anywhere;
there's no need to go there!

DOG [*chuckles*]: No Sir! This comes from Black Whirlwind. . . .

OLD CHAO: Black Whirlwind? Who's he giving orders to?

DOG: Me. Don't misunderstand me. He's told me to come and have
a talk with you.

OLD CHAO: We're liberated now, you know!

DOG: That's just why I want to have a talk with you.

OLD CHAO: Honest folks can hold their heads up now and your sort
are not doing so well; isn't that it? Isn't that what you want to
talk about?

DOG: Now don't get nasty. Tell me, aren't you the local Public
Safety Warden?

OLD CHAO: Certainly I am; they've done me the honor of electing
me.

Doc: They say, you're acting as unofficial police chief so as to catch us, and that you've already got more than thirty of us!

Old Chao: Since everyone has elected me, I must do my best for them. The honest folks, I help them; the others, I'll fight them.

Doc: So you want to be a boss, too?

Old Chao: Black Whirlwind is a gangster, and I'm dead against all gangsters. There's nothing new about that, you know.

Doc: Perhaps you were tied up with Communists before?

[*It is now broad daylight.*]

Old Chao: That's my own business, nothing to do with you.

Doc: All right! You think you're onto a good thing, and you're feeling pleased with yourself!

Old Chao: It's not just luck. I'm a bricklayer—a worker—and this is a workers' government.

Doc: Very well. You're a hero now, but you'd better not get across Black Whirlwind. A starved camel is still bigger than a horse, you know!

Old Chao: What are you really after, coming here? Come on, what is it? Don't talk so much.

Doc: I've brought you something to put away for a rainy day. [*Shows a packet of silver dollars.*] They're from Black Whirlwind. Thirty shining silver dollars; I guarantee you've never had so much money in your life before. Take them, ease up a bit, and don't keep on at us. Do you get that?

Old Chao: And suppose I don't want your money?

Doc: Please yourself. If you don't want it the easy way, you can have it the hard way.

Old Chao: All right then, get out your knife.

Doc: Do you think I dare do that *now*?

Old Chao: Then what *do* you want? [Doc *is silent.*] Speak up! [*Angrily.*]

Doc [*gradually softening*]: Calm down! Take the money, won't you? The well water needn't interfere with the river water.

Old Chao: Oh no! You can't get away with that!

Doc: Just as you like then. [*Moving off.*]

Old Chao: Wait a bit! From now on only honest business will be allowed in the markets. There's going to be no more robbing, stealing, and swindling. They'll all be looking out for it and they'll all help each other. If you so much as raise a finger, someone will grab you. You always used to have your own agents to back you;

now you'll have to reckon with the stall-holders and the buyers as well; they'll all be out to catch you!

DOG: Chao, don't finish us off completely. If I'm driven too far, I'll . . . .

OLD CHAO: You'll what? The country belongs to all us people now and not the gang bosses, you know!

DOG [*solemnly and slowly*]: Black Whirlwind says . . . .

OLD CHAO: What does he say?

DOG: He says . . . [*Looking round, in a low but threatening voice.*] Chiang Kai-shek will be coming back before long!

OLD CHAO: Him? The biggest crook of them all? You'd have to kill off all the people first!

DOG: Why are you so sure about it?

OLD CHAO: Why? Because the people threw him out! That's why I'm so sure! Now look here, Dog, you're still young. You could make a fresh start and find some honest work to do.

DOG: Me? [*Hesitant and confused, but pretending to be confident.*]

OLD CHAO [*seeing that he won't see the point, changes his tone*]: You talk big, but you're weak really. I want to give you a chance to go straight. As for Black Whirlwind, he ought to be shot! But you are only one of his little dogs. There's still hope for you, if you're only willing to try. Now go back home and think it over very carefully. If you follow my advice, I'll help you to get on the right track. If you don't, then you'll be finished. Now be off home!

DOG: All right, see you again. [*Pulls down his hat again and exits.*] [*OLD CHAO meditates a moment and then resumes his sweeping. MAD CHENG holding the goldfish bowl in both hands comes out of his room. NIANG-TSE pulls at his elbow.*]

NIANG-TSE [*seriously*]: Have you got one of your turns again, or what? What are you trying to do? Come back. If you go and make a scene, you know you'll only upset the Tings again!

MAD CHENG: Don't interfere. I'm not going to make a scene. I won't upset them. I'm going to tell Uncle Chao that it's a year ago to-day since Little Niu died.

NIANG-TSE: You needn't do that either.

MAD CHENG: Go back to bed, dear. I shall feel I have a weight on my heart until I've told Uncle Chao.

NIANG-TSE: A grown man like that and he's just like a child! [*Enters room.*]

68

MAD CHENG: Uncle Chao, look. [*Shows the bowl.*]

OLD CHAO [*straightening his back*]: Oh! [*In a subdued voice.*] Little Niu, a year ago today she . . . such a lovely child; quick as a wild animal she was! . . . And then . . . .

MAD CHENG: Uncle Chao, you are always fighting our enemies these days. Why don't you fight the worst of them all?

OLD CHAO: The worst? You mean Black Whirlwind?

MAD CHENG: No! The Ditch that drowned Little Niu! Isn't that the worst of them all? Why don't you do something about it?

OLD CHAO: I will! Of course I will! You'll see, whenever they get to work on the Ditch, I'll be there! You see if I don't keep my word!

MAD CHENG: But when *is* it going to be cleaned out? Tomorrow? If you can tell me the day, then I'll really respect this government. I'm just going to buy two goldfish—the two Little Niu gave me to look after died. There's only the bowl left. I'll go to her grave and put the bowl on it with the red fish and green weeds in it, and I'll mourn for her. I've already made up the words. Listen!

OLD CHAO: All right, all right! I don't need to hear it all!

MAD CHENG: Yes! Listen! Listen!

[*Singing sadly, low, and slowly to a traditional tragic tune.*]

> By Dragon Beard Ditch, I tell you true,
> There lived a sweet girl called Little Niu.
> The Ditch was stinking and foul, but she
> Blossomed down there like a wild apple tree.
> Wild apple tree, your days are few,
> Who cares what becomes of you.
> Our city is freed, our sadness gone,
> Our streets are resounding with dance and song.
> But you, little friend, in my dreams I see;
> You don't sing or dance, you don't answer me.

[*He is too moved to go on.*]

OLD CHAO: Stop! Stop! Don't sing any more. Poor Little Niu! How terrible it was! But don't be so sad. Listen to me. This government is all right. It's not going to forget us; it's sure to put the Ditch right for us!

MAD CHENG: When? It must be soon!

OLD CHAO [*a little impatient*]: It's not something I can do on my own, you know!

MAD CHENG: I know, I know. I shouldn't press you. What I'm trying to say is, you're the only one who's got ability and ideas. But

69

the more I admire you, the more I want to push you to do things, don't I?

OLD CHAO: I don't mind, Mad Brother. You go in now and hide the bowl away; it'll make Sze-sao cry if she sees it.

MAD CHENG: I'll go in. But I've something else to talk to you about. You remember you said that everyone must work now? Before, I was always afraid of being set on again; I didn't dare go out; I had no strength at all and any work made me tired. But people are all kinder now, couldn't I do something? But what? Sell sweets or something? That wouldn't be enough for me to live on myself. Get a job as a servant? I couldn't wait on people!

OLD CHAO: Don't be in too much of a hurry. As long as you are willing to work, there will be opportunities.

MAD CHENG: I am willing. It's just that I have so little energy!

OLD CHAO: I'll think up something for you by and by. We're going to have running water here, aren't we? We shall need someone to take charge of the tap and sell the water. I'll go and find out about it; if they haven't got someone for the job already, I'll ask if you'll do.

MAD CHENG: That would be wonderful. Thank you in anticipation! I must tell Little Niu this as well. That's settled then. [Turns to go.]

OLD CHAO: Don't thank me yet; I don't know if it can be done or not.

[SZE-SAO with her hair down and shoes carelessly slipped on comes out of their room. MAD CHENG quickly hides the bowl behind his back.]

OLD CHAO: Oh, you're up, Sister.

SZE-SAO [sadly]: I didn't sleep the whole night. How could I sleep?

OLD CHAO: You mustn't feel so sad, Sister. How is Ting Sze?

SZE-SAO: He didn't come back at all last night. Yesterday evening I tried to persuade him to change his job. We had a few words. And besides, he saw I was thinking of Little Niu. That upset him and he took himself off.

OLD CHAO: He felt it, too. After bringing her up safe from a baby, right up to that age. This stinking Ditch—what a murderous devil it is! [Seeing SZE-SAO about to cry.] Don't cry, Sister!

SZE-SAO [trying to control herself]: No, I won't cry. Don't try to hide it from me, Mad Brother. My own child that I bore, how can I help grieving for her. Still, the dead are dead. The living have to

70

go on living. There's nothing you can do about it. People like us haven't got much, but we *have* got the strength to struggle on.

MAD CHENG: Sze-sao, don't let's cry. [*As he speaks, he is about to himself.*] I . . . I . . . . [*Quickly turns and rushes into his room.*]

SZE-SAO: [*wiping away her tears, turns to* OLD CHAO]: Uncle Chao, Little Niu can't come to life again, it's no use crying. But what can we do about Ting Sze? You must think of something for me.

OLD CHAO: He's all right at heart.

SZE-SAO: I know. Otherwise I wouldn't bother to talk to you about him. When he started to drive the pedicab, I didn't like it. It wasn't a proper job, not respectable, and didn't bring in a regular income. Ever since Little Niu died it's worse than ever; one night he doesn't come home at all; the next night he comes home drunk. Uncle Chao, don't you always say that it's most respectable to be a worker nowadays? Can't you persuade him to take up regular work? It doesn't matter what it is, cleaning out ditches or repairing roads, I should know where to find him. As it is, once on his cab he may be at the West Gate, he may be at Nanyuan on the southern outskirts, he may be anywhere; I haven't a hope of finding him. And even when he does earn a lot, he says he hasn't got a penny. I can't get at the truth! Do talk to him and find him a regular job, so that even if he only earns a little I shall know where to find him!

OLD CHAO: Sister, leave it to me, I'll talk to him. But you mustn't nag him any more. Quarreling only makes things worse; it doesn't do any good, does it now?

SZE-SAO: I promise! But if you talk to him and I scold him, won't it be even more effective?

OLD CHAO: No, no! That won't do. You must be gentle with him and show some affection, and I'll use my authority. That's the way!

SZE-SAO: I don't know whether to laugh or cry! [*Laughs sadly.*] Anyway I'm going to mourn for Little Niu. [*Puts shoes on properly.*]

OLD CHAO: I'm coming with you!

MAD CHENG [*running out*]: I'm coming with you, too, Sister!

[*They go out together.*]

Scene 2

Time: 1950, *spring. About four o'clock one afternoon.*
Place: *Same as Scene 1.*
Curtain Rises: *There is no one in the yard.* Erh-chun *rushes in from outside, all out of breath.*

Erh-chun: Hallo! where's everybody gone to? . . . Sze-sao, where's Ka-tse?
Sze-sao [*in her room*]: Gone to school.
Erh-cun: Then why is his teacher looking for him everywhere?
Sze-sao [*coming out*]: Is she? If the child isn't at school, he must have gone off to play somewhere!
Erh-chun: Then I'll go and have another look for him. [*Runs out of gate.*]
Mother Wang [*coming out of her room*]: Erh-chun, come back!
Sze-sao [*rushing out to the gate*]: Erh-chun, come back! Your mother wants you!
Erh-chun [*comes back, wiping her forehead*]: He'll be missing school!
Sze-sao: Don't you worry, he'll go; he hasn't missed school at all. He's studying very hard these days. I'll try and find him on my way to get my sewing.
[*Exit.*]
[Erh-chun *fetches wash-basin from her room and wipes face and neck with damp cloth.*]
Mother Wang [*looking displeased, comes out from her room*]: Erh-chun, why were you looking for him? You're always dashing about like a fly without a head these days instead of working!
Erh-chun: Who says I'm not working? I've done my full share!
Mother Wang: A big girl like you dashing about the whole time! I'm not used to it!
Erh-chun: Times have changed, Ma! If we young people stay at home, who's going to run things? Tell me that?
Mother Wang: Don't be so unkind! You know I can't go out and run things!
Erh-chun: Then why not let us go? [*Changing to a conciliatory tone.*] You know Miss Chi, Ka-tse's teacher; after teaching in a school the whole day she takes an evening class for illiterates, without pay. And not only that; if the pupils don't turn up, she goes to their houses to fetch them out. Did you ever see people

72

like that before? Just after I'd delivered our work, I ran into her
going from door to door to fetch her pupils. So I told her to rest
a little and I would go and find them for her; I got them all
except Ka-tse.

MOTHER WANG: Don't bother about him! What does it matter if
the son of a pedicab driver studies books or not. He's not going
to get a doctor's degree, is he?

ERH-CHUN: What are you talking about, Ma? We all have the same
rights now, and it's just people like the sons of pedicab drivers
who need to study more than anyone else. Otherwise, how can
they *really* stand up?

MOTHER WANG: A girl like you is going to marry a high official, I
suppose!

ERH-CHUN: Oh you! You're old fashioned! You only think of officials.
If I get married, it'll be to a Labor Hero!

MOTHER WANG: You shameless girl! How dare you talk about such
things when you're not married!

ERH-CHUN: Not married? Don't speak too soon. I can get married as
soon as I want to!

MOTHER WANG: You're getting worse and worse. It's really indecent!
The more you learn, the looser you get.

[NIANG-TSE *enters hurriedly from outside.*]

ERH-CHUN: Niang-tse, have you seen Ka-tse?

NIANG-TSE: Why, of course I've seen him; he was minding my stall
for me!

ERH-CHUN: Minding your stall? That's all very fine, but didn't you
know he ought to be at school? I've been looking for him everywhere!

NIANG-TSE: He didn't tell me!

ERH-CHUN: Oh, that child!

MOTHER WANG: He is so careless; can he look after your stall all
right?

NIANG-TSE: A child of three could do it nowadays! Prices are fixed;
no more bargaining. Pilferers will soon be extinct. [*Lowering her
voice.*] I hear they're tightening up to catch Black Whirlwind.
Once he's caught, the whole market will be quiet. He's the ring-
leader! Well, when he and that Dog Feng are caught, I'm going
to have my revenge. If I get a chance, I'll let them have it! I'll
bash them! If I can't get near enough, I'll spit in their faces, the
dirty swine! They stole my things, they hit my poor old man.
. . . By the way, where is he? Is he in?

ERH-CHUN: There isn't a sound from him, if he is!

NIANG-TSE: He's been very full of himself lately. I don't know what new bee he's got in his bonnet! He worries me.

[MAD CHENG *comes slowly out of his room.*]

ERH-CHUN: So you are in, Mad Brother!

MAD CHENG: The saying goes:

It's good to stay at home a year,
It's hard to go away an hour!

NIANG-TSE: Crazy again! Whatever's happened to you the last two days?

MAD CHENG: Nothing!

NIANG-TSE: I don't believe it! Tell me!

MAD CHENG: I'll tell you, but don't stare at me so! I can't stand rows. Well then, I've got a job!

ERH-CHUN: Congratulations, Mad Brother! Tell us what it is!

MAD CHENG: Someone from the Popular Education Center came to ask me if I would go and sing for them.

ERH-CHUN: Oh, isn't that wonderful! You've been kept down for years, and now you're invited to work *there!* Doesn't it feel as if you've come to life again?

NIANG-TSE: Yes, do go! Everyone will have a chance to see you then! Mother Wang, Erh-chun, can you lend me any money? I want to dress him up and make him look as nice as he used to in the old days!

MAD CHENG: But I can't go.

ERH-CHUN }
NIANG-TSE } : Why? Whyever not?

MAD CHENG: It's more than ten years since I sang last. If I were a failure, it would be terrible!

NIANG-TSE: You haven't gone yet, how do you know you'll be a failure? Really! You're being specially honored and you want to turn it down!

MOTHER WANG: I think, if there's any pay, go; if there isn't, don't go!

ERH-CHUN: You don't have to talk, you know, Ma! No one's going to try and pass you off as a dummy!

MAD CHENG: Besides, what can I sing?

"Green Screen Hill"—not at all decent,
"Wishing for a Baby"—it just isn't elegant!

ERH-CHUN: We'll make one up! Let's have a meeting this evening and everybody produce ideas and make something up together! A *shu-lai-pao* will do fine!

MAD CHENG: Will it?

ERH-CHUN: Yes! Everyone likes them and you sing them so well.

MAD CHENG: No, it can't be done.

[SZE-SAO *comes in through the gate, with a big bundle of sewing under her arm.*]

SZE-SAO: Niang-tse! Erh-chun! They've got Black Whirlwind!

NIANG-TSE: No! Have they really? Where is he?

SZE-SAO: I saw him being taken to the police station.

NIANG-TSE: I'm going to go and spit in his face!

ERH-CHUN: Let's go and let him have it! Tell everyone what he's been doing all these years, and give him his deserts, the beast!

MOTHER WANG: Ehr-chun, I forbid you to go!

ERH-CHUN: Don't worry, he can't eat me!

NIANG-TSE [*to her husband*]: You come too!

MAD CHENG [*shaking his head*]: No, I don't want to go.

NIANG-TSE: But they hit you, didn't they, till your mouth bled and your face was swollen for days? Haven't you any backbone?

MAD CHENG: I'm not going. I'm afraid of fighting. I'm terrified of those people.

NIANG-TSE: You're behind the times. Come on, Ehr-chun!

ERH-CHUN: Coming! [*Runs out with* NIANG-TSE.]

MOTHER WANG: Erh-chun, stand well away from Black Whirlwind! Really! That girl's getting crazier and crazier!

SZE-SAO: Don't be so rigid, Old Lady. Women are respected nowadays; they can go anywhere they like, just as men can. Why, ever since New Year the girls here are being vaccinated and inoculated free and going to school too, just like the boys! Oh, if only Little Nui were still alive. . . .

MAD CHENG: Wouldn't it have been wonderful!

SZE-SAO: She was too . . . . [*Bows her head and rushes into the room.*]

MOTHER WANG: Oh! . . . . [*Walks toward her own room.*]

MAD CHENG: [*pacing up and down, to himself*]: The world is changed, changed! Your men used to bully me and hit me; now you are down yourself. The poor, the simple and the downtrodden can hold their heads up; your sort have to bow your heads! You go to jail; I go to meetings! Changed, the world is changed! I must go! I must go and sing! One man singing for everyone's pleasure, isn't it wonderful! [DOG FENG's *head appears stealthily at the gate; seeing no one else there, he enters quietly.*]

DOG [*in a low voice*]: Mad Brother! Mad Brother!

MAD CHENG: Who is it? Oh, it's you! Have you come to hit me again? Go on then, I won't run away, I won't hide, and I'm not afraid of you either! Strike me; I won't return your blows. I will remember you in my heart, and hatred will grow there. When it's grown big enough, the striker of others will suffer for it. Come and strike me!

SZE-SAO [Coming out of her room]: Who is it? Oh, it's you! You still come and bully people? How dare you! Don't you know Black Whirlwind has been downed? All right then! If you so much as touch him, I'll smash you to pieces!

DOG [grinning, very embarrassed]: Who says I've come to hit people?

SZE-SAO: I suppose you daren't after all! What have you come to do then, rob us? You try that!

DOG: I'm being watched. I haven't done any business for two months.

SZE-SAO: You call yours "business," too! What a cheek!

DOG: I'm trying to learn. I'm not going to make any more trouble.

SZE-SAO: So you're afraid now!

DOG: Mr. Chao's got a plan for me; he says I should go to the police station and tell them all my doings in the past. If I don't, I shall always be on the black list. Then he says I can go and attend a course for a few months. After that I can earn my living, even if it's only driving a pedicab.

SZE-SAO: So you despise the pedicab drivers, do you? At least they don't steal or rob; they're much better than you. My husband is one!

DOG: No offense meant; please excuse me. [Bows in apology.] Mr. Chao says, if I really want to make a fresh start I must first come and apologize to Brother Cheng for hitting him. He says if I'm in earnest, he'll help me; if not, he won't trouble about me.

SZE-SAO: Mad Brother, don't let him off with an apology. Now it's your turn to give him a slap in the face!

DOG: Mrs. Ting, Mad Brother hasn't said anything; why do you want to rub salt in my wounds! Uncle Chao is fair and he's kind, and he says the new government is fair and kind, too; otherwise I shouldn't have dared to come. Well, I hope you'll forgive me, too.

SZE-SAO: Why weren't you fair and kind before? Why did you beat people up all the time?

DOG: It wasn't really me that struck him.

SZE-SAO: Not you? Was it some animal then?

Dog: It was the boss's orders; I was just acting for him. No one is born like that! I've beaten people up, but I've never killed anyone.

Sze-sao: You mean to say you were born good! If Black Whirlwind weren't finished, you wouldn't be talking so sweetly!

Mad Cheng: Sze-sao, let him go away. Uncle Chao's ideas must be right, and any way *I* can't hit people!

Sze-sao: Isn't that letting him off too lightly?

Mad Cheng: You can go now, Dog!

Sze-sao: [*stopping him*]: Have you said you're sorry? Have you apologized?

Dog: I tell you straight this is the first time I've ever given in to soft talk!

Sze-sao: So you're still not really giving in?

Dog: Oh all right, I give in! Mr. Chao keeps saying, from now on I must use my hands to work with and not to hit people with. Mad Brother, let's be friends now; I apologize! [*He bows, and then walks towards the gate, shamefacedly.*]

Mad Cheng: Come back! Show me your hands! [*Looking at them.*] Oh, your hands are just ordinary human hands! I shan't worry now. You can go.
[*Exit Dog.*]

Sze-sao: Oh, Mad Brother, how like you! You're too kind to him!

Mad Cheng: Even those who used to hit people have stopped; how can I start learning? [*Enters room.*]
[*Ka-tse runs in through gate.*]

Ka-tse: Ma! Ma! They're coming, they're coming!

Sze-sao: Who are coming, scatterbrain?

Mother Wang [*in her room*]: Erh-chun's been looking for you everywhere to send you to school. Why haven't you gone yet?

Ka-tse: I'm going in a moment. Let me finish first! Ma! They just went past here, with small red flags and long red and white poles and a funny thing like a camera on a tripod.

Mother Wang [*coming out*]: Well, what are they doing? What's all the excitement about?

Ka-tse: People are saying that they're a survey team, coming to measure the land for us.

Sze-sao: What for?

Mother Wang: Is it to ride round and enclose land?

Ka-tse: Ride round and enclose land—what's that?

Mother Wang: When the dynasty changed, the Princes, Ministers, and Imperial guards used to seize land to collect grain and rents, and build barracks on. This district of ours was originally the barracks of the Imperial Blue Banner.[11]

SZE-SAO: But we don't have Princes and Imperial Ministers now!

MOTHER WANG: Never mind whether we have them or not. They may be called by different names but they're all the same!

SZE-SAO: Mother Wang, people like us haven't been done down once since this government came in!

MOTHER WANG: Maybe, but perhaps they're giving us the sugar first! I've lived many more years than you have; I *know*. When the Japanese first came . . . . Oh! Is it safe to talk about the Japanese now?

SZE-SAO: Go on! If there's any trouble I'll look after it!

MOTHER WANG: You are brave, Sze-sao! . . . Well, didn't they start off by giving sweets to the children and then afterwards kill whole masses of people? As soon as *they* left, there was all that fuss about "taking over." It all sounded very nice at first, arresting collaborators and so on, but in a few days the collaborators themselves became high officials, and our kind of people were still kept down!

SZE-SAO: Do you think it'll be the same this time? Look, the gangsters have all been arrested, and there's nothing to stop us earning money. You know it as well as I do!

KA-TSE: Ma, don't listen to Granny Wang; she's an old diehard!

SZE-SAO: Rubbish! What do you know about it? Get off to school!

KA-TSE: I am going! You can't say I cut school! [*Exit.*]

MOTHER WANG: What a child! [*Hurriedly enters room.*]

[*OLD CHAO enters the gate, looking very pleased.*]

SZE-SAO: Uncle Chao, Dog Feng has been here and apologized to Mad Brother. Do you think he can really make a fresh start?

OLD CHAO: We won't let the real gang bosses get away, but we'll give the ones like him who aren't too bad another chance. My old eyes are sharp enough to see the difference. . . . Sze-sao, I've another piece of good news for you!

SZE-SAO: Oh! What is it?

OLD CHAO: The survey team is here, surveying the land for remaking the Ditch!

SZE-SAO: Remaking the Ditch? Our Dragon Beard Ditch?

OLD CHAO: Yes, this stinking Ditch, that no one has ever bothered about.

78

SZE-SAO: Uncle Chao, I . . . I kowtow! [*Kneels down and knocks her head on the ground.*]

MAD CHENG [*opening the door of his room*]: Uncle Chao, do you mean to say they're really remaking the Ditch? You are far-sighted! You've been saying all along they would do this. You were right!

ERH-CHUN [*running in*]: Ma! Ma! I didn't see Black Whirlwind. He'd been locked up. But I saw the survey team. They're going to remake the Ditch!

MOTHER WANG [*opening the door*]: I still have my doubts.

ERH-CHUN: Why?

MOTHER WANG: They haven't come to collect any money! Do you mean to tell me they're coming to remake the Ditch without saying a word? We shan't get off so cheaply!

OLD CHAO [*to MAD CHENG*]: Mad Brother, do you believe it?

MAD CHENG: Yes, I believe it, never mind what Mother Wang says!

OLD CHAO [*to SZE-SAO*]: And you do, don't you?

SZE-SAO: Of course! Haven't I kowtowed?

ERH-CHUN: It'll be wonderful! Just think, no more filthy water, no more stench, no more flies and mosquitoes. Oh, too, too wonderful! Uncle Chao, the gangsters have gone; when the Ditch is remade this place of ours will be transformed. In future, if anyone dares to say a word against the government, I'll split his skull open!

OLD CHAO [*to MOTHER WANG*]: And what do you say, Madam?

MOTHER WANG: Me? [*Smiling, embarrassed.*] Just as you all say, I say the same.

ERH-CHUN: Why are we all standing here? Why don't we dance the yang-ko?[12] [*Leading them in the dance.*] Chiang, chiang, chi-chiang-chi!

ALL [*except MOTHER WANG*]: Chiang, chiang, chi-chiang-chi. [*All dance.*]

MAD CHENG: Stop! I've got it! I *will* go to the Popular Education Center! I'll sing about "Remaking Dragon Beard Ditch."

SCENE 3

Time: 1950, early summer. Before the midday meal.
Place: The same.
Curtain Rises: MOTHER WANG is sitting on a stool under the eaves, working. Not feeling quite settled, she keeps on looking towards the gate.
[OLD CHAO enters.]

OLD CHAO: You're here all alone?

MOTHER WANG: Yes, they've all gone out. Haven't you anything to do today?

OLD CHAO: The new lavatory on the west side was finished yesterday; there's nothing doing today. [Sits down on stool.] I just went over to have another look at it; I'm not boasting, but it's good work. When the government is building it for us, of course we put more into it!

MOTHER WANG: Was only that one lavatory built?

OLD CHAO: Eight at least! Everyone used to say, in Dragon Beard Ditch we had places to eat but nowhere to do the other thing! But now we're even going to have running water!

MOTHER WANG: Really? I have been puzzled—how is it the officials are so fond of doing things nowdays, building lavatories for us and such like? What are they getting out of it themselves?

OLD CHAO: This is the people's government, Old Lady. Look here, I'm a bricklayer and I'm earning more than an official!

MOTHER WANG: I've been keeping my eyes open this last year or so. Your Communist Party is really not so bad!

OLD CHAO: You say so? Now you're really saying what you feel at last!

MOTHER WANG: But they have some bad points too!

OLD CHAO: Then you must tell them so. People and governments that are any good aren't afraid of criticism.

MOTHER WANG: Last night I had a few words with Erh-chun, and early this morning she disappeared.

OLD CHAO: Where would she go, except to her sister's to have a good grumble?

MOTHER WANG: I thought of that, and I asked Mad Brother to go and look for her.

OLD CHAO: That's all right. But what's it got to do with the Communist Party?

80

MOTHER WANG: They are very sharp.

OLD CHAO: Sharp?

MOTHER WANG: You see, in the old days, all the fuss in the city about new ideas never reached us here on the Ditch. There was a lot of talk in the city about marriage from choice, and free love, and such like; but here in Dragon Beard Ditch, never mind if it was filthy and stinking, we still had proper marriages, arranged by matchmakers and decided by parents—not just done anyhow.

OLD CHAO: Mother Wang, I understand you now. Erh-chun wants to choose her own husband; isn't that it?

MOTHER WANG: I'd never have thought it! The Communist Party build lavatories and catch thieves for us, and now they're going to rebuild the Ditch. That's all very fine. But then they go and encourage the young people to choose for themselves; don't you think that's sharp? They not only talk about it in the city but the talk has reached us here!

OLD CHAO: That's what real revolution is! It comes up from below and works down again.

MOTHER WANG: If you had a grown-up daughter, would you let her choose her own husband? Do you think that would be decent?

OLD CHAO: Me? Well, although we've been neighbors all this time, I've never told you. My wife . . . .

MOTHER WANG: You're married? You are a close one! All these years you've never let on!

OLD CHAO: We were married in the north city, by arrangement through a matchmaker. But in less than six months she went off with a merchant. She was fond of eating and drinking and having a good time. She was a pretty girl—I wasn't bad looking in those days either—and my earnings weren't enough for her. After she left, I hadn't the face to live in the city and I moved here. Of course I had no children. If I *had* a daughter who wanted to choose a boy for herself, I'd say to her: "Look around carefully, my girl, don't choose the wrong one."

[MAD CHENG comes in, in high spirits.]

MOTHER WANG: Is Erh-chun at her sister's?

MAD CHENG: Yes, she'll be back very soon.

MOTHER WANG: Oh, I am relieved. Thank you very much. What did you say to her?

MAD CHENG: I said, "Come back, my dear, everything can be arranged satisfactorily."

MOTHER WANG: What did she say?

MAD CHENG: She said, "If Ma won't agree, I'll never go back. I'll run away altogether."

MOTHER WANG: The miserable creature! How utterly shameless! What did you say to her then?

MAD CHENG: I said, "Don't be in too much of a hurry. If you go home first and then run away, won't that do just as well?"

MOTHER WANG: You said that? You're really half mad!

OLD CHAO: Mother Wang, you must be more reasonable. You can express your views about Erh-chun's affairs, but don't on any account stop or obstruct her. I suffered from an arranged marriage and I know free-choice marriage is best!

MOTHER WANG: Oh! I simply don't know what to do! [TING SZE enters, walking with excessive care.] What's the matter with you?

TING SZE: Nothing. I'm not drunk!

OLD CHAO: Give him some water to drink, and don't tell Sze-sao, or she'll flare up again!

MOTHER WANG: I'll go and pour some out. [Goes across.] Not midday yet and you're drunk already!

MAD CHENG [helping TING SZE to sit down]: Sit down.

MOTHER WANG [with water]: Drink this first. [Hands him water.]

TING SZE: There's nothing wrong with me. I'm not drunk!

OLD CHAO: You're not drunk; you've had a drop too much, that's all!

MOTHER WANG: Don't go on at him, he's feeling bad. [To TING SZE.] Have another drink of water.

TING SZE: No more, thank you, Mother Wang. I just felt a bit dizzy. I'm all right now. [Hands bowl back to MOTHER WANG.] I felt depressed. I didn't drink much.

[MOTHER WANG resumes her work. MAD CHENG sits down again.]

OLD CHAO: I don't understand, Ting Sze; your wife's earning more than before; why is it you don't work steady yourself? With you going on like this, I can't face her. It isn't the first time she's asked me to have a talk with you about it!

TING SZE: You're always going on about this government, how marvellous it is!

OLD CHAO: It's facts that convince people. I'm not biased either way.

TING SZE: Listen to me: It's true that Ka-tse's mother is earning a little more, but I hardly ever get a fare. Nowadays the People's Liberation Army men don't use pedicabs, and office workers either walk or ride bicycles. I'm pushing an empty cab!

OLD CHAO: That's only one side of the story. The Army men don't ride in pedicabs? But in the old days when soldiers rode they never paid up, and they knocked you about into the bargain. You were treated like an animal then. Now you're a man. Isn't that a fair picture?

TING SZE: I suppose so!

OLD CHAO: In the old days, the police didn't dare to interfere with motorcars; they only went for pedicab drivers and rickshaw pullers. Do they do that now?

TING SZE: No!

OLD CHAO: Very well then! Some time ago I did my very best to persuade you to change your job, but you wouldn't listen.

TING SZE: I'm over thirty now. What job can I change to? And I don't want to leave Peking.

OLD CHAO: If you're not afraid of work, you can easily change. You don't want to leave Peking; yet you detest this stinking place. You make excuses not to work. What's the matter with you? People who have gone to hew coal or open up new land are all happy doing productive work. The government doesn't let people down.

TING SZE: They do!

OLD CHAO: When, for instance?

TING SZE: Well, some time ago, they were surveying our place. That's weeks ago now, and they haven't started work yet.

OLD CHAO: Remaking the Ditch isn't like going out and buying a pound of flour. You've got to appoint engineers, draw plans, and get materials. A whole lot of things have to be done first. I'll have a bet with you, Ting Sze; how about it?

TING SZE: No need to bet on it. If they do start to clean out the Ditch, I'll get down to it. You keep on saying, this government is the people's government. I want to see if they'll do things for the people! This Ditch drowned Little Niu. I hate it! It's my enemy!

OLD CHAO: You just remember that!

TING SZE: You'll see.

OLD CHAO: All right, I'll be waiting for you! When they start to remake the Ditch, if you don't listen to me then, I'll give you a good hiding!

TING SZE: Yes, you could hit me all right, because I wouldn't hit you back!

83

OLD CHAO: You rascal! You won't listen to reason! You're hopeless!

KA-TSE [dashes into the gate carrying a basket of coal cinders]: Daddy, they're for you; half a basketful; enough to last till evening! [Rushes away again immediately.]

TING SZE: Hey! Where are you off to in such a hurry—someone's funeral?

KA-TSE: To Mouchia Well.

TING SZE: What for?

KA-TSE: They've put up huts; there are lots of workmen there already. They're talking about a lot of carts and lorries coming with bricks and cement and sand. And there's a big cement bucket, as high as a man. I'm going to creep in and see how tall it really is! [Runs out.]

OLD CHAO: They've come to remake the Ditch! They've come!

MAD CHENG: Wait for me, Ka-tse; I'm coming too! [Runs out.]

MOTHER WANG [standing up and running a few paces forward]: They're really going to remake the Ditch? Without even asking a copper from us?

OLD CHAO: Now do you believe me, Old Lady?

MOTHER WANG: It's unheard of! It's unheard of!

OLD CHAO: What do you say, Ting Sze?

TING SZE: I . . . I . . . .

OLD CHAO: [pulls him up and speaks earnestly, face to face]: Ting Sze, look here, the government is not rich—the gold and silver were taken away by Chiang Kai-shek and his dirty crew—but they are remaking the Ditch for us. Rebuilding this Ditch isn't a matter of a few dollars. We ought to be very grateful!

TING SZE: All right . . . .

OLD CHAO: The East Arch, the West Arch, the Drum Tower—everywhere needs repairing. Why does the government come to our stinking Ditch first? Instead of improving the appearance of the city first, they have come to look after us, because this Ditch gives me malaria every year and because it killed Little Niu. When it rains, Niang-tse can't put up her stall, you can't go out with your cab, stinking water floods our rooms with maggots. The government knows about these things, and they're doing something for you and me, and everyone in this district, so that we shan't have to be ill, and die, stink, and be filthy, and go hungry, any more. You and I are the people, and the government cares for the people; they're remaking the Ditch for us! Do you believe me now?

84

TING SZE: I believe you! I believe you!

OLD CHAO: Are you coming if the government asks you to go and remake the Ditch? It is your Ditch and your enemy. Are you going to get down to it and clean out that stinking Ditch?

TING SZE: Uncle Chao, please don't ask me any more questions. I swear before heaven I'll come the moment work starts!

Curtain

ACT III

SCENE 1

Time: 1950, summer; small hours of the morning, before dawn.

Place: *The San Yuan, a small teashop on higher ground by the Ditch.*

Setting: *The teashop consists of two rooms facing east, with a door between. In summer, an extra shelter is put up outside, consisting of old matting supported by poles. Under this there is an earthen structure serving as a table, beside which stands an oblong wooden table. On the latter are teapots, cups, and small winepots, snacks to go with the wine, cigarettes, and two or three glass jars containing little paper packets of tea, shelled peanuts, etc.*

Curtain Rises: *It has rained during the early part of the night and now has just stopped. Water is still heard dripping from the matting. One or two cocks crow. The proprietor, MR. LIU, lights a paraffin lamp, looks at the stove and kettles, and then looks outside as if expecting somebody. A POLICEMAN walks into the shelter; his cape is soaking wet; he wears goloshes but no socks, and his trousers are covered with mud; he has a flashlight.*

POLICEMAN: Mr. Liu, you've taken a lot of trouble.

PROPRIETOR: Oh, it's nothing!

POLICEMAN: How are you getting on?

PROPRIETOR: Nearly ready now; when the neighbors arrive there'll be hot tea and a comfortable place to sit.

POLICEMAN: That's good. The chief asks me to tell Uncle Chao not to start digging yet; get the neighbors here first, in case any house should collapse and somebody get hurt.

PROPRIETOR: That's new. It used to be nobody's business if people were drowned or buried alive! Now the police have even prepared a place for people to evacuate to, just in case houses might collapse and crush people to death.

POLICEMAN [*as he listens, shines the flashlight into the two rooms*]: Yes, that's so. Everyone's helped this time, luckily. If we'd had to depend on us few police and the construction gang, we couldn't have done it so quickly. I'm going now; when Uncle Chao comes with the neighbors, you look after them. Oh, here they are! [OLD CHAO *leads a group of people up.*] Is everyone here now, Uncle Chao?

OLD CHAO: One lot's here. The rest'll be here in a moment.

POLICEMAN: I'll leave it all to you now. I'm going to help dig. [*To all.*] Neighbors, you rest here. [*Exit.*]

OLD CHAO: Women and children go inside, there's a fire there, dry your feet first. [*Women and children go in; men stand about or sit.*] Erh-chun! Erh-chun! Isn't she here yet?

ERH-CHUN [*answering from outside*]: Coming, Uncle Chao, I'm coming. [*She runs in, a torn raincoat on her shoulders, carrying a small bundle which she puts down, speaking as she takes off raincoat.*] Oh! I nearly fell down. It's awful slippery!

OLD CHAO: Don't talk; get to work!

ERH-CHUN: What shall I do?

OLD CHAO: First boil some water and make tea so that everyone can have a hot drink. Then heat more water and find a tub and see that the children soak their feet in hot water so they won't catch cold.

ERH-CHUN: Right! [*Picks up bundle and goes into the room.*]
[*A* YOUNG MAN *comes in carrying* MOTHER WANG *on his back, her arms full of things.*]

MOTHER WANG: Erh-chun, Erh-chun! Where are you? You don't care a bit about your mother! If I fell down and died, I don't believe you'd even shed a tear!

ERH-CHUN [*to the* YOUNG MAN]: Come in and rest a bit.

YOUNG MAN: I can't, I've got to carry more people here. [*Hurries out.*]

ERH-CHUN: Warm yourself by the fire inside, Ma. [*Starts to take things from her.*]

MOTHER WANG: I'm not staying here! [*She is unwilling to hand over things.*]

86

ERH-CHUN: Where are you going, then?

MOTHER WANG: Home, I've forgotten the iron.

OLD CHAO: Now don't be silly, Mother Wang. The iron won't be swept away by the flood! An old lady like you should set an example to the others and not make more bother for us.

MOTHER WANG: Oh dear! [*Sits down.*] I knew there'd be trouble. In the old days they always asked the astrologer for an auspicious day before starting work. Now, as soon as they say they're going to do it, they do it, without bothering to find out whether its an auspicious day or not. No wonder we've got this flood if the Dragon King has been disturbed!

OLD CHAO: Erh-chun, get on with your work; let the old lady get it off her chest.

ERH-CHUN: Ma, make yourself comfortable here; don't grumble. Nowadays, whatever day the work is done is an auspicious day; you needn't bother about the Imperial calendar! [*Enters room.*]

[MAD CHENG *comes in, supporting* NIANG-TSE.]

NIANG-TSE: Let me go! Are you supposed to be helping me or pinching me?

MAD CHENG: Anything to please you, dear!

NIANG-TSE: What can I do, Uncle Chao?

OLD CHAO: You go and help Erh-chun inside. Mad Brother, you leave your things with Niang-tse; you'd better be a messenger, going back and forth.

MAD CHENG: Yes, I can do that. Is there enough water here? I have the key to the water tap.

PROPRIETOR: It's all right, we've got plenty.

[MAD CHENG *goes out.*]

NIANG-TSE [*seeing* MOTHER WANG]: Oh, why are you sitting here and not going inside, Old Lady?

MOTHER WANG: I won't go in. They are asking for trouble. They *would* go and dig the Ditch. Now they have dug up a mess, haven't they?

NIANG-TSE: You've forgotten; it was like this every time we had heavy rain.

OLD CHAO: Besides, after the Ditch has been remade, we'll never have any more trouble.

ERH-CHUN [*from the door*]: Uncle Chao, Niang-tse, don't listen to her. Ma, if you're going to go on being so unreasonable, I'm going to get married straight away and not look after you any more!

87

MOTHER WANG: H'm! If you don't let me have a good look at him first, you needn't think of getting into the bridal chair!

ERH-CHUN: You've had a good look at him already!

MOTHER WANG: Me? Nonsense! When have I seen him?

ERH-CHUN: You've ridden on his back! [Goes inside again.]

MOTHER WANG: Was that him?

OLD CHAO ⎫
         ⎬ : Ha! Ha! Ha!
NIANG-TSE ⎭

NIANG-TSE: It's fixed up all right now, this marriage!

MOTHER WANG: I . . . I . . . I can't argue against all of you. I still want to go back home. Even a tumbledown home is worth a fortune. I can't sit around in a teashop in the middle of the night!

NIANG-TSE: Never mind, Old Lady; this flood was no worse than those we had before, but the government and the police have taken precautions in case any house should collapse and bury people, and so they've brought us here. You'd better go in and have a rest.

ERH-CHUN [from inside]: Come along! Tea's made. Who'll have some hot tea?

NIANG-TSE: Let's go and have some. [Pulls MOTHER WANG in with her.]

MAD CHENG [calling from a distance]: Come this way, all come this way! Uncle Chao, another lot has arrived.

OLD CHAO [running out]: This way, this way! [A group of people enter, more men than women.] Women, go inside. Men, put down your things; they won't be lost. Let's organize a bit. Let's send more people to help clean out water from houses and dig. We can't let the government people do all the heavy work while we just stand by and watch.

RESIDENT A: They're working so hard; we really ought to go back and help!

OLD CHAO: That's right. With Mr. Liu and me here you needn't worry about missing your people or losing anything. I suggest those over forty should clean out water and those under forty should dig; how's that?

RESIDENT B: That's right!

ALL: Let's go! [Exeunt.]

[SZE-SAO runs in alone.]

SZE-SAO: Uncle Chao, Uncle Chao, have you seen Ka-tse?

OLD CHAO: No; but he's too big to get lost.

SZE-SAO: That child never gives me a moment's peace of mind!

OLD CHAO: Where's Ting Sze?

SZE-SAO: Gone to dig.

OLD CHAO: Good chap, he's improved!

SZE-SAO: Improved? You wait and see! When he comes home tired, I have to suffer! He finds fault so, but he thinks *he's* done great deeds, and I ought to get down on my knees to welcome him back and see him off again!

OLD CHAO: Humor him a little and bear with him. Do as he wants. However you look at it, at least he's working for us all, and he *is* working very hard. It isn't easy for him.

NIANG-TSE [*Calling from the door*]: Sze-sao, come in and drink some hot tea!

SZE-SAO: Niang-tse, will you keep an eye on my things for me? I must go and look for Ka-tse. For heaven's sake, he mustn't go after Little Niu. . . . [*Exit.*] [MAD CHENG *runs in.*]

MAD CHENG: Brother Ting is back.
[TING SZE *comes in, a shovel on his shoulder, his clothes covered with mud, very tired.*]

OLD CHAO: You're back, Ting Sze?

TING SZE: I'm dead tired. Why shouldn't I come back?

MAD CHENG: How's the Ditch getting on?

TING SZE [*sitting down*]: Nearly dug through.

NIANG-TSE [*handing him tea*]: Have a hot drink! [*She hands tea to others.*]

MOTHER WANG [*coming out*]: Ting Sze, what's really happening? Has the water gone down yet? Have any houses collapsed? When can we go back? Have they really moved the things on to the beds?

ERH-CHUN [*coming out*]: Oh Ma! You can't talk without asking strings of questions! He's worked half the night. Let him rest now.

MOTHER WANG: I won't say another word. Treat me as if I were dumb. Will that be all right?

TING SZE: Don't squabble. If anyone wants to be kind, give me some water to wash my feet.

ERH-CHUN: I'll go! [*Goes inside.*]

TING SZE [*yawning*]: Uncle Chao!

OLD CHAO: Yes, what is it?

TING SZE: Ever since they started remaking the Ditch, I've done my share, like you said. The government has played fair by us and we must play fair by them, isn't that right?

OLD CHAO: That's it! You're able-bodied; when they're rebuilding the Ditch for us, how could a young chap like you not get down to it?

TING SZE: But now, after sweating away the whole day, I have to get soaked at night. Even a plaster dummy goes to pieces in water, and I'm not made of plaster! I can't stand it. I'm going to give it up. I'll go back to my pedicab and leave this stinking place!

ERH-CHUN [carrying water]: Soak your feet in this!

TING SZE [putting his feet in basin]: I'm going to give it up!

ERH-CHUN: Give what up?

MAD CHENG: I'll wash your feet, Brother Ting! You're rebuilding the Ditch; you're as good as the government; I'm happy to wash your feet! Uncle Chao often says everyone who works for the community is a hero. You're a hero. I'm glad to wait on you, and you know I'm not at anyone's beck and call!

NIANG-TSE: Brother Ting, Mad Cheng is often muddle-headed, but this time he's right. Let him wash your feet for you.

TING SZE: Mad Brother, that would never do; I can't let you!

SZE-SAO [running in]: No, certainly not! Get up, Mad Brother. I'll wash them for him. [Squats down and washes his feet.]

TING SZE: Where have you been?

SZE-SAO: I've been looking and looking for Ka-tse, and I still haven't found him!

TING SZE: Yes, if we lost our son, too, that'd be a fine thing! I ought to leave this cursed place; nothing good ever happens here!

SZE-SAO: At it again? You're tired and sleepy and cross. After you're washed, I'll find a place for you to sleep. Ka-tse can't be lost; he's a big boy now.

OLD CHAO: Ting Sze, now you're digging the Ditch for us all, isn't everyone doing this? [Thumbs up.]

TING SZE: Oh yes? My feet are soaked till they're nearly rotted a-way; I should think they ought to say a good word for me!

[A POLICEMAN comes in, carrying KA-TSE, fast asleep, on his back.]

SZE-SAO [turning towards them]: Ka-tse, where have you been?

POLICEMAN: He was so keen, he's been going round with me for hours. Now he can't keep his eyes open any more, so I've brought him here.

KA-TSE [opening eyes, gets down]: Ma, I was so sleepy!

[SZE-SAO takes him into the room.]

90

POLICEMAN: Mr. Chao, you must be tired, you've been going at it so hard. How's everything here now?

OLD CHAO: Fine! Have some tea; you're dead tired too.

ERH-CHUN: Here you are. [Hands him tea.]

POLICEMAN: Thank you. You've been working as hard as anyone! [To MOTHER WANG.] Madam, are you being put upon?

MOTHER WANG: Never mind whether I'm being put upon; what's really happening?

POLICEMAN: I'll tell you presently. Mad Brother, Niang-tse, you've had a tough time, too!

NIANG-TSE: It's you who must be really worn out! Still, my old man hasn't done too badly as the messenger either!

POLICEMAN: You must have had about enough tonight, Ting Sze?

OLD CHAO: H'm! He's in a bad temper, talking about going back to his pedicab and not bothering any more about our stinking business!

TING SZE: No, no, Uncle Chao, that's past! I'm all right again now. Comrade, you carried Ka-tse back here yourself, and I'll do whatever you tell me to! We're men; it's no use our acting like a lot of old women!

ERH-CHUN: Women! We aren't like you, sensible at one moment and muddle-headed the next!

POLICEMAN: All right, all right! Don't argue! Ting Sze, go and find a place to sleep.

TING SZE: Here's good enough; I'll just have a nap.

ERH-CHUN: Isn't he nice! When he stops being cross, he's more obliging than anyone!

[Some of the men who went out earlier come in.]

POLICEMAN: You must be tired, all of you. Is the Ditch through now?

ALL: Yes, it's through!

POLICEMAN: Are there any more people inside?

ERH-CHUN: Yes, the women and children are there.

POLICEMAN: Don't wake the children up. If the grown-ups want to hear about it, ask them to come out.

ERH-CHUN: I'll go and tell them. [Runs to the door and calls.]

POLICEMAN: Neighbors! [Women, including SZE-SAO, follow ERH-CHUN out.] Neighbors, please sit down. We're going to ask Uncle Chao to tell us about what happened last night. Some of you know about it already, but others aren't very clear. Uncle Chao, please tell us.

[Some people sit down, others remain standing.]

OLD CHAO: You sit down, too. You've been at it half the night as well!

POLICEMAN: I'm all right. I can stand.

OLD CHAO: Neighbors, the plan was to make an underground drain first, and then fill in the old Ditch. You all know about this.

ALL: Yes.

OLD CHAO: When they started to dig out the Ditch, the engineers' department made careful plans to shore up the sides with props and boards, so as to prevent our houses and walls from falling down if the soil got loose underneath; none of our houses here are very strong. You know about this, too.

ALL: Yes.

OLD CHAO: But in spite of all these precautions we had this trouble last night. In the first place, nobody dreamed that such torrential rain would come so early in the season. In the second place, the earth dug out of the old Ditch, which there hadn't been time to move yet, blocked it up just where the new drain joins it. We were all taken by surprise, and some damage was done. The local authority and the police both feel very responsible about this. As soon as they heard the news, the district head and his fellow workers all rushed here. The head himself carried people and saved things from the flood. The police chief is still cleaning water out from people's houses. Now, if any of you have anything to say, tell us, and we'll pass it on to the district head and police chief.

[*Nobody speaks.*]

POLICEMAN: Speak up; anything you've got to say, compliments or complaints, let's hear it. We're all one family here!

ERH-CHUN: It seems to me . . . .

MOTHER WANG: Erh-chun, there are plenty of people here. Why should a girl like you speak first?

ERH-CHUN: All right, if you've anything to say, go ahead!

OLD CHAO: Speak up, Old Lady. Nowadays policemen are glad to listen to what we've got to say.

MOTHER WANG: I've nothing to say except this: Next time it rains, don't ask me to come out! It's terrifying to have to come out in the middle of the night.

POLICEMAN: The district head and police chief were afraid that some houses might collapse and kill people, Madam!

RESIDENT A: If they hadn't dug the underground drain, we shouldn't have had all this trouble, should we?

92

ERH-CHUN: You are talking nonsense!

RESIDENT A: Anyone who likes can talk here, can't they?

ERH-CHUN: Yes, but not nonsense! Without digging the drains how could the Ditch be filled up, and without doing away with the Ditch, however do you think we can get rid of the filth and stink?

NIANG-TSE: Besides . . . .

RESIDENT B: Ha! The Women's Army![13] [*Laughter.*]

NIANG-TSE: What I say is, weren't we flooded out by torrents of rain last year, the year before, every year? People were drowned and buried alive, and who cared? Let's be fair; this time it certainly isn't any worse and yet the district head himself gets soaked from head to foot rescuing us! We ought to thank them!

SZE-SAO: Never mind about anything else, just look at that husband of mine. [*Points to* TING SZE, *fast asleep with his head on the table.*] If it weren't for the Ditch being rebuilt, how could he ever have become a worker, doing something useful for all of us? Just think, when it's all finished, and people have changed for the better too, how wonderful it'll be then!

ERH-CHUN: Well said, SZE-SAO!

[*Applause.*]

POLICEMAN: Tell us some more, Uncle Chao.

ALL: Yes, Uncle Chao, go on!

OLD CHAO: All right, I'll say a little more. The government hasn't repaired Wangfuching Street or the West Arch; they're rebuilding our Ditch first. That's something quite unheard of. And now that this has happened, the government has taken special care of us. In all my sixty years I've never seen anything like it! Besides, when the new drain is finished we'll never have any more trouble, shall we? Kindness deserves kindness. The government cares for us; we must care for them. Isn't that right, neighbors?

ALL: That's right!

MAD CHENG: If there hadn't been this trouble, we shouldn't have realized what a good government we've got!

POLICEMAN: I just want to add this. Nobody was hurt this time; it might have been much worse. We moved as many of your things on to the beds as we could. Now it's stopped raining and it's light. Those who want to go home and see what things are like can go. For those who want to rest we've reserved two small inns on the west side. You can all do as you please.

OLD CHAO: Those who go home and find they can't rest or sleep there can still go to the inns, can't they?

POLICEMAN: That's right. The inns are the Dragon and the Phoenix. Erh-chun, you take the girls and the old ladies to the Dragon and look after them. Uncle Chao, you go with the men comrades to the Phoenix.

ERH-CHUN: Ma, Niang-tse, Sze-sao, everybody, let's go.

NIANG-TSE: I'll just get my things. [*Enters room followed by a few other women.*]

SZE-SAO [*coming out with* KA-TSE]: This gentleman [*pointing to* TING SZE] is still asleep. We'd better not wake him up; let him sleep. [*She puts a jacket over his shoulders.*]

ERH-CHUN: Come on, Ma.

MOTHER WANG: I've never in my life stayed in an inn! I'm not going, I'm going home!

ERH-CHUN: The room's still full of water!

MOTHER WANG: I'd rather be in my own home, even if it's soaking wet!

ERH-CHUN: You're out to make trouble! You really are the limit, Ma!

SZE-SAO: Ka-tse, go with Granny Wang. If it isn't fit to stay there, then take her to the inn. Do you understand? Carry her things for her.

KA-TSE: Granny Wang, if I walk too fast, don't scold me!

MOTHER WANG: When did I ever scold anyone? You little demon!

POLICEMAN: Mother Wang, are you going? Walk slowly; it's very slippery.

MOTHER WANG [*turning back*]: I've lived in Dragon Beard Ditch for years; you think I don't know how to walk carefully?

ERH-CHUN [*to the women*]: Shall we go now?

ALL: Let's go. [*To* POLICEMAN.] Comrade, give our thanks to the district head and police chief. [*They go out.*]

OLD CHAO [*to the men*]: Shall we go too?

RESIDENT A: Let's give a cheer for those who dug the Ditch!

ALL [*including those women who haven't yet gone*]: Hurrah! Hurrah!

94

SCENE 2

Time: 1950, end of summer. The new drain is finished and a road built over it.

Place: The same courtyard as in Act I.

Setting: The courtyard is very clean; the brokendown wall has been repaired, and the rubbish has all gone. The flower trellis is covered with pink and purple morning glory. A vase of fresh flowers stands on the water-butt in front of OLD CHAO's door. There is a new water-butt outside the TINGS' window. The whole courtyard is bathed in sunshine.

Curtain Rises: MOTHER WANG is sitting on the small bench outside her room sewing a jacket of patterned cloth for ERH-CHUN. A sewing basket is on the ground by her. SZE-SAO comes out of her room, looking at her own appearance, especially her new shoes and stockings.

MOTHER WANG [seeing SZE-SAO come out, starts to grumble]: Sze-sao! That wretched creature Ehr-chun's gone gadding off somewhere again today! I'm making this new jacket for her, and I can't get hold of her even to try it on!

SZE-SAO: She's busy. You know there's going to be a big meeting today to celebrate the finishing of our new drain; it's like a wedding celebration! She says you and I and Niang-tse must all go. That's why I've put on my new shoes and stockings. Look how well these shoes fit!

MOTHER WANG: I'm not going to any meeting. I can't understand what people say.

SZE-SAO: There's nothing difficult to understand. It's all about building the drain, anyway. Building the drain's a good thing, and we must clap our hands for any good thing, and clapping our hands can't be wrong, can it, Old Lady?

MOTHER WANG: H'm! You're just like Erh-chun, smiling the whole day long just because of the new drain!

SZE-SAO: I've got something to smile about! Everyone used to urge Ting Sze to get a proper job, but he wouldn't listen. When the work on the Ditch started, the Ditch moved him!

MOTHER WANG: When did the stinking Ditch ever speak to *him*?

95

SZE-SAO: It's a manner of speaking. The Ditch seemed to say, "I stink, what will you do to me? I drowned your child, what will you do to me?" But when the government started to rebuild the Ditch it was Ting Sze who seemed to say, "Yes, you stink, and you drowned my child, and now I'm filling you in, you devil!"

[NIANG-TSE *comes in with her basket.*]

SZE-SAO: Niang-tse, how did you come to finish so early?

NIANG-TSE: Have you forgotten the meeting's today! This is something that doesn't happen once in a hundred years. I'm taking a half-day off to go to it. Ah! You're dressed up already, Sze-sao! I must put on a clean jacket myself. It's like celebrating our Dragon Beard Ditch's birthday. The new drain's finished, and the old Ditch is finished, too!

MOTHER WANG: Seeing's believing! The old Ditch is still yawning there, not filled in yet!

NIANG-TSE: But it's going to be filled in! What on earth should we keep it for? You don't take an active enough interest in local affairs, Old Lady!

MOTHER WANG: What do you mean by "an active interest"? I keep to myself certainly. I don't flatter people, and I don't go looking for trouble.

SZE-SAO: I know why you're feeling down; it's because Erh-chun's wanting to get married. You've got this worry on your mind, so nothing suits you; that's it, isn't it?

MOTHER WANG: It's true, I shouldn't stop you all being happy just because of my own worries. It's quite right, you should be happy. Why even Mad Brother has work to do. Who would have thought it possible?

NIANG-TSE: Don't mention him. He'll be the death of me!

MOTHER WANG ⎫
SZE-SAO   ⎬ : Why?
           ⎭

NIANG-TSE: Ever since he got this wonderful job of looking after the water, he wakes me up several times every night. He keeps on asking me, "Niang-tse, hasn't the cock crowed yet?"

MOTHER WANG: He's really active!

NIANG-TSE: Then a little while later, "Niang-tse, isn't it light yet?" Looking after the water, he acts as if he were the Imperial Minister of War, always afraid of holding up His Majesty's business!

SZE-SAO: Don't grumble, Niang-tse. If it weren't for his single-mindedness, always doing what he says he'll do, they wouldn't

96

have chosen him for this job. It seems to me, as he hasn't the strength to fetch and carry, this job really suits him!

NIANG-TSE: That's true; whatever we say, at least he's got a job and nobody calls him useless any more! I am glad really, but it would be even better if he wouldn't disturb me at night!

SZE-SAO: You can't have everything perfect; you're not doing too badly. It's just the same with that husband of mine. No one outside calls him "Ting Sze" any more, they call him "Mister Ting." Why, he can't stop smiling! And when he gets back home, he's as pleased as a dog with two tails!

NIANG-TSE: I should say so! There's any amount of work for men in his trade. In our own district alone there's the big ditch leading to the Yungting Gate, and the one by the East Market; these will take months to do. The Communist Party really gets things done! They say the Palace Lakes, Back Lake, and Shih Cha Lake, as well as the whole city moat, are all to be dug out and new stone embankments built. Then all the roads will be repaired in turn. *He'll* never have to worry about being out of a job! As for Ka-tse, he's going to do even better. When he finishes school, he'll start in a factory; if he does well, he may end up as a factory manager for all you know!

SZE-SAO: You are in a hurry! But, anyway, we shan't have to wait long for better times. Oh, I haven't sewed that collar on Ka-tse's jacket yet. [*Goes into her room to get her work.*]

MAD CHENG [*outside, singing*]:

> Water I'm selling, sweet and bright,
> Drink it and the devils in your belly won't fight;
> Water I'm selling, bright and sweet,
> At a farthing a bucketful, I call it cheap.

NIANG-TSE: Look at that lunatic! Mother Wang, I'm going in now to change my dress. [*Exit.*]

MAD CHENG [*enters, still singing*]:

> Fresh and fragrant, the tea you brew,
> Not like it used to be, brown as stew.
> For washing clothes or washing your face,
> It's easy on the soap, and of dirt it leaves no trace!

SZE-SAO [*coming out with her work, sews*]: Mad Brother, why are you home and not looking after the water?

MAD CHENG: Mother Wang, Sze-sao, I've come back to practice that *shu-lai-pao.* I'm going to sing it at the big meeting. Ka-tse is

looking after the water for me. He can read and write now; he's
even more businesslike than I am!

SZE-SAO: You're a smart pair, I'll say!

MAD CHENG: Sze-sao, don't look down on us. Whenever we sit down
together we discuss problems.

SZE-SAO: Just you two?

MAD CHENG: Listen, just now I said, "Ka-tse, we've got two drains
now, the new one in front of our yard and the old Ditch at the
back. The new one is underground, its pipes are laid and it's all
finished; and on top of it there's a fine level road." And he said,
"When the old Ditch is all filled in, there'll be another road."
And I said, "Then there'll be two roads, one in front of our houses
and one behind. What shall we do when the roads are finished?"
He's really clever, Sze-sao. He said, "We must plant trees," and
he asked me, "What trees shall we plant?" "Willows," I said,
"weeping willows, how beautiful!" And he said, "Pooh!"

SZE-SAO: Really! What a bad boy!

MAD CHENG: He says we must plant peach trees, so we can have big
honey-peaches to eat. Isn't he clever!

NIANG-TSE [inside room]: Don't chatter any more! Hurry up and
make up your rhymes!

MAD CHENG: There's plenty of time. I'm just coming to the most
important part. Sze-sao, I've gone into it with Ka-tse. We must
have a park here. He proposed that we should change the Goldfish Pond into a park with trees all round it, and a swimming
pool and some pavilions as well. It would be wonderful!

NIANG-TSE [coming out in a new dress]: Don't waste time dreaming!

SZE-SAO: He isn't just dreaming. Who'd have thought we'd have a
fine road outside our gate, and proper clean lavatories, and running water? Why shouldn't we have a park here, too?

MAD CHENG [in the Peking opera recitative style]: Sze-sao's words
are weighty indeed! Mother Wang, Sze-sao, Niang-tse, for the
present I take my leave! [Enters his room.]

SZE-SAO: No wonder children love him! He's like a Granny to them!

NIANG-TSE: Don't praise him; he's like a child, the more he's praised
the more unbalanced he gets! [TING SZE comes in, very gay, carrying a new blue cotton jacket and trousers under his arm.]

TING SZE: Mother Wang, Niang-tse, look at my new suit!

[They surround him; MOTHER WANG feels the cloth for its quality,
NIANG-TSE looks at the length of the trousers, SZE-SAO examines
the stitching.]

TING SZE [seeing his wife's new shoes and stockings]: Ha! You're a stranger below the waist!

SZE-SAO: Don't be so silly! [Holding up the jacket.] Put it on and see if the length's right.

TING SZE [putting it on]: How does it look?

NIANG-TSE: Fine! It's a very good fit.

MOTHER WANG: I'm afraid it will shrink in the wash, though.

TING SZE: You're always an optimist, aren't you!

MOTHER WANG: It isn't that! If you men can all do the shopping, what will there be left for us women to do?

SZE-SAO: Never mind how much it shrinks. Enjoy it today while it's new!

MOTHER WANG: If you don't mind my saying so, that's not the way to manage. You should have bought the cloth, and let us all help to make the suit for him; then one suit would have lasted as long as two like this!

TING SZE: But, Mother Wang, there are some things even you don't know about. The man who sold it to me only asked four-fifty for this suit, and no bargaining either.

NIANG-TSE: Yes, there's no bargaining at all now. Prices are fixed.

TING SZE: I put the suit down and had a chat with him. I bragged a bit. I said, "I'm buying this for the big meeting; I've helped to build the drain and I can't stay away from the opening ceremony, can I?" Then I said, "In that blazing heat, the upper half of my body was grilled and the lower half soaked in black mud, the old Ditch stinking beside me, flies and mosquitoes biting me the whole time, and rank sweat streaming down into my shoes!" Well, before I could finish, what do you think he did? He pushed the suit into my hands and said, "Take it, give me four yuan. If I'm not losing fifty fen on the deal, you can bury me in the old Ditch when you fill it up!" Mother Wang, would you ever have thought this kind of thing could happen?

MOTHER WANG: Oh, that's really cheap! I'm going to buy a new dress, too!

TING SZE: Have you worked on the drain?

MOTHER WANG: That's right! Me work on the drain! Wouldn't it look nice! I give up; I can't talk to you people. [Returns to her sewing.]

[ERH-CHUN runs in with a red silk badge inscribed "steward" on her lapel, and her hair done up with a silk ribbon.]

99

ERH-CHUN: Ting Sze, why are you still here? Your mates are assembling already!

TING SZE: I must change my trousers first! [*Runs into room.*]

MOTHER WANG: Erh-chun, quick! Come and try your jacket on! [*Holds it for her to try on.*]

ERH-CHUN [*trying it on*]: Ma, it's going to be grand today! The Mayor and a comrade from the municipal Party committee are coming! Are you going?

MOTHER WANG: No, I'm not going; I'll stay at home and look after things.

ERH-CHUN: Still the same as ever! There's no need at all for you to stay at home! A policeman will be coming soon to look after all the street. Go and put your new dress on, for the Mayor to see!

NIANG-TSE: Come on, Old Lady! Dragon Beard Ditch doesn't have such a big do every day, you know!

SZE-SAO: Do come! I'll look after you!

MOTHER WANG: All right, I'll go. [*Enters room.*]

SZE-SAO: Put that small red pomegranate flower in your hair!

ERH-CHUN: Niang-tse, Sze-sao, we must be prepared. There'll be people from the newspapers coming to see us soon. They may photograph us. Niang-tse, if they ask you what are your impressions about the reconstruction of the Ditch, what will you say?

NIANG-TSE: *What are "impressions"?*

MOTHER WANG [*from inside room*]: Don't press her. The more you press her, the less she'll be able to think what her "impressions" are!

ERH-CHUN: "Impressions"—I suppose it means what you think about it.

TING SZE [*rushing out from his room*]: See you at the meeting! [*Runs out, happily singing "The Sky in the Liberated Areas Is Bright."*]

NIANG-TSE: Would it be all right if I said, "When the work on the Ditch was started, even my crazy husband had work to do, and I'm grateful to the government?

ERH-CHUN: All right! How about you, Sze-sao?

SZE-SAO: If they ask me, I'll say, "If the government goes on like this, Dragon Beard Ditch will soon be one big garden! But there's one thing, when it is a garden, they must still let us go on living here!"

ERH-CHUN: You're quite a speaker, Sze-sao! Don't worry, we lived here when the Ditch stank; we'll go on living here when it smells sweet! . . . Ma! Aren't you ready yet?

100

MOTHER WANG: Don't hurry me. [*Comes out, pointing to her dress.*] Does it look all right?

ERH-CHUN [*looking her mother up and down*]: It's all right! . . . Ma! What will you say if they ask you?

MOTHER WANG: I . . . .

ERH-CHUN: Go on, what will you say?

MOTHER WANG: Now the new drain is finished, my married daughter can come back here and visit me!

ERH-CHUN: Is that all?

MOTHER WANG: I don't know what to say when I meet strangers. [*Suddenly remembering something.*] Erh-chun, I'm not going to have my photograph taken. Every time we have a photograph taken, we lose a soul!

ERH-CHUN: Ma, you do bring up old tales, don't you!

NIANG-TSE: I'll take your place, I'm not afraid of losing my soul! Let them take my photograph, so that people everywhere will know there's a Cheng Niang-tse in Peking! I've got another idea, too. Let's all subscribe a little money to put up a stone, and have the words "There used to be a stinking Ditch here; the people's government made it into a fine road" carved on it.

ERH-CHUN: That's a really good idea; I must tell Uncle Chao. We'll all subscribe to it.

SZE-SAO: Yes, so we can let our children and grandchildren know about it, too. I'll contribute!

[*The distant sound of waist-drums is heard.*]

ERH-CHUN: The waist-drummers are coming! Let's go!

KA-TSE [*rushes in carrying a small red flag*]: Commander Uncle Chao is coming! Get into line!

[*OLD CHAO enters, very dignified, in a new suit, with a red silk badge on his breast.*]

ERH-CHUN: Look at Uncle Chao, just like a Commander-in-Chief!

OLD CHAO [*laughing*]: You minx!

ERH-CHUN: Uncle Chao, you must be prepared, the press reporters are sure to come to interview you!

OLD CHAO: As if I needed you to tell me! I prepared three days ago!

ERH-CHUN: Well, let me be a reporter then. [*Mimicking.*] What are your impressions about the reconstruction of the Ditch?

OLD CHAO: Briefly or in detail?

ERH-CHUN [*mimicking*]: Briefly, please.

OLD CHAO: As the saying goes, the Five Blessings have come to our door.

101

ERH-CHUN: Which Five Blessings?

OLD CHAO: In front of our gate, there's the underground drain; at the back the old Ditch is going to be filled in; that's the first. Fine roads at front and back, that's the second. The running water is the third. Later, when handicraft industry is established here, everybody will have work and livelihood; that's the fourth. And then, when the Goldfish Pond has been turned into a park where we can relax after the day's work, that'll be the fifth. Five Blessings!

ERH-CHUN
SZE-SAO
NIANG-TSE   } [together with OLD CHAO]: Five Blessings!
MOTHER WANG

[The neighbors, like those living in the courtyard, have all put on new clothes, and are going past the gate to the meeting. A POLICEMAN comes in and greets everyone. Some of the crowd wait outside the gate; others come in. Military music and waist-drums sound in the distance.]

POLICEMAN: Come to the meeting! It's nearly time to start!

[MOTHER WANG turns round to lock her door, but SZE-SAO and NIANG-TSE hasten to stop her. As they are pulling her toward the gate, MAD CHENG runs out of his room, a pair of bamboo castanets in his hand.]

MAD CHENG: Wait a moment please, all of you! I've made up a new ballad, and I want to try it out on you first!

ALL: Yes, yes! Sing it for us!

MAD CHENG: Listen, then!

> To all you people, I joyfully state,
> The People's Government is truly great.
> Is truly great, for it mended the Ditch,
> And took great pains for us though we're not rich.
> Think well of this, I beg you all,
> East Arch, West Arch, Drum Tower tall,
> Five Altars, Eight Temples, old Altar of Grain,
> Summer Palace too needed mending again.
> All needed repairing, I grant you this,
> But why should they first mend Dragon Beard Ditch?
> Simply because it was dirty, it stank,
> When the Government saw it their very heart sank.
> A first-rate Government, loving all poor men,

Helped us to stand up proudly again.
They repaired the Ditch, made a road besides,
Helped us to stand straight and march with great strides.
To march with great strides, and go laughing on,
All workers must strive with their hearts as one.
Must strive together, and work without cease,
Then our land will be great, the people happy,
And the world at peace!

ALL: Peace for us all!
[Outside joyful shouts of "Long live Chairman Mao!" The crowd
pours out of the gate. A military band strikes up.]

Slow Curtain

NOTES

1. The expression translated as "popular entertainer" denotes a person who recites popular stories in verse or prose, a singer of popular songs, an actor who sings in folk opera, and so on. There is a great variety of these traditional popular entertainments, many of which nearly died out before 1949. Since the establishment of the People's Government their high artistic value has been recognized, the entertainers have been encouraged to develop their art, and they have achieved wider popularity than ever before.

2. A kind of folk-ballad, the basic meter of which is
A b A, A b A
A b A b A b A
("A" representing a stressed syllable and "b" an unstressed one.) The number of lines may be varied, and the last line lengthened, to fit what the singer has to say. The last syllable of each line should rhyme. The shu-lai-po is recited by the entertainer to the accompaniment of a pair of bamboo castanets.

3. A tricycle rickshaw ridden by the driver in front, with the passenger seat behind.

4. The center of a crowded district in the southern part of Peking.

5. A kind of unleavened and steamed bread made of flour ground from coarse grain (especially maize) which until recently was a staple food of the poor in North China.

6. The word "shaoping" translated as "girdle-cake" denotes a round leavened cake made of wheat flour, generally about three inches across and half an inch thick, coated with sesame seeds.

7. The word translated as "bed" is "kang," which in reality is a raised platform made of bricks or clay, in houses in northern China, which can

be heated by means of flues running through it. It is used for sleeping on at night, and for sitting on by day.

8. This gesture indicates the Eighth Route Army (the forerunner of the People's Liberation Army), and hence, in popular speech, Communists.

9. The expression here rendered as "a loaf" is "a pound of *taping.*" *Taping* (literally "big cake") is a large, slightly leavened girdle-cake made of wheat flour; it may be a foot or more in diameter and about an inch thick, and is therefore often cut for sale by weight.

10. This was formerly a notorious place for robberies and fights.

11. One of the eight divisions in which the Manchu army was organized, the color being that of the banner under which they fought.

12. A traditional peasant dance which had almost died out but was revived in the liberated areas and has since become an expression of the new freedom throughout China.

13. The expression here translated (literally) as "The Women's Army" could equally well be translated as "The Lady's Army." It is double joke: (a) at the expense of the women in general, who are doing all the talking, and (b) at the expense of Niang-tse in particular, who is so full of ideas. It is also a historical allusion, to the Princess of Pingyang, who led an army known as "The Lady's Army" and, by defeating the last of her father's opponents, enabled him to become the first emperor of the Tang Dynasty (A.D. 618–907).

THE WHITE-HAIRED GIRL*

(An Opera)

By Ting Yi and Ho Ching-chih

Translated by Yang Hsien-yi and Gladys Yang

CHARACTERS

YANG, *tenant of* LANDLORD HUANG, aged over fifty.

HSI-ERH, YANG's daughter, aged seventeen.

AUNTY WANG, YANG's neighbor, a peasant woman of over fifty.

TA-CHUN, AUNTY WANG's son, about twenty.

UNCLE CHAO, YANG's old friend, a tenant peasant of about fifty.

LI, a peasant, over forty.

TA-SO, a young peasant.

HUANG, a landlord in his thirties.

MRS. HUANG, LANDLORD HUANG's mother, over fifty.

MU, the HUANG family steward, in his thirties.

AUNTY CHANG, a servant in the HUANG family, in her forties.

TA-SHENG, a servant in the HUANG family, in his twenties.

TWO THUGS EMPLOYED BY THE HUANG FAMILY.

THE DISTRICT HEAD.

HU-TZU, a young peasant.

FOUR PEASANTS.

FOUR PEASANT WOMEN.

CROWD.

---

*Reprinted from *Chinese Literature*, No. 2 (1953), p. 38–109.

ACT I

Time: Winter, 1935[1]

Place: *Yangko Village in Hopei. There is a plain in front of the village, and hills behind.*

SCENE 1

[*It is New Year's Eve in the Yang home, and heavy snow is falling. HSI-ERH, daughter of the tenant peasant YANG, comes on through the snowstorm carrying maize flour.*]

HSI-ERH [sings]:

> The north wind blows, the snowflakes whirl,
> A flurry of snow brings in New Year.
> Dad's been hiding a week because of his debt,
> Though it's New Year's Eve, he's still not back.
> Aunty's given me maize flour, and I'm waiting
> For Dad to come home and spend New Year.

[*Pushing open the door, she goes in. It is a humble room, containing a stove with a kitchen-god beside it and firewood and pots stacked in one corner. On the stove stands an oil lamp.*]

HSI-ERH: Now it's New Year's Eve, everybody's steaming maize cakes and dumplings, burning incense and pasting up door-gods for New Year. Dad has been away for a week, and still isn't back. We've nothing in the house for New Year. [*Pauses.*] There are only Dad and I at home; my mother died when I was three. My father cultivates one acre of land belonging to rich Landlord Huang. Dad works in the fields with me at his heels, in the wind and in the rain. . . . Every year we're behind with our rent, so just before New Year he always leaves home to escape being dunned. [*Anxiously.*] Now it's New Year's Eve, and getting quite dark—why isn't he back yet? Oh, I went to Aunty's house just now, and she gave me some maize flour which I'm going to mix with bean cake to make cakes for Dad to eat when he comes back. [*She fetches water, mixes the dough, and starts making cakes.*]

[*The wind blows open the door. HSI-ERH runs over, but finds no one there.*]

HSI-ERH: Oh, it's the wind that blew open the door. [*Sings.*]

> Wind whirls the snow against our door,
> Wind batters the door till it flies wide open.

> I'm waiting for Dad to come back home,
> And step inside the room again!

When Dad left, he took beancurd to sell. If he's sold the bean-curd and brings back two pounds of flour, we could even eat dump-lings. [Sings.]

> I feel so restless waiting for Dad,
> But when he comes home I'll be happy.
> He'll bring some white flour back with him,
> And we'll have a really happy New Year!

[She continues making cakes.]

[Enter YANG covered with snow. He has his peddler's pole and kit for carrying beancurd, and over his shoulders the cloth used to cover the beancurd. He staggers along.]

YANG [sings]:

> Three miles through a snowstorm I've come home,
> After hiding a week from the duns.
> As long as I can get by this time,
> I don't mind putting up with hunger and cold.

[After looking round apprehensively he knocks at the door.] Hsi-erh! Open the door!

[HSI-ERH, overjoyed, opens the door.]

HSI-ERH: You're back, Dad!

YANG: Yes. [He signs to her not to talk so loudly.]

HSI-ERH [brushing the snow from her father's clothes]: It's snowing very hard outside, Dad! Look how thickly you're covered!

YANG: While I was away, Hsi-erh, did the landlord send anyone to press for payment?

HSI-ERH: On the 25th, Steward Mu came.

YANG [taken aback]: Oh? He came? What did he say?

HSI-ERH: When he found you were away, he left again.

YANG: And then?

HSI-ERH: He hasn't been back since.

YANG [rather incredulous]: Really?

HSI-ERH: Yes, Dad.

YANG [still unconvinced]: Are you sure?

HSI-ERH: Why should I fool you, Dad?

YANG [reassured]: Well, that's good. Listen, Hsi-erh, how strong the wind is!

HSI-ERH: And it's snowing so hard!

YANG: It's growing dark, too.

HSI-ERH: And the road is bad, Dad.

YANG: I don't think Steward Mu will come now. I owe the landlord one and a half piculs, and my debt with the interest amounts to twenty-five dollars; but this time I've got by.

HSI-ERH [happily]: So we've got by again, Dad!

YANG: Hsi-erh, fetch some firewood so that I can dry myself. Have you still not finished that maize flour?

HSI-ERH: I finished that long ago. This is some Aunty Wang gave me just now.

YANG: So you've been to the mountain for firewood again in such cold.

HSI-ERH: I went just now with Ta-chun. [She fetches firewood.] You must be hungry, Dad.

YANG [warming himself by the fire]: I'm hungry all right. [Chuckles.]

HSI-ERH: The cakes are mixed; I'm going to steam them.

YANG: Just a minute, Hsi-erh. What do you think this is? [Producing a wallet from his pocket.]

HSI-ERH [clutching at it in delighted surprise]: What is it, Dad?

YANG [sings]:

> With the money I made by selling beancurd,
> I bought two pounds of flour at the fair;
> But I didn't want Landlord Huang to see it,
> So it's been in my wallet the last few days.

HSI-ERH [sings]:

> With the money he made by selling beancurd,
> Dad bought two pounds of flour at the fair.
> He's brought it home to make dumplings,
> So now we'll have a happy New Year!

Dad, I'll call Aunty Wang over to make dumplings.

YANG [stopping her]: Wait a bit, Hsi-erh! Look what this is.

HSI-ERH: What, Dad?

YANG [takes a thickly wrapped paper packet from his pocket. When all the paper wrappings are removed, a red ribbon is disclosed. While taking off the wrappings, he sings]:

> Other girls have flowers to wear,
> But your dad can't afford to buy flowers;
> So I bought two feet of red ribbon
> To tie in my Hsi-erh's hair!

[HSI-ERH kneels before YANG who ties the ribbon in her hair.]

108

HSI-ERH [sings]:

> Other girls have flowers to wear,
> But Dad can't afford to buy flowers;
> So he's bought two feet of red ribbon
> For me to tie in my hair!

[HSI-ERH stands up.]

YANG [laughs]: Turn round and let me have a look at you. [HSI-ERH turns.] Good. Presently we'll ask Ta-chun and Aunty Wang to come and have a look, too. [HSI-ERH tosses her head shyly yet coquettishly.] Oh, I brought two door-gods, too. Let's paste them up. [He takes out two pictures.]

HSI-ERH: Door-gods! [They paste them up and sing]:

> The door-gods ride roan horses!

YANG:

> Pasted on the door they'll guard our home!

HSI-ERH:

> The door-gods carry such big swords!

YANG:

> They'll keep out all devils, great and small!

BOTH:

> They'll keep out all devils, great and small!

YANG: Aha, now neither big devils nor little devils can get in!

HSI-ERH: I hope that rent collector, Steward Mu, will be kept out, too!

YANG: Good girl, let's hope we have a peaceful New Year.

[They close the door.]

[Enter AUNTY WANG from next door.]

WANG: Today Ta-chun bought two pounds of flour at the fair. I'm going to see if Uncle Yang has come back or not, and if he's back, I'll ask them over to eat dumplings. [Looks up.] Ah, Uncle Yang must be back; the door-gods are up. [Knocks.] Hsi-erh! Open the door!

HSI-ERH: Who is it?

WANG: Your aunty.

HSI-ERH [opens the door and WANG enters]: See, Aunty, Dad's back!

WANG: How long have you been back, Uncle Yang?

YANG: Just the time it takes to smoke one pipe.

HSI-ERH: Aunty, Dad's bought two pounds of flour. I was just going to ask you over to make dumplings, and now here you are. Look, look!

109

WANG: Ta-chun has bought two pounds of flour too, child, and for half a pint of rice he got a pound of pork as well. I was going to ask you both to our home.

HSI-ERH: Have them over here!

WANG: No, come on over.

HSI-ERH: Do stay here, Aunty!

YANG: Yes, stay here.

WANG: Look at you both! Why stand on ceremony with us! [*Turns and whispers to* YANG.] Uncle, after New Year Hsi-erh and Ta-chun will be one year older. I'm waiting for you to say the word!

YANG [*afraid lest* HSI-ERH *hear, yet apparently eager for her to hear*]: Don't be impatient, Aunty. When the right time comes, we'll fix it up for the youngsters. Ah . . . .

HSI-ERH [*pretending not to understand, interrupts them*]: Aunty, come and mix the dough.

YANG: That's right; go and mix the dough.

[AUNTY, *chuckling, goes to mix dough.*]

[*Enter the landlord's steward,* MU. *He carries a lantern bearing the words, "The Huang Family—House of Accumulated Virtue."*]

MU [*sings*]:

> *Here I come collecting rent*
> *And dunning for debt!*
> *I've four treasures as tricks of the trade:*
> *Incense and a gun,*
> *Crutches and a bag of tricks.*
> *I burn the incense before the landlord,*
> *I fire the gun to frighten tenants,*
> *With my crutches I trip folk up,*
> *And with my bag of tricks I cheat them!*

This evening the landlord has sent me on an errand to the tenant peasant Yang—a secret errand, not for everybody's ears! The landlord has given me instructions to take Yang to him for a talk. [*Knocks.*] Old Yang, open up!

YANG: Who is it?

MU: I, Steward Mu!

[*The three inside start, and* AUNTY WANG *and* HSI-ERH *hastily hide the flour bowl.*]

MU: Old Yang, hurry up, and let me in!

[*There is no help for it but to open the door, and* MU *enters. All remain silent.*]

110

Mu [*makes a round of the room with his lantern,* Hsi-erh *hides behind* Aunty Wang]: Old Yang! [*With unusual politeness.*] Are you ready for New Year?

Yang: Oh, Mr. Mu, we haven't lit the stove yet.

Mu: Well, Old Yang, I have to trouble you. Landlord Huang wants you to come over for a talk.

Yang: Oh! [*Greatly taken aback.*] But . . . but . . . Mr. Mu, I can't pay the rent or the debt.

Mu: Oh no, this time Landlord Huang doesn't want to see you either about the rent or your debt, but to discuss something important. It's New Year's Eve, and the landlord is in a good humor, so you can talk things over comfortably. Come along!

Yang [*pleadingly*]: I . . . Mr. Mu . . . .

Mu [*pointing to the door*]: It's all right. Come along. [Yang *has to go.*]

Hsi-erh [*hastily*]: Dad, you . . . .

Mu [*shining the lantern on* Hsi-erh's *face*]: Oh, don't worry, Hsi-erh. Landlord Huang will give you flowers to wear. Your dad will bring them back. [*Laughs.*]

Wang [*putting the beancurd cloth over* Yang's *shoulders*]: Put this over you, Uncle! The snow is heavier now . . . . When you get there, go down on your knees to Landlord Huang, and he surely won't spoil our New Year.

Mu: That's right. [*Pushes* Yang *out.*]

[Yang *looks back as he goes out.*]

Hsi-erh: Dad! . . .

[Yang *sighs.*]

Mu: Hurry up! [*Pushes* Yang *off.*]

Hsi-erh: Aunty, my dad! . . . [*Cries.*]

Wang [*putting her arms round her*]: Your dad will be back soon. Come on, come to our house to mix dough.

[*They go out.*]

Curtain

Scene 2

Landlord Huang's *house*.

[*The stage presents the entrance and a small room near the reception hall, furnished with a table and chairs. The candle in a tall candlestick on the table lights up an account book, abacus, inkstone and old-fashioned Chinese pipe.*

Sounds of laughter, clinking of wine cups, and the shouts of guests playing the finger-game are heard offstage. Landlord Huang *comes in, cheerfully tipsy, picking his teeth.*]

Huang [*sings*]:
> With feasting and wine we see the Old Year out,
> And hang lanterns and garlands to celebrate New Year's Eve!
> There are smiles on the faces of all our guests
> Who are drunk with joy, not wine.
> Our barns are bursting with grain,
> So who cares if the poor go hungry!

[*The servant* Ta-sheng *brings in water, and* Huang *rinses his mouth.*]

Huang: Ta-sheng, go and tell your mistress I have a headache and can't drink with the guests. Ask her to entertain them.

Ta-sheng: Very good, sir. [*Exit.*]

Huang: Well, I haven't lived in vain! I have nearly a hundred hectares of good land, and every year I collect at least a thousand piculs in rent. All my life I've known how to weight the scales in my own favor and manage things smoothly both at home and outside. During the last few years our family has done pretty well. Last year my wife died. My mother wants me to marry again, but I feel freer without a wife at home. Women are cheap as dirt. If one takes my fancy, like this one tonight, it's very easy to arrange.

[Mu *leads* Yang *on.*]

Yang [*sings timidly*]:
> The red lanterns under the eaves dazzle my eyes,
> And I don't feel easy in my mind.
> I wonder what he wants me for?
> Hsi-erh is waiting for me at home.

Mu: Old Yang, Landlord Huang is here. This way.

[*They enter the room.*]

112

HUANG [politely]: So it's Old Yang. Sit down, won't you? [Indicates a seat.]

[YANG dare not sit.]

MU [pouring tea]: Have some tea.

[YANG remains silent.]

HUANG: Have you got everything ready for New Year, Old Yang?

YANG: Well, sir, you know how it is. It's been snowing more than ten days, and we have no firewood or rice at home. I've not lit the stove for several days.

MU: Bah. See here, Old Yang, there's no need to complain about poverty. Landlord Huang knows all about you, doesn't he?

HUANG: Yes, Old Yang, I know you're not well off. But this year is passing, and I have to trouble you for the rent. [Opens the account book.] You cultivate one acre of my land. Last year you were five pecks short, this summer another four and a half pecks, in autumn another five and a half pecks.

MU [reckoning on the abacus]: Five times five . . . two fives makes ten . . . .

HUANG: And remember the money you owe us. In my father's time your wife died, and you wanted a coffin, so you borrowed five dollars from us. The year before last you were sick and borrowed two and a half dollars. Last year another three dollars. At that time we agreed upon five per cent monthly interest. At compound interest it amounts to—

MU [reckoning on the abacus]: The interest on the interest amounts to—five times five, twenty-five. Two fives is ten . . . . Altogether twenty-five dollars fifty cents. Plus one and a half piculs' rent.

HUANG: Altogether twenty-five dollars and fifty cents, and one and a half piculs' rent. Right, Old Yang?

YANG: Yes, sir. . . . That's right.

HUANG: See, Old Yang, it's down here quite clearly in black and white, all correct and in order. This is New Year's Eve, Old Yang; the rent must be paid. If you've got it with you, so much the better; you pay the money and the debt is canceled. If you haven't got it with you, then go and find some way of raising it. Steward Mu will go with you.

MU: So it's up to you. I'm ready to go with you. Get going, Old Yang!

YANG [pleadingly]: Oh, Mr. Mu . . . . Sir . . . . Please let me off this time! I really have no money; I can't pay the rent or the debt. [His voice falters.] Sir . . . Mr. Mu . . . .

HUANG: Now, Old Yang, that's no way to act. This is New Year's Eve. You're in difficulties, but I'm even worse off. You must clear the debt today.

YANG: Sir . . . .

HUANG: Come, you must be reasonable. Whatever you say, that debt must be paid.

MU: You heard what Landlord Huang said, Old Yang. He never goes back on his word. You must find a way, Old Yang.

YANG: What can I do, sir? An old man like me, with no relatives or rich friends—where can I get money? [Beseechingly.] Sir . . . .

HUANG [seeing his opportunity, signals to MU]: Well . . . .

MU [to YANG]: Well, listen, Old Yang, there is a way. Landlord Huang has thought of a way out for you, if you will take it . . . .

YANG: Tell me what it is, Mr. Mu.

MU: You go back, and bring your daughter Hsi-erh here as payment for the rent.

YANG [horror-stricken]: What!

MU: Go and fetch Hsi-erh here as payment for the rent.

YANG [kneeling beseechingly]: Sir, you can't do that! [Sings.]

> The sudden demand for my girl as rent—
> Is like thunder out of a cloudless sky!
> Hsi-erh is the darling of my heart,
> I'd rather die than lose her!
> I beg you, sir,
> Take pity on us, please,
> And let me off this once!
> She's all I have,
> This is more than I can bear!

HUANG [stands up in disgust]: Well, I'm doing you a good turn, Old Yang. Bring Hsi-erh to our house to spend a few years in comfort, and won't she be better off than in your home, where she has to go cold and hungry and has such a hard time of it? Besides, we are not going to treat Hsi-erh badly here. And this way your debt will be cancelled, too. Isn't that killing two birds with one stone? [Laughs.]

YANG: No, sir, you can't do that. . . .

MU: Well, Old Yang, it seems to me you poor people try to take advantage of the kindness of the rich. Landlord Huang wants to help your family. Just think, Hsi-erh coming here will have the time of her life. She will live on the fat of the land, dress like a

114

lady, and only have to stretch out her hand for food or drink! That would be much better than in your house where she goes cold and hungry. In fact Landlord Huang is quite distressed by all you make Hsi-erh put up with. So you'd better agree.

YANG: But, sir, Mr. Mu, this child Hsi-erh is the apple of my eye. Her mother died, when she was three, and I brought her up as best I could. I'm an old man now and I have only this daughter. She's both daughter and son to me. I can't let her go . . . sir! [Turning to HUANG.]

HUANG [adamant]: Bah!

[YANG turns to MU who also ignores him.]

HUANG [after a while]: I'm not going to wait any longer, Old Yang! Make your choice. Give me your girl or pay the debt.

MU: Old Yang, Landlord Huang is in a good humor now. Don't offend him, or it'll be the worse for you.

HUANG [angrily]: That's enough! Make out a statement! Tell him to send the girl tomorrow! [Starts angrily off.]

YANG [stepping forward to clutch at him]: Don't go, sir!

HUANG: Get away! [Pushing YANG aside, he hurries off.]

MU: All right, better agree, Old Yang. [Goes to the table to write a statement.]

YANG [barring MU's way wildly]: You . . . you mustn't do that! [Sings.]

> What have I done wrong,
> That I should be forced to sell my child?
> I've had a hard time of it all my life,
> But I little thought it would come to this!

MU: Get wise, Old Yang. Don't keep on being such a fool. You've got to agree to this today, whether you like it or not! [Pushes YANG aside and takes up a pen to write the statement.]

YANG [seizing MU's hand]: No! [Sings.]

> Heaven just kills the grass with a single root,
> The flood just carries off the one-plank bridge.
> She's the only child I ever had,
> And I can't live without her!

MU [furiously]: Don't be a fool! Presently if you make the master lose his temper, it'll be no joke!

YANG: I . . . I . . . I'll go somewhere to plead my case! [About to rush out.]

MU [banging the table]: Where are you going to plead your case?

115

The county magistrate is our friend, this is the yamen door; where are you going to plead your case!

YANG [aghast]: I . . . I . . . .

MU: It's no use, Old Yang! You're no match for him. I advise you to make out a statement and put your mark on it to settle the business. [Writes.]

YANG [stopping him again]: You . . . you . . . .

[Enter HUANG impatiently.]

HUANG [in a towering rage]: Why are you still so stubborn, Old Yang! Let me tell you, it's going to be done today, whether you like it or not! [To MU.] Hurry up and make out a statement for him.

YANG [at a loss]: Ah!

MU [reading as he writes]: "Tenant Yang owes Landlord Huang one and a half piculs of grain and twenty-five dollars fifty cents. Since he is too poor to pay, he wants to sell his daughter Hsi-erh to the landlord to cancel the debt. Both parties agree and will not go back on their word. Since verbal agreements are inconclusive, this statement is drawn up as evidence . . . . Signed by the two parties, Landlord Huang and Tenant Yang, and the witness, Steward Mu. . . ." Right, talk is empty but writing is binding. Come on, Old Yang! Put your mark on it!

YANG [frenziedly]: You can't do this, sir!

HUANG: What! All right, then tell Liu to tie him up and take him to the county court!

YANG [panic stricken]: What, send me to the county court! Oh, sir!

MU [seizing YANG's hand]: Put your mark on it! [Presses his fingers down.]

YANG [startled to see the ink on his finger]: Oh! [Falls to the ground.]

MU: Aha, one fingerprint has cleared the debt of all these years. . . .

[Hands the document to HUANG.]

[HUANG makes a gesture to MU.]

MU [ascertains that YANG is still breathing]: He's all right.

HUANG: Old Yang, you'd better go back now, and bring Hsi-erh here tomorrow. [To MU.] Give him that document.

MU [helping YANG up]: This one is yours, here. . . . [Hands him the document.] Tomorrow send Hsi-erh here to give New Year's greetings to Landlord Huang's family. Tell her to come here to spend a happy New Year. Go on. [Pushes YANG out, then shuts the door.]

[YANG collapses outside the gate in the snowstorm.]

116

HUANG: Old Mu, you take a few men there early tomorrow. We don't want the old fellow to go back and decide to ignore the debt and run away. In that case we'd lose both girl and money.

MU: Right.

HUANG: Another thing. For heaven's sake don't let word get about; it wouldn't sound well on New Year's Day. If those wretches spread the news, even though we've right on our side, it would be hard to explain. If anyone questions you, say my mother wants to see Hsi-erh and you're fetching her to give New Year's greetings to the old lady.

MU: Very good. [Exit.]

HUANG: Ah! The only way to get rich is at the expense of the poor. Without breaking Old Yang, I couldn't get Hsi-erh!

YANG [comes to himself outside the gate, and gets up]: Heaven! Murderous Heaven! [Sings.]

> Heaven kills folk without batting an eye!
> The landlord's house is Hell!
> I'm an old fool, an old fool,
> Why did I put my mark on that paper just now?
> I've gone and sold my only daughter,
> Your dad's let you down, Hsi-erh!
> You're happy, waiting at home for me for New Year,
> But I'm in despair!
> With this hand I've sold my only child,
> How can I face you when I get home?

[He staggers off.]

Curtain

SCENE 3

[YANG's old friend, the tenant peasant CHAO, enters with a basket containing a small piece of meat and a pot of wine. He is taking the path by the village.]

CHAO [sings]:

> In the gale the snow whirls high,
> Nine homes out of ten are dimly lit;
> Not that we don't celebrate New Year,
> But the poor have a different New Year from the rich.

> There's wine and meat in the landlord's house,
> While we tenants have neither rice nor flour!

[He hears sounds of merriment from LANDLORD HUANG's house in the distance.] Bah! At New Year the rich could die of laughing, while the poor could die of despair! Old Yang's been away a week to escape paying his debt, but he ought to be back now. I've bought four ounces of wine to drink with him. Getting his troubles off his chest is the poor man's way of spending New Year. [Sings.]

> Just as officials are all in league,
> The poor stick together, too.
> I'm going to spend New Year's Eve with Old Yang,
> To share four ounces of cheap wine with a friend. [Exit.]

[Enter YANG.]

YANG [sings]:

> I feel as befuddled as if I were drunk,
> In such a snowstorm where can I go?
> The deed in my pocket is like a knife
> That's going to kill my own flesh and blood.

Where are you, Hsi-erh? You don't know what your dad . . . . [Falls.]

CHAO [enters and sees a prostrate figure. When he goes to help him up, he recognizes YANG]: So it's you, Old Yang?

YANG: Who's that?

CHAO: It's Old Chao.

YANG: Oh, Old Chao, friend . . . .

CHAO [raising him]: What happened to you, Old Yang?

YANG: Ah! [For an instant he appears to be in a frenzy, but then fights down his feelings.] Nothing . . . . No, nothing. Just now I went to the rich man's house . . . .

CHAO: Oh, so you were badly treated up there. It's snowing faster; let's go back now and talk it over. We'll have a good talk. [Helps YANG along.]

YANG: Talk . . . . Talk . . . . Talk it over . . . . Have a good talk.

CHAO: Here, how is it the door is closed? [Opens the door and helps YANG in.] Why is there no light? [Gropes for the matches to light the lamp.] Where are you, Hsi-erh?

YANG [hearing HSI-ERH's name]: Ah, Hsi-erh, Hsi-erh!

CHAO: What is it, Old Yang?

118

YANG [*controlling himself*]: Nothing, Hsi-erh has gone with Aunty Wang to make dumplings.

CHAO: So this New Year's Eve you have dumplings to eat? Your daughter must be happy. Old Yang, look, I've got a pound of pork for you, for you two to eat tomorrow. And I've brought four ounces of wine. Tonight the two of us can drink a few cups. [*Heats the wine.*]

YANG: Right, drink. Drink a few cups. . . . Drink a few cups. [*Sits by the stove. They drink.*]

CHAO: What happened, Old Yang, in the landlord's house just now?

YANG: That . . . nothing . . . Old Chao.

CHAO: What is it? Tell me. I'm your friend.

YANG: Ah, yes . . . .

CHAO: Go on, Old Yang! What's there to be afraid of?

YANG: I . . . .

CHAO: You'd try the patience of a saint, the way you never take other people into your confidence, but keep all your troubles to yourself! But we two have always talked frankly, and tonight you mustn't brood. Come on, Old Yang, out with it!

YANG: Very well, I'll tell you. I came home today, hoping to have escaped paying the debt. Then Steward Mu called me to the landlord's house.

CHAO: Yes.

YANG: Landlord Huang opened the account book and Mu reckoned on the abacus, and insisted on my clearing the debt. I couldn't pay it, so he . . . .

CHAO: So what?

YANG: He wanted Hsi-erh as payment.

CHAO: Did you agree?

YANG: I . . . No.

CHAO [*excitedly*]: Good for you, Old Yang! You did right. To let Hsi-erh go to his house in payment for the debt would be like throwing your child to the wolves. As the proverb says, "Buddha needs incense, and a man needs self-respect." That's something we must fight for. You've shown the right spirit, Old Yang. [*Raises his cup.*] Come on, Old Yang, drink up.

YANG [*in agony of mind*]: Old Chao . . . Old Chao, you know to-morrow—no, next year—next year the landlord will still want Hsi-erh to go.

CHAO: Next year? Well, Old Yang, I'm considering that. Next year I'm not going to stay here. I'm going north.

YANG: Where? Going north? Ah, even a poor home is hard to give up. If we leave, we'll starve.

CHAO: Not necessarily. Here we cultivate these small plots of poor land, and can't live anyway, what with the rent. This year I worked fifty days for the landlord, but even so I didn't clear all the rent for the melon field; yesterday he was pressing me again. Bah! Why should an old man like me, all alone and without children, end my days on these small fields? I think we'd better take Hsi-erh to the north, until she's grown up. At our age, we can't expect to live long, and our death doesn't matter; but we mustn't ruin the child's life.

YANG [sadly, weighing his words]: Our death doesn't matter, but we mustn't ruin the child's life.

CHAO: Think it over, Old Yang! I consider next year, as soon as spring comes, we should take our things and go. [Raises his cup again.] Drink up!

YANG: Ah!

[Enter AUNTY WANG, HSI-ERH and WANG TA-CHUN, carrying the dumplings.]

WANG: Has Uncle Yang really come back, Ta-chun?

TA-CHUN: I saw him coming out of the landlord's house. [To HSI-ERH.] Hsi-erh, the path is slippery; let me take that.

HSI-ERH: I can carry it, Ta-chun.

[YANG, hearing voices outside, hastily wipes his eyes and pretends all is well.]

HSI-ERH [approaching, sees a light through the door]: Aunty, I think Dad is really back. [They enter.]

HSI-ERH [joyfully]: Dad, you're back!

TA-CHUN: Uncle, you're back!

WANG: Uncle Chao, you're here too . . . .

CHAO: We two have been chatting quite a time.

TA-CHUN: Uncle, what happened in the landlord's house?

YANG: I went, and couldn't pay the rent or settle the debt, so he . . . .

ALL: What did he do?

YANG: Nothing . . . I . . . I went down on my knees to him, that's all, and then came back.

TA-CHUN: Really, Uncle?

HSI-ERH: Really, Dad? That was all?

YANG: Certainly, child. Have I ever deceived you?

CHAO: That's right.

120

WANG [*wiping her eyes*]: Thank heaven! All's well then, and we
can enjoy New Year. Uncle Chao, we have a few pounds of flour
not taken by the landlord, and we made some dumplings. You
and Uncle Yang come and eat.

CHAO: Right.

YANG: Yes.

WANG: Ta-chun, empty out the garlic from that bowl, and give it to
Uncle Yang. Hsi-erh, you take this one to Uncle Chao.

TA-CHUN [*handing the bowl to* YANG]: Try our dumplings, Uncle.
[YANG *takes the bowl in silence.*]
[*They eat.*]

HSI-ERH [*sings*]:
Dad's come home after hiding from the duns!

TA-CHUN and WANG:
We're eating dumplings for New Year!

ALL:
Old and young we're sitting around,
Enjoying a very happy New Year!
Enjoying a happy New Year!

WANG:
The snow's been falling for a week or more,

ALL:
But we're all safely here together!

WANG:
Hoping by the time our young folk grow up,

ALL:
We can all pass some years in peace!
Yes, pass some years in peace!

HSI-ERH: Dad, you aren't eating!

YANG: Yes, I am.

CHAO [*reminiscently*]: Ta-chun and Hsi-erh, today we're celebrating
New Year and eating dumplings, so let me tell you a story about
dumplings. It was 1930,[2] the thirteenth day of the fifth moon,
the day when the War God sharpened his sword. There was a
fine rain falling. That day troops appeared from the southern
mountains. They were called the Red Army.

WANG: So you're harping back to that, Uncle. Better eat now.

HSI-ERH: Let Uncle Chao talk, Aunty! I like to hear.

CHAO: Yes, they had red all over them, their red sashes bound cross-
wise from shoulder to waist; and they were all ruddy-faced, hefty

121

fellows, so they were called the Red Army. They went south of the city to the Chao Village. I was there then, when the Red Army came and killed that devil, Landlord Chao. Then they distributed the grain and land among the poor, so on the thirteenth of the fifth moon all poor folk had basketfuls of white flour, and we all ate dumplings. In every house I went to then they offered me dumplings to eat. . . . [*Chuckles.*]

TA-CHUN: Where did that Red Army go to then?

CHAO: They went to the city, but they hadn't held it long when some Green Army arrived; then the Red Army went to the Great North Mountain, and never came down again. And after the Red Army left, the poor had a bad time of it once more.

TA-CHUN: Tell us, Uncle, will the Red Army be coming back?

CHAO: I think so.

HSI-ERH: When will they come?

CHAO: In good time, a day will come when the War God sharpens his sword again and the Red Army comes back. [*Chuckles.*]

WANG: Don't keep on talking but eat now. [*To* YANG.] Uncle, eat. There's plenty more.

HSI-ERH: Dad, have some more.

YANG [*holding the bowl, unable to eat, after a painful pause*]: Ah, Hsi-erh, isn't Aunty good?

HSI-ERH: Yes, she is!

YANG: Aunty, isn't Hsi-erh good?

WANG: She's a good child.

YANG: Hsi-erh, tell me, is your dad good?

HSI-ERH: What a question! Of course you are, Dad!

YANG: No, no. . . . Dad's no good.

WANG: What's got into you, Uncle Yang? Why are you talking like this?

CHAO: We've been drinking, and he may have had a drop too much. . . . [*Chuckles.*] It goes without saying you two are both good, Hsi-erh and Ta-chun. It won't be long now! [*Laughs.*]

[HSI-ERH *turns away shyly.*]

WANG: Stop talking and eat!

YANG: Yes, eat. . . .

[*They all eat.*]

HSI-ERH [*sings*]:
    Dad's come home after hiding from the duns!

TA-CHUN and WANG:
    We're eating dumplings for New Year!

122

ALL:

>Old and young we're sitting around,
>Enjoying a very happy New Year!
>Enjoying a happy New Year!

WANG:

>The snow's been falling for a week or more,

ALL:

>But we're all here safely together!

WANG:

>Hoping by the time our young folk grow up,

ALL:

>We can all pass some years in peace!
>Yes, pass some years in peace!

[In a state of mental agony, YANG cannot keep still, so he withdraws to a corner, where he clutches the document in his pocket with trembling hands.]

WANG: What are you doing, Uncle Yang? Come and eat.

YANG [startled]: I'm looking, looking. . . . Ah, it's empty, my pocket. Not a single coin. I can't even give the two youngsters money for New Year.

WANG: Come on. To have dumplings is good enough. Come and eat, Uncle.

YANG: I . . . I'll eat later.

WANG: Uncle Chao, have some more.

CHAO: I've had enough.

WANG [to TA-CHUN and HSI-ERH]: How about you two?

TA-CHUN and HSI-ERH: We've had enough.

WANG: Then let's clear away. [They clear the table.] Uncle Yang has been on his feet all day and is tired; he should rest now.

YANG [mechanically]: Rest now.

WANG: We would go on chatting forever, but we can talk again tomorrow. Tomorrow Ta-chun will come to give you New Year greetings.

CHAO: I'll be going too. Hsi-erh, take good care of your dad. Old Yang, tomorrow I'll come and wish you a happy New Year. I'm off now.

YANG: Good night, Old Chao.

[Exit CHAO.]

TA-CHUN: We're going too, Uncle.

YANG: See your mother back carefully, Ta-chun.

HSI-ERH: Are you going, Aunty!

WANG: Good night. [*She and* TA-CHUN *go out.*]

   [HSI-ERH *starts to close the door.*]

TA-CHUN [*at the door*]: Hsi-erh, Uncle is tired! Get him to rest early.

HSI-ERH: Yes. [*Closes the door.* WANG *and* TA-CHUN *go out.*]

YANG: You'd better go to bed, Hsi-erh.

HSI-ERH: So had you, Dad.

YANG: Your dad . . . your dad will see the New Year in.

HSI-ERH: I'll stay up, too.

YANG: Then put on some more firewood.

   [HSI-ERH *adds wood to the stove and sits by the fire.*]

YANG [*coughing*]: Hsi-erh, your dad is old and good for nothing.

HSI-ERH: Whatever do you mean, Dad! Come and warm yourself!
   [*They sit by the stove. The silence is oppressive, while snow falls outside. Time passes.*]

YANG: Are you asleep, Hsi-erh?

HSI-ERH: No, Dad. . . .

YANG: I'll trim the lamp. [*He trims the lamp.*] [*Presently the lamp on the stove burns low, and* HSI-ERH *falls asleep.*] The wick is burnt out, and the oil is used up. [*The lamp goes out.*] The light is out, too. . . . Hsi-erh! [HSI-ERH *is sound asleep.*]

YANG: Asleep? Hsi-erh! [*Sings.*]

> *Hsi-erh, my child, you're sleeping,*
> *Dad calls you, but you don't hear.*
> *You can't imagine, as you dream,*
> *The unforgivable thing I've done.*

Hsi-erh, Dad has wronged you! Aunty Wang, I've wronged you! Old Chao, I've wronged you! I made a statement and put my mark on it. . . . When Hsi-erh's mother died, she said, "Bring Hsi-erh up as best you can." And I brought her up. Hsi-erh has had a hard time of it with me for seventeen years. Today . . . I've wronged Hsi-erh's mother; I've sold our child. . . . Tomorrow the landlord will take her away. Neither the living nor the dead, neither human beings nor ghosts can ever forgive me! I'm an old fool, a criminal! But I can't let you go! I'll have it out with them! [*He runs wildly out, to be buffeted by the wind and snow.*] Ah, magistrates, landlords! . . . Lackeys. . . . Bailiffs! . . . Where can I go? Where can I turn? [*He clutches the document.*] Ah! [*Sings.*]

124

Magistrates, rich men—you tigers and wolves!
Because I owed rent and was in debt,
You forced me to write a deed,
Selling my child. . . .
The north wind's blowing, snow's falling thick and fast!
Where can I go? Where can I fly?
What way out is there for me?

[He pauses, bewildered.] Ah, I still have some lye for making bean-curd—I'll drink that! [He drinks it.] Now I'll drink some cold water. . . . [He takes off his padded jacket to cover HSI-ERH, then rushes outside, falls on the snow and dies.]
[Crackers sound in the village, signaling the arrival of the New Year.]

Curtain

SCENE 4

[In front of the Yang's home the next day. Crackers sound and TA-CHUN comes in gaily.]

TA-CHUN: Uncle Yang! Uncle Yang! I've come to wish you a happy New Year! [He suddenly stumbles on the corpse.] Oh! [Clearing the snow from the face of the dead man he recognizes YANG.] Oh! Uncle Yang! You! What's happened? [He hurries to the door and knocks.] Hsi-erh, Hsi-erh! Open the door, quick! [Hastily turning towards the backstage.] Mother! Mother! Come quick! Come quick!

HSI-ERH [wakened from her sleep]: Dad! Dad! [She looks for her father.]

TA-CHUN: Hsi-erh! [Pushing open the door.] Hsi-erh! Look! Your dad—

HSI-ERH: Has something happened to Dad? [Runs out, and seeing her father's body, falls on it and cries.] Dad! Dad!

TA-CHUN: What happened, Hsi-erh?

HSI-ERH [cries. Then sings]:

Yesterday evening when Dad came back,
He was worried but wouldn't tell me why.

125

> *This morning he's lying in the snow!*
> *Why, Dad, why?*

TA-CHUN [*helplessly turning toward the backstage*]: Mother, come
    quick!

[*Enter* AUNTY WANG.]

WANG: What is it, Ta-chun?

TA-CHUN: Mum, look at Uncle Yang! He—[*pointing to corpse.*]

WANG: What's happened to Uncle Yang? [*She kneels beside the
    corpse and touches it, hoping the dead man will wake up.*] Ta-chun,
    go and call Uncle Chao and the others at once.
    [*Exit* TA-CHUN.]

WANG [*finding the body stiff and lifeless, wails*]: Uncle Yang! Uncle
    Yang!

HSI-ERH: Daddy! [*Cries.*]

[*Enter* TA-CHUN *with* UNCLE CHAO, LI *and* TA-SO.]

CHAO: What's happened?

TA-SO: What happened, Ta-chun?

LI: It's Old Yang.

WANG [*crying as she tells the story*]: Friends, last night when he
    came back he was all right. Who could imagine this morning he
    would—[*Unable to proceed.*]

CHAO [*stoops and examines* YANG]: He's drunk lye.

HSI-ERH: Daddy!

CHAO [*noticing the dead man's clenched fist*]: Ah! [*He starts forcing
    open the fingers.* TA-CHUN *and* TA-SO *help him, and they take the
    deed of sale.*]

LI [*reading the deed*]: Tenant Yang owes Landlord Huang rent . . .
    Since he is too poor to pay, he wants to sell his daughter Hsi-erh
    to . . . [*Unable to finish he lets the deed fall to the ground. They
    are all horror stricken.*]

WANG: Merciful heavens! This . . . .

HSI-ERH [*shrieks*]: Oh, Dad! [*Sings.*]

> *Suddenly hearing that I've been sold,*
> *I feel as if fire were burning me!*
> *Could it be Dad didn't love me?*
> *Or thought me a bad daughter, could it be?*

CHAO [*addressing the corpse indignantly*]: Old Yang, last night you
    only told me half! You shouldn't have died! Because you wouldn't
    leave your little patch of land, you let them hound you to death!

126

TA-SO [*loudly*]: Last night they took away my donkey! Today for this paltry rent they drove Uncle Yang to suicide! They won't let the poor live! It's too much! [*Too angry to speak he turns to rush out.*]

TA-CHUN [*unable to suppress his anger*]: They killed Uncle Yang, and they make Hsi-erh . . . . I'm going to have it out with them! [*He rushes after* TA-SO.]

[CHAO *and* LI *pull* TA-SO *back, while* AUNTY WANG *restrains* TA-CHUN.]

WANG: Ta-chun! Ta-chun!

LI: It's no good, Ta-so, Ta-chun! It's there in black and white! Uncle Yang put his mark on it.

TA-CHUN: His mark? They forced him, didn't they? I'll send in an appeal!

TA-SO: Right!

LI [*sighs*]: To whom can you appeal? The district head? The magistrate? Aren't they hand in glove with the rich? I think we'd better accept it, if we can.

TA-SO: Accept it? I can't!

TA-CHUN: How are we poor folk to live! [*Stamps his foot and strikes his head in despair.*]

CHAO: Ta-chun, Ta-so, blustering is no use. Time's getting on, and the landlord will soon be here to fetch the girl; we'd better hurry to prepare the dead for burial, so that Hsi-erh can at least attend her father's funeral. We all know what goes on nowadays, but they've got the whip hand. Where can we turn to look for justice? . . . [*To* HSI-ERH.] This has happened today because we old people are no good. We've done you a great wrong, child! Ta-chun, Ta-so, we'd better first bury the dead! Aunty Wang, get ready quickly, and put Hsi-erh in mourning!

[*They bow their heads in silence, wiping their eyes in sorrow and anger.*]

[*Enter* STEWARD MU *with thugs.*]

MU: A happy New Year, friends! I wish you good luck and prosperity! [*They are all taken aback.*]

MU [*seeing the dead man in their midst, realizes what has happened, but feigns astonishment*]: Ah! Who's that?

LI: It's Old Yang.

MU: What, Old Yang! . . . Why, last night he was all right, how could he . . . ? Well, well . . . . [*Feigning sympathy.*] Who could have thought it? Such an honest fellow. . . . [*Turns.*] *Well then . . .* let us all help, and prepare his funeral. . . . Oh, Hsi-erh is here. Let's do it this way: let Hsi-erh come with me to beg the landlord for a coffin for her father. Come on, Hsi-erh. [*Tries to lead* HSI-ERH *off.*]

TA-CHUN [*unable to contain his anger, darts forward and shakes his fist at* MU, *who steps aside*]: I know why you've come. You shan't take her!

TA-SO [*stepping forward too*]: You dare!

THUGS [*stepping forward to cover* TA-CHUN *and* TA-SO *with their guns*]: Hey, there! Don't move!

MU [*changing his tune*]: All right, let's put our cards on the table. Old Yang has sold Hsi-erh to Landlord Huang! Here's the deed. [*Taking the deed from his pocket.*] Old Yang put his mark on it, so justice and reason are on our side. . . . Sorry, Wang Ta-chun, but Hsi-erh belongs to the landlord now.

TA-CHUN: Steward Mu, you dog aping your master, bullying the poor!

MU: So! You are cursing me? Very well, fellow, just wait and see!

CHAO: Mr. Mu, this is too much. The child's father has just died, and you want to carry her off, on New Year's Day, too.

MU: Too much? [*Pointing to the deed.*] Here's our reason. Better mind your own business.

WANG: Mr. Mu, let the child attend the funeral first. . . .

MU: Can't be done. Landlord Huang wants the girl taken back immediately. [*Sizing up the situation he adopts a more conciliatory tone.*] Well, actually I can't make any decisions; you must talk to Landlord Huang. Still, I think Hsi-erh will enjoy herself later on. [*He takes hold of* HSI-ERH *again.*] Come on, Hsi-erh.

TA-CHUN, TA-SO: You! . . . [*They want to rush forward again, but are stopped by the guns of the thugs.*]

[AUNTY WANG *timidly steps in front of* TA-CHUN.]

CHAO [*signing to them to stop*]: Ta-chun! Ta-so!

HSI-ERH [*shaking off* MU's *hand, darts back to* CHAO *and* AUNTY WANG]: Uncle! Aunty! [*Rushing to the dead man, she cries bitterly.*] Daddy! Daddy! . . .

MU [*pulling at* HSI-ERH *again*]: Well, Hsi-erh, we're all mortal. It's no use crying, better come with me. [*Pulls hard.*]

HSI-ERH [*frightened, screams and struggles*]: Uncle! Aunty!

WANG: Steward Mu, do let the child put on mourning for her father.

128

Mu: All right, put on mourning.
  [AUNTY WANG goes inside and fetches out a piece of white cloth which she ties round HSI-ERH's head.[3]]
CHAO [holding HSI-ERH, speaks to the dead man]: Old Yang, Hsi-erh can't attend your funeral today. This is all the fault of us old folk; we've done her a wrong. [To HSI-ERH.] Come, Hsi-erh, kowtow to your father.
HSI-ERH: Uncle! Aunty! [Kneels and kowtows.]
  [MU drags HSI-ERH off crying and screaming, followed by AUNTY WANG. TA-CHUN and TA-SO want to pursue them, but are stopped by CHAO.]
CHAO: Ta-chun, Ta-so . . . . They have the whip hand, what can we do? Let us remember how many people the Huang family has killed. Their day of reckoning will come! A day will come when power changes hands. . . . [They sob.] Don't cry, but come and bury the dead! [They carry YANG off.]

Curtain

ACT II

SCENE 1

Time: As in the last scene.

Place: The Buddhist shrine of LANDLORD HUANG's mother. Big, bright candles are lit, and incense smoke wreathes the air.

  [MRS. HUANG comes in bearing incense sticks in her hand.]
MRS. HUANG: Yesterday my son told me our tenant Yang was sending his daughter here as payment for the rent. Why hasn't she come to see me yet? [Sings.]
  At New Year our family gains in wealth and we old folk in
    longevity,
  Thanks to the virtues of our ancestors and holy Buddha's
    protection.
  I carry incense to the shrine where bright candles are lit on
    the altar,
  And bow three times in all sincerity.
  One stick of incense I offer Ju-lai of the Western Heaven—

May we grow wealthy, and our rents increase!
The second stick I offer Kuan-yin of the Southern Seas—
Grant peace in the four seasons, and may all our house grow
    rich!
The third stick I offer Chang Hsien, giver of children—
Protect us, and may we increase and multiply!

[*She closes the door and sits down.*]
Now money is depreciating, one maidservant costs so many years'
rent! Last year was better, when we bought that girl Hung-lu for
only eight dollars; while that girl bought by the northern household only cost five dollars and fifty cents. But this year everything
is expensive!
[*Mu comes on with Hsi-erh.*]

Mu: Come along, Hsi-erh. [*Sings.*]

What a queer girl you are!
Why act so strangely here?
Just now, when we saw the landlord,
You wouldn't look up or say a word,
And when he gave you a flower,
You wouldn't wear it!
Now that we're going to see the old lady,
You'll have to be on your best behavior!

Look happy now!
[*Hsi-erh gives a frightened sob.*]

Mu: Don't cry! If you make the old lady angry, even with her fingers
    she can scratch holes in your face. [*They enter the room.*] Ah,
    Mrs. Huang, the Yang family girl, Hsi-erh, has come to give you
    her New Year greetings.
Mrs. Huang: Oh, it's Old Mu. Come in. [*Enter Mu and Hsi-erh.*]
Mu [*to Hsi-erh*]: Kowtow to the mistress! [*Pushes her down on her
    knees.*]
Mrs. Huang: All right, get up.
Mu [*raising Hsi-erh*]: Get up, and let the mistress look at you.
Mrs. Huang: H'm, a good-looking child. Come over here.
Mu [*to Hsi-erh*]: Go on. [*He drags her again.*]
Mrs. Huang: The child looks intelligent. What's her name?
    [*Hsi-erh remains silent.*]
Mu: Answer the mistress. You're called . . . called Hsi-erh.
Mrs. Huang: Hsi-erh? Well, that's an auspicious name.[4] It needn't

130

be altered much to match Hung-fu and Hung-lu; we'll just add the word Hung in front. Let her be called Hung-hsi.

Mu [to Hsi-erh]: Thank the mistress for your new name. From now on you won't be called Hsi-erh but Hung-hsi.

Mrs. Huang: How old is the child?

[Hsi-erh remains silent.]

Mu: Seventeen.

Mrs. Huang: Ah, seventeen. Good girl, better than Hung-fu. Hung-fu is a regular scarecrow; she looks like nothing on earth! This girl is good. Old Mu, presently you tell my son I shall keep her with me.

Mu: Oh! That's too good for her.

Mrs. Huang: Well, her family is poor. Think of the hardships her father made her suffer—nothing to eat, no clothes to wear. Now that you've come to our house, Hung-hsi, you'll live in comfort. Are you glad?

[Hsi-erh remains silent.]

Mu: Speak up. . . . You are glad, you are glad! You are a lucky girl!

Mrs. Huang: See, the girl is dressed like a beggar! Old Mu, tell my maid Chang to change her clothes and bring her cakes to eat.

Mu [calling]: Ta-sheng! [There is a response offstage.] The mistress orders Chang to change Hung-hsi's clothes and bring cakes for Hung-hsi! [Voice offstage: "Yes, mistress! Visitors have come from the north village to pay their respects to you and Landlord Huang."]

Mrs. Huang: All right. [Stands up. To Hsi-erh.] Hung-hsi, soon Chang will come to change your clothes and look after you. [Starting out.] Ah, whoever does good deeds in his life will become a Buddha and go to the Western Paradise. [Mrs. Huang and Mu leave.]

[Voices off: "We've come to pay our respects to Mrs. Huang!" "We've come to wish Landlord Huang a happy New Year!"]

Hsi-erh: Oh dear! [Sings.]

    Oh, Dad!
    I hear so many voices here,
    I'm all of a tremble!
    So many bolts, so many doors!
    I call my dad, but he doesn't answer.
    Who'll wear mourning for my dad?
    Who'll cry at his funeral?

[Enter Ta-sheng holding a plate, and Chang with clothes.]

TASHENG: So this is Hung-hsi. Here, come and eat your cake.

CHANG: You must be hungry; have something to eat.

TA-SHENG: Hurry. I have to go and look after the guests.

[Out of nervousness HSI-ERH drops the plate and breaks it.]

TA-SHENG: What a bad girl you are, breaking a plate on New Year's Day! I'm going to tell the old lady.

CHANG: Don't, Ta-sheng! [Picks up the broken pieces.] The old lady's in a good temper today; don't make her angry. The girl's just come. She doesn't know how to behave. Let her off this time.

TA-SHENG: Huh, little wretch! We'll wait and see how she behaves in the future. [Exit.]

CHANG: Hung-hsi, come with me to change your clothes. [Taking her arm.] Child, this is not your own home, not like with your own parents; you'll have to fit in with these people's ways. . . . Come, don't be afraid. I'm Aunty Chang; I'm a servant too. We shall be together a long time; if there's anything you can't do, I'll help you. If you have any trouble, let me know. . . . Come now, come and change your clothes. [Exeunt.]

Curtain

SCENE 2

One month later.

At the gate of AUNTY WANG's house.

[Enter TA-CHUN.]

TA-CHUN [sings]:

> Uncle Yang's been dead for a month, and Hsi-erh
> In the landlord's house is treated like dirt;
> My mother's in tears the whole of the time,
> And it's harder than ever to make ends meet.
> How can I ever get even with them?
> My whole heart seems to burn with hate!
> When I went just now to look for Hsi-erh,
> Huang's thugs wouldn't let me in at the gate!

[Stamps.] Today I wanted to go and see Hsi-erh in my spare time, but that gateman saw me. . . . It was Ta-so who suggested that some day, when I had time, I should fetch Hsi-erh out; but although I've been there several times, I haven't been able to see her. Yesterday Landlord Huang pressed me to pay my debt, saying if I didn't pay they'd evict me, and drive me away. This evening Steward Mu's coming again. Bah! [*He pushes open the door and goes in.*] Mother! [*No one answers.*] She must have gone over to see Uncle Chao. When she gets back, there'll be more sighing and sobbing. [*Enter Ta-so.*]

TA-SO: Ta-chun!

TA-CHUN: Who is it?

TA-SO: Me! [*Coming forward.*] My! That bastard Mu has got his knife into us! Just now when I was out, he went to my home and took away five pints of kaoliang seeds, driving my mother nearly frantic. Some day that bastard's going to get what's coming to him. . . .

TA-CHUN: I've just come back from the Huang house. It was no good, I still couldn't see Hsi-erh. . . . [*Pauses.*] Presently Steward Mu is going to throw me out. . . .

TA-SO: What, is he coming soon? [*Looking at the sky.*] It's getting dark. . . . [*Looking at the door.*] Is your mother home?

TA-CHUN: No.

TA-SO: Ta-chun, I think we ought to have a fling at him tonight!

TA-CHUN: What do you mean, Ta-so?

TA-SO: When the bastard comes, we'll [*Makes a gesture and whispers.*] . . . .

TA-CHUN [*worked up*]: Yes . . . but . . . if it leaked out, my mother and Hsi-erh . . . .

TA-SO: Don't be afraid. It's dark, and when we're through with the rogue we'll drag him to the North Mountain gully to feed the wolves!

[*He whispers again.*]

TA-CHUN: All right, we'll be ready for him this evening! [*The watch sounds. Ta-chun and Ta-so take cover, and Ta-chun fetches a rope from the house.*]

[*Enter Mu, weaving tipsily.*]

MU [*sings*]:

> Kings and queens, kings and queens,
> And all the aces too!
> I don't care for kings or queens,
> All I want, my knave, is you!

[*Laughing he reaches the gate.*] Ta-chun! Ta-chun! Why haven't you gone yet, you rascal? Clear out of the house and be off with you!

[TA-CHUN *remains angrily silent.*]

MU: You want to spend all your life here, don't you, you rogue! You won't give up! Today you were hanging about the Huangs' gate again! Do you still want another man's girl? True, Hsi-erh was promised to you before, but she belongs to our Landlord Huang now. . . . Ah, that wench! Let me tell you, Landlord Huang knows you won't keep quiet, you rogue, so he says we've got to get rid of you. You clear out of this house now, and look sharp about it! [*He advances as he speaks.* TA-CHUN *does not answer, and as* MU *approaches he falls back.*] Where are you going, fellow? Why don't you say something? . . . Where are you going? [*Pressing* TA-CHUN.]

[TA-SO *suddenly seizes* MU *from behind and throws him to the ground.*]

MU: Who's that?

TA-SO: Don't you dare shout! [*To* TA-CHUN.] Stop his mouth, Ta-chun.
[MU *struggles.*]

TA-SO: You're going to dun for debts in hell! [*As they beat* MU, *two of* LANDLORD HUANG's *thugs enter.*]

THUGS: What's up?

[TA-CHUN *and* TA-SO, *seeing them, start to make off but are seized. However* TA-CHUN *breaks loose and escapes.*]

THUGS [*helping* MU *up*]: Well, Mr. Mu, you've had a fright!

MU [*panting*]: Lao San, Lao San—go after him! Go after Wang Ta-chun! [*Pointing to* TA-SO.] Well, so it was you, Ta-so, my fine fellow! . . . Old Liu, take him back for questioning.
[TA-SO *is pushed off by the thugs, kicking and struggling.* MU *also leaves.*]

[*The inner curtain falls.*]

[TA-CHUN *hurries to Uncle Chao's house, and hammers at the door.*]

TA-CHUN: Uncle Chao! Uncle Chao!

[CHAO *enters.*]

TA-CHUN: Uncle Chao, where's my mother?

CHAO: She's gone home, Ta-chun. Why have you got the wind up like this?

TA-CHUN: Uncle, something's happened! Ta-so and I beat up Steward Mu, but we were found out, and Ta-so was caught. Now they're after me!

134

CHAO: You young fellows! Just rashness is no use. I knew you were
    smoldering with rage, but our time hasn't come yet, Ta-chun.
    You can't stay here now; you'd better make off quickly.

TA-CHUN: Uncle . . . .

CHAO: Go northwest quickly!

TA-CHUN: Uncle . . . my mother and Hsi-erh . . . .

CHAO: I'll look after them. Go now. When times change, you can
    come back and see your mother and me.

    [TA-CHUN *runs off, and* CHAO *goes out.*]

Curtain

SCENE 3

The HUANG *house.*

[*Enter* LANDLORD HUANG *holding a lantern.*]

HUANG [*sings*]:

> Fate's been kind to me, I'm rich and respected,
> My barns are stuffed with grain and my chests with gold.
> The poor, of course, must go cold and hungry,
> Because that's their destiny, fixed by Fate!
> If cattle won't budge, I whip them;
> If pigs won't die, I slaughter them;
> And if the poor set themselves against me,
> They'll find out to their cost what fools they've been!

A few days ago Ta-so and Ta-chun refused to pay their rent, and
beat up Steward Mu. Tch! It's really preposterous! They should
remember who I am. . . . Even rats think twice before coming
out of their holes. Do they think they can get anywhere by making an enemy of me? Ta-so I have sent to the district jail. Ta-chun
ran away, but let him go! I don't think he dares to come back
even if he wants to. As for Hsi-erh . . . . [*Chuckles.*] The only
trouble is she's kept by my mother, so I've not been able to get
hold of her yet, which is beginning to make me impatient. . . .
Today I went to the north village to feast with some friends, and
I'm feeling rather restless. Now that it's dark I'll go and have
another try at it—try, try, and try again! . . . [*Laughs.*]

[*The second watch sounds, showing that it is after ten.*]

[*Sings.*]

> Hearing the second watch,

135

> *I tiptoe to my mother's room.*
> *I've hit on a fine plan*
> *To get my way tonight.*

[Exit.]

[The back curtain rises, disclosing Mrs. HUANG's bedroom.]

[Enter HSI-ERH, carrying broth.]

HSI-ERH [sings]:

> The few months I've been here,
> My life has been so bitter—
> First I am cursed, then beaten,
> They treat me all the time like dirt.
> But I have to swallow my tears,
> My only friend is Aunty Chang.

[She approaches the left side of the bed, and calls timidly: "Mistress!" Then approaches the right side of the bed and calls again, "Mistress! Mistress!"] Ah! [Sings.]

> Rich people are hard to please,
> I haven't a minute to myself;
> And if I'm careless and annoy her,
> I'm afraid she may do me in!

[Voice from within the bed curtains: "Hung-hsi, is the lotus-seed broth ready?"]

HSI-ERH: Coming, mistress! [A hand comes out from the curtain to take the bowl.]

[Voice from the bed: "So hot! Do you want to scald me? You damn slave! Cool it!" She passes the bowl back.]

HSI-ERH [holding the bowl, sings]:

> It's either too hot or too cold,
> She's never satisfied.
> I'm so tired and sleepy,
> But it's more than my life's worth to sleep!

[Voice from the bed: "Give me the broth!"]

HSI-ERH: Coming, mistress! [A hand from the bed takes the bowl.]

[Voice from the bed: "What, so bitter? You can't have taken out the roots properly. You make me furious, damn you! Kneel down!"]

HSI-ERH [frightened]: I . . . I . . . . [Kneels.]

[Voice from the bed: "You bitch, who can drink such bitter broth? Open your mouth!" Reaching out with an opium pin she slashes at HSI-ERH's mouth.]

HSI-ERH: Oh! [*Cries.*]

[HUANG *steals on, and listens at the door.*]

[*Voice from the bed:* "Don't cry! You really are infuriating!"]

HSI-ERH: I . . . I . . . . [*Cries.*]

[*Voice from the bed, angrily:* "Damn slave!" *She parts the bed curtain and emerges.*]

MRS. HUANG: Damn slave! [*Beats her again and again with a feather duster.*]

HUANG [*coming in quickly to stop her*]: Mother, Mother, don't be angry! Mother! [*Helps her to the bed.*]

MRS. HUANG: What brings you here? . . . [*To* HSI-ERH.] Get up. [HSI-ERH *gets up.*]

HUANG: Don't be angry, Mother. You're not feeling well these days, and Hung-hsi has offended you. . . .

MRS. HUANG: What brings you here so late?

HUANG: I came to see you, and . . . I would like Hung-hsi to sew something for me.

MRS. HUANG: I need Hung-hsi to make my broth.

HUANG: Oh . . . .

MRS. HUANG: My, how you reek of wine! Better go to bed at once!

HUANG: Yes, Mother. . . . Yes . . . er . . . Mother, you rest and have some opium. Don't be angry. [HUANG *prepares the opium pipe for his mother, who smokes; then he puts down the bed curtains.*]

HUANG: Come, Hung-hsi, come.

HSI-ERH [*in alarm*]: Young master, you . . . .

MRS. HUANG: Son, what are you doing? Haven't you gone yet?

HUANG: Mother, I was saying that Hung-hsi is quite clever, isn't she [*Taking* HSI-ERH's *hand.*] at looking after you! . . . [*Pinches her arm.*]

[HSI-ERH *gives a scream.*]

MRS. HUANG [*angrily getting out of bed again and sitting down*]: You wretched slave, have you gone crazy again?

HUANG: Er . . . er . . . Mother, I think tomorrow I'd better ask Dr. Chen from the town to examine you again.

MRS. HUANG: Humph!

[*Enter* CHANG, *and sets a teapot on the bed.*]

CHANG [*sizing up the situation*]: Has Hung-hsi offended you again, mistress? [*To* HUANG.] Why are you here, sir? It's getting late, you should rest now.

HUANG [*to himself*]: Huh, this servant Chang . . . .

CHANG: The old lady is not feeling well and it's getting late. . . .
Better go to bed, sir.

MRS. HUANG: Go to bed, son.

CHANG [nudging HSI-ERH]: Sir, here's your lantern. [Passing him the lantern.]

MRS. HUANG: Go on back, son. Hung-hsi, prepare that broth for me.

HUANG: Well, Mother, you'd better sleep. [To CHANG.] Tomorrow you wash those clothes of mine.

CHANG: Yes, sir.

[Exit HUANG.]

CHANG: Hung-hsi, come and heat the old lady's broth.
[HSI-ERH moves to take the bowl, but CHANG signs to her to be seated, and heats the broth herself.]
[HSI-ERH remains silent, and they watch the broth.]

CHANG [softly letting down the curtains]: How did you offend the old lady, Hung-hsi?

HSI-ERH: She said I hadn't taken the roots out of the lotus seeds, and they tasted bitter; but I had picked them clean. . . .

CHANG [indignantly]: Well! She feels bitter because she's had too much opium. . . .
[Voice from the bed: "Chang! What are you talking about?"]

CHANG: I was telling Hung-hsi not to cry, so as not to wake you. . . .
[Voice from the bed: "Oh. . . ."]
[Silence.]

CHANG [softly]: Hung-hsi, you couldn't have had enough to eat this evening. [Taking a dumpling from her sleeve.] Have this.

HSI-ERH [biting eagerly into the dumpling, gives a cry because her mouth hurts]: Oh!

CHANG [surprised]: What's the matter? [Looks at the wound.] Oh, so she's hurt you with the opium pin again. . . . [Indignantly.] Well! Presently I'll go to the kitchen and get some soup for you.

HSI-ERH [in pain]: No . . . no need.

CHANG [looking at MRS. HUANG]: Well, the old lady is asleep. . . . [Sits by HSI-ERH and fans the fire.] Ah, Hung-hsi, it's a hard, hard life. Only we two know it. It was because my family couldn't pay our rent either that I was sent to work here in payment for the rent. The things I've seen during these years! Every single maidservant like us has a wretched life of it. [She sighs, then pauses.] Hung-hsi, I'll tell you something, but you mustn't let it upset you. . . .

138

HSI-ERH: Yes, Aunty.

CHANG: Ta-chun and Ta-so, because the landlord pressed them for rent, beat up Steward Mu. Ta-so was caught and put in jail, and Ta-chun ran away. . . .

HSI-ERH: Oh! [She starts crying from the shock.]

CHANG [comforting her]: It happened nearly a month ago; but I didn't tell you for fear it might upset you. . . .

HSI-ERH: Then . . . Aunty Wang?

CHANG: Don't worry, your Uncle Chao's looking after her. . . . That's how it is, and it's no use crying over spilt milk. We're all in the same boat; although life is so hard, we have to stick it out. . . .

[HSI-ERH cries.]

[The third watch sounds.]

CHANG: That's the third watch now. . . . The old lady is asleep, and the master should have gone to bed, too. When the broth is ready, Hung-hsi, come back to bed; don't run around. I'll wait for you. [Exit.]

HSI-ERH [goes on watching the broth, and sings]:

> It's after midnight now,
> The more I think, the sadder I grow.
> Poor Dad was hounded to death,
> And Ta-chun forced to leave home.
> Why must we poor folk suffer so?
> Why are the rich so cruel?
> How can we go on living like this?
> Will these hard times never end?

[She dozes and the broth boils. She starts up to remove the pot from the fire, but lets it fall. The pot is broken and the broth spilled. MRS. HUANG snores.]

HSI-ERH [sings]:

> I'm dizzy and I feel so frightened;
> I've broken the pot and spilt the broth!
> Now I've done such a dreadful thing,
> I'm afraid I shan't escape with my life!
> Where can I hide myself?
> Oh, Heaven, save me!

[As she runs out, the back curtain falls. HSI-ERH re-enters from the side of the curtain, and sings]:

> At dead of night it's so dark,
> The road is black and everywhere there are dogs.

I can hear someone coming after me;
I can't escape this time!

[Enter HUANG with a lantern to confront her. HSI-ERH halts in dismay.]

HUANG [overjoyed]: Aha, what luck! What brought you here, Hung-hsi?

HSI-ERH [frightened]: I . . . I . . . [Wants to leave.]

HUANG [seizing her]: Ah! Hung-hsi, sew something on for me! I need it now. Come, come on over! [Pushes open the door. The back curtain opens. He pushes HSI-ERH in and bolts the door behind him. This is LANDLORD HUANG's study. A painting of a big tiger hangs there. The tiger is crouching, ready to spring.]

HSI-ERH [terrified]: Oh! [She turns to fly, but is pushed aside by HUANG.]

HUANG [seizing HSI-ERH's hand]: Come, Hung-hsi. [His eyes gleam with lust, as he pushes HSI-ERH.] Come on!

HSI-ERH: Oh! [Struggling.] Aunty! Aunty! [She starts running, but is pushed into the inner room.]

HUANG: You! Ha! Still shouting! You won't escape now! Come on! [Follows HSI-ERH inside.]

[The fifth watch is heard. Day gradually dawns.]

Curtain

SCENE 4

The next morning in Landlord Huang's study.

[CHANG enters hurriedly.]

CHANG: Hung-hsi! Hung-hsi! [Sings.]

Last night she was beaten and frightened,
So I stayed with her till it was late.
Only when all was quiet, at midnight,
And she had calmed down, I came back.
But this morning she's not to be found,
Though I've looked for her everywhere.
Hung-hsi! Hung-hsi! [Exit.]

[Enter HSI-ERH with dishevelled hair and crumpled clothes. Her face is tear-stained, and she walks with difficulty.]

HSI-ERH [comes to the door, but shrinks from opening it. Sings]:

> Heaven!
> You could kill me with a knife or axe,
> But you shouldn't have shamed me!
> I little thought of this
> When I came to the Huang house. . . .
> Mother bore me, Dad brought me up,
> Was it all for nothing?
> Now—how can I face people?
> How can I live on?

Oh, Dad, Dad, I've let you down! Aunty Wang, Ta-chun, I can never face you again! [Having decided to commit suicide, she finds a rope in a corner of the room, and picks it up.] Oh, Dad, Dad, I'm coming. [Ties the rope to a rafter.]

[CHANG enters and sees her through a crack of the door.]

CHANG: Hung-hsi, let me in!

HSI-ERH [startled]: Oh! [The rope falls from her trembling hands.]

CHANG: Hung-hsi! Open the door for me, quickly!

HSI-ERH [opens the door, and runs to CHANG as she enters]: Aunty! [Cries.]

CHANG: Hung-hsi! You—

HSI-ERH: I . . . I . . . .

CHANG [seeing the rope, understands]: Hung-hsi, how could you think of such a thing? You must never . . . never . . . .

HSI-ERH: Aunty! [Cries.]

CHANG: Child, how could you be so foolish as to think of such a thing! You must on no account do that.

HSI-ERH: Aunty, I . . . I can't face people any more.

CHANG: I understand. It's my fault for not looking after you better.

HSI-ERH: Aunty, I can't go on living. . . .

CHANG: Don't talk nonsense, child. What's done is done, but you have to live anyway. You're young, child, and there is hope. I'll look after you, and later on we two will live together. The day will come when we shall avenge your father. . . . [Helps her up, wiping her eyes.]

[HSI-ERH remains silent.]

CHANG: Stop crying now, and come and rest.

[TA-SHENG enters.]

TA-SHENG: Hung-hsi, Hung-hsi! [Seeing them.] Oh, there you are,

Hung-hsi! Last night you made such trouble, the old lady is asking for you!

[HSI-ERH looks frightened.]

CHANG: Go now.

HSI-ERH: Aunty! [She clings to CHANG.]

CHANG: I'll go with you, Hung-hsi. [They go out together.]

Curtain

ACT III

SCENE 1

Time: Seven months after the second act.

Place: MRS. HUANG's room.

[Enter HUANG and MU carrying wedding invitation cards. The servant TA-SHENG follows, holding a teapot; and after him come thugs dressed in military uniform. CHANG comes on carrying colored silk. MRS. HUANG enters holding a teacup from which she is sipping. The atmosphere is lively.]

HUANG [sings]:

Cassia trees in autumn—

ALL [sing]:

Make the whole courtyard fragrant!

HUANG [sings]:

Preparing for the wedding—

ALL [sing]:

We all work with a will!

MU: Our young master is now promoted captain of the militia, and getting married. This is truly a double happiness!

HUANG and MRS. HUANG [sing]:

The masters are busy!

ALL [sing]:

The servants are busy!

All busy and happy together!

MU: The preparations for our master's wedding have made every member of the household happy, whether young or old, master or servant!

142

MRS. HUANG [sings]:
> New clothes and coverlets must be quickly made!

[CHANG and TA-SHENG tear up the silk, while HUANG, MRS. HUANG and MU sing cheerfully.]

TOGETHER [sing]:
> Red silk and green, like ten thousand flowers!

MRS. HUANG [sings]:
> Measure it quickly! Cut it straight!

ALL [sing]:
> Some for our master and some for his bride!
> And some for quilts and covers for the bed!
> To deck the bride!
> To spread the bed!
> Let's all hurry to get them made!

MRS. HUANG [sings]:
> Send cards at once to our relatives!

MU [sings]:
> I take my pen and quickly write!

HUANG: To Secretary-General Sun of Kuomintang County Headquarters, to Magistrate Liu and Captain Li. . . .

MRS. HUANG: To the Seventh Aunt, and to Uncle. . . .

MU [sings]:
> One card is written and then another. . . .

ALL [sing]:
> When the time comes, guests will gather,
> Men and women, old and young,
> To feast here in our hall together!

MRS. HUANG: Chang, go to the servants' quarters, and see how the sewing is getting on.

CHANG: Yes, mistress.

MRS. HUANG: Ta-sheng, go and see how the preparations for the feast are going forward.

TA-SHENG: Yes, mistress.

ALL [sing]:
> Cassia trees in autumn make the whole courtyard fragrant,
> The whole household's busy preparing for the wedding!
> We're just waiting for the happy day to come,
> When with flutes and cymbals we welcome the bride home!

[MU, CHANG, and TA-SHENG leave.]

143

MRS. HUANG [*in a low voice*]: Son, has that procurer from the city arrived?

HUANG: Not yet. I'm so worried, yesterday I sent for him again.

MRS. HUANG: Better hurry. Her condition is more obvious every day, and your wedding is drawing near. If you don't make haste, and word gets out, our family reputation will be ruined.

HUANG: How about this, Mother—for the next day or two let Old Mu keep an eye on her, and stop her running around. Later we can find a quiet place, and lock her up.

MRS. HUANG [*approvingly*]: Good. [*Exeunt.*]

[*Enter Mu.*]

MU [*picking up the invitations and glancing round prior to going out again*]: Ah, here comes Hung-hsi. Landlord Huang told me to keep an eye on her. Let's see what she's up to. . . . [*Hides behind the door.*]

[*Enter HSI-ERH, carrying a wooden pail. She is seven months pregnant, looks haggard, and walks with difficulty.*]

HSI-ERH [*sings*]:

> Seven months have passed—
> Like a twig crushed beneath a stone,
> I bear the shame, swallowing my tears.
> I can't say how ill I feel.
> Things have gone so far, there's no help for me,
> I'll just have to bear it and swallow my pride.

[*Entering the room she sees the red silk and invitation cards on the table.*]

HSI-ERH: Ah, there's going to be a wedding. Does it mean Landlord Huang? . . .

[*Mu coughs. HSI-ERH steps aside. Enter Mu.*]

MU: Oh, Hung-hsi, what are you doing here?

HSI-ERH: Fetching hot water for the old lady.

MU: You must be happy now. What do you think I'm doing?

HSI-ERH: How should I know?

MU: Well, look at this! [*Picking up the invitation cards.*] What are these?

HSI-ERH: Those?

MU: Wedding cards, for the wedding! Ah, these days we're all busy preparing, didn't you know? As for you . . . you ought to be pleased now! You ought to be laughing! The old lady says you mustn't run around these days. . . . Just wait! [*Exit.*]

144

HSI-ERH: What? Steward Mu said I . . . .

[*Enter* HUANG.]

HSI-ERH [*seeing* HUANG]: Oh, it's you.

HUANG: Ah, Hung-hsi! [*Wants to turn back.*]

HSI-ERH [*stopping him*]: You—wait! I want to ask you something. . . .

HUANG: Well, but I'm busy now, Hung-hsi. . . .

HSI-ERH: Let me ask you—

HUANG: All right. [*Taking up an invitation card, and listening helplessly.*]

HSI-ERH: I'm growing bigger every day, what can I do? People laugh at me and despise me. But I can't die, however much I want to. Tell me, how shall I live on? . . .

HUANG: Er . . . . [*Wanting to make off.*]

HSI-ERH [*stopping him*]: Sir, you . . . . [*Weeps.*]

HUANG: Now, Hung-hsi don't cry. Er, you know, Hung-hsi, the time has nearly come. Just keep calm. Keep quiet, Hung-hsi, and don't run about. I'm going now to make preparations. [*Exit hastily.*]

[*Enter* CHANG *with silk.*]

HSI-ERH [*bewildered*]: Aunty . . . .

CHANG: So you're here.

HSI-ERH: What's that you're carrying, Aunty?

CHANG: Clothes I made for the bride.

HSI-ERH: Is there going to be a wedding, Aunty?

CHANG: I was just going to talk to you, Hung-hsi. Come along to our room for a talk. . . .

[*She leads* HSI-ERH *out of the door, to their own room. The back curtain falls.*]

HSI-ERH: Aunty—

CHANG: You know, Hung-hsi, the time is getting near. . . .

HSI-ERH: I know.

CHANG: You ought to realize.

HSI-ERH: I do realize, Aunty: it's seven months now. But what can I do? At least now he's . . . .

CHANG [*surprised*]: What are you talking about, Hung-hsi?

HSI-ERH: Just now Landlord Huang said he was going to marry me. . . .

CHANG: What! You're dreaming, Hung-hsi! You've got it wrong, child!

HSI-ERH [*greatly taken aback*]: What do you mean, Aunty?

145

CHANG [sings]:

> Oh, Hung-hsi, you foolish child,
> He's not going to marry you,
> But a girl called Chao from town;
> Her family's rich and powerful. . . .
> Child!

Just think, Hung-hsi, how could he dream of marrying a servant like you or me?

HSI-ERH: No need to go on, Aunty. I lost my head for a moment. Landlord Huang is my enemy; even if he married me, he would make me lead a wretched life. Oh, it's just because I'm getting bigger every day, and can't do anything about it. So I thought—

CHANG: Ah, I meant once the child was born you should give it to me to bring up for you; then one day when you left the Huang family you could marry someone else. I didn't think to tell you about the wedding. Who could imagine you would suppose . . . .

HSI-ERH: I understand now, Aunty. Now he's going to be married, and he's cheating me, too. What a devil he is! I'm not a child. He's ruined me, so that I can't hold up my head again; but I'm not like my father! Even a chicken will struggle when it's killed, and I'm a human being! Even if it kills me, Aunty, I'm going to speak my mind!

CHANG [crying]: I never thought of you as a child, love. I like your spirit—

HSI-ERH: Aunty! [Too moved to speak she falls into CHANG's arms.] [Voice offstage: "Aunty Chang, the mistress wants you."]

CHANG: Someone's calling me. Wait a little, Hung-hsi. I'll be back soon. [Crossing the threshold she turns back.] Don't go out again. [Exit, closing the door.]
[HSI-ERH watches CHANG go. Presently she can no longer contain herself for anger, and rushes out, just as HUANG enters from the other side.]

HSI-ERH [fiercely]: Sir!

HUANG [startled]: Hung-hsi, why are you here?

HSI-ERH [stepping forward]: Sir, you . . . .

HUANG: Now, Hung-hsi, go back quickly. It doesn't look good if you're seen in the courtyard.

HSI-ERH [loudly]: Landlord Huang!

HUANG [startled]: What! You—

HSI-ERH: On New Year's Eve you forced my dad to commit suicide!

146

On New Year's Day you got me to your home. Since I came, you've never treated me as a human being, but as dirt beneath your feet! Your mother beats and curses me! [*Coming nearer.*] And you— you ruined me!

HUANG: You . . . why bring that up now?

HSI-ERH [*coming nearer*]: I'm seven months gone, but you're getting married and deceiving me! I ask you, what do you mean by it! [*Bites and tears at him.*]

HUANG [*throwing* HSI-ERH *down*]: You fool! Mad! [*He shakes her off and hurries out.*]

HSI-ERH [*getting up*]: I'll have it out with you! I'll have it out with you! [*Runs out after him.*]

Curtain

SCENE 2

MRS. HUANG's room

HUANG [*enters hastily.*]

HUANG: Mother! Mother!

MRS. HUANG [*putting down her opium pipe*]: What is it, son?

HUANG: Mother, I was too careless. I didn't have Hung-hsi watched, and now she's making trouble.

MRS. HUANG [*sitting on the bed*]: What's she been doing?

HUANG: She's after me now! Look, Mother, she's coming here! The guests will be here directly. If this gets known, it will be too bad.

MRS. HUANG: The fool! She must be mad! Well, you go. Send Old Mu here.

[*Exit* HUANG.]

[MRS. HUANG *picks up a broomstick and stands waiting angrily.* HSI-ERH *runs in.*]

HSI-ERH: I'll have it out with you! . . . [*Enters the room.*]

MRS. HUANG: Silly girl! You are mad! Kneel down!

HSI-ERH: You! [*Refusing to kneel.*]

MRS. HUANG [*fiercely*]: Kneel down!

[HSI-ERH *looks at her angrily, trembling with hate.*]

MRS. HUANG: Wretched girl! Do you admit your guilt? I ask you, who got you with child?

HSI-ERH: What!

MRS. HUANG: Wretched girl! Carrying on with men, you've spoiled

147

our family's reputation. Speak! Who is your lover? Speak up, who is it?

[Mu *comes in behind* HSI-ERH's *back.*]

HSI-ERH [*loudly*]: It's your son! [CHANG *is listening from one corner and* HUANG *from another.*]

MRS. HUANG [*furiously*]: What! You liar! You are accusing my son? You are asking for trouble! [*Steps forward to strike her.*]

HSI-ERH [*starts to rush forward but is seized by* Mu. *She shrieks*]: It's your son! It's your son! You've ruined my whole family! There isn't one good person in your Huang family! Not a single man or woman in your family for generations has been any good! You're all bitches and . . . .

MRS. HUANG: Old Mu! Stop her mouth, quickly!

[Mu *gags* HSI-ERH *with a handkerchief.*]

MRS. HUANG: Quickly shut her in the inner room and whip her! [Mu *drags* HSI-ERH *to the inner room and whips her. The strokes of the lash and muffled cries are heard.*]

MRS. HUANG [*listening*]: Good, good. Today she must be well beaten. [CHANG *listens in distress outside the door.*]

[*There is a pause.*]

MRS. HUANG [*taking out a lock*]: Old Mu, lock the door for me. [*As* Mu *locks the door,* HUANG *enters hastily.* CHANG *hides herself and listens at the door.*]

HUANG: Mother, it's time now. I think we'll have to find a way to get rid of her. The guests will soon be here. If outsiders hear of this, it will be too bad.

MRS. HUANG: You're right. The bride is coming. If the bride's family hears of it, we'll be in an awkward position. . . . Old Mu, is there anybody outside?

[*As* Mu *looks outside the door,* CHANG *hides herself.* Mu *re-enters the room, closing the door, and* CHANG *listens again.*]

Mu: No one.

MRS. HUANG: Good. We mustn't lose any time. Tonight when they are all asleep, Old Mu, you get a horse and take her away.

HUANG: Yes, Old Mu. When you get to the city, take the girl to the procurer for him to get rid of quickly. On no account must people know.

Mu: Very good, sir. I'll do that. [*Exit.*]

HUANG: Don't be angry, Mother. Let's go to inspect the preparation of the bridal chamber. [*Takes his mother's arm to help her out.*]

148

[CHANG hides herself as HUANG and MRS. HUANG leave. Then she runs into the room and tries to open the inner door, but finds it locked.]

CHANG: The key? [She looks for the key on MRS. HUANG's bed, and finding it, opens the door. A voice is heard offstage: "Aunty Chang!" Enter TA-SHENG. CHANG hides the key, and pretends nothing is amiss.]

TA-SHENG: Aunty Chang! [He comes in.] Oh, there you are, Aunty Chang. The mistress wants you to go to supervise the sewing.

CHANG: All right, I'm coming. [TA-SHENG goes out, followed by a distracted CHANG.]

[Voices are heard offstage]:

> MU: Old Kao, what a drunkard you are!
>
> KAO: It's the young master's wedding. Why shouldn't I drink?
>
> MU: Saddle a horse for me at once. Quickly!
>
> KAO: Why do you want a horse so late?
>
> MU: Never you mind. Just get it ready.
>
> KAO: All right. All right.

[CHANG re-enters, carrying cakes, and hastily closes the door. She puts the cakes on the table, then opens the door of the inner room.]

CHANG: Hung-hsi! Hung-hsi! [After dragging HSI-ERH out, she locks the door and puts the key back on the bed.]

CHANG: Hung-hsi! [Undoing the rope binding HSI-ERH's arms.] Hung-hsi! Hung-hsi! [Removing the gag from her mouth.] Hung-hsi! Wake up, Hung-hsi!

HSI-ERH [coming to herself]: Who are you?

CHANG [softly]: It's Aunty.

HSI-ERH: Ah, Aunty! . . . [Falls on CHANG.]

CHANG: Hung-hsi, Hung-hsi, I know all that happened. [Helping her up.] You must go quickly. They want to ruin you.

HSI-ERH: Ah!

CHANG: They're murderers! They've sold you! They'll be coming to fetch you, you must go at once! If you fall into their hands, you'll never escape again.

HSI-ERH: Aunty, they . . . they . . . . [She wants to rush out.]

CHANG [pulling her back]: Don't be foolish, Hung-hsi. You're no match for them. Go quickly. You must fly for your life.

[HSI-ERH says nothing.]

CHANG: Go by the back door. Along the gully. I've opened the door for you. Quick! [*They start out.*]
[*Voice from offstage:* "Aunty Chang! Aunty Chang!" *Taking fright they hide. The voice grows fainter.*]

CHANG [*urgently*]: Hung-hsi, soon you won't be with me any more. In the future you'll have to make up your own mind. I can't go with you. They're calling me.

HSI-ERH: Aunty!

CHANG [*giving HSI-ERH the cakes from the table*]: Here are some cakes to eat on the road. Mind you only drink running water. However hard life is, you have to go on living. Remember how they destroyed your family. A day will come when you can avenge yourself.

HSI-ERH: I shall remember, Aunty.

CHANG [*giving HSI-ERH money*]: Here's some money I've saved. You'll need it on your journey. Soon I'll be leaving their family. One day we shall meet again.

HSI-ERH [*takes the money and kneels down*]: Aunty—

CHANG: Ah, Hung-hsi, get up. Go quickly. [*Opens the door and runs out, leading HSI-ERH.*]
[*Voice from offstage:* "Aunty Chang! Aunty Chang!"]
[*After a while CHANG comes back by the way she went out, walking calmly. The third watch sounds. Enter HUANG and MU.*]

HUANG [*taking the key from his mother's bed, unlocks the inner room, goes in, and discovers HSI-ERH has gone. In surprise*]: What! Where's Hung-hsi? She's disappeared!

MU: What!

HUANG: Old Mu, Hung-hsi has escaped! The back window is open. She must have climbed out through the window. Go and catch her, Old Mu. When you've caught her, strangle her with a rope and throw her into the river, so we won't have any more trouble. [*They leave the room.*]

MU: She won't dare leave by the front gate, sir. Let's go by the back gate. [*Exeunt.*]

Curtain

SCENE 3

[Hsi-ERH *is escaping by the back gate. There are stars in the sky.*]
Hsi-ERH [*falls down and gets up again. Sings*]:

> They want to kill me, to murder me,
> But I've escaped from their tigers' den!
> Mother bore me, Dad brought me up,
> I want to live, I want to live!

[*She runs off.*]
[HUANG *and* MU *enter in pursuit, carrying ropes.*]
HUANG: Hurry up after her, Old Mu!
MU: Right.
HUANG: If she took this road, there's a big river in front, and she can't get away.

[*They pursue. A mountain looms in front. On one side is a rushing river flanked by marshland.* Hsi-ERH *hurries in.*]
Hsi-ERH [*sings*]:

> I'm going on, I'll not turn back,
> I've been wronged and I want revenge!
> They killed my dad and ruined me,
> I'll remember it in my grave!

[*The sound of running water is heard.*]

> I can hear running water,
> There's a river gleaming under the stars;
> It's a great river flowing east,
> I've lost my way—where shall I go?

[*Suddenly the sound of heavy footsteps behind throws her into a panic.*] Ah! I'm being followed! [*She stumbles and falls in the mud. When she extricates herself her shoes have fallen off; but her pursuers are near, and she has no time to pick up her shoes.*] There are some reeds. I'd better hide myself there. [*She crawls into the reeds.*]
[*Enter* HUANG *and* MU.]
HUANG: Can you see her, Old Mu?
MU: No. [*They search.*]
HUANG: The river's in front. Where could she have gone?
MU: The mountains on both sides are steep, and there's no path.
HUANG: A girl, and so near her time, where can she go?
MU: She won't get away, sir. [*They search again.*]

MU [suddenly discovering a shoe]: Ah, sir, isn't this Hung-hsi's shoe?

HUANG [taking the shoe]: Yes, it's hers allright.

MU: Then she must have jumped into the river.

HUANG: Ah, well, she brought it on herself. Well, that saves us trouble. Let's go back, Old Mu. If questions are asked, we'll just say she stole things and ran away. Don't let anyone know the truth.

MU: Right. [They leave by the way they came.]

HSI-ERH [emerges from the reeds and sings]:
>   They want to kill me, how blind they are!
>   I'm water that can't be drained dry!
>   I'm fire that can't be quenched!
>   I'm not dying, I'm going to live!
>   And live to be avenged!

[She hurries into the mountains.]

Curtain

ACT IV

SCENE 1

Time: Three years later—the autumn of 1937.[5]

Place: On the hillside overlooking the river, not far from the Goddess' Temple. It is dusk. The sun is setting.

[Enter UNCLE CHAO with a long whip, leading his flock.]

CHAO [sings]:
>   Year after year passes,
>   And the road's overgrown with wild grass;
>   Houses crumble and the place is empty,
>   Some have died and some have gone.
>   When cold winds blow, the lonely grieve;
>   Water flows eastward never to return.

[He stands at the river's edge watching the water flow eastward, then speaks with feeling.] Ah, how quickly time passes. It's three years since that child Hsi-erh drowned herself in the river. . . . [Sits on a boulder.]

[Enter LI from one side carrying incense.]

152

LI [*seeing* CHAO]: Ah, Uncle Chao, watching the flock?

CHAO: Well, Li, where are you off to?

LI: I'm going to burn incense before the White-haired Goddess.

CHAO: Burn incense before the White-haired Goddess? . . . Oh, yes, it's the fifteenth of the moon again today. . . .

LI [*sitting down beside* CHAO]: It's quite some time now since the White-haired Goddess appeared in these parts. . . .

CHAO: Well, we shall see. Something must be going to happen. . . . [*Leans forward a little, as if he heard something.*]

LI [*suddenly standing up*]: Listen, Uncle Chao!

CHAO [*after a pause*]: Oh, it's only the wind in the reeds.

LI [*relaxing. Softly*]: Tell me, Uncle, have you seen it?

CHAO: Seen what?

LI: The White-haired Goddess, Uncle. Old Liu met her once in Uncle Yang's land, and Chang Szu saw her when he was cutting wood in the North Mountain gully. They say she was all white, in the shape of a woman; but she was gone in a flash. . . . [*Shivers.*] [*Pause.*]

CHAO [*thinking back*]: Ah, if the White-haired Goddess were any good, then Hsi-erh's family should have been avenged.

LI: May the fairy help us; [*Pauses.*] Say, Uncle, wasn't it that autumn Aunty Chang sent Hsi-erh . . . . [CHAO *hastily stops him and looks around.*]

LI [*in a lowered voice*]: Didn't you say Aunty Chang sent her away?

CHAO: Ah, how could a girl run far? She drowned herself in the river, poor thing. . . .

LI [*sighs. They are silent. He looks at the sky*]: Uncle, I must go to burn incense now. A storm is coming. [*He moves toward the temple.*]

CHAO [*sighs sadly. Sings*]:

> *Is there no good judge*
> *To right the wrongs of old?*
> *What we suffered in the past*
> *No words can tell!*
> *But if the goddess were any good at all,*
> *She'd avenge the ghosts of those unjustly killed!*

[AUNTY WANG, *leaning on* AUNTY CHANG's *arm, enters from the direction of the temple.*]

CHANG: Uncle Chao!

CHAO: Oh, Aunty Chang, Aunty Wang! You've been all that way to burn incense?

CHANG: Well, Aunty Wang insisted I come with her. Ah, when you're brooding over something, you can't forget it.

WANG [crying]: Uncle Chao . . . I want nothing else, great goddess, but let my child come back. . . . I've never done a bad deed in my life. Why should this have happened to me? All these years have passed, Uncle Chao, yet every day as soon as I close my eyes, I see Hsi-erh on one side and Ta-chun on the other. Oh, son, why have you forgotten your mother? Poor children! One drowned herself, and the other ran away. . . . [Cries bitterly.]

CHANG: Now don't cry, Aunty Wang. [Comforting her.] Don't take on so, Aunty Wang.

CHAO: Nothing can bring the dead to life. What's the use of crying? . . . Although Hsi-erh died, she died well. . . . As for Ta-chun, although there's been no news of him since he left, he'll come back some day. . . .

CHANG: That's right. Every day since I left the Huang family, I've reasoned with her, saying, "Wait, Aunty. Although Hsi-erh is dead, Ta-chun is sure to come back. Don't complain of fate. Our fate is the same. I'll help you, and you help me. Then we shall struggle along in spite of difficulties."

CHAO [nodding sadly]: Struggle along, struggle along. One day Heaven will stop being blind.

[Li enters hurriedly, in consternation. There is a gust of wind.]

LI [looking pale]: Uncle Chao! Uncle Chao!

CHAO: What is it?

LI: She's coming! She's coming!

THE OTHERS: What is it?

LI: Behind the temple! White! All white! The White-haired Goddess!

THE OTHERS [panic-stricken]: What, is it true? Let's go quickly! [They run off. CHAO follows with his sheep. The sky grows dark, thunder rolls and the storm breaks.]

[A chorus sings offstage]:

> The storm is coming,
> The storm is coming,
> THE STORM IS COMING!
> Heaven and earth grow dark
> With lightning and with thunder!

154

> Heaven and earth grow dark
> With lightning and with thunder!
> God has grown angry,
> And the world's in chaos!
> A gale has sprung up, and from the mountain
> The White-haired Goddess is coming down!

[A great clap of thunder and flash of lightning.]

[Enter the WHITE-HAIRED GODDESS—HSI-ERH—with dishevelled white hair, rushing through the storm.]

HSI-ERH [sings]:

> I came down to gather fruit and berries,
> When this sudden thunderstorm broke.
> The mountain's steep and the path is slippery,
> I can't get back to my cave, so I'll take shelter
> In the Goddess' Temple nearby.

[She slips and falls and her fruit rolls to the ground. She hastily picks it up.] I've spent more than three years out of the sun. Today I came out to get some maize and potatoes and steal some food from the shrine for my winter store. . . .

[Thunder and a downpour. HSI-ERH sings]:

> Lightning makes me close my eyes
> Thunder makes me lower my head
> Wind tries to sweep me off my feet,
> And I'm drenched in the pouring rain!
> But never mind the thunder and lightning,
> The wind and the pouring rain!
> I clench my teeth
> And step by step
> Push on—
> The temple's close ahead!

[Exit in the direction of the temple.]

[MU enters running through the storm with a lantern and umbrella.]

MU [sings]:

> Thunder's crashing, lightning's flashing,
> This storm broke out of the blue!
> Master went to town on business,
> What's keeping him so long?

[At a clap of thunder he crouches down.] Ah, what weather! . . . Really, what is the world coming to! Recently I heard the

155

Japanese fought their way across from Lukouchiao and have occupied Paoting.[5] They may even be here in a few days. Landlord Huang went to town for news. He ought to be back by now. . . . [*He is restless and anxious. Thunder rolls again. He stares ahead, not knowing what to do.*] Ah, during the last few years the villagers have been talking about some white-haired goddess, and ghostly noises are heard at midnight. [*Sighs.*] What can I do? . . . [*Shivers.*]

[*He suddenly sees a shadowy figure on the left, and gives a start.*] Who is it?

[*After a pause,* LANDLORD HUANG's *voice is heard in the dark:* "Oh. . . . Is it Old Mu?"]

MU [*reassured*]: You're back at last, sir!

[HUANG *hurries in holding an umbrella, followed by* TA-SHENG.]

MU: Are you all right, sir?

HUANG: Things look bad, Old Mu! [*Sings*]:

> I set out for the county town
> The day before yesterday;
> But I'd only reached the market town
> When I heard some dreadful news!
> The Japanese have taken the county town,
> So I hurried right back,
> Hurried back like mad today!

MU [*startled*]: What! Is it true?

TA-SHENG: Yes.

HUANG: It's appalling! The Japanese kill people and set fire to houses! All my in-laws have fallen into their hands!

MU [*more alarmed*]: Heavens! Then what can we do, sir?

HUANG [*reassuringly*]: Don't worry, Old Mu. Whatever changes take place, we'll always be able to find a way out. Come on, let's go home first.

[*There is a clap of thunder, and the rain pours down more heavily.*]

MU: The storm's growing worse, sir. Let's take shelter first in the temple. [*The three battle their way toward the temple. On the way they meet* HSI-ERH. *A flash of lightning lights up the* WHITE-HAIRED GODDESS.]

HUANG [*panic-stricken*]: What!

[*There is another flash of lightning, and* HSI-ERH *recognizes* HUANG.]

HUANG: Ghosts! Ghosts!

[*The three men hide in terror.*]

HSI-ERH [*in rising anger rushes at* HUANG *and the others, throwing the sacrificial fruit at* HUANG *and shrieking*]: Ahh!

HUANG and MU [*flying in terror*]: Help! ... Help! ... Ghosts! Ghosts! [*They rush off, followed by* TA-SHENG.]

[*A pause.*]

HSI-ERH [*halting in alarm and uncertainty*]: Ghosts? Ghosts? [*She looks round, then is silent for a moment.*] Oh, you mean I'm a ghost? [*She looks at her hair and clothes.*] So, I don't look like a human being! [*Her voice trembles with indignation and grief.*] This is all your doing, Landlord Huang! You brought me to this! And you call me a ghost? ...

[*Wind, rain, and thunder are heard, and lightning flashes, as* HSI-ERH *sings.*]

> I'm Hsi-erh whom you ruined,
> I'm not a ghost!

[*Thunder crashes even closer.*]

> ... I've lived in a cave for more than three years,
> Gritting my teeth for misery;
> Hiding by day for fear folk see me,
> While at night there are tigers and wolves;
> I've only rags and leaves to wear,
> Only temple offerings and berries to eat,
> So my hair and skin have turned white!

[*Accusingly.*]

> I was brought up by parents, too,
> But now I've come to this pass!
> It's all through you, Landlord Huang,
> You brought me to this, yet now you call me
> A ghost! All right—
> I'm a ghost!
> The ghost of someone cruelly killed!
> The ghost of someone hounded to death!
> I'm going to scratch and pinch you!
> I'm going to bite you!

[*Shrieks.*]

[*She rushes headlong into the storm.*]

[*Lightning and sheets of rain.*]

[*The chorus sings "The Storm ..." offstage, the sound gradually dies away in the distance.*]

Curtain

SCENE 2

The following afternoon.

Under a big tree at one end of the village.

[OLD CHAO *and two peasants enter. They are obviously upset.*]
ALL [*sing*]:
>A storm's sprung up. The world's
>In a bad way, we can't live in peace.

FIRST PEASANT:
>Landlord Huang has practically squeezed us dry!

SECOND PEASANT:
>The White-haired Goddess is making trouble!

CHAO:
>The Japanese are fighting their way over!

PEASANTS:
>It's said they've taken Paoting city!

FIRST PEASANT:
>Hu-tzu has gone to town for news.

SECOND PEASANT:
>Why isn't he back yet?

ALL:
>It's enough to distract one, such goings on!

CHAO: Ah, Hu-tzu went to town three days ago; how is it he's not back yet?

FIRST PEASANT: Could he have met the Japanese?

SECOND PEASANT: Surely they can't be there already? [*Sighs.*]

[*As the three are waiting impatiently,* AUNTY CHANG *hurries in.*]

CHANG: Oh, you're here. Have you heard the news?

ALL [*startled*]: What's happened?

CHANG: Yesterday evening when Landlord Huang was coming back from town and took shelter in the temple from the rain, he saw a ghost!

ALL [*amazed*]: Really?

CHANG: It's true. He's ill now from the shock.

CHAO: Well! Now the Huang family's sins are finding them out, if ghosts come out to confront him!

CHANG: And I heard those Japanese have occupied the county town!

ALL [*startled*]: No! Then what's to be done?

CHAO [*stamping impatiently*]: Why isn't Hu-tzu back yet?

158

FIRST PEASANT: Oh, look! Isn't that Hu-tzu coming?

ALL [shouting]: Hu-tzu! Hu-tzu!

[HU-TZU hurries in.]

HU-TZU [panting]: You're all here. Things are in a bad way! [Sings.]

> The Japanese have taken the county town,
> And smashed the Kuomintang troops!
> The county head's fled, the commissioner too,
> Leaving just the people, with nowhere to turn!

ALL: Ah! Only the people are left to bear the brunt!

HU-TZU [sings]:

> When the Kuomintang troops fled from the market town,
> There was cursing, conscripting, beating and looting!
> And when the Japanese come, so they say,
> There's always burning, raping, shooting!

ALL: Heavens! Only the people are left with no one to care for them!

HU-TZU [sings]:

> But I heard some good news too—
> Troops have come from the west, with banners flying.
> They'll fight the Japanese and save us all!
> They march sixty miles in a single night,
> They're super men and officers, they really fight!

ALL [astounded]: Really?

HU-TZU [sings]:

> At Pinghsing Pass they won a great victory,
> Killing several thousand Japanese,
> Then fought their way north. . . .

ALL: What army is that?

HU-TZU [sings]:

> They call it the eight—eight—
> Eighth Route Army!

ALL [at a loss, echoing him]: What—the Eighth Route Army?

HU-TZU [emphatically]: Yes. They're called the Eighth Route Army.[6] I heard they're very good to the people—

[LI rushes in before HU-TZU has finished, carrying a hoe.]

[The "Eighth Route Army March" is heard.]

LI [showing amazement]: Quick! Quick! I was just coming in from the fields, when I saw troops coming down the Southern Hill!

ALL [alarmed]: What! Troops?

FIRST PEASANT: Could it be the Japanese?

159

Li: No, they didn't look like Japanese. They're Chinese troops!

SECOND PEASANT: Ah, they must be retreating.

Li: They don't look like retreating either. You look! [*All stare in the direction he points.*] They're in good order, heading briskly due north.

ALL [*looking*]: Ah, there are so many of them!

Li: Ha! That's a funny army! They're all youngsters, wearing big straw hats, and with no puttees, only shoes. And there's a figure "eight" on their sleeves.

ALL [*in unison*]: Oh, they must be the Eighth Route Army!
[*The martial music grows louder.*]
[*They watch anxiously.*]

SECOND PEASANT [*suddenly catching sight of them*]: Ah! Here they come! Here they come!
[*An armyman's voice offstage:* "Hey! Countryman—countrymen!"]
[*They all take cover in fright.*]
[*Enter* TA-SO, *ragged and unkempt, leading a soldier who proves to be* TA-CHUN.]

TA-SO: By calling out like that, Ta-chun, you frightened them all away! Say, Ta-chun, just now there was someone here who looked like Uncle Chao.

TA-CHUN: Let's call him then.

TA-SO: Uncle Chao! Uncle Chao!

TA-CHUN [*calling too*]: Uncle Chao!
[*After a pause,* CHAO *and others enter; but the sight of the soldier makes them fall back a few steps in fear.*]

TA-CHUN [*advancing*]: Uncle Chao, don't you know me? I'm Ta-chun!

TA-SO: I'm Ta-so!

ALL [*incredulously*]: What? Ta-chun! Ta-so! [*After a second they recognize them, and are overjoyed.*] Well! Well! Ta-chun! Ta-so! You've come back! [*Other peasants crowd in.*]
[*They sing happily in unison*]:
> A clap of thunder,
> And then a sunny sky!
> The stars in heaven
> Are falling from on high!
> Ta-chun! [*Some:* Ta-so!] You've been away so long,
> Who could tell you would come home today!
[*Enter a peasant:* "Ta-chun! Your mother's coming!"]
[*TA-CHUN goes to meet her.*]

ALL [*following* TA-CHUN *to meet her, sing*]:
>   Now mother and son will meet,
>   And be together from now on!
>   All we country folk are happy, too;
>   All we country folk are happy for you!

[AUNTY WANG *runs in, calling* "Ta-chun! Ta-chun!"]

TA-CHUN [*shouts*]: Mother!

WANG [*unable to believe her eyes, hesitates, then rushes forward, crying*]: Ta-chun! My boy!

TA-CHUN: Mother! [*He breaks down, too.*]

SOME PEASANTS [*comfortingly*]: Aunty Wang . . . . [*Sing.*]
>   Don't take on so!

OTHERS [*sing*]:
>   Don't be so upset, Ta-chun!

CHANG: Don't make your mother sad, Ta-chun!

CHAO [*wiping his eyes*]: Don't take on so, Aunty. Ta-chun's back, isn't he?

WANG [*wiping her eyes*]: Oh . . . I'm not . . . not sad. [*Cries again.*]

CHAO: Well! [*sings.*]
>   You waited day after day so many years,
>   Now Ta-chun's here, isn't he?

ALL [*sing*]:
>   Isn't it grand that he's back!

CHANG: Your day of rejoicing has come, Aunty.

CHAO: Tell us, Ta-chun, how did you come back?

TA-CHUN and TA-SO: Right!

TA-CHUN: Mother, Uncle—

TA-SO: Aunty Chang, neighbors—

TA-CHUN and TA-SO [*sing*]:
>   When we left that year,
>   Landlord Huang—

TA-CHUN:
>   Drove me out with nowhere to go!

TA-SO:
>   Threw me into the county jail!

TA-CHUN:
>   I fled to Shansi province,
>   And joined the army there!

TA-SO:
>   Life was misery in that jail!

161

TA-CHUN:

> Today our troops have come to the front,
> Determined to fight the Japanese invaders!

TA-SO:

> They stormed the county town and opened the jail doors,
> Letting us out after all we'd suffered!

BOTH:

> So we came back together,
> Home to see our old neighbors!

ALL [*to* TA-CHUN]: What army do you belong to then?

TA-CHUN [*sings*]:

> I'm in the Eighth Route Army.

TA-SO [*simultaneously*]:

> He's in the Eighth Route Army!

ALL [*delighted, crowding round him*]: Oh, so you joined the Eighth Route Army then! [*Sing*]:

> The Eighth Route Army! The Eighth Route Army!
> You've come from the west!
> It was you who won the battle of Pinghsing Pass,
> You're the army with the super officers and men!

TA-CHUN: Yes, the Eighth Route Army, led by the Communist Party, is like one family with the common people. Do you remember, Uncle Chao, you used to talk about the Red Army? That Red Army is the present Eighth Route Army!

CHAO: Eh? What's that you say? The Eighth Route is the same as the Red Army? [*Wildly happy, to all.*] Ho! Have you all forgotten the Red Army that came to Chao Village on the thirteenth of the fifth moon that year, the day the War God sharpened his knife? . . . It's too good to be true; It's too good to be true! Everything will work out all right now. The Red Army's come back again!

TA-CHUN [*correcting him*]: The Eighth Route Army—the Eighth Route Army's come back!

ALL [*in unison*]: The Eighth Route Army—the Eighth Route Army's come back! Now there'll really be a change for the better! [*Laughter.*]

[*The "Eighth Route Army March" sounds loudly offstage.*]

[*All go to meet the troops.*]

Curtain

ACT V

Scene 1

Time: Spring, 1938.

Place: *Under the big tree in front of the village. The tree has come into leaf. This village has become one of the Eighth Route Army's anti-Japanese bases behind the enemy's lines. The early morning sun lights up the sentry box of the Self Defense Corps. From a tree beside it hangs a reading board on which is written: "Resist Japan and Reduce Rents."*

[Hu-tzu, *carrying a lance with a red silk tassel, is on sentry duty.*]

Hu-tzu [sings]:

> The first clap of thunder in spring!
> The first lamp lit in the valley!
> The poor are going to be masters,
> Now the Communist Party's come!
> We mustn't be afraid, we must fight
> To build up our new people's power.
> Since the government's ordered rents reduced,
> We must all rally round and work hard!

[*Cheerfully.*] Ah! At last the time has come for us poor folk to be masters! Last year when Ta-chun was transferred here from the army he became assistant officer of our district. When the village held an election for political officers in the first moon, Uncle Chao was elected village head and Ta-so chairman of the Peasants' Union. Now an order has come that rents be reduced, so we shall have to settle old scores with Landlord Huang. [*Sighs.*] Only the villagers don't all see eye to eye yet. Folk are still so afraid of Landlord Huang and that "White-haired Goddess" that nobody dares stick his neck out. There was to be a meeting today, but I'm sure they won't all come. [*Walks to one side to look round.*]

[Enter Uncle Chao *and* Ta-so.]

Chao *and* Ta-so [sing]:

> If everyone rallies round,
> Our struggle is sure to succeed!

163

> *The government will back us up,*
> *They're sending us cadres today.*

TA-SO: Hu-tzu!

HU-TZU [*turning round*]: Oh, Ta-so! . . . Oh no—[*Hastily correcting himself.*] Peasant Union Chairman and Village Head. [*Laughs.*]

CHAO [*laughing, too*]: Have you seen anybody from the district, Hu-tzu?

HU-TZU [*impatiently*]: Not yet!

TA-SO: They said they'd come today; why aren't they here yet? [*Goes to one side to look.*]

CHAO: Hu-tzu! This time we're going to demand rent reduction and settle old scores with Landlord Huang. How about it, youngster? Do you dare stand out and speak up?

HU-TZU: Need you ask, Village Head? Of course I want to attack Landlord Huang. [*Raising his thumb.*] I'll be the first! . . . But one person isn't enough. See here, this looks bad; a meeting was announced for today, but so far nobody's shown up! Bah! I think it'll be a washout.

CHAO [*reassuringly*]: Now, Hu-tzu, don't you worry. It's always darkest before dawn. Today cadres are coming from the district with Ta-chun; we've already thought out a good plan, and we're not afraid of Landlord Huang's tricks! . . . Keep cool, youngster, and wait and see. It won't be long now!

HU-TZU: All right. [*Smiles contentedly.*]

TA-SO [*seeing figures on the road to the village*]: Hey, Uncle Chao, is that Ta-chun and the district head there?
[CHAO *and* HU-TZU *look.*]

HU-TZU: Yes, it is. It's Ta-chun. And the district head!
[*Two figures approach, and they go eagerly to meet them, calling "District Head!" "Ta-chun!"*]
[*The district head and* TA-CHUN *walk briskly in.*]

HU-TZU: Hey! Ta-chun . . . Oh no, it's our Assistant Officer Wang who's come!
[TA-CHUN *mops his head and smiles at* HU-TZU.]

CHAO [*to the district head*]: We've been waiting a long time. Why are you so late?

DISTRICT HEAD [*wiping his face*]: Ta-chun and I came by way of Liu Village; otherwise we'd have been here much earlier.

CHAO: How about it? I suggest we go first to the village office.

164

TA-SO: Yes, let's go to the village office first.

[*They start for the village.*]

[*Sound of villagers singing in unison offstage.*]

DISTRICT HEAD [*seeing the villagers approaching*]: Hullo! What are these folk doing?

HU-TZU [*stepping forward*]: Bah! They're going again to sacrifice to the "White-haired Goddess," damn them! See there's that rogue Steward Mu, too!

TA-CHUN [*to the district head*]: Suppose we step out of sight for a second, District Head, and watch them?

CHAO: Yes, just come over here. [*They hide on one side. HU-TZU takes cover, too.*]

[*Enter the villagers—an old man, an old woman, two peasants and two women, carrying incense and offerings. MU follows.*]

ALL [*sing*]:

> The world is out of joint,
> And troubles never cease;
> But the White-haired Goddess has power
> To protect and give us peace!

MU [*seeing there is no one about, addresses them craftily*]: Ah, do you know? Another strange thing happened yesterday evening!

ALL [*startled*]: What?

MU: The White-haired Goddess appeared again! [*Sings.*]

> Yesterday, at the dead of night,
> The White-haired Goddess appeared again!
> "You shan't reap what you've sown," she said.
> "There's great trouble ahead!
> Ruin will stalk the land,
> Everywhere men will die,
> Everywhere fires will break out,
> The sound of weeping will reach the sky!"

ALL [*aghast*]: Oh! What can we do?

MU [*sings*]:

> Then she warned men:
> "To be safe and sound,
> You must do good deeds!
> Don't meddle in things that aren't your concern,
> And offer more incense in the temple.
> If you do this you'll be safe!"

ALL [*pray*]: Oh, Goddess, help us!

MU: And the goddess said, too—[*Sings.*]

> The Eighth Route Army won't last long,
> It'll vanish like dew in the sun!
> When the sun comes out the dew disappears,
> And the Eighth Route Army will soon be gone!

[*Hu-tzu has already appeared behind* Mu. *Now he rushes forward, snatches* Mu's *incense and candles, and dashes them to the ground.*]

HU-TZU: You bastard, what rumors are you spreading?

MU [*taken by surprise, is at a loss for words*]: I . . . I . . . . [*Stoops to pick up his incense and candles.*]

HU-TZU: Get out! [*Kicks him off, stamping on the candles and incense.*]

[*Exit* MU *in alarm.*]

[*The others make as if to leave, but* HU-TZU *stops them.*]

HU-TZU [*angrily*]: Stop! No one must pass! Well! When you are summoned to a meeting, you won't come, but you have plenty of time for burning incense.

CROWD [*protestingly*]:

> What are you doing, Hu-tzu?
> What if you offend the goddess?
> This concerns us all, not just you.

HU-TZU [*not yielding*]: The goddess, indeed! Where is the goddess? No, I won't let you go! [*He is spoiling for a fight.*]

[*The district head,* TA-CHUN, CHAO, *and* TA-SO *come in hastily.* CHAO *pulls* HU-TZU *aside and restrains him.*]

CHAO: Hu-tzu . . . .

TA-SO: Don't be angry. No need to get excited.

DISTRICT HEAD: That's right, friends. Don't get heated . . . .

[*The crowd quiets down.*]

OLD MAN: Now the district head is here.

CROWD: Ah, District Head, Ta-chun . . . .

DISTRICT HEAD: Friends, weren't you talking about the White-haired Goddess? Let's hear what miracles the goddess has worked.

TA-CHUN: That's right. Just what?

OLD MAN: District Head, Ta-chun . . . . [*Sings.*]

> The White-haired Goddess often shows herself,
> It's three whole years now we've seen her.

FIRST PEASANT [Sings]:
> We've all seen her,
> She comes and goes without a trace. . . .

SECOND PEASANT: She's all in white! A flash—and she's gone! [Sings.]
> She's often in the Goddess' Temple,
> Where she comes out at dead of night!

THIRD PEASANT [sings]:
> The sacrifice set out one day
> Will be gone by the next!

FOURTH PEASANT [sings]:
> She declares truths in the temple,
> Every word can be heard distinctly!

FIFTH PEASANT: It's true. She said—[Sings.]
> Men are wicked, sinful creatures,
> That's why we can't have peace!

SIXTH PEASANT: And Steward Mu told us—[Sings.]
> The White-haired Goddess is so powerful,
> We must all mend our ways!

ALL [sing]:
> Otherwise we'll offend her, and that'll be the end of us!

HU-TZU [impatiently]: That's a pack of lies! Where is the White-haired Goddess? Why haven't I seen her?
[The crowd shows fresh indignation.]

FIRST: How can you say that, Hu-tzu?

SECOND: Everybody knows how powerful the goddess is.

THIRD: Who will bear her anger if you offend her?

DISTRICT HEAD [intervening persuasively]: Friends, don't lose your heads. Let's look into the business of the goddess. We must get to the bottom of it. . . . If you want to burn incense, we won't stop you. But I hope you'll give some thought, too, to the matter of reducing rents. Our government will always work for the people.

TA-CHUN: Just think what we've suffered all these years. Now the communists are here, leading us to become our own masters. We must stand up and act!

OLD MAN: Well, yes, District Head, Ta-chun. . . . We'll leave you now.

DISTRICT HEAD: All right. In a few days we'll get together and have a talk. [The villagers leave.]

DISTRICT HEAD [to CHAO and TA-SO]: Village Head, Ta-so, it's clear what's happening. We've studied the relevant materials in our office, too. [*In a low voice.*] This is no simple matter . . . .

TA-CHUN [*following him up*]: That's right. Landlord Huang is involved. The district office has decided to get to the bottom of the mystery of the "White-haired Goddess." . . . Tonight there'll be a full moon. I think Ta-so and I should go to the Goddess' Temple . . . .

[*They confer in whispers.*]

DISTRICT HEAD [*to* CHAO *and* TA-SO]: What do you think? Do you agree?

CHAO: Yes. A good idea.

TA-SO: Right, let's see what happens tonight.

DISTRICT HEAD: Better be on your guard, Village Head.

CHAO [*eagerly*]: That goes without saying. . . . [*Turns to* HU-TZU.] Hu-tzu, you keep a sharp watch in that direction tonight. Our day of vengeance is coming, youngster.

TA-CHUN: Then let's go quickly and prepare.

[*They walk briskly out.*]

[HU-TZU, *holding his red-tasseled lance, climbs onto a mound to stand guard.*]

Curtain

SCENE 2

Evening.

The Goddess' Temple. There are offerings on the shrine. It is dark and eerie.

[*Enter* TA-CHUN *carrying a pistol, and* TA-SO *with an unlighted torch and a big knife. Approaching the door, they look around, then whisper together and enter the temple.* TA-CHUN *points out a corner to* TA-SO, *and both hide themselves. The wind roars. The temple lamp sheds an eerie light. Pause.*]

[TA-CHUN *peers out from the gloom, then shrinks back into the shadows. There is musical accompaniment throughout.*]

TA-SO [*nervously*]: Ta-chun! Ta-chun!

TA-CHUN [*stopping him*]: Quiet! [*Makes a gesture, and they keep silent again.*]

[*Enter the "White-haired Goddess" from outside. She darts behind the shrine. After a while, seeing there is nobody there, she comes out to collect the sacrifices on the shrine.*]

[TA-CHUN *and* TA-SO *leap out from the darkness.*]

TA-CHUN [*shouting*]: Who are you?

HSI-ERH [*taken by surprise, is bewildered. She shrieks and rushes at* TA-CHUN]: Ah!

[TA-CHUN *fires.* HSI-ERH *is hit in the arm and falls, but she gets up and runs out in fright.*]

TA-CHUN: Ta-so! After her, quick!

[*The scene changes. On the mountain path.*]

[HSI-ERH, *clutching her wounded arm, runs with difficulty, and jumps over a ditch and runs off.*]

[TA-CHUN *and* TA-SO *follow.*]

TA-SO: Which way? She's vanished again!

TA-CHUN [*looks around and down at the ground*]: The trail of blood has disappeared, too.

TA-SO [*looking down*]: There's a valley beneath us. We have come a long way.

TA-CHUN [*making a discovery*]: Look, Ta-so! There's a gleam of light!

TA-SO: Ah, it must be a cave!

[*The crying of a child is heard.*]

TA-CHUN [*listening hard*]: There seems to be a child crying. . . . Let's go after her, Ta-so.

[*The two jump across the ditch.*]

TA-CHUN: Ta-so, light the torch! [*Exeunt.*]

[*The music continues. There is a gust of wind.*]

[*The scene changes again. Inside the cave. An oil lamp gleams on a ledge of the rock, its flickering light revealing the gloom and horror of the cave. On one side are piled firewood, wild fruit, maize, and temple offerings. The child is struggling and crying on the firewood as* HSI-ERH, *panic-stricken, crawls into the cave, and blocks the entrance with a rock. Seeing its mother the child crawls over, crying "Ma!" Outside the cave* TA-CHUN's *voice is heard "Ta-so! Here! Here!" They push at the rock, which crashes down. They enter the cave,* TA-SO *holding the torch.* HSI-ERH *hastily steps to one side to shield her child with her body.*]

169

TA-CHUN [*covering* HSI-ERH *with his pistol*]: Are you man or spirit? Speak!

TA-SO: Quickly! Man or spirit?

TA-CHUN: Speak or I'll fire!

HSI-ERH [*with hatred, fiercely*]: I . . . .

TA-CHUN: Speak! Speak and I'll let you go.

HSI-ERH: I . . . I . . . [*Explosively.*] I'm human, human, human! [*Sings.*]

> I'm flesh and blood! I've a heart like you!
> Why do you say I'm not human?

TA-CHUN: Where did you come from?

HSI-ERH [*sings*]:

> Under the mountain a stream flows by,
> From Yangko Village my family!

TA-CHUN and TA-SO [*startled*]: Then how did you come here?

HSI-ERH: All because of your Huang family! [*Sings.*]

> You hounded my dad to death!
> You forced Ta-chun to leave home! [TA-CHUN *and* TA-SO *stand dumbfounded.*]
> You want to kill me, but I won't die!
> I came and lived in this cave,
> Each day I traced a line on the stone,
> But they're not enough to express my hate!
> Such hate, such burning for revenge
> Is cut in my bones and engraved on my heart!
> Ah! [*Cries.*]
> Did you think I was dead?
> You were wrong, wrong! [*Laughs loudly.*]
> I'm a fire you'll never put out!
> I'm a tree you'll never uproot!

TA-CHUN and TA-SO: What is your name?

HSI-ERH [*sings*]:

> I'm the fire in the waste, I'm the tree on the hill!
> And I am Hsi-erh—who is living still!

[TA-CHUN *and* TASO *exclaim in amazement.*]

HSI-ERH: Well, now you've come again, I'll have it out with you! I'll have it out with you! [*Rushes wildly at them.* TA-CHUN *and* TA-SO *stand there at a loss. The torch in* TA-SO's *hand is still*

burning, and by its light she sees TA-CHUN's *face.*] Ah, you, you!
[*To her amazement she recognizes* TA-CHUN.] Are you Ta-chun?
[*Faints.*]
[*The child cries over her.*]
[TA-CHUN *and* TA-SO *step forward hastily and look at her.*]

TA-CHUN [*speaking as if in a dream*]: Yes . . . . It is Hsi-erh. [*He
    pauses, not knowing what to do, then sees the wound on her
    arm.*] Ah! [*Taking a towel, he binds it up very sadly, calling
    softly.*] Hsi-erh!

TA-SO: Hsi-erh!
    [*The pain of her wound brings* HSI-ERH *to herself. She sighs and
    opens her eyes. When she sees* TA-CHUN, *she knows all is well, and
    listlessly closes her eyes again.*]
    [*Musical accompaniment.*]

TA-CHUN [*looks from* HSI-ERH *to the cave. He remembers all the past,
    and his tears flow. Then he grows angry*]: Now I understand every-
    thing! Ta-so! Go back quickly to tell the district head. Have Land-
    lord Huang arrested! Tell Old Chen to report to the district!

TA-SO: Right!

TA-CHUN: Hold on! And tell my mother and Aunty Chang to bring
    some clothes to fetch Hsi-erh back!

TA-SO: Right! [*Hurries off.*]

TA-CHUN [*to* HSI-ERH]: Hsi-erh! Hsi-erh! [HSI-ERH *comes to herself.*]
    We've come to ask you to go back.

HSI-ERH: Eh? To go back? [*Shakes her head.*]

TA-CHUN [*vehemently*]: You don't realize, Hsi-erh, how things have
    changed outside. Do you remember the Red Army Uncle Chao
    spoke about that year? Well, now the Red Army's come—it's
    called the Eighth Route Army now. They've come, and we poor
    folks have become masters! You must go out; we must take re-
    venge!

HSI-ERH [*after a pause, in a low voice*]: Ah . . . changed . . . changed!
    Revenge! [*She nods.*] Revenge!
    [TA-CHUN *takes off his jacket and puts it over* HSI-ERH's *shoulders,
    then picks up the child and leads* HSI-ERH *out of the cave. Dawn
    is breaking and birds can be heard. There is sunlight outside the
    cave.*]
    [*Singing offstage.*]

    The sun's come out! The sun's come out!
    The sun so bright—a blaze of light!
    For generations till today
    We suffered pain and grief;

But today we've seen the sun rise
To drive away the gloom of night!
Where did our Hsi-erh disappear to?
She's left us many a year.
But today—
We'll trample down the hill,
We'll tear open the mountain cave,
To rescue Hsi-erh!
To rescue her!

[TA-SO leads the district head, AUNTY WANG, AUNTY CHANG, OLD CHAO, and others up the mountain path. They enter singing.]

ALL [sing]:

Where is Hsi-erh?
Where is Hsi-erh?

TA-SO: Over there—ah, look!

ALL [sing]:

Hsi-erh has come! She's coming home!

[They advance in welcome.]

[HSI-ERH's appearance dumbfounds them. After a moment AUNTY WANG goes up to her.]

WANG: Hsi-erh!

CHANG [going to her]: Hsi-erh!

CHAO: Hsi-erh!

[Seeing these familiar faces, HSI-ERH is at first unable to speak. Presently she calls: "Uncle Chao! Aunty Chang! Aunty Wang!" Finally she falls into AUNTY WANG's arms and sobs bitterly. All are moved to tears. AUNTY WANG and AUNTY CHANG straighten HSI-ERH's hair.]

DISTRICT HEAD: Don't be sad, friends! Today we've rescued Hsi-erh! That's good! Tomorrow we'll hold a mass meeting to accuse Landlord Huang, avenge Hsi-erh, and vent our anger. Let's go back now.

ALL [sing]:

Country folk, comrades, don't shed tears!
The old life forced men to turn into ghosts,
But the new life changes ghosts back into men,
It's saved our unhappy sister here!
The new life changes ghosts into men,
She's been restored to us again!

[While singing they help HSI-ERH off.]

Curtain

SCENE 3

The following morning at sunrise.

At the gate of the HUANG *family ancestral hall, chosen as the meeting place for the peasants' mass meeting.*

[*Gongs sound offstage. Shouts are heard:* "Come to the meeting!" "The meeting's at the gate of the Huang family ancestral hall."]
[*Singing offstage*]:

> Age-old injustice must be avenged,
> And a thousand years' wrong be set right!
> Hsi-erh, who was forced to become a ghost,
> Becomes human again today!
> Crushing rents must be reduced,
> The grain extorted must be restored!
> Those who suffered their whole lives long,
> Will stand up and become the masters today!
>
> How much of our blood have you sucked?
> How much have you drunk of our sweat?
> How much of our grain did you steal?
> How much of our gold did you get?
> How long have you tricked and oppressed us?
> How many deaths lie at your door?
> Today we shall settle scores with you,
> Settle every old score!

[*The curtain parts.*]
[*Innumerable peasants have stood up to accuse* LANDLORD HUANG.]
[*The district head,* TA-CHUN, UNCLE CHAO, *and others are standing on the platform. Self Defence Corps guards, armed with red-tasseled lances and swords, surround the meeting place.* LANDLORD HUANG, *in mourning for his mother, stands with bent head below the platform, while* STEWARD MU *has hidden under the table.*]
[HUANG *has just spoken, and now it is the turn of the masses to question him. Feeling is running high.*]

FIRST PEASANT [*sings*]:
> You pretend to reduce the rent, but it's all a lie!

ALL [*in chorus*]:
> You pretend to reduce the rent, but it's all a lie!

SECOND PEASANT [sings]:
> You take the land back on the sly!

ALL [in chorus]:
> You take the land back on the sly!

THIRD PEASANT [sings]:
> When you've rumors to spread, you rattle away!

ALL [in chorus]:
> When you've rumors to spread, you rattle away!

FOURTH PEASANT [sings]:
> When you hound folk to death, you've nothing to say!

ALL [in chorus]:
> Then you've nothing to say!
> Then you've nothing to say!
> So much rent you squeezed, so much money too,
> There's no counting the tragedies caused by you!

Speak, Landlord Huang! Speak up, you!

[HUANG mumbles and wants to justify himself. The crowd grows angry.]

CHAO [sings]:
> Landlord Huang, do you argue still?
> To pretend to be crazy will serve you ill!

ALL [in chorus]:
> Serve you ill!

TA-CHUN: Landlord Huang, I tell you— [Sings.]
> The bad old times have got to stop!
> We common folk are up on top!

ALL [in chorus]:
> Today the world is ours instead!
> Murderers must atone for the dead!
> Pay what you owe to the folk you've bled!
> We'll have your blood for the blood you've shed!

[Two peasant women rush forward.]

FIRST WOMAN [sings]:
> That year—in the ninth moon,

SECOND WOMAN [simultaneously]:
> That year—in the twelfth moon,

FIRST WOMAN [sings]:
> You came to our door for the rent!

SECOND WOMAN [simultaneously]:
> You came to our door for the debt!

174

FIRST WOMAN [sings]:
   You beat my boy till he nearly died!
SECOND WOMAN [simultaneously]:
   You beat my dad till you broke his legs!
TOGETHER [sing]:
   We'll have your blood for the blood you've shed!
ALL [sing]:
   Murderers must atone for the dead!
   Pay what you owe to the folk you've bled!
   We'll have your blood for the blood you've shed!
   [THIRD and FOURTH PEASANTS rush forward.]
THIRD PEASANT [sings]:
   The wrong you did me I'll never forget!
FOURTH PEASANT [simultaneously]:
   The hatred I bear you I'll never forget!
THIRD PEASANT [sings]:
   My son must repair the dike, you said!
FORTH PEASANT [simultaneously]:
   My brother must build you a tower, you said!
   My brother fell to his death from the tower!
THIRD PEASANT [sings]:
   My son was swept off and drowned in the flood!
TOGETHER [sing]:
   Your crimes will be visited on your head!
ALL [sing]:
   Murderers must atone for the dead!
   Pay what you owe to the folk you've bled!
   We'll have your blood for the blood you've shed!
   [The crowd roars]:
   Make Landlord Huang speak!
   Landlord Huang! Answer us!
   [HUANG continues to mutter.]
CHAO [loudly]: Neighbors! Since he won't confess, let's not waste our
   breath on him! Hu-tzu! You fetch Hsi-erh here!
ALL [echoing him]: Right! Fetch Hsi-erh!
   [HU-TZU runs off. HUANG and MU stand aghast.]
PEASANT WOMAN [tearfully, sing]:
   Hsi-erh! . . .
ANOTHER GROUP OF WOMEN [sing]:
   Hsi-erh! . . .

PEASANTS [sing]:
>   Hsi-erh! . . .
>   Hsi-erh! . . .

PEASANT WOMEN [sing]:
>   The poor child suffered bitterly,
>   But a new life starts for us poor folk today!

ALL [sing]:
>   A new life starts! A new life starts today!

[HU-TZU's voice offstage: "Hsi-erh is coming!"]

[All turn to see HSI-ERH. Sing]:
>   Today the world belongs to us,
>   We'll take revenge for past wrongs!
>   Past wrongs!
>   We'll accuse!
>   We'll accuse!
>   And avenge Hsi-erh for all past wrongs!

[Enter AUNTY WANG and AUNTY CHANG supporting HSI-ERH, who is wearing a new dress.]

THE CROWD [shouts]: We want vengeance for Hsi-erh!

[Seeing HUANG, HSI-ERH rushes across like a mad thing to scratch him, but her thirst for vengeance overcomes her, so that she falls fainting into the arms of AUNTY WANG and AUNTY CHANG.] [Pause.]

CHAO [moved to tears]: Child, don't be upset! The time has come for you to speak!

TA-CHUN: Hsi-erh! Did you hear? The time has come for you to speak!

HSI-ERH [as if in a dream]: What? The time . . . has come . . . for us to speak?

ALL [thunderously]: Yes! Hsi-erh, the time has come to speak!

WANG and CHANG: Speak, child!

HSI-ERH: I'll speak, I'll speak, I—will—speak! [Sings.]
>   I want vengeance for all that happened,
>   My wrongs are too many to tell!
>   They're a mountain that can't be leveled,
>   A sea that can't be drained!
>   But what's caused such a great change
>   That I can beard my enemy today?
>   Landlord Huang—
>   To be cut into pieces is too good for you!

176

ALL [sing]:
> To be cut into pieces is too good for you!
> To be cut into pieces is too good for you!
> To be cut into pieces is too good for you!

HSI-ERH [sings]:
> That year—[Her voice falters.]

WANG [sings]:
> That year on New Year's Eve,

HSI-ERH [sings]:
> In storm and snow—

WANG [sings]:
> Mu came and pressed for rent!

HSI-ERH [sings]:
> And hounded my dad to death!

WANG [sings]:
> Our good Old Yang was hounded to death!

ALL [sing]:
> Those hounded to death
> Are too many to count!
> Too many to count!

HSI-ERH [sings]:
> On New Year's Day—

CHANG [sings]:
> They took her to the Huangs' house that day—

HSI-ERH [sings]:
> I led a wretched life there—

CHANG [sings]:
> She was raped by Landlord Huang!

PEASANT WOMEN [shocked, sing]:
> Ah! Ah!

HSI-ERH [cries and sings]:
> Ah! . . .

CHANG [sings]:
> Then they wanted to sell her—

HSI-ERH [sings]:
> As a prostitute!
> Landlord Huang! Landlord Huang!
> Murderous brute!

177

ALL [sing]:
> You man-devouring beast!
> The day of reckoning has come!

[Unable to control their anger, the villagers rush forward to beat HUANG.]

[The district head and others stop them.]

DISTRICT HEAD: Friends, don't beat him yet! Let Hsi-erh finish.

HSI-ERH [sings]:
> But Aunty Chang, she saved me,
> So I could leave the tiger's den.
> It was pitch black!

ALL [sing]:
> It was pitch black!

HSI-ERH [sings]:
> And the way was dark!

ALL [sing]:
> And the way was dark!

HSI-ERH [sings]:
> I didn't know where to turn!

ALL [sing]:
> Where did you go?

HIS-ERH [sings]:
> I stayed in a cave in the mountain,
> Far from people and out of the sun,
> Eating raw fruit and offerings,
> Till I seemed neither ghost nor man!
> But I refused to die,
> Though stones rot or streams run dry!
> I bore my hardships till today,
> And today they have vanished away!

WANG, CHANG and PEASANT WOMEN [sing]:
> In the light of the sun . . . .

HSI-ERH [sings]:
> Let vengeance be done!

PEASANT WOMEN [sing]:
> She'll be avenged in the light of the sun!

ALL [sing]:
> Now our time has come,
> We must be revenged!

178

> We want justice done,
> Hsi-erh must be avenged!

[No longer to be stopped they rush forward and beat HUANG and MU.] [The district head and other cadres try to stop the crowd. The district head stands on a table.]

DISTRICT HEAD [shouts]: Friends! I represent the government. I support your charges against Landlord Huang. We will certainly avenge Hsi-erh. First, let us arrest Huang and Mu for public trial according to proper legal procedure.
[All cheer excitedly.]
[Members of the Self Defense Corps tie up HUANG and MU.]
ALL [sing]:

> Landlord Huang, you have bowed your head!
> You quake with dread!
> You have bowed your head!
> You quake with dread!
> Age-old feudal bonds
> Today are cut away!
> Crushing iron chains
> Will be smashed to bits today!

[The song is repeated.]
[The sun rises. It shines brightly on HSI-ERH and the surging crowd, who shout for joy and sing]:

> We, who suffered in days bygone,
> Shall be our own masters from now on!
> Shall be our own masters from now on!
> Our—own—masters—from—now—on!

[LANDLORD HUANG crouches before the crowd like a felled tree.]
[The peasants stand proudly under the sun, countless arms raised high.]

Curtain

NOTES

1. A confusion in dates exists. If time lapses between subsequent acts are accurately described, this date should read "Winter, 1934."

2. At this time the main force opposing the Communists was the Nationalist Government of China (1927–1937), with its capital at Nanking.

3. White is the color for mourning in China.

4. "Hsi" means "joy."

5. On July 7–8, 1937, the Japanese forces attacked Lukouchiao and continued on to Shanghai which they attacked on August 13, 1937; Paoting lies between these two points. Technically, only one year has passed, but the dramatists have evidently suggested a three year period to add to the effect of the play.

6. In the early fall of 1937 the Red Army was reorganized as the Eighth Route Army and the New Fourth Army.

THE WOMEN'S REPRESENTATIVE*

By Sun Yu

Translated by Tang Sheng

Time: Winter, 1952.

Place: A village in Northeast China. In the home of WANG CHIANG, a peasant.

CHARACTERS:

CHANG KUEI-YUNG, twenty-six years old, newly elected chairman of the women's association.

MRS. WANG, KUEI-YUNG's mother-in-law, in her fifties.

TSUI-LAN, a girl about eighteen.

AUNT NIU, an old-style midwife, about forty-five, distant relative of MRS. WANG.

WANG CHIANG, KUEI-YUNG's husband, a peasant in his late twenties.

Scene: An average peasant home. A door on the left leads to the outer room of the house. Near this door there are a vat for water (kept indoors in the winter to prevent the water from freezing), and a kitchen cupboard. Another door on the right side leads to an inner room. Alongside the door stands a table with drawers and a few chairs. On the table is a vase holding a feather duster, etc. Facing the audience and beneath the window, there is a kang. At the foot of the kang is a small chest on which folded quilts are stacked. A lighted brazier sits on the kang.

[As the curtain rises there is no one in the room. TSUI-LAN, whose voice is heard offstage, comes on hurriedly, a small bunch of straw in her hand.]

---

*Peking, Foreign Languages Press, 1956, 44-94.

LAN [*calling*]: Kuei-yung, Kuei-yung! [*Discovers that the room is empty. Still calling, she walks toward the innerroom.*] Kuei-yung, Kuei-yung . . . ! [MRS. WANG *comes hurriedly out of the innerroom holding a cloth shoe sole which she has been working on. She motions* TSUI-LAN *to lower her voice.*]

MRS. WANG [*looking slightly annoyed and in a hushed voice*]: What are you shouting about? Do you want to wake the baby?

LAN [*preoccupied*]: Mrs. Wang, where is Kuei-yung?

MRS. WANG: She's gone to draw some water. She'll be back in a minute. [*Coldly.*] What do you want with her now?

LAN: I want to tell her I've tried everywhere but couldn't get any good straw.

MRS. WANG: Straw? What kind of straw?

LAN: The rice straw our handicraft group uses to weave into sacks. We had a large stack put by, but working in two shifts from early in the morning till after dark, we finished it off in a couple of days. Kuei-yung told me to get some more from the families on our street. I've been to several houses but everyone seems to have used theirs up as fuel. All that's left is this short kind.

MRS. WANG [*offhandedly*]: Well, what if you can't get any more? Why get yourselves all worked up? [*Sits down on the kang and starts to stitch the cloth sole.*]

LAN [*seriously*]: But don't you see, we won't have anything to work on this evening.

MRS. WANG: So much the better. You can just drop the whole business. You can't go on weaving sacks all the time.

LAN: But everybody's just in the right mood for work. How can we drop it? [*Puts the straw down on a chair.*] Kuei-yung said as soon as we get another batch of sacks made we'll be signing a contract with the co-op.

MRS. WANG [*peevishly*]: She wants to do everything. Making sacks all day and going to literacy class at night. She can't spend a minute at home. Why do you girls listen to her?

LAN: Why indeed! We elected her the chairman of our women's association and our representative so that she'd lead us in study and in work.

MRS. WANG [*disappointed*]: I really can't understand why you do it. None of your families need your support. Young girls like you, dashing all over the place, and in this cold weather, too!

LAN [*explaining patiently*]: This happens to be the time when people pay their tax in grain. They need the sacks we're making. The

182

more sacks we make the better it is for the country. And we're earning a bit on the side, too.

MRS. WANG [*impatiently*]: Humph! As if the grain wasn't sent in before you girls started this sack making. [*Turns away.*]

[*The door outside bangs; TSUI-LAN walks over to the door on the left and lifts the curtain. KUEI-YUNG enters with two buckets of water. Puts her carrying-pole in a corner.*]

KUEI: Did you get the straw?

LAN: I've been to all the people with rice fields, but only one family had this bit of short straw left. [*Points to the straw.*] Everyone burns it for fuel.

KUEI [*walks over to her and examines the straw*]: Too short, and not very strong either. I'm afraid we can't use it. [*Drops the straw back on the chair.*]

LAN: What shall we do? No one else on our street has any more.

[*KUEI-YUNG empties the buckets into the water vat, ponders.*]

KUEI: I know someone who has.

LAN: Who? Every little bit helps.

KUEI: We've got some straw!

[*MRS. WANG gives KUEI-YUNG a displeased sidelong glance.*]

LAN [*joyfully*]: That's wonderful! Your rice crop this year was better than anyone's. I'll get Chang Yu-chen. We'll have him cart it back. [*Starts to leave.*]

KUEI [*calling her back*]: Wait a second.

LAN: He's back. I've already arranged it with him. He's to pick up our straw first and when he's delivered that he'll take our sacks to the co-op. [*Again starts to go.*]

KUEI [*pulling her back*]: I know all that. [*Indicates to her that they must first ask MRS WANG. TSUI-LAN pauses and KUEI-YUNG turns to the old lady.*]

MRS. WANG [*unable to hold her tongue any longer*]: You know you mustn't touch that bit of straw of ours.

KUEI: The group can't get rice straw anywhere. They only want a little from us, Ma.

LAN: We'll pay for it as soon as we've sold the sacks. It won't be for nothing.

MRS. WANG: I can't give it to you whether you pay or not. When Chiang was leaving, he didn't say anything about the straw. Nobody can touch it without his permission.

KUEI: Ma, our family's in this handicraft business, too. It's a shame

to burn up our fine straw in the stove. Let's send it to the handicraft group.

MRS. WANG [*reprovingly*]: I won't let you have your way this time.
Didn't Chiang tell you not to stick your neck out and bother
about things that are none of your business? Didn't his words
sink in at all? As it is, I'll be blamed for plenty when he returns, without you trying to cart our things off. Stop making
trouble for me. [*Gets off the kang and goes toward inner room.*]

LAN: If Chiang comes back and makes a fuss, I'll handle him! Please,
Mrs. Wang, let us have some of the straw now. We've got nothing to work on!

MRS WANG: Good, just break up the group and stop all this nonsense. You girls quiet down and stay home for a change. Then
we can all have a little peace of mind. [*Goes into inner room.*]

LAN [*exchanges a glance with* KUEI-YUNG]: Oh, damn! I'm fed up.
[*Pushes the straw off the chair and sits down angrily.*]

KUEI [*after much thought walks to* TSUI-LAN *and pats her on the
shoulder*]: Take it easy. Let's go out and have another look. Old
Li at the east end of the village planted five *mou* of rice. You go
see if he has any straw left. I'll try Old Huang on the west end.

LAN: I doubt if there's a chance.

KUEI: Even if they haven't much, it'll still be something. Anyhow,
we can ask.

LAN: Let's go then!

[*They leave through door on the left.* MRS. WANG *enters.*]

MRS. WANG: Ai! I can't do a thing with them!

[*A pause.* AUNT NIU *enters from the door on the left.*]

NIU: Mrs. Wang!

MRS. WANG: Ah, it's Aunt Niu. Come and sit down!

NIU [*still standing and full of concern*]: Is my nephew back?

MRS. WANG: No. No sign of him yet. It's nearly three months since
he went to the mountains for timber.

NIU: But the people who went with him are home already. They
said he came back with them. They left him at the station. Maybe he's been delayed.

MRS. WANG: Maybe. Did they say how he was?

NIU: I hear that all of them are fine.

MRS. WANG [*pushing* AUNT NIU *into a chair*]: Do sit down a while.
[*Fills a pipe with tobacco and offers it to* NIU.] Why haven't you
been visiting us lately?

NIU: I find it hard enough keeping out of your precious daughter-

184

in-law's way as it is without coming here to visit! Today I heard that Chiang is back, that's why I've come.

MRS. WANG [puzzled]: Why do you want to keep out of her way?

NIU [about to speak, stops. In a whisper]: That was she and Tsui-lan who went out just now, wasn't it?

MRS. WANG: Yes. But why? What's the matter?

NIU: You and I have been neighbors for years. We're relatives, too. I feel I can tell you what has to be said. A few days ago, Old Yu's child got sick and they asked me to take a look at him. I did what I could, and left some medicine. Somehow or other your daughter-in-law got wind of it. She told them my treatment was no good and talked Old Yu into bringing the child to the district clinic. And as if that wasn't enough, she also took away the two packages of medicine I had left. After all, you and I are so close. I don't know what to say.

MRS. WANG [angrily]: That daughter-in-law of mine is a plain fool. She does anything the leaders tell her to do.

NIU: Other chairmen of the women's association never bothered me. Why should she be so nosey?

MRS. WANG: Now, now, don't you mind her.

NIU: Mrs. Wang, you know how it is with us. The family depends on what money I manage to scrape together. This medicine for the Yus meant sure cash for me. But she had to go and spoil everything!

MRS. WANG: Don't be angry, Aunt Niu. When she comes back, I'll have her return the medicine to you.

NIU: Do you think she'll listen to you?

MRS. WANG: Ah . . . well, my son is coming back. She won't be having her own way much longer.

NIU [pleased]: Oh, that's fine. [Explaining.] You see, she's the chairman, elected by the people. If she wants to do things officially and stick to the rules, I can only turn to you and your son. You talk to her; tell her to go easy on me. You know the saying: "The clever official helps his friends." If she'll only keep one eye shut, I'll be all right.

MRS. WANG [complacently]: From now on, I won't let her make any more trouble. When Chiang comes home, I'll make her give up all this women's chairman and representative nonsense.

NIU: That's not exactly . . . .

MRS. WANG: If Chiang had been here, she'd never have become a representative in the first place.

NIU: You're quite right. "The General should not leave his post," how true it is. It's a case of "When the cat's away, the mice will play." But now the cat has come back. . . . [*The outside door creaks. Startled, she whispers.*] Your daughter-in-law . . . . [KUEI-YUNG *enters with a bunch of fairly long straw.*]

KUEI: Hello, Aunt Niu. How are you?

NIU: Mm.

MRS. WANG: Chiang is coming home. Do you know?

KUEI: Yes, I've just heard.

MRS. WANG [*in a commanding tone*]: Aunt Niu has come for her medicine. Give it back to her.

KUEI [*surprised*]: Her medicine! [*Puts the straw down. To* AUNT NIU.] Didn't you say yesterday "The medicine's no good. Throw it away"? How come you want it again?

NIU [*glances at* MRS. WANG, *emboldened*]: Well, now that we're talking before your mother-in-law, I'll tell the whole story. Yesterday, because all of you were picking on me, I had to say that. Actually this medicine of mine was prepared from a secret prescription that cures nine times out of ten. It's made of first-grade herbs. I bought them long ago. Three yuan a package they cost me, but I did not get a penny from the Yus.

KUEI [*seriously*]: Aunt Niu, you know perfectly well your doctoring made the Yu child worse.

NIU [*trying to justify herself*]: I can't be blamed for that. After all, "Accidents can happen to anyone; even horses get sick." I cure one thing, but I can't help it if the patient gets something else.

KUEI [*suppressing her anger*]: Then you still want that medicine back to use on other patients?

NIU [*righteously*]: I know my trade. I've been at it for years!

MRS. WANG [*cutting in and addressing herself to* KUEI-YUNG]: Why do you butt into other people's business? Give her the medicine and be done with it!

KUEI [*after some reflection, with determination*]: All right. [*Turns to the table, gets out a key and opens a drawer.*]

[AUNT NIU *thinks she has won her point, goes to* KUEI-YUNG *and stands behind her, a broad smile on her face.*]

NIU [*flatteringly*]: Don't think Aunt Niu is mad at you. Not a bit. She knows how hard it is for you. What with the government on the one side and your own relatives on the other, you're stuck in the middle. But you're quite right to give the medicine back. As they say: "Friendship is more important than the govern-

186

ment's laws." I won't forget your help. When Chiang comes home and starts finding fault, depend on me. I'll put in a good word for you. . . .

KUEI [turning to her with some money in her hand]: Here!

NIU [puzzled]: But why are you giving me money? Where's my medicine?

KUEI: I'm buying it from you.

MRS. WANG [not understanding]: No one's sick in our family. What do you want the medicine for?

KUEI [with determination]: I want to send it to the County Hospital to be analyzed, to see if it isn't some quack concoction.

NIU [greatly alarmed]: But niece, that . . . that'll put me in an awful fix. [Begging her.] You, you mustn't do that!

KUEI: What are you afraid of? After it's been analyzed, you can sell it all over the country.

NIU [in a panic]: No, no, I don't want your money; give me back the medicine.

KUEI: I have to get to the bottom of this.

NIU [cornered, suddenly hits on an idea. Slightly menacing]: After all, we're relatives. If you do this to me, your husband won't like it.

KUEI [with deep feeling]: Just think of the things you've been doing. We told you that a midwife should work properly. When you deliver babies, you should sterilize everything. But you won't listen. Quite a few of the babies you delivered in our village got blood poisoning. You've been forbidden to hand out medicine, but you still sell your stuff on the sly. When Old Yu's child caught pneumonia, you insisted on calling it a "cold fever." You punctured the poor little thing all over with needles and left some foul medicine. If I hadn't made them take the child to the clinic, he would have died. Now that the danger's past, you think you can just forget it.

MRS. WANG: This is none of your business, Kuei-yung. Why meddle?

KUEI: It's a matter of life or death. How can I stand aside?

NIU [beseechingly]: Believe me, niece, I'll never sell the stuff again.

KUEI: Then why not let me have it analyzed? Make yourself clear!

NIU [with hesitation]: Oh, uh . . . uh, a relative of mine once took this medicine for dysentery and got well. I learned the prescription from him. Anyway, I know it's harmless; it won't poison anybody.

187

KUEI: But are you sure it will cure other things, too? When you give a medicine like this, aren't you keeping the patient from getting proper treatment?

NIU: But by luck it might turn out to be just what he needed!

KUEI: So you stake the life of your patients on luck!

NIU: All right, I'll never sell it again.

KUEI: You'll have to really promise. Never again.

NIU: Yes, never again.

KUEI: Let me tell you frankly then. We've already talked things over at a meeting of women representatives from different villages. We're going to set up mother and child care clinics in the villages and teach everyone about health and sanitation. Even if you still try to sell your stuff, no one will trust you any more.

NIU [stands in silence]: . . . .

KUEI [sympathetically]: I know it's hard for you to make ends meet. [Offering her money.] Here, take this. We'll just destroy the medicine.

[AUNT NIU is ashamed to take the money, stands woodenly. A baby is heard crying in the inner-room.]

MRS. WANG [angry]: The baby's crying.

KUEI: Your medicine didn't drop down from the sky, you spent money on it. You'd better take this. [Puts the money on the table; goes into inner room.]

NIU [despondently]: Ai! [Starts to leave. On second thoughts picks up the money from the table. To MRS. WANG as she goes to the door.] I'll take it since she insists. [Goes out.]

[MRS. WANG sits glumly on the kang. KUEI-YUNG comes in with baby in her arms.]

MRS. WANG [severely]: Why are you so fond of meddling? Her business is no concern of ours. The eaves of our houses don't touch; the borders of our land lie far apart. Water from the river needn't mix with the water in the well. What is her business to you anyway? Why are you always offending people?

KUEI: Ma, I'm chairman of the women's association and a member of the health committee. If I don't bother about these things, who will?

MRS. WANG: If you weren't such a show-off, do you think the people would have elected you? You're not the only smart one in this village. It's a dangerous road you're taking—stepping on everyone's toes! Just wait till Chiang comes home! [As she talks, she goes toward the door on the right.]

KUEI: Ma—

MRS. WANG [stopping in her tracks]: What is it?

KUEI [picking up the bunch of long straw]: Look how fine and strong our straw is. It's such a pity to burn it. I've just been out. We simply can't get any decent straw anywhere. Let's sell ours to the handicraft group. With the money they pay we can buy other fuel for the stove. Won't that be just as good?

MRS. WANG: Haven't you made enough trouble? Now you've got your eyes on that bit of straw!

KUEI: But Ma, the girls have no more straw for weaving and here we're burning ours. It hurts me every time I put a handful into the stove. What harm will it do to sell some?

MRS. WANG [stubbornly]: Nothing doing! You're not the one to decide. If you girls have no more straw, wind up your group and stay home where you belong. Otherwise you'll catch it from Chiang. [Goes off.]

[KUEI-YUNG looks worried. TSUI-LAN enters hurriedly.]

KUEI [anxiously]: Well, did you get any?

LAN: No, how about you?

KUEI: No luck! All used up.

LAN: What shall we do? Yu-chen is waiting at the door with his cart. He said he ran into the co-op chairman when he delivered the grain. The chairman said they need more straw sacks and want us to send in what we've finished.

KUEI: Has he fed the donkeys yet?

LAN: Yes, he's got them ready and harnessed to the cart. He wants to pick up our straw before he takes the sacks to the co-op.

[YU-CHEN calling offstage: "TSUI-LAN, hurry up will you? Where do I go for your straw?"]

LAN: Hear that? He's getting impatient.

KUEI [thinking desperately]. . . .

LAN: All right, we'll just have to use second-rate straw then. [Turns to go.]

KUEI [stopping her]: If we use that kind, the sacks will burst with the slightest strain. They won't do!

LAN [getting impatient]: But there's no other kind around. Unless we get some straw, the second shift won't be able to work tonight.

KUEI [resolutely]: Take ours!

LAN [surprised]: Did Mrs. Wang say it's all right?

KUEI: She'll understand by and by. Take two hundred sheaves first.

LAN: Good. We'll load right now. Then we'll have to hurry to literacy class, or we'll be late.

KUEI: I haven't eaten yet. You go first and tell Yu-chen to load. I'll come as soon as I've had a bite.

LAN: All right. [Goes off.]

[KUEI-YUNG picks up the bunch of short straw, tosses it into the outer room. She turns and walks to the cupboard, gets out bowls and chopsticks. The rumbling of the cart, cracking of the whip, and cries of the driver can be heard offstage. MRS. WANG, fuming with rage, comes on.]

MRS. WANG: Did you tell them to take our straw from the court-yard?

KUEI: Yes, I did.

MRS. WANG: You certainly are getting bolder and bolder. When my son comes home . . . .

KUEI [crisply]: When he comes home, then what? I'll be respon-sible for what I'm doing.

MRS. WANG: Oh! I've nothing to say in this house any more! Go ahead, sell everything! Let them take it all away!

KUEI: Ma, I've been trying to explain but you refuse to understand. They need straw sacks for the grain. We earn extra income by making the sacks. What's wrong with that? We've got 600 sheaves of straw; I've told them to take 200. I'll be responsible. You don't have to worry about anything. [Places bowls and chop-sticks on the table, brings out a home-made ledger and makes an entry with a pencil.] [MRS. WANG starts to speak but thinks better of it. Utters a loud sigh and goes into inner room. KUEI-YUNG puts away the account book, brings in a crockery pot of rice, fills a bowl for herself. Is about to eat when TSUI-LAN enters.]

LAN [brushing bits of straw off her clothes]: Well, 200 sheaves are on their way. Let's hurry to class. It's getting late.

KUEI [anxiously]: Is Yu-chen gone?

LAN [suspiciously]: Yes, why? Changed your mind about that straw?

KUEI: No! I know he's going to the co-op next. I want him to buy some things for us with the money I'll be getting for the sacks.

LAN: What do you want?

KUEI: Things for the house, very important things.

LAN: Let's hurry and catch him. After he's delivered the straw, he's going straight to the co-op with the sacks. If you haven't

190

eaten yet, you can have some cold muffins with me at my house. But let's catch him first.

KUEI: Good. Will you hold the baby for me? I'll just put the rice back on the stove. When Chiang comes home, it'll be hot and ready for him.

LAN [taking the baby]: Aiya, how considerate you are. You're so good to him.

[KUEI-YUNG takes the pot of rice and goes out through the door on left. Re-enters, takes the baby and goes to the other door.]

KUEI: Ma!

MRS. WANG [appearing at the door]: What do you want?

KUEI: I'm going to class. Will you take little Pao?

MRS. WANG [displeased]: Are you still going this evening?

LAN: We're having tests every night. She can't miss them.

MRS. WANG [to KUEI-YUNG]: Your husband has quarreled with you more than once because of all these meetings you like so much. When he comes home and hears that you've become the women's representative and go to night school as well, he's not going to like it one bit. You'd better give up all this running around. . . .

LAN: Winter evenings are so long. Why shouldn't people go and study when there's nothing else to do?

MRS. WANG: Are you going to wait till he forces you to stay home? Take the baby with you if you're going out tonight. I'm not going to look after him! [Turns and goes inside.]

LAN [in an undertone]: The old hog! Trying to scare you with her son! Why shouldn't she take the baby off your hands once in a while? Leave the baby with her. She'll have to mind him whether she wants to or not.

KUEI: How can I do that!

LAN: I think you're too meek with her. Why do you let her bully you so?

KUEI: It's not that, Tsui-lan. Put yourself in my place. I'm a member of the Youth League. If people hear that I quarrel with my mother-in-law, it'll hurt the Youth League's reputation.

LAN: Then you mean to say you're going to give up the literacy class?

KUEI: Of course not! If we women don't learn to read and write, if we don't go out and work, we'll be tied hand and foot. What's the use of fighting for equality? Where will our freedom come from? Everyone has difficulties. If I quit, others will feel like giving up, too.

191

LAN: That's right. But what about your baby? Mrs. Wang refuses to mind him.

KUEI [remaining silent]. . . .

LAN [bursting out]: I know! There's the second team's nursery. We'll leave the baby there; old Mrs. Wan is very good with children.

KUEI: It's no use. Ma doesn't trust her with our baby. She'll raise a row if I leave him there.

LAN: She doesn't trust the nursery and won't mind the baby herself, and she still has the brass to make a fuss! Take the baby to the nursery. Don't you care about her. [Pushes KUEI-YUNG toward the door.]

KUEI: Wait, I'll try talking to her again. [Goes inside with the baby.]

[TSU-LAN idly picks up a reader for beginners and practices pronouncing a few phonetic symbols aloud: Bo, poh, mo, foh. . . . KUEI-YUNG re-enters, still holding the baby.]

LAN: Everything all right?

KUEI [shaking her head]: She won't do it!

LAN: What a crab! Won't even mind her own grandson.

KUEI: It's not that she doesn't like to mind the baby. She's trying to use the child to tie me down at home where her son can beat me and she can scold me. I've had enough of all that. Let's go.

LAN: You're right. We'd better hurry though.

[TSUI-LAN goes out of door on the left. KUEI-YUNG stops on the threshold.]

KUEI [loudly, toward the other door]: Ma, I'm going now. I'm leaving the baby at the nursery. [Goes.]

[MRS. WANG comes out, sees that KUEI-YUNG is gone.]

MRS. WANG: Ha! She's really taken the baby! [Calls out.] Kuei-yung! Kuei-yung! [No response. Fiercely.] Wretched girl! She's out of her mind! Eats her fill and off she goes! She makes me so mad . . . !

[Outside, darkness falls, MRS. WANG lights the lamp. A pause. CHIANG enters, a big padded cap on his head and his bedding roll on his back.]

CHIANG: Ma!

MRS. WANG: At last you're back! Why did you take so long coming home? [Rushes to him and helps him put his things down.]

CHIANG [putting down his bedding roll]: I did some shopping in the district center.

192

MRS. WANG: What did you buy?

CHIANG [bringing various articles out of his pocket]: Little things. A pair of stockings for each of you and a cake of scented soap.

MRS. WANG: Isn't our laundry soap good enough? Why buy this fancy kind? [Sniffs at the soap.]

CHIANG: Old women might not care for it, but young ones do! [Picks up the soap lovingly and puts it back in his pocket.]

MRS. WANG [examining the stockings]: Oh, you've bought me a pair of stockings. Why not a pair of felt slippers instead? They're light and warm, too.

CHIANG: I didn't think of that.

MRS. WANG: The brazier's lighted, come and get warm.

CHIANG: I'm quite hot from the walk. [Removes his cap and wipes his brow.] It's given me a terrific appetite. I'm starving! Tell Kuei-yung to hurry and make me something to eat.

MRS. WANG: She's not home.

CHIANG: Where is she?

MRS. WANG [letting off steam]: She's always busy with something. Can't ever keep her at home.

CHIANG: Where did she go?

MRS. WANG: She said she was going to the literacy class.

CHIANG [displeased]: Stuff and nonsense! [Goes to the cupboard to get the rice pot.] Why isn't there any rice left?

MRS. WANG: I suppose she ate it all. Running around so much, she has to eat more, you know. I'll cook you something.

CHIANG: Let her do it when she comes back.

MRS. WANG: When will that be? I can't let you go hungry. [Exit.] [CHIANG seats himself on the edge of the kang, his face showing displeasure. MRS. WANG brings in hot food.]

MRS. WANG: Here's some rice and a left-over dish. Put the little table on the kang.

[He does so, and she places food on the table.]

CHIANG [eating]: Is little Pao asleep?

MRS. WANG: He's not home either. She took him with her.

CHIANG [anxiously]: Took him where? [Stops eating.]

MRS. WANG: Over to old Mrs. Wan's. There's a sort of nursery there. These three months you've been away, Kuei-yung's going out much more. Her program's really big, I can tell you. I keep telling her, "Your husband's away. You should stay home, not go gadding about poking your nose into this and that." But she won't listen. Today she walked out in a huff—with the baby, too.

193

CHIANG [thoughtful a minute, then indignantly]: I knew once she got some backing, she'd come to this. When she joined the Youth League, I didn't like it at all.

MRS. WANG [grumbling]: Why didn't you stop her?

CHIANG: I was going to, but people made such a fuss. I know it's a good thing for a man to join the Communist Party or the Youth League, but what does a woman want to get mixed up in them for? While I was still thinking about it, she went and joined.

MRS. WANG: Now she's in her glory! Been elected a representative in the women's association. What's more, she's their chairman!

CHIANG: Who gave her permission? Why didn't you stop her?

MRS. WANG: Do you think I could do anything with her when you weren't home? [Plaintively.] This village is too small for her. When a husband and wife quarrel, she must go and interfere; when some woman doesn't feel like working, she must go and interfere. Aunt Niu delivers babies and sells medicine—she must look in on that, too. We're a respectable family. What are we coming to?

CHIANG: Why didn't you put her in her place?

MRS. WANG: How could I out-talk her? Since you went away, she's learned to talk like a stream at those meetings of hers. In the past, the mother-in-law managed the daughter-in-law. Now it looks as if pretty soon the daughter-in-law will be running the mother-in-law. Today, for instance, she sent off 200 sheaves of our rice straw.

CHIANG [anxiously]: What for?

MRS. WANG: They're weaving sacks out of straw at the east end of the village. She's in charge of collecting it. I said to her, "We have enough to eat and enough to wear. You needn't bother about such things. You don't have to run around to earn pin money!" But do you think she'd listen to me? She seems to be doing things just to spite me. [Sadly.] My words no longer count. What can I expect from her when I become old and weak. [Starts to sob.]

CHIANG [throwing the chopsticks down in rage]: I told her that she was to stay home. Damn the woman! She's getting bolder and bolder; doesn't even listen to her husband's orders. Ma, bring her home. I'm not going to let her go on like this.

MRS. WANG: Those women in the literacy class will snap my head off if I try to call her out.

194

CHIANG: I'll go myself then. [*Gets ready to go.*]

MRS. WANG [*stopping him*]: You rest a while first. You must be tired after the long trip home.

CHIANG: If I don't take her off her high horse right away, she'll be even harder to handle in the future. [*Again is about to go but is pulled back by his mother.*]

MRS. WANG: She'll come back after class.

CHIANG: Damn her! I suppose I can wait till then to settle with her. She's not going to get away with this!

MRS. WANG: They say: "Teach your son openly but lecture your wife privately." Punish her at home, if you've got the nerve to do it. Don't make a scene outside and have everyone laughing at you.

CHIANG: What about the baby? Can't we bring him home at least?

MRS. WANG: I'll go and get him right now. You finish your food and lie down for a while. [*Looks at food.*] You've hardly touched anything. It's all getting cold. I'll warm it up on the brazier. [*Carefully puts the metal bowl containing meat and vegetables on the brazier.*] Come over and eat it hot by the fire. I'll get the baby. [*Goes off.*]

[*CHIANG finishes his meal, reaches for bowl on the brazier and burns his fingers. Lets the bowl drop to the ground with a clatter. Exasperated, he stands motionless a few minutes, then begins to stack the dishes on the cupboard. This done, he goes back to the kang and lies down. He gets up again soon after and reaches for the wicker tobacco tray to roll himself a cigarette. Notices the reader, takes it up.*]

CHIANG [*turning over the first few pages, discovers only phonetic symbols, which he can't read*]: What queer stuff is this? [*Tears out a page and rolls himself a cigarette, lights it and puffs vigorously.*]

[*AUNT NIU enters from the door on the left.*]

NIU: Ah, so you're home again, nephew. When did you get back?

CHIANG: Just now. Do sit down, Aunt Niu.

NIU [*looking around the room and full of concern*]: Where's your mother and your wife?

CHIANG: They're not home. Is there anything you want?

NIU [*producing some money out of her pocket*]: I've brought the money back for your wife.

CHIANG: What money?

195

NIU: Oh, just a bit of money I shouldn't have accepted. I was wrong to take it. Your mother knows all about it. [*Puts the money on the table and turns to go.*]

CHIANG [*detains her*]: Aunt Niu, my mother will be home in a minute. Why not wait for her? Please sit down. I'd like to ask you something.

NIU: Ask me what? [*Sits down on the edge of the kang.*]

CHIANG: I hear that Kuei-yung offended you when I was away. What was it about?

NIU [*embarrassed*]: Uh, about me . . . I . . . uh, I don't know how to say it. I suppose it was all my fault.

CHIANG: What was the matter?

NIU: Why ask? Your wife is a big shot now. She's the women's chairman. The way I make my living doesn't please certain people, so I've got to quit. "Everybody kicks a person when he's down," the saying goes. How true it is. Even my own relatives will do nothing to help me.

CHIANG [*impatiently*]: What exactly has my wife been doing in the village these days?

NIU [*begins to say something but changes her mind*]: Your mother knows everything. You'd better ask her.

CHIANG [*knitting his brows and very anxious*]: Aunt Niu, let me ask you—

NIU: Yes?

CHIANG: We're relatives. You can speak frankly. Tell me, with all her running around, are people talking about me behind my back?

NIU [*taking up her tobacco pouch nonchalantly and filling her pipe*]: Why ask? Some things it's better not to know.

[*Listening suspiciously, CHIANG becomes exceedingly angry and flushes a dark crimson. He pulls out the cake of soap, looks at it, snatches up the pair of stockings he had bought for KUEI-YUNG and flings them all to the ground. Startled, AUNT NIU lifts her head and discovers that MRS. WANG is just coming through the door on the left with the baby in her arms.*]

MRS. WANG: Here we are. Come and see your son.

CHIANG [*too angry to hear what she's saying*]: Ma, I'm going out to look for her. [*Rushes off.*]

MRS. WANG [*going after him and shouting*]: What's your hurry? She'll be back sooner or later! [*Unable to stop him, she walks back from the door. To NIU.*] When did you come?

196

Niu: Just a few minutes ago. I've brought the money back.

Mrs. Wang: What for?

Niu: I went home and thought it over. It didn't seem right. Of course she insisted that I take it, but I can't be spending your money for no good reason. That's not being fair to any one. [Picks up the money and hands it over to Mrs. Wang.]

Mrs. Wang: No, keep it. You don't have to give it back. [Pushes money away.]

[While they are trying to force the money on each other, Kuei-yung enters.]

Kuei [as soon as she steps into the room]: Ma, is Chiang back?

Mrs. Wang: Yes. He just went out to look for you. Didn't you meet him on the way?

Kuei: No. I was called to the Party secretary's as soon as I got to literacy class. I came straight home from his office.

Mrs. Wang: Chiang cut across the threshing ground just a minute ago. He can't have gone very far. I'll bring him back. [Hands the baby to Kuei, hurries off.]

Niu: Kuei-yung, I'm returning the money. But I'm very grateful for your good intentions. I know I was wrong. I'll mend my ways from now on.

Kuei: No, no Aunt Niu. Take it. Your family is hard up.

Niu: It's true that we're not well off. Still I can't take that money. [Gets ready to go.]

Kuei [stops her, makes her sit on the kang]: Aunt Niu, I was going to look for you. I've some important news to tell you.

Niu: Niece, you don't have to keep explaining things to me. Everything's as clear as crystal already. All the women have joined the women's association. You only have to call a meeting and everyone listens to you. At any rate no one will trust me any more, so there's no use my trying tricks on the sly.

Kuei: Aunt Niu, I want you to keep on with your profession.

Niu: You don't have to console me, niece. I'm not blind to the changes going on. Women are gradually learning things. If I should make a real blunder with my old methods, wouldn't I just be asking for trouble!

Kuei: What you say is true, of course, but let me ask you. There are only two in your family. Uncle Niu ruined his health working for the landlords as a hired hand. He's been sickly for years. Although you two got thirty mou of good land during the land reform, you haven't the labor power to till it properly. Everyone

197

else is much better off than before, but you two can't even make
ends meet. What are you going to do?

NIU [*sadly*]: Ai, what can we do? I can only curse fate.

KUEI: It's no use blaming fate. Man must find ways for himself.

NIU [*forlornly*]: I have no sons and no daughters. I can carry neither
buckets nor baskets. I'm no good behind the plough. Where
can I turn?

KUEI [*warmly*]: Don't you worry, we've thought of something good
for you.

NIU: Something good for me?

KUEI: The Party secretary, the village head, and I worked it out
together. You'll be sent to the district center to be trained as a
midwife. When you finish the course, we'll set up a maternity
station here. You'll do nothing but deliver babies, and the village will take care of you and your husband.

NIU [*surprised but delighted*]: Oh, this can't be true!

KUEI: I've already arranged everything with Comrade Yang from
the district.

NIU: But I can't even read or write. How will I keep up with the
course?

KUEI: You've had lots of experience. You'll get along fine.

NIU: Aiya, how wonderful!

KUEI: But Aunt Niu, you must be sensible after this. You'll have
to put everything into your job.

NIU [*feelingly*]: Nobody's heart is made of stone, niece. You've
thought of everything for me. How can I fail to do my very best?
You're so good to me.

KUEI: It's not me. It's the government and the people.

NIU: Ah, but you're doing a lot, too.

KUEI: Listen to me, Aunt Niu. When people ask you to deliver a
baby, they're putting the lives of mother and child in your hands.
A slip may mean the loss of a life. I hear that you had several
babies yourself, but none of them lived. . . .

NIU [*sobbing*]: Ai. . . .

KUEI: I'm sorry, Aunt Niu.

NIU: I'm past forty, niece, but in the old days who could I tell my
troubles to? Do you know how I became a midwife? When I
was young, I gave birth to sons two years in succession. Both
times it was Granny Kuo who delivered my baby. I don't have to
tell you what I went through with her! Both babies died before
they were a month old. I made up my mind then that I was not

going to have Granny Kuo again, no matter what happened. When I was having my third baby, I didn't ask anyone in. I just gritted my teeth and managed everything myself. The news spread. People said I was good at delivering babies. When women here and in neighboring villages neared their time, they began to send for me. I muddled along and I've been muddling along ever since. . . . I must find out how it should be done now that I have this chance to get some training.

KUEI [gentle and considerate]: That's the spirit. If you learn right this time, it will be good for you and even better for the women of our village. Comrade Yang from the district said you are to go to the District Women's Federation tomorrow. She hasn't left the village yet. Perhaps she's gone to see you.

NIU: Really? In that case I must get back and see about refreshments for her.

KUEI: Never mind the refreshments; just talk to her. I'll take care of the papers you'll be needing to join the training class.

NIU: Good. [Takes a few steps towards the door, turns back again.] My bark is worse than my bite. Don't be angry about anything I've said.

KUEI: Of course I won't. Oh, the money! I still think you'd better take it. [Offers her the money.]

NIU: No. I've troubled you enough as it is. I won't touch it. No, no! [Hurries off.]

[KUEI-YUNG, holding the baby in her arms, notices the tiny socks scattered on the kang, picks one up and plays with the baby.]

KUEI: Look, Baby Pao, your papa's come home. What pretty colored socks he's brought you.

[MRS. WANG, panting, suddenly bursts in.]

MRS. WANG [toward door, in a tone full of annoyance]: Come quickly and get them mended.

KUEI [anxiously]: Has something happened?

MRS. WANG [plaintively]: Chiang went to look for you, and tore his pants crossing the fence.

[CHIANG enters. Bits of cotton padding are dangling from a big tear on his right trouser leg. He is fuming with rage. KUEI-YUNG immediately puts the baby down on the kang, hurries to him, and bends down with concern to examine his torn trousers.]

KUEI: I hope you haven't scratched your leg.

CHIANG [glares at KUEI-YUNG and remains sullenly silent] . . . .

199

KUEI [bringing out needle and thread]: Sit down on the kang; I'll
  mend it for you.
CHIANG [angrily shoving KUEI-YUNG to one side]: Get away from me.
KUEI [patiently]: What's the matter? Why are you acting like this
  as soon as you come home?
CHIANG [taking a step toward her menacingly]: Like what? It's a
  hell of a lot better than the way you're acting! What made you
  finally come back?
KUEI [ignoring his threatening tone and trying to speak gently]:
  Why shouldn't I come back? This is my home, isn't it? [Picks
  up the baby and gives him a kiss. In an affectionate tone to
  CHIANG.] Haven't you come home, too? [Solicitously.] Have you
  eaten?
MRS. WANG [coldly]: He's eaten. Why couldn't you come home
  earlier to attend to him?
KUEI [putting down the baby]: I'll boil you some water to drink.
  [Starts towards door.]
CHIANG [stormily]: Don't be so kind-hearted! What did I tell you
  before I left? You were to stay home and look after the house.
  A woman shouldn't be going out getting mixed up in all sorts of
  things. But you paid no attention.
KUEI [stooping to pick up the baby]: I only organized the women for
  spare-time work and learning to read and write. You don't expect
  me to stick in the house all day, do you?
MRS. WANG [unable to stay quiet]: You shouldn't talk like that.
  The old saying is right: "Men may roam the country, but wom-
  en should only travel round the stove." No wonder Chiang is
  angry.
KUEI: I can't travel round the stove all the time! When I've finished
  the household chores, why can't I go and do some studying?
CHIANG [strides up to KUEI and shouts]: Suppose you don't study,
  then what?
KUEI [clasping the baby closer to her and backing away from CHI-
  ANG]: Don't scare the baby.
MRS. WANG [to KUEI]: Must you two start bickering the minute you
  get together? The baby's not offending anybody. Why should he
  suffer with you? [Snatching the baby from KUEI, she takes him
  into the inner room.]
CHIANG: Now you listen to me. Starting from today, you're going
  to stay home. Unless I say so, don't you dare think of going

anywhere. In my house, there'll be no hens crowing at dawn or mares becoming battle-chargers.

KUEI: You can stop trying to bring back the old set of rules. I'm not a pig to be shut up in a sty whenever you give the word. If you try to trample me underfoot again, I'm not going to take it!

CHIANG: Why, you, you dirty shameless wench!

KUEI [*very earnest about it*]: How have I behaved shamelessly? I walk straight and I do what is right. What have I done for you to call me shameless?

CHIANG [*in a towering rage*]: Damn you, how dare you answer me back? I'll teach you a lesson, see if I don't! [*Looks around wildly for something to hit her with, finds nothing in the room, dashes through door on left.*]

[*KUEI-YUNG quickly bolts the door. CHIANG shouts outside and pounds on the door. MRS. WANG hurries in from the inner room.*]

MRS. WANG: What are you two up to now, what are you doing?

CHIANG [*offstage*]: Open up, open up I say!

KUEI: He wants to beat me.

MRS. WANG: Why must you offend him?

KUEI: Who's offending him? He's being unreasonable.

CHIANG [*offstage*]: I'll show you who I am! Open up, open up this minute! [*Ferociously kicking the door outside, sound of pounding and the handle of a whip knocking on the door. The bolt is gradually giving way.*]

KUEI [*a bit worried now*]: Don't kick the door down. I'll open it. [*Goes bravely to the door but is pulled away by MRS. WANG.*]

MRS. WANG: He'll have a stick in his hand. He's liable to smash things.

[*The bolt gives way with a crash. CHIANG bursts into the room with a horse whip in his hand. He tries to lash out at KUEI-YUNG but his mother holds him back.*]

MRS. WANG: Enough. You've had your row and she's given in. What good will raising lumps all over her do?

CHIANG: Who says she's given in? I say one word and she answers back with ten!

MRS. WANG: She may not say so, but in her heart she's given in. She knows you're the master of the house. She doesn't dare go against you. Come on now, give me that whip. [*Takes the whip out of CHIANG's hands, tosses it through the door on the left and turns to* KUEI-YUNG.] It's your cussedness that gets you into trouble all the time. The best swimmers are always the ones who get drowned and the best talkers are always the ones who get beaten up. There's no use trying to out-talk him. I was a young wife myself once. I never got anything out of arguing with my husband. You'd better just do what he tells you.

[KUEI-YUNG *realizes that it's no use trying to reason with them. She stands against the kang in one corner and keeps silent.*]

CHIANG [*lecturing her triumphantly*]: You don't think men like me let themselves be run by their women, do you? I told you one thing and you did the exact opposite. I told you to stay away from that women's association. But you had to take the lead in all their trouble-making! [*Pressing near* KUEI-YUNG *and shouting.*] Did you think I wasn't coming back?

KUEI [*indignantly*]: You're back now, but that doesn't mean you can do everything without any help. A man can't block out the sky with one hand. Ask anybody: is it a crime to attend literacy class and do women's welfare work? I haven't done badly with the work either. I not only sew and cook, I did the ploughing and weeding, too.

MRS. WANG: Tut, tut, Kuei-yung. You ploughed and weeded because you wanted to. Your husband didn't force you, and neither did I. A woman ought to act like a woman. Ploughing and weeding is a man's job. I don't like to see a woman out in the fields.

CHIANG [*to his mother*]: Stop wasting words on her. [*To his wife.*] You'd better get this straight. Don't think you can put on airs just because you gave a hand in the fields. That doesn't mean a thing to me. From now on you're not to do it, and I want you to resign from the women's association and the Youth League. If I catch you running around again, I'll break your legs!

KUEI: You wouldn't dare!

CHIANG: You'll see if I dare. Just try gadding about again.

MRS. WANG [*to* KUEI]: Aiya! Can't you stop goading him? He's in a temper already. Must you talk so much? You two act as if you're afraid life's getting too dull for me. [*To* CHIANG.] You've been away working for three months. Now that you're home, you ought to get some rest. You've had your quarrel; now forget it. [*Glances at* KUEI.] She'll have to give up this women's representative thing sooner or later. Must you make her admit defeat this minute? Let's all go to bed. [CHIANG *notices that* KUEI-YUNG *is silent, seats himself on the kang arrogantly and starts to unlace his boots.* MRS. WANG *turns to* KUEI-YUNG.] You should know his temper by now. Don't argue any more. It's getting late, time for bed.

CHIANG [*taking off his boots, to* KUEI]: Bring my slippers.

MRS. WANG: Where're his padded ones? Get them. [*While the mother and son watch her intently,* KUEI-YUNG *brings a pair of slippers from the chest and puts them beside* CHIANG's *feet. She looks around and takes up a wash basin.*]

KUEI: Want to wash your feet?

CHIANG: Yes!

[KUEI *goes out with the basin.*]

MRS. WANG [*in a whisper*]: Just give her a little scare so that she'll behave; that's enough. But don't you hit her!

CHIANG: If I don't act a little tough, she'll get even harder to handle.

MRS. WANG: I'm afraid you can't do anything just by force. Haven't you heard there's a Marriage Law now? The government won't let you beat her. There'd be what they call "divorce."

CHIANG [*a bit hesitant, ponders, then resolutely*]: She must obey the man who feeds her. I'm not going to pamper her.

MRS. WANG: We're a respectable family. Don't make a scene. All our neighbors will laugh at us.

[KUEI *enters.*]

KUEI: The basin's waiting for you in the next room. [CHIANG *goes out.* KUEI *picks up his boots, carefully takes out the felt socks and tucks them under the mat at one end of the kang.* CHIANG *finishes washing, comes in and sits on the kang.*]

MRS. WANG: Well, don't sit up and waste lamp oil. Go to bed. [*Goes into the inner room.*]

[CHIANG *sits back on the kang. His hands brush against the torn part of his trousers.*]

CHIANG [*looking at his wife and still rather resentful*]: Damn it, a nice pair of pants torn all because of you, you jinx!

KUEI [*checking her anger and walking over to her husband*]: Why do you treat me like this the minute you get back? What have I done wrong?

CHIANG: Don't play innocent. Did you obey my orders at all?

KUEI [*doing her best to say it gently*]: But maybe your orders weren't quite right. I'm leading the handicraft group, but after all I

203

also earned extra income for the family. I've learned a little in the literacy class and it'll come in handy. We're already using new farm implements, and the time is coming when we'll be using tractors. How will we work then, if we can't even read and write? Just look around. Everyone is studying. Everyone is trying to improve.

CHIANG: That's got nothing to do with you! Just because you can scribble a few lousy words is no reason for you to go rushing around making a fool of yourself. I suppose our home isn't good enough for you!

KUEI: How have I been making a fool of myself? You've only just come back. Why don't you find out what I've really been doing before you say things like that?

CHIANG: I've found out all I want to know. I saw through you long ago!

MRS. WANG [coming from the inner-room]: Time to go to bed! Quit your squabbling! [Goes up on the kang, takes down two quilts and begins to make up the bed.]

KUEI: Don't you bother, Ma. I'll do it soon.

MRS. WANG: No, I'll do it. Young people are so stubborn! [Finishes rolling out one quilt, starts on the other one but is interrupted by CHIANG.]

CHIANG: Don't make the bed for her. Why should you serve her?

MRS. WANG: Get away. I don't mind.

CHIANG [glares at his wife and turns to his mother]: I'm not going to let you! [Disarranges the quilt his mother has just spread.]
[MRS. WANG, pretending to be angry, gives him a light thump on the back.]

MRS. WANG: You're a big boy; don't act wild! [Waves him off and rolls out the quilts side by side. This done, she gets off the kang and goes back into her own room.] It's time you turned in. A little quarrel between husband and wife. There's nothing to get excited about. [Exit.]
[Silence. Then TSUI-LAN's voice is heard.]

LAN [offstage]: Kuei-yung, Kuei-yung, Aunt Niu wants you.

KUEI: Yes, I know, I'll be right over.

LAN [offstage]: Hurry up, will you!
[Her voice fades into the distance. MRS. WANG hurries in.]

MRS. WANG: She's the very devil! What's she trying to tempt you into now?

KUEI: Aunt Niu wants to see me.

MRS. WANG: Must you go? Haven't you offended enough people?

KUEI: I've arranged for her to study in the district center. I want her to reform.

CHIANG [*shouting*]: So you want to reform others! Who do you think you are? All the time I was away, you were all over the place, offending everyone in the village, mixing with all sorts of people! Stay home, do you hear! You're not going to stir a single step out of this house tonight!

KUEI [*ignoring him, picks up her scarf, drapes it over her head and ties it beneath her chin. Turning to* MRS. WANG]: Ma, I've talked it over with Aunt Niu. She wants to go and study midwifery. She's leaving tomorrow. I must write a letter of introduction for her and help her fill out some forms.

[CHIANG *immediately jumps off the kang, groping for his slippers with his feet.*]

CHIANG: Stop! Who said you could go? How dare you walk out just like that? We'll see who makes decisions in this family! [*Pulls* KUEI-YUNG *back roughly. She stumbles against the table.*] As if I can't handle the likes of you!

KUEI [*exploding*]: It's time you stopped acting the fool! I've put up with all your tantrums, but now you're keeping me from my duties. I won't stand for it.

MRS. WANG: Aiya! Kuei-yung, if he doesn't want you to go, don't go. Why must you cross him?

KUEI: This is my job. What right has he to stop me?

MRS. WANG: Never mind. Just consider that you've backed out of the whole business. You don't really want to bother about it.

KUEI: I've been doing this work because everyone's asked me to. I'm not going to quit halfway. [*Prepares to go.*]

[MRS. WANG *tries to stop her.* KUEI-YUNG *steps away from her.* CHIANG *dashes out and returns with the whip.*]

MRS. WANG: Don't you know an egg can't crush a stone? He's your husband; you belong to him. What's the use of your crossing him?

KUEI: Who belongs to him? I have my freedom. [*Walks with determination towards the door.*] Today I wouldn't let my own father treat me like this.

CHIANG: I'll have to show you what I'm like! [*Drags* KUEI *back and raises the whip.*]

[MRS. WANG *tugs frantically at his arm.* CHIANG *pushes his mother*

205

to one side and lashes out at KUEI *who steps agilely out of the way.* CHIANG *tries again but is again stopped by* MRS. WANG.]

MRS. WANG: Kuei-yung, hide in the next room! Don't stand here and wait for him to hit you!

KUEI: Let him! Even if he puts a knife to my neck, I'm not going to obey him.

CHIANG: I don't care if I go to jail for this. I'll teach you a thing or two about "freedom"!

MRS. WANG [*frantically*]: Aiya! Heaven! What are you two coming to?

[CHIANG *continues to swing the whip.* KUEI-YUNG *jumps on to the kang. The lash hits the window, tearing the paper panes.* KUEI *pulls the whip out of* CHIANG's *hands, breaks it into two and tosses the pieces to the ground.*]

MRS. WANG: Enough, enough. Don't forget you two are husband and wife!

KUEI: What kind of husband and wife are we? He swears at me and beats me whenever he feels like it. I haven't even the freedom to attend meetings and classes. Is a husband supposed to behave like that?

MRS. WANG: Everyone has his own temperament.

KUEI: What do you mean—temperament? Bullying a woman, hitting her—do you call that temperament? It's quite a few years since liberation now. He'll have to change whether he wants to or not.

CHIANG: I am what I am. I'll not let you have your way.

MRS. WANG [*apprehensive of worse things to happen, to* CHIANG]: No one would ever mistake you for a dumb mute. You can keep your mouth shut for a minute. [*Pushes him into the inner-room. Turns to* KUEI *in an affectionate tone.*] Stop arguing with him, Kuei-yung. This business of Aunt Niu's; if you must do it, do it tomorrow. It's too late tonight. Now that Chiang is home, you'd better quit the women's association. Have you ever seen an office-holder who doesn't have to offend people left and right? If things turn out well, you get nothing for it, but if things go wrong you get all the blame. Is it worth annoying your husband about? You've been living with us a couple of years. Ma knows you're proud and capable. You do very good work around the house. Ma hasn't a thing against you there. Today, let Ma tell you something straight from the heart.

KUEI: Go ahead, Ma. [*Jumps down from the kang, gets a towel and washes her face while she listens to* MRS. WANG.]

206

MRS. WANG [*sincerely*]: Ma's got one foot in the grave now, but she's seen a few strong-minded wives in her time. In the end, they're the ones who suffer. When I was young, I had to take plenty of blows from your father-in-law because I wasn't meek. Later on I resigned myself; I just let him have his way in everything. It was much simpler all around. Of course now there's been a liberation, but a woman's still a woman. She can't really be equal to a man. Kuei-yung, you've taken the wrong path, but you can always turn back. Don't go on being obstinate.

KUEI [*tossing her towel aside and speaking with feeling*]: Ma, I haven't taken the wrong path. It's you who can't get things straight. You spent half your life at your husband's beck and call. You took his curses and took his blows. If he knocked your teeth in, you'd have had to swallow them without a word. Think, Ma, think. Is that fair?

MRS. WANG [*has no answer*]: Ai, why bring all that up?

KUEI: That was in the old days when women didn't dare raise their heads, but how can you still think like that today? . . .

CHIANG [*tearing out of adjoining room*]: You get out of here. There's no place for you in my house. [*Comes close to* KUEI.] Get out! My house isn't good enough for you any more!

MRS. WANG [*tugging at* CHIANG]: What's all this?

CHIANG: I can't manage her. I'm not going to feed a woman who won't listen to me!

KUEI: Open your eyes and take a good look! I don't have to depend on you for my meals!

CHIANG: Get out or I'll throw you out! [*Snatches up* KUEI-YUNG'S *quilt from the kang and flings it toward the door. MRS. WANG brings it back.*]

MRS. WANG: Are you crazy?

CHIANG [*to his wife*]: You can leave right now. The way you're acting—don't think I'm going to let you stay in my house another day.

KUEI [*unable to stand it any longer, with determination*]: All right, you forced me into this. I won't stay where I'm not wanted. If you're sorry later, don't come looking for me! [*Jumps onto the kang, opens the chest, and starts searching through a flat box.*]

CHIANG [*a little worried*]: What are you doing with my title-deeds?

KUEI: We've got two title-deeds. One of them belongs to me. And one of the three rooms in this house is mine, too. The Communist

207

Party and the people's government gave them to me. My title-deed
I'll take along. I won't be using the room. I'll have it torn down!

MRS. WANG [*dumbfounded, goes to* KUEI-YUNG *on the kang and
tries to take the title-deed from her*]: Aiya, you can't do that! If
you don't care about him, what about me? You can't really leave
us! [*Takes the title-deed, puts it back into the flat box and closes
the chest.*]

KUEI: I've got two hands. Why should I be so spineless and hang
around here when I'm no longer wanted?

MRS: WANG: You don't mean it!

KUEI: The way he's treating me, I can't stay. [*To* CHIANG.] I'm your
wife, but I'm a person too, a free citizen of our country. I'm not
your ox or your mule. The days when women weren't human
beings are over. [*Turning back to the kang she takes up a quilt.*]

MRS. WANG: Why are you taking the quilt?

KUEI: I'll bundle up the baby and go. [*Jumps down from the kang
and hurries into the inner-room.*]

MRS. WANG [*in a frenzy, comes down from the kang and chides her
son*]: You, you're a real curse to me! You can't even tell which
way the wind's blowing. What have I been telling you? Today
when a woman goes, she takes her share of the land and the house.
My sister's daughter-in-law went off like that. They lost the
daughter-in-law and her property, too. You, oh you! What shall
we do? [*Hurries off in despair.*]

[CHIANG *begins to feel uneasy, paces around the room nervously,
occasionally peeping into the inner room through a slit in the
curtain.* MRS. WANG *comes rushing out of the room, bumps right
into* CHIANG *who backs away.*]

MRS. WANG: Blockhead! Why are you so dense? She's wrapping up
the baby. I tried to stop her but she won't listen to me. Hurry now,
go in and make up with her.

CHIANG [*unable to conquer his pride, dejectedly*]: I . . . I . . . heck!
[*Turns away from his mother and stands facing one wall.*]

MRS. WANG [*tugging at* CHIANG's *sleeves*]: This is no joke! If she
goes off with her share of the land and house, how will we manage? Her wings are strong and she's got a mind of her own. Once
she leaves the nest she won't come back!

CHIANG [*weakening but still putting up a bold front*]: I . . . I can't
apologize to her!

MRS. WANG [*worried*]: Must you be so pig-headed? Once she leaves
and the news gets around, it won't be so easy to get her home

again. Suppose she becomes interested in someone else? Do you want to be a bachelor again?

CHIANG: I . . . [*in despair*] I can't back down!

MRS. WANG [*helpless and sad*]: I suppose I just wasn't fated to keep a good daughter-in-law. [*Dabs at her eyes, then rushes back to* KUEI.]

LAN [*offstage*]: Kuei-yung, why didn't you go?

NIU [*offstage*]: I've come to you, Kuei-yung.

[MRS. WANG *comes on from door on right at the same time as* TSUI-LAN *and* AUNT NIU *enter from door on left.*]

MRS. WANG [*welcoming them like long lost friends*]: Aunt Niu, I'm so glad to see you! Please talk to them.

NIU: What's the matter with you people?

[KUEI-YUNG *comes on with the baby snugly wrapped in the quilt.* MRS. WANG *goes to her and takes the baby out of her arms.*]

MRS. WANG: I won't let you go. Here, give the baby to me. Talk it over with Aunt Niu. Let her say who's in the right.

KUEI: He refuses to talk sense. There's no use trying to reason with him.

NIU: What's all the excitement about?

[MRS. WANG *wants to explain but finds that she's not sure of where she stands now. Mumbles.*]

LAN [*taking the bull by the horns*]: Mrs. Wang, don't bother to explain. I can guess everything. It must be that Chiang is mad at Kuei-yung because she joined the literacy class and is doing women's work. As soon as he came home, he got tough to prove that he was still the boss. Right?

MRS. WANG [*turning on her*]: Tsui-lan! Don't think I want to blame you, but if you girls hadn't egged her on, Kuei-yung would never have become so worked up about women's welfare and we wouldn't have had such a terrible row.

KUEI: I've taken up this work because I want to. They had nothing to do with it. What's wrong with being a representative?

MRS. WANG [*emboldened by the sight of* AUNT NIU]: Kuei-yung, the old law says the smart ones judge things for themselves; only fools need a magistrate. Think of what you've been doing. Even if you are a representative, was it right not to help your Aunt Niu? Let's ask her.

LAN: Ask me! It's perfectly plain—

MRS. WANG [*cutting her short*]: You're biased. Let Aunt Niu be the

209

judge. [*To* NIU.] She's become a representative but she doesn't help you. Is that the right way to act?

NIU [*earnestly*]: Kuei-yung, don't you want to help me?

MRS. WANG: We're all here. Let everyone listen closely. [*To* AUNT NIU.] Go ahead, speak up. Your nephew is here. You can speak freely.

[CHIANG *and his mother look at* AUNT NIU *expectantly.*]

NIU [*turning to* KUEI]: Since you're helping me, you shouldn't stop halfway. I asked Tsui-lan to call you but you didn't come. Have you changed your mind?

MRS. WANG: What are you talking about?

NIU [*to* KUEI]: Comrade Yang is waiting for you at my place. She wants you to fill out my papers so that she can take them with her. What's keeping you? You're chairman of the women's association. When you promise something, you're supposed to do it!

[*The whole thing suddenly dawns on* MRS. WANG. *Extremely embarrassed, she hurries off with the baby.*]

KUEI: Aunt Niu, it's not that I don't keep my word. I was coming to fix your papers, but he [*Pointing to* CHIANG.] wouldn't let me leave the house. When I tried to reason with him, he took a whip to me. He insists that I leave the women's association. Because I don't agree, he wants to drive me out of the house. What do you think of that?

NIU [*turning quickly to* CHIANG]: So it was you who wouldn't let her come. You want to spoil things for me, eh? [*With righteous indignation.*] Let me tell you, Wang Chiang, I understand things much better now. If you won't let her do this you are—you are— [*Can't think of the right words, looks to* TSUI-LAN *for help.*]

LAN [*finishing for her*]: You are violating the rights of women!

NIU: That's it. You are violating the rights of women, and I won't stand for it!

LAN: How can you be so wicked? Beating her the minute you come home! Kuei-yung's been elected the women's representative. What harm does that do you? All of us elected her. How dare you try to force her to resign! Not only do you beat her—you want to throw her out as well! You're nothing but a brute!

NIU: Kuei-yung, you're our chairman. We need you. Don't let him get away with this. Hit you, did he? Well, you just stand right up to him. [*Gets more and more indignant.*] If he dares to lay so much as a finger on you again, we'll make him pay for it with his head!

210

LAN [*walks across to the kang, and picks up the broken whip handle. To* CHIANG *indignantly*]: Wang Chiang, you're a tyrant. What right have you to use a whip on a woman?
[Mrs. WANG *enters, without the baby.* KUEI-YUNG *produces two account books and a bunch of keys.*]

KUEI [*to* CHIANG]: I'm not going to leave things in a muddle. You'll find our family budget worked out in these. I haven't spent a single cent without reason or been idle a single day. Take a good look! [*Places the account books and keys on the edge of the kang near* CHIANG. *Adjusts her head-kerchief and goes into inner-room.*]

Mrs. WANG [*again in a flutter*]: She's gone to get the baby. I can't let her go! [*Goes after* KUEI *but turns back after a few steps. To* AUNT NIU.] Please, Aunt Niu, see if you can talk her around. [*Pulling* AUNT NIU *with her,* Mrs. WANG *goes in.*]

LAN [*holding the broken whip. In a loud voice to those in the next room*]: Kuei-yung, don't leave yet. I'm going for the welfare officer. [*Goes toward the door on the left.*]
[Mrs. WANG *dashes out from the other door and stops her.*]

Mrs. WANG: Don't go stirring everyone up, Tsui-lan!

LAN: There's no telling when he'll decide to beat her again.

Mrs. WANG: He didn't put a mark on her.

LAN: Piffle.

Mrs. WANG: If you don't believe me, ask her yourself.

LAN: I don't have to. Just look at this whip.

Mrs. WANG: Kuei-yung snapped it with her own hands.

LAN: You're biased. I don't believe you.

Mrs. WANG: Tsui-lan, you don't think I'd lie to you.

LAN: He's beaten her before.

Mrs. WANG: He was wrong then.

LAN: What about now? Wasn't he wrong this time, too?

Mrs. WANG: Yes, of course, very, very wrong. Tsui-lan, please go in and persuade Kuei-yung to stay. [*Takes the whip out of* TSUI-LAN'S *hands and throws it down. Pushes her into the inner room and is about to follow.*]

CHIANG [*holding one of the account books in his hands*]: Ma . . . .

Mrs. WANG [*turning to him*]: Yes?

CHIANG: Did she work out the budget all by herself?

Mrs. WANG: Yes. She'd never have had the nerve to try it if she hadn't learned to read and figure. [*Goes into the inner-room.*]

CHIANG [*to himself*]: When I left, she couldn't even write a simple account slip for the mutual-aid team. [*Alone in the room, he thumbs through the account books. The expression on his face changes from surprise to respect and finally, uneasiness. He looks at his hands and sits down, dejectedly on the kang.*] [*Outside, a dog barks.* YU-CHEN, *the carter, is heard offstage,* "To WANG CHIANG's *place . . . . Hold your dog . . . oh, the women's chairman . . . ."* TSUI-LAN *hurries out of the inner room, followed by* MRS. WANG.]

LAN [*calls through window*]: Put it in the courtyard.

MRS. WANG: Who is it? Who is it?

LAN: It's Yu-chen, bringing your things.

MRS. WANG: What things?

LAN: You'll know in a minute. Come with me.

[TSUI-LAN *and* MRS. WANG *exit through the door on the left.* AUNT NIU *comes on from the next room, goes to* CHIANG.]

NIU: You know how I like to chatter, nephew. Don't be offended if I seem to scold you. You're very lucky to have a wife like Kuei-yung, so good and capable. But still you're not satisfied! Ever since she became the women's chairman, there's not one of us who isn't all for her. She does such a good job. How can you treat her so badly?

CHIANG [*slowly lifting his head*]: Weren't you dissatisfied with her, too?

NIU: She works for us women and she's done so much to help me; I don't know how I can thank her enough! It's you I'm dissatisfied with. You wouldn't let her come to me.

CHIANG [*mumbling*]: From what you said before, I got the idea that you were a little annoyed with her.

NIU: That's because I was upset over a small personal problem. People have sharp eyes these days, I can tell you. Kuei-yung would never have been elected representative if she weren't a fine woman. Why do you want to beat her? Let me hear!

CHIANG: I . . . I . . . she just galled me.

NIU: What do you mean, galled you? There's something wrong with you—imagining all sorts of nonsense. How has she wronged you? [MRS. WANG *comes in with a piece of pork, a package of noodles, and a pair of felt slippers in her hands. Her sleeves and the front of her jacket are sprinkled with flour. She turns to her son as she enters.*]

MRS. WANG: Quick, go to the door and bring in that sack of flour. Tsui-lan is trying to carry it.

CHIANG [*takes a few steps towards the door, stops*]: Where did the flour come from?

MRS. WANG [*in a low voice as if to remind him*]: Kuei-yung bought it. She and the girls made straw sacks and sold them to the co-op. She bought a lot of things with her share of the money. Go and bring them in. [CHIANG *looks shamefaced. His mother pushes him towards door. In his pride, he refuses to budge.* MRS. WANG *places her armful of things on the table, and in a loud ingratiating voice to the door on the right.*] Yu-chen has brought all the things you asked for and Chiang is bringing them in. There's sixteen yuan left. I'll give it to you in a minute. [*Turning her head, she discovers that* CHIANG *is still standing there, gives him an impatient nudge.*] Why don't you go and help bring the things in?

[CHIANG *remains where he is. Meanwhile* TSUI-LAN *enters, carrying a sack of flour on her shoulder and a package of insecticide and two thick notebooks in her hand. She puts the sack on the ground and the other things on the table. While* MRS. WANG *busies herself dusting the flour off* TSUI-LAN's *jacket, the girl turns to* CHIANG.]

LAN [*pointing to the things on the table*]: Just look at the things Kuei-yung got for your homecoming. Pork, noodles, fine flour, and here are slippers for Mrs. Wang and insecticide for the wheat field. She's used the money she earned by hard work to buy provisions for the whole family. She's so considerate of you, but you only want to tie her down, to beat her. Ask yourself honestly, is that the way to treat a wife? [CHIANG *stands in silence with bowed head.*] Kuei-yung worked hard for your family and for all of us while you were away. Nothing was too much trouble for her. And in the evenings she often went without sleep rather than fall behind in her studies. Why, she can read the newspaper now! She tried so hard. But now that you're back, you haven't even a kind word for her, not even a smile. Instead, you beat her. How can you be so cruel? [MRS. WANG *is moved by* TSUI-LAN's *words. She urges* AUNT NIU *to go inside and talk to* KUEI-YUNG. AUNT NIU *goes.* MRS. WANG *remains where she is. But she is extremely uneasy, and keeps glancing towards the inner room.*] You forbid her to go out. You threaten to break her legs. Don't you know that she's the representative elected by all the women in the village? If she doesn't go to meetings and manage things, do you think people will keep working so well on their spare-time jobs? If she stays away from literacy class herself, how can she get others

213

to take an interest in learning? It's bad enough that you're backward yourself without standing in the way of someone else's progress. You're trying to make your wife backward, too. Aren't you afraid that people will laugh at you? Kuei-yung's a thoughtful woman. She knew that you've been working hard the past three months and that you must be tired. So when you came home she humored you all she could. But nothing pleased you. You treated her worse and worse. How far do you think you can force her? [Mrs. WANG picks up the broken whip.]

Mrs. WANG [trying to clear herself in TSUI-LAN's eyes]: Don't say any more to him, Tsui-lan. [Raising her voice.] Let me square things for Kuei-yung. [Strikes her son with the whip handle.] Don't you dare beat her again, do you hear; don't you dare!

LAN [stopping her]: You can't do that. It's against the law.

Mrs. WANG: Just a few cuts to clear that thick brain of his. Now he'll remember your words. [Tosses away the whip. Beseechingly.] Please talk to Kuei-yung. Ask her to cool off and stay with us.

LAN [to CHIANG]: Then you don't want to drive her out any more? [Ashamed, CHIANG hangs his head in silence.] Come on, say something! A nod for yes or a shake for no. If you want her to stay, just nod. [Embarrassed, CHIANG remains motionless.] Unless you nod, I'm not going to go and plead your case.

Mrs. WANG: He's nodding, he's nodding!

LAN: I didn't see it.

Mrs. WANG: I did—very plainly. Hurry, go in and talk to her.

[TSIU-LAN does not stir. AUNT NIU enters from door on the right.]

NIU: Tsui-lan, Kuei-yung is filling out my papers. She wants to borrow your fountain pen.

[TSUI-LAN unclips her fountain pen, hands it to AUNT NIU who goes back into the other room.]

LAN: Anyway his nod alone doesn't solve anything. It takes two parties to make a contract. Maybe she doesn't agree. [Takes two steps toward the inner room, then turns back suddenly.] Mrs. Wang, I have to ask you something.

Mrs. WANG: Me?

LAN: Today, when we were short of rice straw, you had plenty but wouldn't sell it to us. Rather use it for the stove, you said. Aren't you afraid people will say you're mean? Do you want to cut yourself off from everybody?

Mrs. WANG [in an aggrieved tone]: Aiya, Tsui-lan, I'm not as bad as

214

all that. It's just that I was thinking . . . . [*Too ashamed to utter the truth. A pause and finally.*] I was thinking . . . ai! . . . I was all mixed up. I thought if family questions were decided by the daughter-in-law, where would the mother-in-law stand? That was why I wouldn't let her sell the straw.

LAN: Then you were undemocratic. Trying to ride roughshod over people! Confess now, wasn't her idea a good one?

MRS. WANG: Yes, yes. She was quite right. And I was wrong.

LAN: In the future you should talk such things over first, and consider other people's ideas, too. [*Exit.*]

[*Mother and son stare at each other. There is a long silence.*]

CHIANG [*his eyes on the things KUEI-YUNG bought. Speaks slowly*]: Ma, tell me, did she . . . .

MRS. WANG: Did she what?

CHIANG: Did she think of buying these things herself?

MRS. WANG: Of course. It's all your fault. You're too hasty.

CHIANG: I was afraid she was getting flighty. But she cares for the family more than ever. [*His eyes move from the whip on the ground to the torn paper on the windows and light on the broken whip handle. Notices the cake of soap and the stockings on the ground, hastily picks them up, blows off the dust and carefully tucks them into his pocket.*]

[*AUNT NIU comes on with a letter in her hand followed by KUEI-YUNG who this time has left the baby inside.*]

NIU [*talking as she enters*]: Don't worry about me, niece. All kinds of quacks got by in the old days, but today you really have to know something. I'll work hard at this training.

MRS. WANG: Papers all filled out?

NIU: Yes. I'll be starting tomorrow. Mrs. Wang, let me offer you some advice before I go. You're too old-fashioned. You ought to ask your daughter-in-law about these new things more. Your old mossback ways won't do, you know.

MRS. WANG: I think I've learned my lesson.

NIU [*to CHIANG*]: Nephew, remember what I told you. [*Gets ready to leave.*]

MRS. WANG: Don't go yet, Aunt Niu. Won't you help talk to . . . . [*Indicates KUEI.*]

LAN [*quickly interjects*]: Aunt Niu, let's go together. [*Turning to KUEI.*] We must be leaving, Kuei-yung. It's getting late. The one who's wrong knows it in his heart. Let him think things over and act accordingly. [*Goes off with* AUNT NIU *in spite of* MRS. WANG'S *efforts to keep them.*]

MRS. WANG [*loudly to the departing guests*]: Everything's all right now in our family. Please say nothing about what's happened. [*Walks uneasily to* KUEI-YUNG. *Shamefacedly.*] Don't be upset any more. Pay no attention to that blockhead. Ma's treated you badly too sometimes. That's because Ma's an old fool. Forget what's happened. In the future, do what you think right. [*To* CHIANG.] Tomorrow, don't forget to send all our straw to the weaving group. [*Takes out some money and hands it to* KUEI.] This sixteen yuan is what's left of your money for the sacks. Here's the list of things you gave Yu-chen to buy. [KUEI *takes the list, gives it a cursory glance, and puts it down.*] It's getting late! [*Goes up on the kang and once more rolls out the quilts.*] You two go to bed.

[*Turns and starts to go to her room.*]

[KUEI-YUNG *picks up the felt slippers.*]

KUEI: Ma! [MRS. WANG *turns back.*] You once said padded shoes aren't warm enough. I bought these for you. [*Gives her the slippers.*]

MRS. WANG [*taking the slippers, very moved. Tears come to her eyes*]: Ah! [*Gazes at* KUEI-YUNG, *unable to speak. After a pause, she wipes her tears with the hem of her padded tunic. Walks slowly into her own room.*]

[KUEI-YUNG *stands facing one wall. For a long time she is silent.* CHIANG *slowly approaches until he is standing behind her.* TSUI-LAN, *still uneasy about the couple, puts her head in the door on the left, then disappears. Tongue-tied,* CHIANG *quietly retraces his steps.*]

CHIANG [*looking at the quilts*]: You sleep near the fire; it's warmer on that side. [KUEI-YUNG *makes no reply. His words hang in awkward silence. Slowly,* CHIANG *takes a roll of money out of his pocket, offers it to* KUEI. TSUI-LAN *again pokes her head in at the door.*] Here, take all the money. From now on you manage things in the family. Your word will be final.

KUEI [*earnestly*]: Why should my word be "final"? I don't want to lord it over anyone. I'm not going to turn around and treat you the way you treated me. We both want things to go well in the family, to have a happy life. Why can't we decide problems by talking them over together? You learn to be democratic, too.

CHIANG: I'm all for that. But you take the money anyhow. You can

read and write now but you have no fountain pen. Even Tsui-lan
has got one. Take this and buy yourself a fountain pen.

KUEI [pointing to the money on the table]: I have enough here. You
don't have to give me any more.

CHIANG [finds it hard to withdraw his outstretched hand]: Never
mind the expense. Get yourself a really good pen.

[TSUI-LAN again peeps in. She signals to KUEI-YUNG who does not
see her. TSUI-LAN can no longer control her giggles. She laughs.
CHIANG and KUEI are startled. CHIANG is greatly embarrassed. The
money falls from his hand.]

CHIANG [abashed]: You, you're still here?

LAN [smiling teasingly]: This time I really must go. [Withdraws her
head from the doorway. Her footsteps are heard fading into the
distance.]

CHIANG [suddenly shouts uneasily toward the door]: Tsui-lan, Tsui-
lan!

LAN [again poking her head in and in a serious tone]: What do you
want?

CHIANG [looking embarrassed, glances at KUEI and then at LAN]:
When you get home . . . .

LAN: Yes?

CHIANG [shamefaced, in a low voice]: When you get home, please
keep things to yourself. Don't talk about . . . .

LAN: Oh, that's all right. I'll keep my tongue in check and you hold
on to your temper. But if you ever let go again, don't blame me
if I let go, too. Everything depends on you.

[CHIANG listens with bowed head as TSUI-LAN's footsteps echo into
the distance. He is still not reassured. Goes out of the door on the
left for a final inspection, returns and closes the door. He discovers
that the bolt is broken. Glances at KUEI-YUNG.]

CHIANG [to himself, more or less ashamed]: The door is coming to
pieces. I'll have to repair it tomorrow. No, we'll get a new one.
[Bending down, he picks up the roll of money and hands it to
KUEI.] You take care of the family's money. Everyone in the
village is for you. How can I be different? It's time you took a
turn at running the family.

KUEI: That's silly. [Picking up the money on the table.] We'll do the
work. Let Ma take care of the money. [Hands the money to
CHIANG. He ponders a moment, then cheerfully takes the money
to the inner-room. KUEI-YUNG goes up on the kang, brings out the

217

flat box from the chest. *She is rummaging for something when* CHIANG *comes back.*]

CHIANG [*alarmed*]: What are you looking for?

KUEI: Some paper to mend the windows with.

[CHIANG *breathes a sigh of relief.* KUEI-YUNG *notices* CHIANG's *torn trousers. Brings a pair of new cotton-padded trousers out of the chest.*]

KUEI: I finished these a few days ago. You can wear them tomorrow.

CHIANG [*accepts the trousers. Takes out the scented soap and stockings from his pocket and presents them to* KUEI]: I bought these for you.

[KUEI-YUNG *takes them.* MRS. WANG, *trying out her new slippers, walks in.*]

MRS. WANG: Kuei-yung, the slippers fit beautifully.

KUEI [*repressing a little smile*]: That's fine, Ma.

MRS. WANG [*feeling herself in the way*]: Oh . . . uh . . . I must be getting to bed. [*Goes back into her room.*]

KUEI [*watches* MRS. WANG *retire, turns to* CHIANG]:
We mustn't ever quarrel like that again.

CHIANG: It was my fault, not yours. From now on, I won't stand in your way.

Curtain

YESTERDAY*

(A Comic Dialogue)

By Chao Chung, Chang Pao-hua and Chung Yi-ping

Translated by Sidney Shapiro

A: It's been ages since we met.

B: It certainly has.

A: Why haven't you come around to the house to see us?

B: Who's got time!

A: My paternal uncle mentions you a lot.

B: Your paternal uncle?

A: My father's brother, that is.

B: Everybody knows that! But where did you get a paternal uncle, all of a sudden?

A: You met him when you were a kid. Don't you remember?

B: Oh. But how come I didn't see him the last time I went to your house?

A: He's been in the hospital all this while.

B: Then I really must visit the old fellow. What was wrong with him?

A: Off his rocker.

B: I'm not going! He's liable to hit me!

A: He's cured now!

B: What made him go crazy?

A: Ah, don't ask. It happened back in '48, before liberation. My aunt and uncle were both living in the country.

B: Oh, peasants.

A: He was a landlord's hired hand. Not enough to eat, not enough to wear, beaten and pushed around all the time—my uncle just

*Reprinted from *Chinese Literature* (April, 1961), pp. 127–139.

219

couldn't take it any more. He came to Peking and looked up my father.

B: Oh! And how was your family getting along then?

A: Getting along? My pa and ma were both sick.

B: Everything depended on you.

A: I was still very young.

B: What did you do?

A: We pawned what we had for food. Soon there was nothing left to pawn, nothing left to sell. As if that weren't enough, my uncle came.

B: He'd better find a job.

A: So much unemployment, where was a poor man going to look for work?

B: Why not become a peddler?

A: No capital.

B: He could have borrowed a little money?

A: Borrow? Poor men didn't have any rich friends. H. H. Kung, T. V. Sung—they were rolling in wealth. Did you have any contact with them?

B: We never met.

A: In the big compound where we lived, we had several neighbors. But which could we touch for a loan? The man in the east wing was a scissors-grinder.

B: You couldn't borrow from him.

A: In the south wing was a merchant.

B: Ah, the very man.

A: He wasn't a very big merchant.

B: What was his line?

A: Selling ear cleaners.

B: Much too small!

A: In the west wing was a college graduate, a young fellow named Wang. But we couldn't borrow from him.

B: A college graduate should have had a good job.

A: He sold farmers almanacs for a living.

B: A college graduate sold almanacs?

A: The only rich person in our compound was the landlady.

B: You could have gone to her for a little money.

A: My uncle did. She understood the minute she saw him, "What's wrong? Need money? There's nothing to worry about. First take a hundred thousand. If that's not enough, come back for more."

B: What a nice woman!

A: "Five-part interest."

B: You had to pay interest, too? Five for every hundred? That's five thousand yuan.

A: Not five thousand. Fifty thousand. Five for every ten.

B: A devil of a debt!

A: My uncle took the money and counted it. "Excuse me, land-lady," he said. "I'm borrowing a hundred thousand. There's only fifty thousand here." "That's right," she said. "I've deducted the first month's interest."

B: She collected the interest in alvance?

A: Holding the money, my uncle felt very bad. "What else can you do in times like these?" he said to himself. But the more he thought about it, the less he liked it. "With the interest so high, how will I ever be able to repay when the debt becomes due?" he wondered. So a few minutes later he gave the money back to the landlady. Very pleased, she complimented him. "You're the kind of borrower I like," she said. "You've only just taken the loan and here you are already with next month's interest."

B: What!

A: "A hundred thousand gone before I've even turned around?" cried my uncle. Wang, the college graduate, came over to our room and said to my uncle, "How can you borrow from the landlady? Her son is known as the neighborhood emperor. No one dares rub him the wrong way. What can one do in times like this? Although I'm a college graduate, I have to peddle al-manacs for a living. Not long ago I sold my things and bought a rickshaw to try and earn some money as a puller. After two days of hauling fares I started to spit blood. Uncle, why don't you go out with the rickshaw and see what you can do?" My uncle was very moved. "It's only the poor who help the poor."

B: There really are good men in this world.

A: He had no experience as a puller, so he wandered through the quiet lanes, but he couldn't find a fare. At last he saw in the distance someone carrying a sack, all in a sweat and looking around. My uncle ran up to him with the rickshaw, "Ride, sir?" he just started to say, when he saw what the fellow was doing—picking coal out of a cinder heap!

B: How could he afford to ride!

A: After my uncle wandered around all morning without finding

221

a fare, his stomach was growling with hunger. So he spent five hundred and bought a muffin.

B: Five hundred yuan for an ordinary muffin?

A: The Kuomintang "gold" yuan weren't worth the paper they were printed on. My uncle didn't have the heart to finish the muffin all at one go. So he ate half and put the rest in his pocket. Then he came to Legation Street. He was just resting the shafts of his rickshaw when some foreign patrolmen and Kuomintang cops all descended on him. "Is this the place for the likes of you? Eh? Just look at you. These tall buildings are where the foreigners live. They all have automobiles when they want to go anywhere. Who would ride in your rickshaw? Are you trying to get us into trouble?" Crash! With one stroke of the club, a cop broke his mudguard. My uncle picked up his rickshaw and ran.

B: A good thing he did. Otherwise, they'd have beaten him up.

A: By then it was getting dark. He knew that at home we'd had nothing to eat all day.

B: At least he could buy a little flour.

A: He came to a flour shop and parked his rickshaw by the side. Counting off the price of three catties, he went into the shop and said, "Three catties of flour, please." The proprietor looked at his money and asked, "Are you crazy? Who's going to give you three catties for the price of two?" "But this is what three catties cost." "The price has gone up."

B: It certainly rose fast. So he took the two catties?

A: "Where's your sack?" asked the proprietor. Not having a sack, my uncle went out to the rickshaw and got a couple of sheets of newspaper from the box. "All right. Give me my two catties," "What do you mean two? One!"

B: Wasn't he paying for two catties?

A: In the time he went for the paper, the price had gone up again.

B: It rose again?

A: My uncle said, "How could the price go up so fast?" "Cut the chatter. Do you want the flour or not? Better take it now before it goes any higher."

B: What!

A: My uncle decided—buy! Otherwise this little bit of money would soon give him only enough flour for a bowl of paste. He paid the proprietor and came out of the shop, carrying his flour. Across the street, a wounded soldier, walking with crutches and clutching a medicine bottle, rushed over and bumped into him.

222

B: Deliberately!

A: The soldier dropped his medicine bottle to the ground. Crash, and it was broken. "Why don't you look where you're going? You broke my medicine bottle. That's imported American stuff I need for my injections! Sloppymycin . . . ."

B: What?

A: Sloppy—ah, he didn't know himself.

B: An outright swindler!

A: "Pay me!" He grabbed for the flour. My uncle said, "Captain, I can't give you this. . . ." "What do you mean you can't? It's mine!"

B: A fine wounded veteran!

A: My uncle burst into tears. A man standing on the side said, "It's just your tough luck, old man. Those wounded soldiers, no one dares cross them. You'd better remember—the next time you see a soldier, get out of his way!" "Open robbery," cried my uncle, "and no one does anything about it! Isn't there any place I can get justice?" Before he could say another word, someone clapped a hand over his mouth and hissed, "It's forbidden to discusss national affairs!"

B: They didn't even let you talk then!

A: My uncle turned round for another look [startled]—

B: What happened?

A: His rickshaw had disappeared.

B: What a day he'd had!

A: He sat down on a step, his eyes staring straight ahead. He was speechless.

B: Overcome with troubles.

A: His nerves had snapped.

B: Driven mad!

A: How could we cure him in those days? We could only let him roam the streets. Only after liberation were we able to get him into the Hospital for Mental Diseases.

B: His ailment must have been serious.

A: He'd lost his reason completely. He stayed alone in his room, afraid to meet people. If anyone came near him, he got worse.

B: He'd been tormented too much.

A: In the hospital, they did everything to cure him. Recently, they tried a new method and succeeded; suddenly his mind became clear. "What am I doing here? Did that wounded soldier beat me up? How was I brought to a hospital?"

223

B: He was thinking quite rationally now.

A: "When did I get here? Yesterday?"

B: Yesterday?

A: He'd lost track of time. "It must have been yesterday. What a fancy hospital! A day here must cost a lot of money." Just then a nurse came in with his lunch. [*Imitating a nurse tiptoeing into the room.*]

B: Why walk like that?

A: You see, he was afraid to meet people. The nurse put his lunch down and was leaving when my uncle said, "I don't want lunch, doctor, I'm better. I must be going." When the nurse heard him talking so sensibly, she ran out, delighted. In a few minutes the hospital superintendent, the doctor, the head nurse and the medical director all came. "Why aren't you eating your lunch, grandpa?" said the superintendent. "Oh . . . I don't want this. I've still got half a muffin."

B: He hadn't forgotten that muffin!

A: "Doctor, who brought me here yesterday?"

B: Still talking about yesterday!

A: Everyone laughed. "It wasn't yesterday, grandpa," said the superintendent. "You've been here ten years." My uncle was startled. "What! Ten years?" "Yes. And now, thanks to injections, medicine, acupuncture, electrotherapy, and the treatment of Western type and traditional Chinese doctors, you've been cured at last." My uncle thought to himself, "Trying to saddle me with a load of phony charges!"

B: He thought the hospital was padding the bill.

A: "Doctor, I'm a poor man." "Don't worry, grandpa," said the superintendent. "Here in this hospital you get treatment free of charge. Stay and rest a few more days. See you later." And they all walked out. The more my uncle thought, the more puzzled he became. "Free of charge? Never heard of such a thing. When the time comes, they'll add everything to the bill. I'll have to go to the neighborhood emperor for another loan. No, there's only one thing to do. I'll make a run for it!" He slipped out.

B: Did he still know his way home?

A: Chienmen Gate was right outside the hospital. He started through it, but didn't dare go any further.

B: What was the matter?

A: "This can't be Tien An Men! Is it or isn't it? [*Asks B.*] Is it?"

B: Don't ask me!

224

A: A little boy wearing the red scarf of the Young Pioneers came along and my uncle stopped him. "I say, young master!"

B: Young master?

A: "Is this Tien An Men?" "It certainly is, grandpa," the boy said. "So the foreigners have put up these fine buildings and laid out these beautiful gardens," my uncle mused.

B: Foreigners?

A: "They weren't built by foreigners, grandpa, we built them ourselves." "Who's we?" "Why all of us. You have a share in it too." "Me? Where would I get the money to build such mansions?"

B: Oh!

A: The child said, "See, there's the Monument to the People's Heroes, and that's where the deputies to the People's Congress meet. . . ." "People's Congress?" "Of course. The place where we people conduct the affairs of our nation—" My uncle clapped a hand over the boy's mouth. "Shhh. It's forbidden to discuss national affairs!"

B: The old Kuomintang prohibition!

A: The youngster laughed. "We must understand our national affairs, grandpa, in order to—" "Hush. Go away. Move on, quickly!" The boy raised his hand over his head in a Pioneer salute and said, "Goodbye." My uncle nearly jumped out of his skin. "That kid wanted to hit me!"

B: Why did he scare so easily?

A: We all were very worried after he ran away.

B: How come?

A: The hospital called up our house and said that my uncle was cured, so I rushed down in a taxi. But when I got there, they said he had run off alone. They were out searching for him, and I started to search, too.

B: How did you find him?

A: It was easy. He was the only man at Tien An Men in pajamas. I spotted him immediately. I got out of the cab and walked up to him. "Do you remember me, Uncle?" "Iron Egg!" he cried.

B: Your nickname as a kid!

A: "You are Iron Egg, aren't you?" "That's right, I'm Iron Egg," I answered. "There's something wrong here. How did you get so tall in one day?" he asked.

B: I never heard of such a thing!

A: I said, "Let's go home and I'll tell you all about it. Get into the car." "What! We're going to ride in an automobile?"

B: Was that such a novelty?

A: Who could afford taxis in the old days? I said, "Please get into the car." I pushed him in. He sat there, very uneasy. "Are you sure we can ride in this contraption?" he asked. I said, "Anyone can ride in a car nowadays." "Then how do the rickshaw pullers earn a living?"

B: He hadn't forgotten pulling a rickshaw.

A: I said, "We don't have any more rickshaw pullers." "Aiya! they've all become beggars?" he asked. The taxi driver put in a word. "I used to be a rickshaw puller myself."

B: See, and he'd become a taxi driver.

A: My uncle kept getting more and more puzzled. When the taxi reached our door, the driver helped him into our courtyard. My uncle thanked him. "It's very good of you, brother. But don't bother about me. Get back before someone swipes your car!"

B: Who would do such a thing?

A: At the door of our flat, my uncle hesitated.

A: Didn't he recognize it?

A: Hard to say. Our place was very different before. After the liberation we moved into the north wing, where the landlady used to live. Three rooms facing south, spacious and sunny, and we'd bought a lot of new furniture.

B: Quite a change.

A: My uncle stared when we went inside, then asked, "What are we doing here?" I said, "This is our home." "Our home? But aren't you on the kang practically the minute you step in the door?" he asked.

B: He was thinking of the tiny room where the kang took up almost all the space.

A: I said, "Don't you remember? This is where the landlady used to live." My uncle got angry. "Have you become the neighborhood emperor?" he asked. "Out with it. How did you get so rich?"

B: Rich?

A: "Now listen to me," he said. "We may be poor, but we can't do bad things and hurt people." "Uncle," I said, "you're still thinking of the time when we had nothing to eat." "How can I forget," he said . . . .

226

B: That was years ago.

A: "It was only yesterday."

B: Still yesterday!

A: "Uncle," I said, "you've been in the hospital ten years." "Ten years?" he said. "Things couldn't change so much even in twenty." "It will take a little time to make clear to you everything that's happened in the past ten years, Uncle," I said. "As to that neighborhood emperor, he's long since gone to a court of law." "All the more reason why we can't afford to cross him," he insisted. "Hah!" I said. "He's been put under control." "What!" said my uncle. "Are there people who dare to control emperors?" "We all have jobs now," I said. "My aunt, back in the village, has entered a Home of Respect for the Aged. She's very happy." "My wife, happy?" he retorted. "Am I dreaming?"

B: It's all real.

A: "You're not dreaming," I said. As we were talking, Mr. Wang, the college graduate, came in. "How wonderful, Uncle," he said. "You're out of the hospital! Do you remember me?" "Oh, Mr. Wang," my uncle cried. "A thousand apologies!"

B: Why?

A: "I've lost your rickshaw!" Wang laughed. "Forget it. That's ancient history. We're all doing well now. Take me—I'm in the Construction Bureau." "You mean you're selling your farmers almanacs there?"

B: Hah!

A: "Why don't you go out and show your uncle around a bit?" suggested Wang. I thought, "That's a good idea. I'll take the old boy out for a stroll." Then I remembered. "You'd better put some regular clothes on!"

B: He was still in his pajamas!

A: After he changed, I said, "You'd better take some money." "What for? I won't be able to buy anything with it." "Take a little along for convenience, sake." "All right. Give me two thousand yuan for the time being."

B: Two thousand!

A: "Here's ten." "Ten? A plain muffin costs five hundred!" "This isn't the Kuomintang's 'gold' yuan, Uncle. Take it."

B: Today we have real money.

A: We got to the shopping district on Wangfuching Street and were just about to cross when my uncle pulled back. "Here

227

comes a cop!" "But he's a people's policeman," I said. "A cop's a cop, and he's carrying a club!"

B: That was his traffic baton!

A: I said, "You see, Uncle. He's helping that old lady across the street and he's carrying her packages. Isn't that nice?" "Must be his mother!" said my uncle.

B: Our people's police are the same to everyone!

A: When we reached the State Department Store, my uncle looked at it in amazement. "What a business they're doing! Iron Egg, what company owns this?" I said, "It belongs to all of us."

B: That's right, all the people.

A: "Let's go in," I said. "Such a beautiful place," he said. "Won't they chase us out?"

B: The things he could think of!

A: "Look at the crowds," I said. "They're all the same kind of people as us. Nobody will chase us out. Come on." Only then would he go in. Inside, he took one look and said, "How crowded it is. Hold on to your money, Iron Egg."

B: What was the matter?

A: "Someone may grab it!" "Don't worry," I said. "Nobody steals any more." "Oh no? They even swiped a big thing like my rickshaw!" I couldn't convince him. He kept taking his money out every few steps to make sure he still had it.

B: That's what his experience in the old society had taught him.

A: I took him up to the second floor and said, "We'll buy you a pair of shoes." "Let's go to Tienchiao market," he said. "It's too expensive here."

B: The prices are the same all over the city!

A: The salesman brought out six or seven pairs of shoes. "I only want one pair, Mr. Manager!" said my uncle. "That's all right," said the salesman. "If you can't find a good fit, you needn't buy."

B: He wanted your uncle to try them on for size.

A: My uncle tried on a pair. "These are fine. Iron Egg, pay the man the money, quick!"

B: What was his hurry?

A: He was afraid the price would go up.

B: He thought we still had inflation!

A: After we bought the shoes, I said to him, "Come and sit down for a while." I led him to one of the lounges. A young fellow who was sitting there stood up and said, "Take my chair, grand-pa." My uncle sat there uneasily. He pulled his money out of his pocket. "Still got it," he muttered. [*Motion of putting money back but dropping it.*]

B: He was still afraid of losing it.

A: "Wait here, Uncle," I said. "I'll get you a drink." As I was bringing it to him, he started to run. "What's the matter?" I asked. "There's a soldier in there!" he said. "That's a comrade from our Liberation Army!" I told him.

B: What was he afraid of?

A: "I've been warned—when you see a soldier, get out of his way!" I said: "Our Liberation Army men are the soldiers of the people—" He said "Don't say any more! Here he comes! He's after me!"

B: What was going on?

A: I looked. Sure enough the PLA man was coming our way. Running for all he was worth, my uncle flew down the stairs to the ground floor. A crowd gathered round him to ask what was wrong.

B: He really started something.

A: The PLA comrade went up to him and said, "What are you running for, grandpa? Here, this is yours." "Eh?"

B: What was it?

A: "You dropped your money." "Aiya. . . ." My uncle searched his pocket, reached out for the money, then pulled his hand back. "Ah . . . captain, keep it for yourself!"

B: What kind of talk was that?

A: Everybody laughed. "How can I take your money, grandpa?" the PLA comrade asked. My uncle was moved to tears. Just then the loudspeaker made an announcement. "Attention, comrades. A fountainpen and a purse have been found. Will the owners please claim them on the second floor? On the second floor." "Did you hear that, Uncle?" I asked. "Anything you lose, you can get back." My uncle thought for a moment, then rushed for the stairs. Chasing after him, I called, "Uncle, where are you going?" "Back to the second floor," he shouted over his shoulder. "I'm going to pick up my rickshaw!"

Curtain

MAGIC ASTER*
(A Play in Three Acts for Children)

By Jen Teh-yao

Translated by William C. White

CHARACTERS

DADDY WANG
MAMA
TA LAN
HSIAO LAN
OLD CAT
GRANDPA TREE
ELDER SISTER RABBIT
LITTLE SISTER RABBIT
SPOTTED DOE
DEER FAWN
MONKEY
LITTLE SQUIRREL
MORNING GLORY
DOG'S-TAIL GRASS
MAGIC ASTER
LITTLE BIRD
MERMAIDS
DADDY WANG'S NEIGHBORS

---

*Reprinted from *Foreign Languages Press*, Peking, 1963.

ACT I

SCENE 1

[It is dawn. From over the horizon the sun gradually brings the silhouette of the tree-clad mountains in the distance into view and sparkles on the rivulet in the valley below. Cocks crow. DADDY WANG's quaint ivy-covered cottage on the mountainside becomes more distinct in the morning glow. With her sleeves rolled up and lifting the hem of her skirt in her hand, HSIAO LAN comes on the stage with two buckets of water on a carrying-pole.]

HSIAO LAN [putting the buckets down quietly, dipping up water and pouring it over the flowers as she croons a tune]:

> Up with the sun and
> Over the dewy mountain I go.
> Every day listening to the birds' song,
> I make friends with the wind, frost, rain, and snow.
> Flowers grace the mountain all the year round,
> Vying with each other in beauty.
> Only the clusters of asters stand
> Nodding by the roadside without a sound.
> When in March the asters awake,
> The valley is tinged as blue as the sky.
> Frosts have gone but spring is late,
> For the asters have still not appeared.

[DADDY WANG emerges from the house.]

DADDY WANG: Not so loud, daughter! Mama is still asleep.

HSIAO LAN [putting her tongue out in a childish gesture]: Good morning, Father!

DADDY WANG: Good morning! You're an early bird. Hurry now and make some griddlecakes for my breakfast. I've got to go up the mountain for firewood.

HSIAO LAN: Yes, Father. [Runs toward the house.]

DADDY WANG [as HSIAO LAN is about to enter the house]: Be careful not to wake your mother. [DADDY WANG inhales the fresh air and goes to open the chicken coop behind the house. The chickens and ducks run out noisily. He shoos them farther away from the house. Black smoke rises from the kitchen chimney. Sparrows chirp. As DADDY WANG sits down on the moss-covered bank of a

231

small pond near the house and begins to sharpen his axe, he hums one of his woodcutters' ditties.]

[A short while later, MAMA comes dashing out of the room carrying a basket.]

MAMA: Goodness me! I overslept this morning. [Discovering DADDY WANG is already up, she runs over to him.]

MAMA: Have you been up long? Why didn't you call me?

[DADDY WANG smiles but says nothing. He merely throws a glance at her and goes on singing.]

MAMA: Are you still trying to sing? You sound like a duck!

DADDY WANG [laughing heartily]: Don't be upset, Mama. I only meant to let you get another forty winks.

MAMA: And let the chickens and ducks go unfed? [She runs over to the chicken coop and finds it open. Not a chicken or a duck is inside. She becomes flustered.]

MAMA: Heavens! Where are my chickens and ducks?

DADDY WANG: What's the matter?

MAMA: They aren't here! Not a one! [Looks around for them.]

DADDY WANG: What's not here?

MAMA: My goodness! You're really something! The chickens and ducks are gone and you don't turn a hair.

DADDY WANG: No, they're not. Ha, ha, ha! Come here. [Pulling her over to the bank of the river.] What's that in the river there? [The ducks are blithely swimming in the river behind the house.]

DADDY WANG [pulling her around to see the chickens]: Look, there in the backyard. [The cheeping of baby chicks is heard in the backyard.]

MAMA [letting out a suppressed giggle]: You're really a devil, you old fellow. . . . [Then she suddenly remembers something.] Oh, that's right! I've got to make some griddlecakes for you to eat on the way.

[Just as she is turning to go to the kitchen to make the griddlecakes, the kitchen window flies open and HSIAO LAN leans out. She has dough on her hands.]

HSIAO LAN: There's no need for you to come, Mama. I've made them already. See, I'm putting the last of the dough on the griddle now. [She turns and goes back into the kitchen. MAMA does not know what to say. Black smoke pours from the chimney.]

MAMA: I see! So this is the game you two are up to!

DADDY WANG: We only wanted to let you get a little more sleep,

Mama! You've not been well lately and last night were up so late weaving that rug. You're entitled to a rest. By the way, why are you in such a hurry to get that carpet woven?

MAMA: Father, you don't know what's on my mind. Our daughters are big girls now and there's no telling when or where they'll select their husbands. It would be too bad if we had nothing to give them as a wedding present when they decide to get married.

DADDY WANG: Good gracious, Mama! People are right when they say the only two things in an old woman's mind are her chickens and her sons-in-law.

MAMA: What's wrong with that? Can't I think like that if I want to?

DADDY WANG: Of course you can!

MAMA: Hey, is Ta Lan up yet? Have you called her?

DADDY WANG: No, I haven't.

MAMA: That girl—if you don't call her, she'll sleep till noon. [*Shouting into the room.*] Ta Lan! It's time to get up, Ta Lan!

DADDY WANG: Get up, Ta Lan! I have to go up the mountain to gather firewood.

TA LAN: Oh-h-h-h, I'm getting up now.

MAMA: Get up, girl! The sun is high in the sky.

[*TA LAN pushes open the window and stretches.*]

TA LAN: Oh-h-h, I'm up already. You would have to wake me. I was having such a good sleep. What do you want?

MAMA: Hurry up, daughter! Your father has got to go up the mountain to gather firewood and your sister is making griddlecakes for him while you're still yawning there.

DADDY WANG: Come out and water the pumpkins before it gets too hot.

TA LAN: All right. [*She promises, but does not make a move, just leans on the window sill as though glued to it. A short while later she falls fast asleep again and her long black hair falls down over the window sill to the pond.*]

MAMA: Father, our two daughters seem not to be born of the same mother.

[*A cat jumps upon the window sill and wakes TA LAN. She gives a start, but upon seeing that it is the cat, she caresses it. Being a tame pussy, it draws close to her and begins to purr.*]

MAMA: That blasted cat has come back again. Ta Lan just sits around stroking it and does nothing else all day.

DADDY WANG: Where does it come from anyway? It hangs around here and just won't leave.

233

MAMA: It belongs to an official in the village up the road. When its master goes out, it comes over here. Ta Lan is so keen to hobnob with the official's family that she simply won't do a lick of work in the house. In fact, she expects to be waited on. It looks as though she's going to become a member of the official's family before long.

DADDY WANG: There is no need to upset yourself, Mama. After all, she's no longer a child. Why don't you have a talk with her?

MAMA: You can talk until you're blue in the face and she won't listen to you. But just let someone from that official's family say something and she never forgets it.

[HSIAO LAN comes out of the kitchen carrying the griddlecakes in a bamboo basket.]

HSIAO LAN: Father, here are the cakes.

DADDY WANG [looking at them]: So many! I'll never be able to eat them all.

HSIAO LAN: There aren't many. Only ten. You'll be able to finish them.

DADDY WANG: No, I won't.

HSIAO LAN: Yes, you will.

[Neither will give in.]

MAMA: Now, Father, take them along. . . .

DADDY WANG [mimicking MAMA and cutting her short]: I know, take them along as a token of your daughter's kindness. Right? [They all burst out laughing.]

DADDY WANG: You two always treat me like this. This is really overdoing things. . . . [Puts axe in his belt as he speaks, then picks up carrying-pole and rope, preparing to leave.]

DADDY WANG: Ta Lan! Get up and give your mother a hand with the housework! I'm leaving now.

[TA LAN wakes up, hair still in disorder.]

TA LAN: Are you going now, Father? Oh, all right. [Suddenly remembering something, she comes running out of house.] Hey, Father! After you've sold the firewood, go to the market and buy me a length of cotton print, will you? I haven't a thing to wear.

MAMA: Don't trouble yourself, Father. [To TA LAN.] If you want a new jacket, weave your own cloth; there are plenty of looms around the house.

[TA LAN pouts and walks away.]

HSIAO LAN: It's about time for the asters to bloom, Father. If you see any on the mountain, will you pick a few to bring back for me?

234

DADDY WANG: All right! [*Not too far away from the house,* DADDY WANG *starts to sing one of his woodcutters' ditties.*]

MAMA: Come straight back, Father.

DADDY WANG [*from a distance*]: All right!

MAMA: Mind how you go on those steep paths.

HSIAO LAN: Don't forget the flowers, Father, the asters.

DADDY WANG [*from a still greater distance*]: I won't.

[*His singing fades into the distance. Sitting on the bank of the pond,* TA LAN *gazes languidly at her reflection in the water and combs her hair. The cat is sound asleep on the window sill.*]

Curtain

SCENE 2

[*Deep in the mountains there is a cliff and below it a still pool. The ancient trees are kissing the clouds and wild flowers are every-where.*

SPOTTED DOE *and her fawn are basking in the sun on the moun-tain top.* MONKEY *is swinging about on the vines.* LITTLE SQUIRREL *is in a tree combing his tail. The* RABBIT SISTERS *are absorbed in a game.*]

LITTLE SISTER RABBIT [*jumping and speaking in a clear ringing voice*]: Ha, ha, ha . . . ELDER SISTER! Don't press me so hard. I'm quite out of breath. . . .

ELDER SISTER RABBIT: Ha-ha . . . I don't care . . . if you're caught, you lose. . . .
[*Playing around Grandpa Tree, they brush against him, convuls-ing him with laughter, so that the vines shake. Monkey, who is swinging on the vines, is startled.*]
[*The two* RABBIT SISTERS, *paying no heed to all this, continue chasing each other.* LITTLE SISTER RABBIT *runs towards the cluster of flowers so fast that she runs head-on into* MORNING GLORY *who is just growing out of the ground.*]

235

MORNING GLORY [*speaks angrily*]: Watch where you're going, you
little imp!
[*Frightened,* LITTLE SISTER RABBIT *runs over to her elder sister.*
MORNING GLORY *pouts. From all appearances she had been angry
when she was under the ground.*]
LITTLE SISTER RABBIT: What's wrong with her, Sister? Should I
apologize?
ELDER SISTER RABBIT: Don't say anything; she's not angry with us.
[*A short while later,* DOG'S-TAIL GRASS *sticks his dejected face
above the ground.*]
DOG'S-TAIL GRASS: Just look at you! What's there to be so angry
about? I was only joking, but you took me seriously.
MORNING GLORY: Who took you seriously? You're only a blade of
grass, and dog's-tail grass at that; but me, I'm a flower, a morn-
ing glory.
DOG'S-TAIL GRASS: What's the difference between flowers and grass
anyway? We both sprang from the same soil, didn't we?
MORNING GLORY: Humph! We're not the same!
DOG'S-TAIL GRASS: Don't flowers and grass make good mates?
MONKEY [*cutting in abruptly*]: Yes, they do! [*Everyone shouts "Hear,
hear!"*]
LITTLE SISTER RABBIT [*laughing along with the others*]: What do
they mean by "make good mates"?
ELDER SISTER RABBIT: I don't know either. . . .
LITTLE SQUIRREL: Ha-ha-ha . . . you mean to say you don't know what
is meant by "make good mates"! That's rich! Ha, ha, ha, ha!
MORNING GLORY: What's so funny? [*To* DOG'S-TAIL GRASS.] Let's
go over there and talk. [DOG-TAIL GRASS *grimaces at everyone and
obediently follows* MORNING GLORY. *Everyone laughs uproarious-
ly*] [*The distant sound of woodcutting and* DADDY WANG's *singing
ring out in the valley. The inhabitants of the mountains are alarmed over this. The two rabbit sisters prick up their ears.* LITTLE
SQUIRREL *climbs up to the top of the tree, exposing only his tail.*
MONKEY *lithely bounds onto a vine and looks in the direction of
the singing. Protecting her fawn,* SPOTTED DOE *stands frozen in
watchfulness.*]
[*The singing becomes louder and louder. Blocking* DOG'S-TAIL
GRASS's *way,* MORNING GLORY *motions for him to hide with her
behind a rock. The little animals are in a flutter and are preparing
to flee.*]

GRANDPA TREE [after making a survey]: Don't be afraid, children!
That's Daddy Wang who always comes to this mountain for firewood. Don't run away; he wouldn't harm a soul.

[Not hearing clearly what he said, they all hide in a trice.]

[After the flurry, silence prevails in the valley. The tree leaves
quiver, the flowers and grass bob, and the little birds wing through
the air.]

[The sound of DADDY WANG's singing becomes louder, and a short
while later he arrives on the scene. He puts his half load of firewood to one side and picks up some more dead branches. Here
he pauses, walks over to the pool, dips up some water to drink,
takes out some griddlecakes from his basket and begins to eat.
That finished, he lies down on a slope to rest a while. He sees the
tail of LITTLE SQUIRREL, picks up a pebble, and tosses it gently at
it. LITTLE SQUIRREL merely wriggles his tail a couple of times,
DADDY WANG then pokes at the tail with a stick. LITTLE SQUIRREL
turns around, throws an angry glance at him, then hides among the
leaves. DADDY WANG bursts out laughing. At this two pairs of rabbit ears appear over the top of a mound, followed gradually by two
rabbit faces. Their gaze is fixed on DADDY WANG.]

[DADDY WANG, delighted to see the two rabbits, strokes their ears.
The two RABBIT SISTERS agilely hop over in front of him.] [A short
while later LITTLE SQUIRREL, MONKEY and even SPOTTED DOE and
her fawn, who are still on the top of the rock, stick their heads
out for a peek at DADDY WANG.]

[With the best intentions, DADDY WANG takes out a griddlecake,
breaks it up into small pieces, and places them on the ground.]

[The daring MONKEY is the first to venture out after a piece.
DADDY WANG does not chase him away. Then MONKEY dares to
come back for a second piece. DADDY WANG still does not move.
One by one the animals come out and crowd around DADDY
WANG. He is extremely kind to them and plays with them.]

[FAWN also wants to come down from the rock to play with
DADDY WANG, but SPOTTED DOE will not let him. FAWN escapes
and comes down hill at the first opportunity.]

[DADDY WANG and the animals are having a gay time together; he
rubs their noses, ears, tails and antlers. Knowing now that he does
not have any bad intentions, the little animals let him pet them.
The little animals gradually come up to DADDY WANG; some rub
his beard, while others run over to grasp hold of his hand. MONKEY

amuses DADDY WANG *so much that he becomes oblivious to every-*
thing and rolls on the ground in laughter with the animals. This
is also a happy sight for GRANDPA TREE *and* SPOTTED DOE.]

GRANDPA TREE: Stop the nonsense, children! Daddy Wang is not a
child any more; he can't stand your being so rough. Stop it!

SPOTTED DOE [*to her* FAWN]: Come here, come here at once!
[*Paying no heed, the little animals continue to sport with* DADDY
WANG. SPOTTED DOE *and* GRANDPA TREE *look at each other help-*
lessly.]
[*Suddenly a melodious sound followed by more music rings out in*
the valley. A sparkling blue flower gradually emerges from the
cranny in a rock on the side of the cliff. The little animals are
startled.]

MONKEY: The aster has bloomed!

THE OTHER ANIMALS: The aster is in bloom! Magic Aster will be
coming again. . . .

DADDY WANG: What flower is this?

GRANDPA TREE: You have come at the right time, Daddy Wang. This
is the aster. It's the first to bloom in the valley this year. Now the
asters on the mountainside and in the dales will all come into
bloom.

DADDY WANG: Oh! It's so beautiful. Isn't that the flower Hsiao Lan
asked me to pick for her? Oh, how wonderful it would be if I
could! [*Talking to himself,* DADDY WANG *climbs up the cliff to*
pick the flower. The little animals are waiting for the asters in
other places to bloom and pay no attention to him. DADDY WANG's
mind is set on getting the flower, and he climbs quickly up the
side of the cliff.]

GRANDPA TREE: Be careful, Daddy Wang. . . . [*His advice is too*
late. At this instant DADDY WANG *falls off the cliff. The little*
animals are thrown into confusion, running hither and thither
trying to devise a way to save him, but everyone is helpless.]
[*At this critical moment, the little animals suddenly fall silent*
and all attention is placed on the movement at the bottom of the
cliff. A cluster of asters on which DADDY WANG *is lying limp*
grows gradually taller, then separates. A handsome young man is
seen emerging from among the flowers holding DADDY WANG *up.*
The little animals are amazed at what they see.]

LITTLE ANIMALS: Magic Aster! Magic Aster! [*Smiling at everybody,*
MAGIC ASTER *comes down from the cluster of asters carrying*

238

DADDY WANG *in his arms and lays him down on a small slope.
The little animals gather around, some rubbing their faces against
DADDY WANG's, others touching his hands. All are quiet in their
demeanor.*]

MAGIC ASTER: Wake up, Daddy Wang! Wake up!

LITTLE ANIMALS [*repeating after* MAGIC ASTER *in a soft voice*]: Wake
up, Daddy Wang! Wake up!

DADDY WANG [*slowly opening his eyes and looking around at everyone*]: My goodness! That was a close shave! Was it you who saved
my life?

MONKEY: No, it wasn't us; it was Magic Aster.

MAGIC ASTER: Where are you hurt, Daddy Wang?

DADDY WANG: I'm not hurt at all. Look! [*Stands up and walks
around slowly.* MONKEY *follows him, taking precautions lest he
should fall. He looks around at the sparkling asters.*] What place is
this?

MAGIC ASTER: This is Mt. Aster.

DADDY WANG: Mt. Aster? [*Pointing to the aster blooming on the
cliff.*] What kind of flower is this?

MAGIC ASTER: This is the first aster to bloom this year.

DADDY WANG: Aster?

MAGIC ASTER: Yes. When it comes into bloom, all the other asters
on the mountainside and in the valley will burst into bloom. You
see!

[*Everywhere* MAGIC ASTER *points, clusters of asters emerge. In
little or no time the mountainside and the valley are a sea of blue
asters.* DADDY WANG *and the other animals look at this panorama
with wide-open eyes.*]

DADDY WANG: Who are you?

MAGIC ASTER: My name is Magic Aster. I raise hundreds of thousands
of asters with my own hands.

DADDY WANG: Are you a man or a flower?

MAGIC ASTER [*standing among the flowers*]: I'm both man and flower.
A flower compared to me is like a drop of dew compared to a
raindrop; the two combined make a drop of water.

DADDY WANG: Will you give me one of these blue flowers?

MAGIC ASTER: Do you want it for yourself?

DADDY WANG: No, for my daughter.

MAGIC ASTER: Your daughter? Is she the young maiden who lives at
the foot of this mountain, rises with the sun and sings with the
birds?

DADDY WANG: Yes, that's she. Do you know her?

MAGIC ASTER: I don't know her, but then again I do know her, because I have heard her sing ever since I was so high. Now I'm always hearing her sing. Listen!

[HSIAO LAN's singing is heard in the distance.]

MAGIC ASTER [beckons to the sparkling aster on the side of the cliff and it comes flying over to him. He receives it and hands it to DADDY WANG]: Take this flower back with you, Daddy Wang, and ask whichever of your daughters who likes it if she is willing to marry me, Magic Aster.

GRANDPA TREE: Congratulations, Daddy Wang! Magic Aster has proposed to your daughter!

DADDY WANG [happily accepting the flower]: All right! All right! I must be going now. I will ask . . . I must be off. . . . [Picks up his wood and prepares to leave.]

[The little animals crowd around and help him gather up his things.]

DOG'S-TAIL GRASS [pulls MORNING GLORY to one side and gives her a blade of dog's-tail grass]: Do you like it? Are you willing?

MORNING GLORY [giving him a playful slap]: Silly, you just guess!

[The little animals overhear them and laugh happily.]

DADDY WANG: I must be off now. Goodbye, little ones.

MAGIC ASTER: See you later, Daddy Wang. That magic aster is a part of my heart. If one of the young maidens agree, we will hold the wedding by the side of the river at the foot of the mountain tomorrow when the moon is high.

[DADDY WANG takes up his carrying-pole and exits. The little animals escort him down the mountain. MAGIC ASTER stands there lost in thought. The little animals stealthily crowd around him and make faces at him. He blushes and hides among the flowers.]

Curtain

SCENE 3

[DADDY WANG's cottage (same as Scene 1). Darkness is falling Birds are winging their way to the forest. The rays of the setting sun tinge the house and trellis orange-red.
The small table under the trellis is set for dinner. HSIAO LAN is doing some embroidery while TA LAN is caressing the old cat and cracking and nibbling sunflower seeds. MAMA is worried about DADDY WANG. He should have returned long since, but now it is almost dark and still he has not come. She looks up the path impatiently, then feels the side of the pot on the table to see if the food is still hot.]

TA LAN: Why isn't he back yet? My stomach is rumbling. [Takes some food from the table.]

MAMA: Just wait a little while longer, Ta Lan.

TA LAN: This is not for myself; it's for the old cat.

MAMA: That old cat has to wait until we've finished eating.

TA LAN: Oh, all right.

MAMA: I think something must have happened to Father because he has never been so late before.

TA LAN: I bet he went to the market, met some old cronies, and is at some inn having a drink. That's definitely what's happened. Let's not wait for him, Mama. Let's go ahead and eat.

MAMA: He couldn't have done that. He knows we're waiting for him. If you're hungry as that, you eat first.

HSIAO LAN [putting aside her embroidery]: Mama, I'll go and look for him.

TA LAN: Who knows where you'll find him at this hour, in the mountain or at the market? Just forget about him, he'll come back sooner or later.

HSIAO LAN: I'll go up the mountain and look for him. [Exit.]

MAMA: Ta Lan, you're the big sister, yet you don't take the initiative in doing anything. It's so late and your father hasn't returned yet, but you're not worrying at all. What you say to looking for him at the market, eh? He might have gone there to buy that cotton print for you.

TA LAN: The market closed long ago. Where should I look for him?

MAMA: Just for good measure, take a look on the main thoroughfare.

TA LAN: I'll go then. Oh, what a bother. [She hardly gets two paces away from the house before the cat mews. She goes back and takes

241

it off the window sill and leaves. Looking about, MAMA is worrying about DADDY WANG. MAMA is on tenterhooks.]

MAMA [*to herself*]: The older he gets, the more muddleheaded he becomes. Just as if he doesn't know we're waiting for him. Now the supper's cold. [*She takes the food back into the kitchen. A few seconds later smoke begins to curl from the chimney.*]

[*DADDY WANG returns with a load of firewood. He is holding the aster as if it's something precious.*]

DADDY WANG: Mama! Girls!

[*MAMA runs out of the kitchen.*]

MAMA: So, you're back at last. You're just like a child. Come over here now and let me smell your breath. I bet you ran into some of your old winebibbers and had a few cups before returning.

DADDY WANG: Mama, Mama, stop fussing. I haven't had anything to drink; neither have I been frittering away my time. I have some good news for you.

MAMA: Stop your nonsense; I don't believe there's any good news. And imagine you coming across good news!

DADDY WANG: Look! [*Holds up the aster.*]

MAMA: What's so precious about that? What's there about a wild flower to get excited about?

DADDY WANG: Now don't go touching it. This is really a wonderful flower.

MAMA: I know what's happened. You went playing around and forgot to come back and now you're trying to find something to cover up with. Come now, tell the truth. You were out drinking, weren't you?

DADDY WANG: Smell my breath! [*Blows in MAMA's face.*] I really haven't had anything to drink. But I did come across some good news. Just listen!

[*As he whispers something to MAMA, her eyes brighten with joy, then she wags her head in wonder.*]

MAMA: Good gracious! I haven't finished weaving that rug. It's just like I said. When it comes it comes, no matter if you're prepared or not. What a mother-in-law I am, not a single gift to give them. What an embarrassing situation!

DADDY WANG: You're rushing things, my dear. They're not married yet and you're thinking of being a mother-in-law. Besides, neither of our daughters has agreed yet.

MAMA: Yes, that's right. The girls have gone out to look for you, one to the market and the other up the mountain. Hurry and call them! The wedding will take place tomorrow; everything's in a rush.

DADDY WANG: Hsiao Lan! Hsiao Lan! Come back quickly. [*No reply.*] Ta Lan! Come back. . . .

TA LAN: Coming, Father.

MAMA: You're back already. How did you get back so quick? Why, you've been here all the time.

TA LAN: I went out to the main thoroughfare to take a look and didn't see anyone, so I came back!

MAMA: Hsiao Lan has probably gone some distance. Father, you go and call her. Oh, I'll go myself. You take a rest; that fall was enough for you. [*Pulling DADDY WANG off to one side purposely.*] You see if Ta Lan is willing or not. When I find Hsiao Lan, I'll ask her. [*Rushes off the stage.*]

TA LAN: Did you go to the market to buy the print cloth for me, Father?

DADDY WANG: I haven't been to the market and I didn't buy the print cloth for you. This is a flower I brought back from the mountain. Do you think it's beautiful? [*Holds it up.*]

TA LAN: Aw, Father! You didn't buy any cotton print for me, so you've just brought me back a flower. I don't want it. Our garden is full of flowers; who wants this! There's nothing beautiful about it!

DADDY WANG: Ta Lan! A handsome and intelligent young man up on the mountain gave me this flower and told me to ask the one of my daughters who liked it if she is willing to marry him; his name is Magic Aster.

TA LAN [*dropping the cat and snatching the flower*]: I like it. Oh, how beautiful it is. [*Smells it.*] And it's so fragrant! I just simply love it.

DADDY WANG: Do you really like it?

TA LAN: Really! Give it to me, Father. [DADDY WANG *hands the flower to her.*] Where does Magic Aster live?

DADDY WANG: Up on the mountain.

TA LAN: Up on the mountain? Does he own a big house? How much land has he got and how many horses does he own? Has he got servants in his house?

DADDY WANG: You're after the wrong man, Ta Lan. Magic Aster is just the same as your father. He doesn't own any land or horses or big mansions, nor does he have servants to wait on him.

TA LAN: How does he make his living then?

DADDY WANG: With his own hands.

TA LAN [*immediately changing her mind*]: Father, I just can't bring myself to leave you and Mama, or this home of ours. Although I do like this flower, I don't think I am ready to get married. [*Throws the flower on the ground.*]

DADDY WANG [*picks the flower up immediately*]: I knew you wouldn't like it.

[MAMA *and* HSIAO LAN *enter the yard and some of the neighbors nearby come over.*]

HSIAO LAN: Father!

DADDY WANG: Look, Hsiao Lan!

[DADDY WANG *holds the aster high. It glows with marvellous radiance, illuminating the yard and seemingly turning it into a wonderland.*]

HSIAO LAN [*enchanted by the flower, stares at it breathlessly then runs over and embraces it*]: I'm willing, Father! I don't know how many times this has been the flower of dreams. [*Turning to* MAMA.] Mama, I'm willing to marry Magic Aster.

[*Soft singing is heard offstage, like the golden voices of thousands of children singing a song of praise.*]

[*The little river in the distance sparkles spectacularly.* HSIAO LAN *walks toward the river carrying the flower.* DADDY WANG *and* MAMA *are moved to tears of joy. Their neighbors congratulate them.*]

[*Assuming an indifferent air and stroking the cat,* TA LAN *is sitting on the bank of the pond. She keeps aloof from all that happens in the yard.*]

Curtain

SCENE 4

[*By the riverside at the foot of the mountain. The earth is bathed in silvery moonlight. The iridescent clouds drifting across the sky are reflected in the river. The sound of music mingled with joyous laughter is heard in the distance.*

A small lotus-leaf boat carrying MAGIC ASTER *and his friends glides into view on the river. They are in smart attire. With them are two little animals dressed as Gods of Harmony in big masks for the wedding ceremony. One is carrying a magic box, the other lotus flowers and leaves.*]

[HSIAO LAN *is standing by the riverside, in a new dress and is carry-ing the aster.* DADDY WANG, MAMA, *and all of their neighbors are there with her. Everyone is neat and clean. They are dumb-founded at the sight in the distance.*]

MAMA: Father! Do you see that? Are those rainbow colors in the distance them?

DADDY WANG: Less noise, Mama! That's them all right.

MAMA: Is that really them? Is Magic Aster among them?

DADDY WANG: Don't get excited! . . .

[MAGIC ASTER *and his friends drawing nearer.*]

MORNING GLORY [*from a distance*]: Daddy Wang! We're coming for the bride.

DADDY WANG: Come on! All is set.

DOG'S-TAIL GRASS: Daddy Wang! Did Mama come, too? Magic Aster has brought a present for her!

MAMA [*to* DADDY WANG]: Didn't I tell you it would be embarrassing if we had no present. [*Straightening up the woven rug and the cosmetic kit in* DADDY WANG'S *hand.*] Be ready with the presents, Father.

[MAGIC ASTER *and the others come ashore.*]

[MAGIC ASTER *and* HSIAO LAN *look at each other. They say noth-ing, but their hearts speak for them. All eyes are fixed on them as they draw closer to each other.*]

[HSIAO LAN *gives the flower in her hand to* MAGIC ASTER, *who puts it in her hair. At this moment the music begins, and innumer-able flower petals fall from the sky, forming a sea of flowers, while the rosy clouds above take on a new glow.*]

GRANDPA TREE: Get on with the wedding ceremony, children!

[*The stage is set. The Gods of Harmony stand at either side of* HSIAO LAN *and* MAGIC ASTER, *creating an ancient traditional mar-riage scene.*]

[MAGIC ASTER *and* HSIAO LAN *bow first to the elders,* GRANDPA TREE, DADDY WANG, MAMA *and* SPOTTED DOE, *then bow to their friends and then to each other.* SPOTTED DOE *pours out glasses of wine for them to toast each other; then the girls and boys dance merrily.*]

[DOG'S-TAIL GRASS *takes* MORNING GLORY *aside for a private talk.*]

DOG'S-TAIL GRASS: Just see how fortunate Magic Aster is!

MORNING GLORY: He's a flower and you're grass.

DOG'S-TAIL GRASS: Aren't we the same?

MORNING GLORY: What are you driving at?

DOG'S-TAIL GRASS: I want . . . I want . . . let's get married along with Magic Aster and Hsiao Lan.

MORNING GLORY: Goodness me! Say no more. It makes me blush to think of it.

DOG'S-TAIL GRASS: What do you say? I've waited all this time . . . let's make this our wedding day, too.

MORNING GLORY: Oh, gracious! I don't know what to say! Go and ask Grandpa Tree.

DOG'S-TAIL GRASS [*running over to* GRANDPA TREE]: Grandpa Tree! Grandpa Tree! I . . . [*in a bashful manner*].

GRANDPA TREE: Go on, tell me what's on your mind!

DOG'S-TAIL GRASS [*pointing to* MORNING GLORY]: I . . . I . . . you ask her.

MORNING GLORY [*turning quickly to hide her face*]: I . . . .

GRANDPA TREE: Ha, ha, ha! What's going on between you two? What are you trying to say?

[*Their friends crowd around.*]

DOG'S-TAIL GRASS: It's like this, I . . . we . . . we're thinking . . . . Aw, come on, you tell him, Morning Glory.

MORNING GLORY: Now just look how useless you are. I'll tell you what it is, Grandpa Tree: he wants to marry me.

GRANDPA TREE: Then that's just fine. How do you feel about it?

MORNING GLORY: I . . . I'm willing.

DOG'S-TAIL GRASS: Hi, hi, hi! [*Runs over and grasps her hand.*]

GRANDPA TREE: A double wedding is pending. Get them dressed, children, and we'll begin the wedding ceremony.

[DOG'S-TAIL GRASS *goes over to* MORNING GLORY *and picks a blade of dog's-tail grass from his head to stick in her hair.*]

[*Their wedding follows in the same manner as* HSIAO LAN'S *and* MAGIC ASTER'S. *The other little animals, however, have to urge them to kowtow to each other before they do so.*]

[*Filled with unlimited joy, all begin to dance and congratulate the brides and grooms.*]

GRANDPA TREE: We'd better be going, children, our clothes are already wet with dew. Let's say goodbye to Daddy Wang and Mama.

[*They say goodbye to one another.* MAGIC ASTER *escorts* HSIAO LAN *onto the boat.*]

[*Their boat gradually sails into the distance.*]

246

MAMA: Don't forget to come back to see us when the asters bloom next year, Hsiao Lan. Your mother will be worried about you.

HSIAO LAN: Ai!

[*The farther they fade into the distance, the less distinct their singing becomes. Finally only a few sparkling flowers are visible floating on the water at the farthest end of the river. They gradually fade out of sight.*]

Curtain

ACT II

SCENE 1

[*Deep in the mountains (same as Act I, Scene 2.) A year has lapsed and the asters are shortly due to bloom. It is early in the morning.* GRANDPA TREE *is sweeping his front yard.* LITTLE SQUIRREL *and* MONKEY *are helping him.*

DEER FAWN'S *long antlers appear over the mountain top. Following this,* DEER FAWN *proudly puts in his appearance. He has grown taller and his voice is huskier.*]

DEER FAWN: Good morning, Grandpa Tree!

GRANDPA TREE: Good morning, Fawn!

DEER FAWN: How many times have I told you now that I've grown up you're not to call me Fawn. My name is Spotted Buck.

[*He stands erect, with his chest out, head high and switches his tail just like a grownup.*]

GRANDPA TREE: Ha, ha, ha. . . .

LITTLE SQUIRREL: Hurry down from there and give us a hand, Fawn.

DEER FAWN: You little imp! . . .

MONKEY: Come on, Fawn, stop fooling around!

DEER FAWN [*pulling a juniper berry and throwing it*]: So you're calling me "Fawn," too, eh? You little devil. I am a year older now. I was younger than you last year, but I'm older than you this year.

LITTLE SQUIRREL: Hi, hi, hi. You're a year older and aren't we, too?

DEER FAWN: You mean to say you're a year older, too?

MONKEY: What a joke! Ha-ha-ha. Do you think you're the only one who advances in age?

[MONKEY *throws a juniper berry at him.* FAWN *throws one back. A fight ensues.* SPOTTED DOE *comes on stage.*]

SPOTTED DOE: Now, what are you fighting about this time, Fawn?

DEER FAWN: They called me "Fawn."

SPOTTED DOE: What's wrong with calling you "Fawn"?

DEER FAWN: My name is Spotted Buck. Can't you see my antlers?

SPOTTED DOE: Just look how proud you are.

GRANDPA TREE: Now that he's a young man, he doesn't like others to call him "Fawn"!

SPOTTED DOE: Good morning, Grandpa Tree! What are you busy at?

GRANDPA TREE: Eh? Have you forgotten? The asters will bloom to-day. Magic Aster and his wife will be coming to see us.

SPOTTED DOE: Gracious! A year has gone by already. Fawn—er—Spotted Buck! Come back quickly and tidy up the place.
[They go back into the cave.]

GRANDPA TREE: Let's get a move on and get things in order, children! From the looks of things, it won't be long before the asters will bloom. I can smell the fragrance rising from the ground.

MONKEY and LITTLE SQUIRREL: Right! Let's hurry and tidy up!
[They busy themselves cleaning the inside and outside of the tree. GRANDPA TREE joins them in their work.]
DOG'S-TAIL GRASS comes on stage cradling LITTLE DOG'S-TAIL GRASS in his arms.]

DOG'S-TAIL GRASS: There, there, don't cry, my little darling! . . .

MORNING GLORY [some distance behind him]: Slow down a bit, Daddy! This path is slippery and the going is hard. Come and give me a hand.

DOG'S-TAIL GRASS: Aiya! What can I do when I have the baby in my arms! Be careful!

MORNING GLORY: Come and help me!

DOG'S-TAIL GRASS: You can see I have the baby in my arms! [Kissing the baby.] My little darling! If I come, I can do nothing. Just watch your step. That's right! Catch hold of that bush. There you are. Now catch hold of that blade of grass. Steady!

MORNING GLORY [still from a distance]: Oh, goodness!

DOG'S-TAIL GRASS: Aw, never mind, just catch hold of that blade of grass.
[MORNING GLORY manages to keep from falling. With great difficulty, she climbs up. Attired in smart clothing, flowers in her hair, a bundle in her left hand, a package wrapped with red paper in her right hand, and carrying a pumpkin in the fold of her arms, she climbs up step by step. As she nears the top, DOG'S-TAIL GRASS

holds out his hand for her. She reaches for it, but before she can grasp hold of it she slips and falls. The things she is carrying fly everywhere.]

DOG'S-TAIL GRASS: Mind!

MORNING GLORY: Oops!

[LITTLE DOG'S-TAIL GRASS begins to scream. This throws DOG'S-TAIL GRASS into a fluster. He tries to lull the baby while at the same time he tries to pull MORNING GLORY up. Helplessly, MORNING GLORY sits there trying to get up but cannot.]

DOG'S-TAIL GRASS: I told you not to bring so many things, but you wouldn't listen.

[The noise brings GRANDPA TREE, LITTLE SQUIRREL, MONKEY, SPOTTED DOE and FAWN rushing to the scene. SPOTTED DOE goes to help MORNING GLORY but she cannot pull her up. She takes the baby from DOG'S-TAIL GRASS and orders him to help MORNING GLORY up.]

SPOTTED DOE: What a rascal you are! Don't you know you're to look after your wife, too?

[Hearing SPOTTED DOE speak like this, MORNING GLORY feels sorry for herself and begins to cry.]

DOG'S-TAIL GRASS [almost in tears]: I had my arms full with the baby, SPOTTED DOE! [At this instant the infant begins to scream again. He drops MORNING GLORY and runs over to SPOTTED DOE.] There, there, don't cry, my little darling. Don't cry. . . .

SPOTTED DOE: Go give your wife a hand! There, there, don't cry. . . .

DOG'S-TAIL GRASS [finding fault]: You're so clumsy you can't even climb this path by yourself. . . . [Helps her up reluctantly.]

MORNING GLORY [jumping up]: Who wants your help anyway! Do you think I can't get up on my own?

DOG'S-TAIL GRASS [starts]: It's a pity you didn't get up before, then.

MORNING GLORY: Just look how proud you are, you blade of dog's-tail grass. Just as if I couldn't get along without you! I am a flower! Understand, a flower!

DOG'S-TAIL GRASS: A flower! Humph! And what if you are a flower! Is a flower supposed to act as you do? . . .

GRANDPA TREE: You two are just like enemies; neither one of you will give in to the other.

MORNING GLORY: Grandpa Tree, you settle this matter! He. . . .

DOG'S-TAIL GRASS [cuts her short]: We have to reason things out, right, Grandpa Tree?

GRANDPA TREE: All right, all right! No more arguing out of you two. You must learn to respect each other.

MORNING GLORY: He's the one. . . .

SPOTTED DOE: Stop it! You've come here to see Grandpa Tree, haven't you?

MORNING GLORY: That's right. Standing here snapping each other's heads off, we've forgotten our purpose in coming. What are you standing there rowing about? Go and pick up the things we brought.

DOG'S-TAIL GRASS [eyes beaming and lips pouted, he goes back down the path, picks up the bundle, package, pumpkin, and the other things and gives them to MORNING GLORY]: Here, take them!

MORNING GLORY: Grandpa Tree, here is a pumpkin for you. It's nice and ripe. [GRANDPA TREE pays no attention to her. She gives DOG'S-TAIL GRASS a shove.] Come on, speak up, you!

DOG'S-TAIL GRASS: I promise not to quarrel again, Grandpa Tree.

GRANDPA TREE: You must keep your word.

MORNING GLORY [cradling the baby in her arms, goes over to GRANDPA TREE]: Don't be angry, Grandpa Tree. Take a look at your grandson.

[Only now does GRANDPA TREE brighten up.] [The RABBIT SISTERS rush on stage. They have grown up. No longer are they a pair of foolish rabbits, but are two beautiful young girls. The ringing, childish laughter of LITTLE SISTER RABBIT, however, has not changed.]

LITTLE SISTER RABBIT: Grandpa Tree! . . . Grandpa Tree! . . .

ELDER SISTER RABBIT: Have the asters bloomed yet, Grandpa Tree?

GRANDPA TREE: Don't rush things, girls! The asters will not bloom without you, ha, ha, ha. . . .

[Just at this moment the valley throws off an iridescent glow and enchanting music is heard. The cluster of asters on the mountain cliff gives off a sparkling light. A blue aster among them unfolds gradually. Following this all the asters on the mountainside and in the valley sparkle and hundreds of thousands of asters gradually come into bloom. This sight is more beautiful and enthralling than the year before. But overshadowing all is the cluster on the mountain cliff, which is beautifully shaped and extraordinarily blue. From a distance it looks like a heap of sapphire.]

[MAGIC ASTER and HSIAO LAN are standing in the center of this cluster of flowers. Everyone on the scene admires this fortunate couple.]

250

LITTLE ANIMALS: How are you, Magic Aster and Sister-in-law Hsiao Lan?

MAGIC ASTER: How are you?

HSIAO LAN: How are you, Grandpa Tree?

GRANDPA TREE: Fine! All of us are just fine!

SPOTTED DOE [to HSIAO LAN]: Are you accustomed to your new life, Hsiao Lan?

HSIAO LAN: Yes, I am.

LITTLE SISTER RABBIT: Do you like our place here, Hsiao Lan?

HSIAO LAN: Very much.

ELDER SISTER RABBIT: What and whom do you like here?

HSIAO LAN: I like you and I like him; I like all of you!

MONKEY: Do you like him? [Pointing to MAGIC ASTER.]
[General laughter.]

MORNING GLORY: Look here, Hsiao Lan! [Lets her see LITTLE DOG'S-TAIL GRASS.]

LITTLE SQUIRREL: Lo! Morning Glory has something precious to show you.

MONKEY: That's not something precious; it's only a precious small blade of grass, a little dog's-tail grass at that!
[All laugh.]

GRANDPA TREE: The holiday for the blooming of the asters has rolled around again. Let's dance our holiday dances in the old spirit of Mt. Aster.
[The music commences and the mountain inhabitants start to dance. In the spirit of the old tradition, they first pay their respects to the elders, then to each other, then give blessings to the younger generation and then praise Nature. All are in high spirits.]
[MAGIC ASTER and HSIAO LAN chat as they dance.]

HSIAO LAN: Goodness, how time flies, Magic Aster! [Plucking an aster.] The asters are once again in bloom all over the mountain and valley.

MAGIC ASTER: Why, of course! This whole path is covered with blue asters.

HSIAO LAN: It looks like the sky and then again it looks like the sea. How beautiful it is!

MAGIC ASTER: Do you still remember? Last year at this very same time you and I walked along this path to our new home.

HSIAO LAN: How could I ever forget! My dress was wet with dew.

MAGIC ASTER: Yes, a year has gone by so quickly.

HSIAO LAN: Magic Aster . . . .

MAGIC ASTER: Yes.

HSIAO LAN: Magic Aster!

MAGIC ASTER: What is it you want to say? Say it!

HSIAO LAN: You mean you haven't guessed what's on my mind?

MAGIC ASTER [looking into her eyes]: Of course, I know you are thinking about your home.

HSIAO LAN: I can't get Mama, Father, and Sister out of my mind. I want to visit them.

MAGIC ASTER: I'll take you back to see them tomorrow.

HSIAO LAN: No, I want to go back now; because today marks the first anniversary of my leaving home. I know they will be worrying about me. I will go now and come back tomorrow. Is that all right with you?

MAGIC ASTER: All right. But you'll have to forgive me for not being able to go with you. I hope you'll be back tomorrow.

HSIAO LAN: I'll be back for sure. Come to the foot of the mountain to fetch me tomorrow morning. I'll be thinking of you, too.

MAGIC ASTER: I'll meet you at the foot of the mountain tomorrow morning.

HSIAO LAN: Then I'll be going now.

MAGIC ASTER: Wait a minute. [He beckons to the asters high upon the mountain and a little blue flower flies over to him. He gives it to HSIAO LAN.] Take this aster with you and whenever you need anything just say:

> "Magic aster! Magic aster!
> Who fears no storm or like disaster,
> Now unfold your petals fair,
> And listen to a toiler's prayer. . . ."

Anything you ask will be granted to you. Dark roads will be lit and rivers will be bridged. [Puts the flower into HSIAO LAN's hair.] You mustn't lose it.

HSIAO LAN: Thank you. I will be careful. Goodbye.

MAGIC ASTER: No, wait a minute. Grandpa Tree! Friends! Stop dancing for a minute. Hsiao Lan is about to leave for home to see her mother and father.

[GRANDPA TREE and their friends run over.]

GRANDPA TREE: What's that? What's that you just said?

HSIAO LAN: Grandpa Tree, I've been away from home for a year now, so I want to go back to see my father and mother.

GRANDPA TREE: That's what you should do.

252

LITTLE SISTER RABBIT: What's the hurry?

SPOTTED DOE: Take my regards to your mother and father.

MORNING GLORY: Hsiao Lan, tell Mama and Daddy Wang we have a fat son.

HSIAO LAN: All right! I'll definitely tell them the good news. Thank you very much, friends. I'll be seeing you tomorrow. Have a good time. It'll be better if you make a night of it, for it will keep Magic Aster from being lonely.

DOG'S-TAIL GRASS: Don't you worry, we won't let him feel lonely!

HSIAO LAN: Goodbye, Magic Aster. Don't forget to come to fetch me early tomorrow morning. Goodbye, friends! [Exits.]

ALL: Goodbye!

MAGIC ASTER: Be careful! And take care not to lose the magic aster on the way.

HSIAO LAN [some distance away]: Ai! [Her friends stand gazing after her.]

Curtain

SCENE 2

[Outside DADDY WANG'S cottage (same as Act I, Scene 1). A moonlight night. The cottage is lit and MAMA is standing outside looking up the road. DADDY WANG comes out of the house and calls her.]

DADDY WANG: Come back, Mama! The dew has fallen and it's turning chilly. Let's go inside; she isn't coming back today.
[This is not what he feels. He keeps looking up the road, too.]

MAMA: She would definitely come back today. A year has passed already without so much as a letter from her.

DADDY WANG: She'll be back in a day or so. Don't worry, Hsiao Lan'll never forget us.
[The cat on the rooftop mews.]

MAMA: That blasted cat has come back again.

TA LAN [hearing the mew of the cat, hurries to open the window and calls]: Here, kitty, kitty. [Sees MAMA and DADDY WANG.] You haven't gone to bed yet? Don't lose any more sleep over Hsiao Lan. She has a new home and has forgotten about us long ago.

MAMA: Nonsense! Hsiao Lan isn't like you!

DADDY WANG: Let's go inside, Mama. It's getting late. She won't be
  back today. Let's go in and get some sleep.
  [DADDY WANG and MAMA enter the room, but do not put out the
  light. The shadow of MAMA doing embroidery is silhouetted on
  the window blind.]
  [HSIAO LAN returns in the moonlight. She has run almost all the
  way back. Everything here awakens her reminiscences. She sees
  MAMA's image.]
HSIAO LAN: Mama—[Stops, goes over to the bank of the pond and
  tidies her hair by her reflection in the water.]
  [The cat on the rooftop mews again. HSIAO LAN looks at it. Just
  as she is about to enter the house, she remembers the magic aster.
  She takes it out of her hair and raises it high.]
HSIAO LAN:

> Magic aster! Magic aster!
> Who fears no storm or like disaster,
> Now unfold your petals fair,
> And listen to a toiler's prayer. . . .

  Please send some gifts for my mother and father. . . .
  [From the iridescent clouds flies a basket loaded with gifts. HSIAO
  LAN looks at the gifts in happy surprise.]
  [OLD CAT mews frantically.]
  [TA LAN opens the window.]
TA LAN: What are you mewing about, Old Cat? [Sees HSIAO LAN.]
  Who is there? Sister! Mama!
  [MAMA hurries out.]
HSIAO LAN: Mama!
MAMA: Hsiao Lan! . . . I knew you would be back. . . .
  [They embrace. Enter DADDY WANG.]
HSIAO LAN: Father!
DADDY WANG: So you come back after all. Why are you so late?
TA LAN: Come in and sit down, Sister.
MAMA: Hsiao Lan, you look so well.
TA LAN: That is really a beautiful dress you're wearing, Sister.
HSIAO LAN: I made it myself.
DADDY WANG: How is Magic Aster?
HSIAO LAN: Fine. . . .
  [Their laughter brings the neighbors over.]
NEIGHBOR A: Hsiao Lan, you're back!
NEIGHBOR B: Your mother has been worried about you.
  [They chat together gaily.]

254

A Young Girl Among the Neighbors: Tell us about your life over there.

Another Young Girl: Sing us one of the new songs that you've learned.

[Hsiao Lan *sings and dances for them.*]

Hsiao Lan:

> Oh, how shall I describe,
> The beauty of my home on the mountainside.
> With my neighbors I live as good friends.
> Magic Aster is forever with me through thick and thin.
> Away from home for one year,
> Been thinking always of my childhood friends, whom I hold
> so dear.
> On the road since early morning, home now I be.
> My parents and friends I've come to see.
> Here is for Father a bottle of wine so good,
> To quench his thirst when deep in the mountain for fire-
> wood.
> To Mama we give silk thread of various colors,
> In hope she'll embroider a thousand different flowers.
> To Sister we give cloth one roll,
> To make herself a changing suit of clothes.
> To everybody we give an aster,
> In hope that happiness on your family will fall.

[*The neighbors are given an aster each. They dance happily.*]

An Old Woman: Go in and take a rest, Hsiao Lan. We must be on our way.

[*The neighbors say goodbye to all.* Hsiao Lan, Daddy Wang *and* Mama *enter the house.* Ta Lan *stays outside alone. She glowers into the room for a long time without uttering a word.*]

Ta Lan [*speaking to herself*]: Just look how arrogant she is, the little minx. Just to see the airs she puts on makes me burn with anger. [*Laughter is heard in the room.*]

Ta Lan: All right, so you're happy and enjoying an easy life, eh? You little baggage. In what way am I inferior to you? [*Goes over to the pond and looks at her reflection.*] I am just as good looking as you are. What is it you've got that I don't have? I can do everything that you can; you've got a brain and so have I; you can think and so can I. But what were my thoughts at that time? Father asked me first. Why was I so foolish? How did I fail to seize this happiness and let it fall into your hands. Oh! how I hate myself! . . .

CAT [on rooftop]: Meow . . . meow. . . .

TA LAN: You good-for-nothing. You are laughing at me?

CAT [crying frantically]: Meow, meow. . . .

TA LAN [picking up a stone and throwing it]: Stop your caterwauling, you stray!

[A puff of black smoke comes up from the place where the stone lands. A black cat jumps out of it. This is not the black cat that TA LAN has been carrying around in her arms, but a black cat the same height as TA LAN.]

CAT: Meow! Meow! Me . . . ha, ha, ha. . . .

TA LAN [frightened]: Who are you?

CAT: Your good friend, Cat.

TA LAN: Cat? How did you grow so big?

CAT: I was never small. Look how long and white my whiskers are. [Strokes his whiskers.]

TA LAN: What have you come here for?

CAT: When I saw your pitiful plight, I thought I'd come to give you a little help.

TA LAN: You! Help me?

CAT: That's right. When an old friend has troubles on hand, one can't just stand by and look on.

TA LAN: What can you do?

CAT: You see these legs of mine; when I use them to jump, it's no less than five to six feet high. Just look how easy it is for me to jump from the floor onto the table to get something to eat. My hands—some people call them paws—are tremendous. When I try them out on a broom, it crackles. [Lowering his voice.] Don't forget, they are not for catching rats. [Loud voice.] I'm very limber. I can turn a somersault without the least effort. Look! [He turns a somersault.] I'm not gasping for breath, and the color of my face has not changed. My brains hatch ideas quickly and effectively. No matter what sort of problem arises I can think of a way to cope with it and I guarantee it'll be effective. Listen to this poem:

> One, two, three; one, two, three,
> All-subduing is Cat's Magic.
> At hatching ideas, turning somersaults
>   and rolling on the ground,
> I am the best to be found.

TA LAN: Do you know what's in my mind?

256

CAT: Don't make me laugh! How could I not know! I wouldn't be your friend if I didn't.

TA LAN: Do you think I can retrieve my lost happiness?

CAT: Why not?

TA LAN: Then how should I go about it?

CAT: Let me tell you one thing, if you want happiness you must have no scruples about letting others suffer.

TA LAN: I have no scruples about letting her suffer! I hate that baggage to the very bottom of my heart.

CAT: That's good! Wait until she gets ready to go home and go part way with her; but you must make her believe that your intentions are good. . . . I'll tell you later what has to be done after that. When they come, you must pretend that nothing has happened. Meow!

[Enter HSIAO LAN. OLD CAT hides. TA LAN pretends to be cleaning up.]

HSIAO LAN: You're tidying up by yourself, Sister. Let me give you a hand.

TA LAN: There is no need, Sister; I can manage it. You get some rest. You must be tired after that journey.

HSIAO LAN: No, I'm not tired.

TA LAN: You really are clever with your fingers, Little Sister. You made that dress yourself, didn't you? No matter how hard I try I can't make one. I really regret I didn't learn how from you when you were at home.

HSIAO LAN: You can learn from Mama.

TA LAN: Anyway Mama knows how, that's good enough. It seems that I'll never learn now, because as soon as I take a needle and thread into my hands, I feel dizzy.

HSIAO LAN: It's not that you can't learn, Sister. . . .

TA LAN: My dear sister, you don't know how much we've missed you. We didn't feel it so much when you were at home, but as soon as you left we thought of you constantly. You must stay with us several days before you go back; I have much to talk to you about.

HSIAO LAN: I'll be leaving tomorrow morning, because I have many things to do at home.

TA LAN: What? You're leaving tomorrow! That won't do. I haven't had a chance to talk with you.

HSIAO LAN: Then tell me what you have to say now.

257

TA LAN: It'll take a long time to tell you what I have to say and besides I don't know where to begin now. I will go part way with you tomorrow morning, then we can talk on the way.

HSIAO LAN: Good!

MAMA [*in the room*]: Hsiao Lan! [*Coming out.*] Where have you disappeared to so quick?

TA LAN: You go in and talk to Mama. I'll have things in order in a few minutes.

MAMA: You come too, Ta Lan; we are going to eat.

TA LAN: I'll be in in a jiffy.

[MAMA *and* HSIAO LAN *go into the house.*]

CAT [*stealthily comes out from his hiding, looks around, then goes over to* TA LAN]: On the way tomorrow, you must think of a way to get her earrings and clothes. When we reach the river we'll— [*He goes through the motion of pushing her into the river.*]

TA LAN: Ai-ya!

CAT: This is the way to your happiness. Ha-ha-ha. . . .

TA LAN [*nodding*]: H'mm.

[*Black clouds blow over the sky. The moon is hidden behind a dark cloud and lightning is seen in the distance.*]

Curtain

SCENE 3

[*At the foot of the mountain by the riverside (same as Act I Scene 4). Early the next morning. The sky is overcast, the river is stirring, and a light breeze has blown up waves.*

CAT *comes shooting over like an arrow. He stealthily looks about, then looks back down the road he came on, and then finds a rock on the river bank to hide behind.*

A short while later, HSIAO LAN *and* TA LAN *come up.*]

HSIAO LAN: Magic Aster! Magic Aster! He hasn't come yet, Sister.

TA LAN: I told you it's early yet. Let's sit down and take a rest.

HSIAO LAN: You must be tired, Sister, coming so far with me.

TA LAN: Oh, that's nothing. After having not seen you for a year, it's a great pleasure.

HSIAO LAN: We've been walking so hard, we've hardly said anything to each other. You said you had something to talk to me about, didn't you, Sister?

TA LAN: Yes, I do, but I don't know where to begin.

HSIAO LAN: Let's hurry and say what we have to say, for Magic Aster will be here in a few minutes and then I'll have to go.

TA LAN: From which direction will Magic Aster come, Younger Sister?

HSIAO LAN: From that direction.

TA LAN: Can we reach your home by going along the river?

HSIAO LAN: We can. You go straight ahead along this river and then cross a mountain where you'll see clusters of asters. That's my home.

TA LAN: Are there any fish in this river? [*Runs over to the bank of the river.*]

HSIAO LAN [*pulling her back*]: What is it you have to tell me, Sister?

TA LAN: Let's go and see, Sister. There are definitely some fish in this river. Come on!

HSIAO LAN: I don't want to. What's so strange about a fish anyway?

TA LAN: There are certainly some rocks in there.

HSIAO LAN: Why do you keep talking about such things?

TA LAN: Don't get excited, Little Sister! I'll stop the nonsense. Tell me, am I plain?

HSIAO LAN: Who said you were plain?

TA LAN: Am I ugly in comparison with you?

HSIAO LAN: I don't know. Why do you want to compare yourself with me?

TA LAN: Oh, nothing, just for the fun of it. Come, let's look at our reflections in the water.

[*TA LAN pulls HSIAO LAN over to a rock on the bank of the river. Their images are reflected in the water.*]

TA LAN: Look, how ugly I am. My clothes are all patched and faded, but yours are so beautiful. As the old saying goes, "Becoming clothes adorn a man; a good saddle beautifies a steed." There is no comparison between us two.

HSIAO LAN: Here, I'll give you this jacket.

[*She takes off her jacket.*]

TA LAN: This won't do! Won't Magic Aster take umbrage, when he finds out?

HSIAO LAN: No, he won't. He'll be most happy when I tell him I gave it to you.

259

TA LAN: All right then, let me try it on.

[HSIAO LAN *hands her the jacket.*]

TA LAN [*having put the jacket on, looks at* HSIAO LAN]: I still don't look so pretty as you because you're wearing earrings and I'm not.

HSIAO LAN [*taking off her earrings*]: I'll give the earrings to you, too. [TA LAN *reaches out for them.*] Magic Aster made these earrings himself.

TA LAN: Then won't he mind when you tell him you gave them to me?

HSIAO LAN: No, of course not.

[HSIAO LAN *puts the earrings on* TA LAN. TA LAN *hurries over to the river bank to look at her reflection in the water.*]

TA LAN: The only thing now is I don't have a flower to wear in my hair. The flower you're wearing is also very beautiful. Little Sister, why don't you give it to me, too?

HSIAO LAN: If you want a flower, I'll pluck one for you, but I can't give you this one.

TA LAN: You've already given me everything, why can't you give me this wild flower?

HSIAO LAN: You don't understand, Sister. This is not an ordinary flower; it is the root of Magic Aster's life and the happiness of our whole family depends on it.

TA LAN: Oh, a magic aster! Then lend it to me to wear for a while.

HSIAO LAN: I can't do that either. I'll give you anything you want except this flower.

TA LAN [*in a joking manner*]: Then I'm going to take it!

HSIAO LAN: Even if you try to take it, I still won't give it to you. Because if I do, it's not even certain that I'll ever see Magic Aster again. But I will give you anything else you ask for; you just name it.

TA LAN: I want the magic aster, but you won't give it to me, so I'm going to take it!

[*She tries to take it.*]

HSIAO LAN [*jumping off the rock*]: Don't go on like this, Elder Sister.

TA LAN: Ha, ha, ha. Little Sister, you really beat all I have seen. I was only teasing you, but you take me so seriously. All right, all right, joking aside. I know that the magic aster is the treasure of your home. I wouldn't take it even if you gave it to me.

HSIAO LAN: But you just tried to.

TA LAN: I was only playing with you, my dear. We are sisters—how

260

can you take a joke so seriously? Come on, let's have a talk. Come and sit down here.

[*Looking up the river and longing for the arrival of* MAGIC ASTER, HSIAO LAN *shows little interest in* TA LAN.]

TA LAN [*looking up the river, too*]: Come here and look, Little Sister! Who is that coming in the distance? Is it Magic Aster?

HSIAO LAN [*quickly climbing up on the rock*]: Where? Where?

TA LAN: Look! Over there, the one wearing the blue suit.

[*On tip toe,* HSIAO LAN *looks up the river.*] [TA LAN *takes this opportunity to snatch the aster out of her hair. This movement brings* HSIAO LAN *back to the scene. At this moment* OLD CAT *comes out from behind the rock and the two of them push* HSIAO LAN *into the river.*]

[*Water splashes up in all directions and* HSIAO LAN *can be heard calling for help.* OLD CAT *picks up a rock and hurls it into the river. A short while later everything returns to normal.*]

CAT: Ha! Ha! Ha! . . . You're really clever, Ta Lan. [*Snatches the flower from her.*] Goodbye! [*Turns to go.*]

TA LAN: Hey, hey! Why are you leaving?

CAT: I've accomplished my mission. You just wait here; little Magic Aster will come for you after a while. From then on you'll have a good life.

TA LAN: He . . . will he believe that I am Hsiao Lan?

CAT: Why shouldn't he? You two sisters look very much alike and besides how can he not believe it when you're wearing Hsiao Lan's clothes and earrings! You just wait, he'll be here in a few minutes. I must be off.

TA LAN: Hold on a minute—I'm afraid. What am I to do if he asks where has Hsiao Lan gone?

CAT: You're Hsiao Lan, you idiot! Why should he ask this anyway?

TA LAN: Oh, that's right. Hey . . . why are you taking the magic aster?

CAT: You lost your happiness by not marrying Magic Aster, and you know it. Now I've helped you to think of a way to retrieve it; you just go on and enjoy it. What I wanted was this magic aster, ha, ha, ha. . . . Enough of this idle talk. I must be shuffling along. Cheerio and good luck!

TA LAN: Hey, what am I to do if Magic Aster asks about the magic aster?

CAT: Just say you lost it. [*Turns to go again, but after a couple of*

261

steps he remembers something.] Now, just look how silly I am; why am I walking when I have this precious thing in my hand? I should enjoy my riches! [*He raises the magic aster high and shouts:*]

> Magic aster! Magic aster!
> Who fears no storm or like disaster,
> Now listen to a toiler's prayer,
> And open up your petals fair.

I want a carriage pulled by eight horses to take me back. [*He closes his eyes and waits in full confidence that a carriage is going to be sent, but when he opens them and looks around, everything is as it was before.*] Has my carriage come, Ta Lan?

TA LAN: Are you fooling? Nothing has come!

CAT [*hitting the magic aster*]: What kind of precious flower are you? You can't even bring me a carriage.

TA LAN: There is no carriage in the world pulled by eight horses.

CAT: Little have you seen. Whenever my master goes out, he rides in a carriage pulled by eight horses or a sedan chair carried by sixteen men. Do you think a wagon pulled by one ox is the only thing that can be called a carriage? If you do, then you really don't know anything.

TA LAN: Anyway the carriage hasn't come!

CAT: Ah, I know what's wrong; I've got the formula wrong. Do you know it?

TA LAN: No.

CAT: Then what use is this flower to me! I might as well throw it away.

TA LAN: Oh, that would be a pity! Give it to me to wear.

CAT: That won't do. If you take it back and it falls into the hands of Magic Aster, everything will be brought to light. He is powerless without the magic aster. No matter what, we can't let him get his hands on it.

TA LAN: What are you going to do then?

CAT [*thinks for a while*]: We'll do it like this; I'll go along with you. You just tell him I am a house cat and can help you work and catch rats. I'll hide the flower on my person and take the first opportunity to get the magic formula out of him.

TA LAN: That's a good idea. If you go with me, I'll have more nerve.

[MAGIC ASTER's *singing is heard in the distance.*]

CAT: He's coming.

TA LAN: Who?

CAT: Your Magic Aster!

TA LAN: Ai-ya! What am I to do? My goodness. . . . What is the first thing I should say to him?

CAT: Calm down!

TA LAN [*prinking and feeling her earrings*]: May God bless us and pray nothing goes wrong. . . . Come and help me, Old Cat. If he discovers what has happened, then everything is finished.

CAT: Don't worry, I guarantee that everything will work out in our favor. Let's go, Hsiao Lan! Remember you're called Hsiao Lan. [*He hides the magic aster, lies on the ground near* TA LAN, *waves his tail and pretends to be tame.*] Meow! Meow!

[MAGIC ASTER *rows the boat over.*]

MAGIC ASTER: Hsiao Lan! Hsiao Lan!

TA LAN [*stands there dumbly*]: . . . .

CAT [*whispering*]: Answer him, you!

TA LAN: Ai!

CAT: Meow!

MAGIC ASTER: Have you been waiting long, Hsiao Lan?

TA LAN: No . . . I just got here.

MAGIC ASTER: I'm late.

TA LAN: Never mind.

MAGIC ASTER: How are your Mama and the rest?

TA LAN: Fine! [*Ill at ease.*]

MAGIC ASTER: Don't be sad. I'll bring you back and let you stay for a few days in another day or so.

TA LAN: There'll be no need to do that; I've had enough of this place already. . . .

CAT: Meow!

MAGIC ASTER: Did you bring this cat with you?

TA LAN: Yes. He's our house cat. He still remembers me after being away for a year. Today, when I was leaving, he wouldn't leave me. I've tried to drive him back, but he won't go. Scat, Old Cat.

CAT: No, meow! I don't want to go back. [*He stays close by* TA LAN's *side. Purring, he rubs himself against* MAGIC ASTER's *legs, hopefully cadging for sympathy and love.*]

TA LAN: Just look at this blasted cat!

MAGIC ASTER: Go back, Old Cat, Daddy Wang is waiting for you.

CAT: No, I want to stay with her. Meow!

[*Lies down at* TA LAN's *feet and won't get up.*]

TA LAN: Well, let's take him back with us. He can catch rats.

MAGIC ASTER: But doesn't Daddy Wang want him?

TA LAN: Oh, never mind about that. Father knows he is with me.

MAGIC ASTER: All right then. Hurry and get on the boat; it looks like rain.

[OLD CAT hastily jumps on the boat. MAGIC ASTER helps TA LAN on the boat, unties the painter, gets on himself, then rows off.]

[A heavy rain follows the flashes of lightning and the roar of thunder. The waves on the river became bigger.]

Curtain

ACT III

SCENE 1

[The home of MAGIC ASTER and HSIAO LAN. MAGIC ASTER comes on stage with TA LAN and OLD CAT.]

TA LAN: Oh! They are bigger than those at home.

MAGIC ASTER: What? Has the room changed?

TA LAN: . . . Er . . . I said that these haws are bigger than those at home. [Takes a haw from the table and begins to eat.]

MAGIC ASTER: Wash your hands, change your clothes, and then eat!

TA LAN: Oh, never mind about that, I'm hungry.

MAGIC MASTER: As hungry as all that?

TA LAN: Goodness! You don't know; besides not getting a good night's sleep last night, I got up before daybreak this morning and walked several miles without any breakfast. Now I'm dead tired and want to sleep for a while.

MAGIC ASTER: All right, you get some rest then. [TA LAN flops onto the bed.] You take a rest, too, Old Cat. Why don't you say something? Do you feel unwanted at our place?

CAT: Oh, I feel quite at home, Young Master.

MAGIC ASTER: Good gracious! You're wet all over.

CAT: Oh, it's nothing. I'll wait until the sun comes out and climb upon the rooftop to dry.

MAGIC ASTER: You can stay in this room, Old Cat.

CAT: You don't have to find me a room, Young Master. I like to

264

sleep on the brick stove where it is warm and comfortable. And it is very convenient there for me to get something to eat when I want it.

MAGIC ASTER: Are you planning to steal food?

CAT: How could I do such a thing? . . . What I meant is that there are plenty of rats in the kitchen for me to catch and eat conveniently.

MAGIC ASTER: You're industrious after all.

CAT: What are you saying! Everybody knows that we cats are the smartest animals in the world. Late at night when everybody else is asleep, our eyes are fixed on the corners and little holes in the walls of the house. You can rest assured, Young Master, now that I've come here every rat in your house will be caught and besides I'll help you do some work. I have nothing further to say. Our miss knows me.

MAGIC ASTER: You're a good talker, Old Cat.

CAT: Yes, I like to talk. I have many stories to tell. One of these days when you're free I will pour them out to you; I'm sure you'll like them.

MAGIC ASTER: All right!

[*Many of their friends come up outside. Their clamor is heard before they come on stage. The clearest voice among them is that of* MORNING GLORY.]

MORNING GLORY: Hsiao Lan! How are Daddy Wang and Mama?

LITTLE SISTER RABBIT: What good things to eat did you bring back for us, Sister-in-law Hsiao Lan?

[*Following this,* MORNING GLORY, THE RABBIT SISTERS, MONKEY, *and* LITTLE SQUIRREL *come on stage.*]

MORNING GLORY: Magic Aster! Is Hsiao Lan back?

MAGIC ASTER: Yes! She's asleep.

LITTLE SISTER RABBIT: Sister-in-law Hsiao Lan!

[*Runs over to the side of the bed.*]

LITTLE SQUIRREL [*frightened at seeing* CAT]: Hey, a cat!

MONKEY [*also frightened*]: Do you belong here?

MAGIC ASTER: Friends! Don't be afraid! He's a cat and a friend of Hsiao Lan. From now on he'll be living with us.

MORNING GLORY: How are Daddy Wang and the rest, Hsiao Lan?

TA LAN: Fine, just fine!

ELDER SISTER RABBIT: Did you bring back anything for us to eat, Sister-in-law Hsiao Lan?

265

TA LAN: Something to eat? If there were anything, I would've eaten it all long ago.

[*The guests are embarrassed. They are at a loss as to what to say next.*]

TA LAN: Old Cat! Did you get a nap?

CAT: No, I've been talking to Young Master. What about yourself?

TA LAN: I had just fallen asleep when they came in and woke me up with all their noise. What a nuisance! . . . [*She stretches.*]

LITTLE SISTER RABBIT: Let's go, Sister!

ELDER SISTER RABBIT: We're sorry to have disturbed you, Sister-in-law Hsiao Lan.

TA LAN: You've already woke me up; what's the use of apologizing!

MORNING GLORY: Let's go! . . .

DEER FAWN [*comes on stage running and shouting*]: Hsiao Lan! How are you, Hsiao Lan?

[*The others grab hold of him. He senses that something is amiss and stops. They pull him outside.*]

MONKEY [*whispering to* DEER FAWN]: Hurry, let's go! She's changed. [*All exit.*]

TA LAN: How annoying they are. Just when I was getting a good sleep.

[MAGIC ASTER *feels there is something strange in all this. A glimmer of doubt comes into his eye, and he looks her up and down.*]

CAT: You were entirely wrong to be so rude to them, Miss. They came to see you with the best of intentions, but you cold-shouldered them.

TA LAN: I didn't invite them here.

MAGIC ASTER: Are you sick or something? How is it that everything about you has changed after one trip back home?

TA LAN: I'm really tired, Magic Aster! I only want to sleep.

CAT: To tell you the truth, she really didn't get any rest while she was at home; for the greater part of the night she sat up talking to Daddy Wang and Mama and then she was up before daybreak this morning and walked several miles without any breakfast. You get some sleep, Miss.

MAGIC ASTER: Wait a minute! Where is the magic aster?

TA LAN: The magic aster?

MAGIC ASTER: Uh-huh! Where is it?

TA LAN: I was wearing it in my hair. [*She feels over her head for it.*]

MAGIC ASTER: It's not there!

266

TA LAN: Then I must have lost it on the bed. [*She pretends to look for it on the bed.*]

MAGIC ASTER [*also looking on the bed for it*]: It's not here either.

TA LAN [*feeling all over her body for it*]: Oh, goodness me, I must have lost it on the way. Don't rush things, let me think. . . . Oh, that's right! I must have lost it in the valley on the western side of the mountain where I took a rest. . . . No, that's not right. I must have lost it when it was raining on my way back.

MAGIC ASTER: Think back carefully. Where did you lose it after all?

TA LAN: How am I to know exactly where I lost it? If I knew, I would go back and get it! Aw, just forget about it, Magic Aster. Why get so excited about an aster, when there are so many of them on the roadside. I'll go out and pick a bunch for you after a while.

MAGIC ASTER: You must be off your head! You've changed! You're not the Hsiao Lan I know.

TA LAN: Ha! Ha! . . . It's you who's off your head. You don't even recognize your wife. Ha, ha, ha . . . isn't that funny, Old Cat? Magic Aster doesn't recognize his own wife. Ha, ha, ha, ha, ha. . . .

CAT: Explain clearly where you could have lost it. I'll go back and look for it. Don't be impatient, Young Master. I'll go and look for it for you. I'm going now.

MAGIC ASTER: There's no need for you to go and look for it, Old Cat. You just help her remember where she could've lost it.

CAT: Hold your horses a minute and let me think. When we left home, she was wearing it in her hair. H'm . . . I seem to have seen it when we were crossing the river, too. . . . What happened after that? Oh, yes! Now I remember. I'm afraid that we must have lost it when we were crossing the river. That's for sure.

MAGIC ASTER: I'm going back to look for it.

CAT: Let me go and look for you, Young Master. However, I don't understand why you're so determined to get that flower back when this whole mountain is covered with flowers. Now that that one is lost, just pluck another one to replace it.

MAGIC ASTER: Old Cat, you don't understand. When you pick a wild flower, you can't keep it long before it withers, but that aster of mine will never wither. All you have to do is to plead to it in time of difficulties and it will find a way for you.

CAT [*taking this opportunity to inquire*]: How are you supposed to plead to it?

267

MAGIC ASTER: I haven't the heart to explain. Don't hold me up any longer. I must be going. I can't set my mind on anything until after I've found the magic aster. [*Exit.*]

CAT: Wait a minute. Let me go with you, Young Master.

MAGIC ASTER [*a long way off*]: There's no need. [*As* CAT *makes gestures of leaving,* TA LAN *pulls him back.*]

TA LAN: Forget about it. Take a rest.

CAT [*turns a somersault*]: Ha, ha, ha. Did you think I was really going with him to look for it? What a joke! I was only pretending so as to make him think I am not such a bad fellow after all. The main thing is to get the magic formula; then I'll be on my merry way. Ha-ha-ha. Let him look for it. Come on, Miss, let's round up the food in the house and have a good meal. Then we can get a good sleep.

[*They merrily jump all over the place with some strange song on their lips.*]

Curtain

SCENE 2

[*At the riverside (same as Act I, Scene 4). A dark cloud covers the moon. With the exception of the sound of the river flowing and the rustling of leaves in a light breeze, all is silent.*]

[MAGIC ASTER *comes on stage much fatigued.*]

MAGIC ASTER [*staring into the river*]: Moving waters of the river, did you happen to see a blue flower on your way down? [*To the sounds of the moving water.*] Oh, if I could understand your language! Ah! Losing the magic aster is like losing my eyes; I can see nothing. [*Looks around.*] What place is this? Isn't this where Hsiao Lan and I were married? . . . But where is Hsiao Lan? Ah! my Hsiao Lan! [*In deep thought, he leans against a rock on the river bank and weeps.*]

[*The moon soars out from behind the dark cloud and the iridescent clouds again appear.* MAGIC ASTER *and* HSIAO LAN *again appear in their wedding dance. But they have no way of contacting one another. Each wants to pour his heart out to the other, but neither can hear the other's voice.*]

[HSIAO LAN *has fallen prey to the dark waves, which dash upon them and cold-heartedly separate them.*]

[*The scene disappears.* MAGIC ASTER *is again alone, leaning against the rock on the river bank.*]

MAGIC ASTER: Hsiao Lan! Hsiao Lan! Has something really happened to you? [*He straightens up and runs shouting in another direction.*] Hsiao Lan! Hsiao Lan!

[*Through the tumbling waves, we see* HSIAO LAN *lying on the pebbles at the bottom of the river. There is a crowd of* MERMAIDS *about her. Awakened by the shouts of* MAGIC ASTER, HSIAO LAN *tries to come to the surface, but she has no way of shaking off the fetters of the water. Like the stem of a water lily, she is borne this way and that by the current. Finally she sinks onto the pebbles.*]

HSIAO LAN [*weakly*]: I want to go back. . . . Magic Aster is calling me. . . . I want to go back. . . .

MERMAID No. 1: Be patient, Hsiao Lan. You won't be able to see each other until he's found the magic aster. Just wait till Magic Aster finds it, then you can reunite.

HSIAO LAN: But who can tell him where the magic aster is? He will never find out like this.

MERMAID No. 2: That's not so. There will come a day when you will get back the magic aster, because it helps only honest, loyal, and kind people.

HSIAO LAN: Kind girl, will you please tell him where it is?

MERMAID No. 1: No, I can't go up to the surface.

HSIAO LAN: Then doesn't that mean everything is finished?

MERMAID No. 2: Don't be upset, Hsiao Lan. We'll think of a way for you.

[*Just as the* MERMAIDS *are putting their heads together, a little bird circles in the air pouring out his song.*]

HSIAO LAN: Little Bird! That's the Little Bird who lives at the entrance of our house. Little Bird!

[LITTLE BIRD *lights upon a rock on the river bank, watching things at the bottom of the river.*]

MERMAID No. 1: Little Bird, Hsiao Lan is beset by misfortune. Will you take a message to Magic Aster for her?

[LITTLE BIRD *listens.*]

HSIAO LAN: Go immediately, Little Bird, and tell Magic Aster that Ta Lan has the magic aster! She cheated me out of my clothes, took the magic aster, pushed me into the river, and disguised herself as me. . . . Hurry now and tell Magic Aster, Little Bird, before he goes far away.

[*After circling in the air,* LITTLE BIRD *lights upon a rock. Just as soon as he lights upon the rock, there is a puff of blue smoke, out of which steps a young man.*]

LITTLE BIRD: Magic Aster! Magic Aster!

[MAGIC ASTER *returns.*]

MAGIC ASTER: Who is that calling me?

LITTLE BIRD: It's me, Little Bird.

MAGIC ASTER: Have you seen a blue flower, Little Bird?

LITTLE BIRD: The magic aster?

MAGIC ASTER: That's right. Have you seen it?

LITTLE BIRD: I know where it is.

MAGIC ASTER: You do?

LITTLE BIRD: Uh-huh.

MAGIC ASTER: How did you come to know where it is?

LITTLE BIRD: Hsiao Lan told me.

MAGIC ASTER: Where is she?

LITTLE BIRD: Ta Lan has killed her.

MAGIC ASTER: What?

LITTLE BIRD: She has not only killed Hsiao Lan, but she has disguised herself as Hsiao Lan and gone to your house to steal her happiness for herself.

MAGIC ASTER: Then where is the magic aster?

LITTLE BIRD: Ta Lan has it.

MAGIC ASTER: Please come back with me to help me find it, will you, Little Bird?

LITTLE BIRD: All right.

MAGIC ASTER: Please fly over here!

[LITTLE BIRD *spreads his wings and alights beside* MAGIC ASTER.]

MAGIC ASTER: Thanks for rendering me help in difficulty, Little Bird.

LITTLE BIRD: We haven't done anything yet, but here you are thanking me! Let's find the magic aster.

MAGIC ASTER: Right!

[LITTLE BIRD *flies ahead of him.* MAGIC ASTER *returns home happily.*]

Curtain

SCENE 3

[*The* home *of* MAGIC ASTER *and* HSIAO LAN (*same as* Scene 1). MAGIC ASTER *and* LITTLE BIRD *enter.*]

LITTLE BIRD: How quiet everything is. Is there no one home?

MAGIC ASTER: Humph! They're still asleep! You'd better stay here, Little Bird. I'm going to look for Grandpa Tree and the others. Now, don't go away, you wait for me here.

LITTLE BIRD: Go ahead. If I happen to find the magic aster, I'll call you.

[MAGIC ASTER *Exit.*]

LITTLE BIRD: You really have no sense of shame! Here you are still lying in bed with the sun shining in on you while everyone else on the mountain has been up and working for hours.

TA LAN [*in bed*]: Who is that making all that noise? [*She looks around and sees* LITTLE BIRD, *but because* LITTLE BIRD *doesn't look at her, she thinks he can't speak.*] How annoying! [*Turns over and prepares to go back to sleep.*]

LITTLE BIRD: Lazybones! Lazybones!

TA LAN [*turning over quickly*]: Who's that? Who's that? At home, Mother and Father made so much noise that I couldn't sleep, but who is it poking his nose in here? I'll sleep as long as I want to and it's nobody's business.

LITTLE BIRD: It's everybody's business, Lazybones, you evil thing. Anyone would find you a nuisance.

TA LAN: You! So, it's you making the noise! This is really a strange place, even a little bird can stick his beak into the affairs of grownups. I think it's best that you mind your own business and leave other people alone. Ha! Ha! Ha! Old Cat! Are you up? Come out at once.

CAT [*lazily crawls out from under the bed, shakes the dust off his body, yawns and stretches*]: Oh-h-h-h. . . .

TA LAN: What are you looking so glum about?

CAT: I can't get used to this place! It's really dull here. I haven't had so much as a smell of fish since I came here yesterday. That's really more than I can take.

TA LAN: Drop it! Stop your grumbling. You'll get a meal of fish sooner or later. [*Pointing to the bird.*] Look.

CAT: Uh—a little bird. [*Drooling.*]

LITTLE BIRD: You lazybones! You evil thing!

271

TA LAN: You shouldn't curse others!

CAT [*hurrying over to stop her*]: He has a right to abuse us, we are late getting up. Look what a mess your hair's in; it really doesn't look nice.

[*TA LAN picks up the comb and begins to comb her hair in the mirror. She breaks out into some ribald old song as she combs her hair. CAT keeps LITTLE BIRD's every movement under watch.*]

LITTLE BIRD: You're a heartless murderess!

TA LAN: What! What did you say?

LITTLE BIRD: How can you, in all conscience, look at your devil's face in the mirror of others and use their comb to comb your dog's hair!

TA LAN: You!

LITTLE BIRD: You don't care a curse about the sufferings of others; all you're concerned about is your own enjoyment!

TA LAN: You devil of a bird! [*Making for him.*] Is it any of your business?

[*LITTLE BIRD nimbly dodges out of the way. TA LAN chases after him. CAT holds TA LAN back.*]

CAT: What are you so angry about, Miss?

TA LAN [*lowering her voice*]: This won't do, Old Cat; he knows our secret. If he tells Magic Aster, then that's the end of us.

CAT: Don't get excited. We have to work things step by step. Go on combing your hair. [*He draws near LITTLE BIRD with a broad smile on his face.*] You really have a kind heart, Little Bird! Why curse her? Hsiao Lan has always been a nice girl.

LITTLE BIRD: Everyone knows that Hsiao Lan is nice. But is she Hsiao Lan?

CAT [*pretending not to have any bad intentions, draws in extremely close to LITTLE BIRD*]: What makes you think she isn't Hsiao Lan? She hasn't changed a bit.

LITTLE BIRD: She can wear Hsiao Lan's clothes and earrings, but she can't steal her heart. What are you trying to do?

CAT: Oh, nothing. You're so nice, Little Bird. You're simply. . . .

[*CAT springs on LITTLE BIRD. LITTLE BIRD spreads his wings to fly, but CAT has him in his paws. CAT suddenly puts on a furious face.*]

CAT: You're going to make me a wholesome breakfast. Ha! Ha! Ha! I haven't had any meat to eat all day, ha-ha-ha.

[*LITTLE BIRD struggles to get free, but CAT has him tightly gripped in his paws. Feathers fall on the floor.*]

272

LITTLE BIRD: Let go of me! You sly devil!

CAT: Let you go? Ha, ha, ha! My mouth's watering.

LITTLE BIRD: You . . . Magic Aster! . . .

[CAT pulls LITTLE BIRD into the courtyard at the back. The cold laugh of CAT and the cries of LITTLE BIRD can be heard.]

[TA LAN continues combing her hair as if nothing is happening. A short while later, OLD CAT comes out, wiping his mouth and washing his face.]

TA LAN: How was it? Did it satisfy your craving?

CAT: Not bad.

TA LAN: Get this place cleaned up, the feathers are all over the floor.

CAT: I'm not used to doing that sort of work.

TA LAN: Magic Aster'll be back in a few minutes. When he sees these feathers, he'll ask about Little Bird.

CAT [enlightened]: It's good that you reminded me. We must act as if nothing has happened. [He gathers up a bundle of feathers and bones, digs a hole and buries them.]

MAGIC ASTER [from a distance]: Little Bird! Little Bird!

TA LAN: Heavens above! Magic Aster is coming back looking for Little Bird. What are we going to do?

CAT: Just keep a cool head! First let's hide and see what he does. [He pulls TA LAN out of sight.]

MAGIC ASTER [running]: Little Bird! Little Bird! Now where has he gone to? [Looks about for him. Notices the feathers on the floor and the empty bed. He concludes that LITTLE BIRD has encountered some evil. He gives way to tears.] My Little Bird!

[Soft music begins to play at this time. To the tune of the music, an apple tree loaded with sparkling apples grows up in the spot where LITTLE BIRD's feathers and bones are buried. LITTLE BIRD's singing is heard mingling with the music.]

THE VOICE OF LITTLE BIRD: Magic Aster! Your Little Bird has been murdered by Cat just the same as your Hsiao Lan.

[MAGIC ASTER hugs the apple tree as he weeps.]

THE VOICE OF LITTLE BIRD: Don't be sad, Magic Aster. Go at once to find your friends. Once you've found the magic aster, everything will come right.

[MAGIC ASTER reluctantly leaves the apple tree.]

[TA LAN and CAT enter.]

TA LAN: Go look for your magic aster, you silly fool, ha, ha, ha . . . .

CAT: Careful, he hasn't gone far.

TA LAN: Who cares. Come, let's pull some apples to eat.

[*Just as she is about to pull an apple, it throws off a dazzling light which knocks her hand back. She tries again and the same thing happens. She then hugs the tree intending to shake down the apples. But, strange as it may seem, the tree catches hold of her arms and will not let go.*]

TA LAN: Ai-you! Old Cat! I can't get my arms free from this tree. . . . Old Cat! . . .

CAT: Don't go getting so excited! [*Picks up an apple and begins to eat.*] Let's think of a way to get you loose.

TA LAN: Ai-ya! Here I am in a stew and you stand there thinking of a way. Damn it, Old Cat, give me a hand!

CAT: I'm coming now. Just keep a cool head. . . . [*Lets out a sudden yell.*] Ai-ya! How sour these confounded apples taste!

TA LAN: Hurry and find an axe, Old Cat, to cut down this apple tree. Hurry! . . .

CAT: I'm coming. . . . I'm coming. . . [*He finds an axe and begins to chop desperately.*]

TA LAN: Put some strength behind it. Quickly! . . .

[MAGIC ASTER *runs up.*]

MAGIC ASTER: What do you think you're doing?

CAT [*suddenly frightened silly*]: Uh . . . Ta Lan . . . er . . . Ta Lan's younger sister can't get her arms free, Young Master.

TA LAN: Don't waste time with him! Hurry, chop it down. There is only a little left.

[CAT *resumes his chopping.*]

MAGIC ASTER: Stop! You're not allowed to cut this tree!

[OLD CAT *turns a deaf ear to him.* MAGIC ASTER *runs over to take the axe, but* CAT *puts up a struggle. Although* TA LAN *cannot get her hands free, she still kicks* MAGIC ASTER *whenever she gets the chance.*]

[*The apple tree has been cut down and* TA LAN *gets her hands free.*]

MAGIC ASTER: You cruel-hearted things. You were not satisfied with killing Hsiao Lan, you had to kill my Little Bird and cut down my apple tree, too. You want to kill us all, you murderers!

TA LAN: All right, now that you know, I won't try to hide it from you any longer. What are you going to do about it? Hsiao Lan is dead and you've lost the magic aster. What other treasures do you have? Ha! Ha! My advice is for you to stop all this running about and settle down with me; better days will follow!

MAGIC ASTER: Get out of my sight! I hate you. I hate your beastly heart. Tell me, right now, where is the magic aster?

TA LAN: I wouldn't know; you didn't give it to me.

CAT: You're going too far, Miss! Don't be angry, Young Master. Does it matter if you don't have the magic aster on you? It may work just by reciting the magic formula. Try it and see, it just might work. Recite it!

TA LAN: That's right! Recite the magic formula and see. You may be saved by doing so.

MAGIC ASTER: Nonsense! Even if you cunning people do come into possession of it, it will be of no use to you. The magic aster helps only honest, loyal, and kind people. You might as well hand it over!

TA LAN: Ha, ha, ha, you find it if you can! Where am I to get it to hand over!

MAGIC ASTER: You cunning fox! It's hidden on your person. [He chases after TA LAN to search her, but she cunningly dodges out of the way. She draws close to OLD CAT.]

TA LAN [whispering]: Hurry and run, Old Cat. Destroy the magic aster. [Shouting.] Come on, Magic Aster, your magic aster is hidden in my hair. Come on! Come on!

[MAGIC ASTER gives chase to TA LAN and she dodges out of the way. He chases her off the stage.]

CAT [alone. Takes out the magic aster and looks at it]: Ha-ha! You fell for the trick, you silly fool!

THE VOICE OF LITTLE BIRD: The magic aster! The magic aster! Magic Aster! Old Cat has the magic aster.

[Hearing the voice of LITTLE BIRD, OLD CAT hides the magic aster in a hurry and escapes.]

THE VOICE OF LITTLE BIRD: Old Cat is trying to escape, Magic Aster!

[MAGIC ASTER comes back and looks around.]

THE VOICE OF LITTLE BIRD: Quick! Give chase to Old Cat. He has the magic aster.

MAGIC ASTER: Fly out and tell our friends to catch Old Cat, Little Bird.

THE VOICE OF LITTLE BIRD: Catch Old Cat, friends, he has the magic aster! . . .

[MAGIC ASTER chases him off the stage.]

Curtain

275

SCENE 4

[*Deep in the mountain (same as Act I, Scene 2). The clatter of* DEER FAWN's *bounding hoofs is heard in the distance.* THE RABBIT SISTERS *stick their heads out from a patch of grass on the roadside.* SPOTTED DOE, *on the mountain top, looks about searchingly.* MORNING GLORY *and* DOG'S-TAIL GRASS *are whispering to each other.* LITTLE SQUIRREL *is watching all movements from a tree-top.* MONKEY *has crawled into a crevice in a rock on the cliff.*]

[GRANDPA TREE *looks about carefully.*]

GRANDPA TREE: That's Deer Fawn's hoof beats. He will certainly be bringing some news. We'd better be ready, children.

DEER FAWN [*bounding up*]: The bad egg is coming. I saw him on top of the mountain over there.

GRANDPA TREE: Be on your toes, children. Let's hide and keep a sharp watch for tricks. That devil has a lot of them up his sleeve. [*All hide.* LITTLE SISTER RABBIT *sticks her ears out, but* ELDER SISTER RABBIT *pulls her down. All around is silence, which is suddenly broken by the squall of an infant. Following this we hear* DOG'S-TAIL GRASS *whisper:* "Hush. Quiet the child!" MORNING GLORY *soothes it.*]

[*All is quiet.* CAT *jumps all in a fluster.*]

CAT [*looking back to see if anyone is after him*]: Damned if I haven't become the rat today. It's the first time in my life I've ever run so far. My legs refuse to obey me and my head feels like lead. [*Remembering the magic aster, he takes it out carefully.*] Venerable magic aster, I, Old Cat, am begging you wholeheartedly to give me a carriage pulled by eight horses. Venerable magic aster, have mercy on me. If a carriage pulled by eight horses is too much, then will you please give me one pulled by four horses and if you can't do that, then just give me one pulled by two horses or even one pulled by one horse will do. If you can't fulfill my request for any of these, then just give me a horse. I am begging you on my bended knees, venerable magic aster. Please have a heart! I, Old Cat, am crying before you, meow, meow, meow!

GRANDPA TREE: What are you doing?

CAT [*opening his eyes and seeing the bearded* GRANDPA TREE *standing over him, he is both surprised and happy, because he takes it as the work of the magic aster. He immediately kowtows*]: Venerable Grandpa, will you do a favor for those in distress!

GRANDPA TREE: What is it you want?

CAT: I want a horse . . . er . . . I mean, I want an eight-horse carriage loaded with gold, silver, pearls, agates, delicacies from the seas and mountains, and silks and satins. . . . Have a heart, Grandpa. Bring it to me immediately, because I need it now. [*Kowtows again.*] Hurry up! Hurry up!

THE VOICE OF LITTLE BIRD: Cat has the magic aster! Catch him, friends! Catch him!

CAT [*in a greater fluster than ever*]: Have a heart, Grandpa! Hurry, hurry! When I get back home, I'll erect a temple to you and have your statue made to be worshipped. Hurry up now with the carriage, gold, silver. . . .

GRANDPA TREE: You swindler! Block the way, children, and don't let him escape!

CAT [*senses that something is amiss, but he has no way to escape, because all paths are under guard*]: Ai-ya! Deuce take it! . . . [MAGIC ASTER *comes chasing after him. Horribly frightened at seeing* MAGIC ASTER *coming, he runs onto the cliff-top.*]

MAGIC ASTER: You swindler! Give me back the magic aster, now!

CAT [*standing on the cliff with the magic aster raised aloft*]: Here is the magic aster! Do you want it? Ha-ha-ha, I can't get anything from it and I am not going to give it to you either!
[MAGIC ASTER *runs up on the cliff after him. A fight ensues. In the end* MAGIC ASTER *raises* CAT *high in the air and throws him into the valley below.* CAT *screams frantically.* TA LAN *comes up just in time to see this sight and is frightened stiff.*]

MAGIC ASTER: Ai-ya, the magic aster fell down there, too.

MONKEY: Don't worry about it so long as I'm around.
[MONKEY *and* DEER FAWN *run down into the valley.*]
[MAGIC ASTER *turns around and sees* TA LAN *standing sickly in a cluster of grass burning with shame.*]

MAGIC ASTER: You?

MORNING GLORY: It takes a heartless creature to kill her own younger sister.

SPOTTED DOE: You're really possessed by the devil.

TA LAN: I. . . .

GRANDPA TREE: Do you have the nerve to open your mouth?
[MONKEY *and* DEER FAWN *come back arguing with each other.*]

MONKEY: Give it to me! I found it first. . . .

DEER FAWN: I was the first . . . Magic Aster! . . . [*Just as he is about to hand it to* MAGIC ASTER.]

MONKEY [snatching it]: Here it is, Magic Aster!

DEER FAWN: You. . . . [Makes ready to tussle for it.]

LITTLE SQUIRREL: Pax! Neither of you will give in to the other.

ELDER SISTER RABBIT: What about Old Cat?

MONKEY: Old Cat is now a dead cat!

LITTLE SISTER RABBIT: Where is he? [She climbs upon the cliff to look.]

GRANDPA TREE: So be it, children! Don't go to look! Let that bad egg and all his dirty deeds perish together. Hurry and bring Hsiao Lan back, Magic Aster.

MAGIC ASTER [raising high the magic aster]:

> Magic aster! Magic aster!
> Who fears no storm or like disaster,
> Now unfold your petals fair,
> And listen to a toiler's prayer. . . . .

Bring Hsiao Lan and Little Bird back together.

[Soft and sweet music is heard in the valley. Iridescent colors again appear in the sky. A little bird wings swiftly through the air. Following this the asters bloom again. HSIAO LAN is standing among them. MAGIC ASTER hurries over to embrace her. Tears of ecstasy well in the eyes of all at this happy reunion.]

[Turning to greet everyone, HSIAO LAN sees TA LAN.]

HSIAO LAN: You—Elder Sister, didn't you say you had a lot to say to me?

[TA LAN hangs her head in shame.]

HSIAO LAN: Much we may say, Elder Sister, but one thing that you should always bear in mind is that we have to create our own happiness.

GRANDPA TREE: Go back and think over what you've done.

[TA LAN leaves in shame.]

GRANDPA TREE: Let's all go back, children. Leave them alone to themselves.

[A rainbow appears in the sky. HSIAO LAN and MAGIC ASTER are standing in a cluster of flowers talking to each other. Their friends hide themselves quietly away again. All becomes quiet on the mountain.]

Curtain

LETTERS FROM THE SOUTH*

By Sha Seh, Fu To, Ma Yung and Chi-huang
Translated by Sidney Shapiro

CHARACTERS

HA, a girl of twenty-four, leader of the party branch of the south Vietnam People's Revolutionary Party in a "strategic hamlet."

TU, a man of forty, member of the branch party committee.

HA'S MOTHER, in her fifties.

NGOC, HA's sister-in-law, about thirty.

GRANDPA, about seventy.

TRAN, TU's daughter, thirteen.

COMMANDER LE, leader of a detachment of the south Vietnam People's Militia.

THANH, a man of sixty-five, member of the militia detachment.

DA, another member.

CHIN, peasant in the "strategic hamlet."

NAM, thirty-seven, soldier in the puppet army.

NAM'S WIFE, in her early thirties.

VAN AN, a man in his thirties, teacher in a normal school.

PHAM, leader of a secret unit of the south Vietnam People's Revolutionary Party in a certain city.

---

*This play is collectively written by Sha Seh, Fu To, Ma Yung and Li-Chi-huang based on some of the contents of *Letters from the South* published in Chinese in 1964 by the Vietnamese Foreign Languages Publishing House. Sha Seh is the director of the Modern Drama Theater of the Kwangsi Chuang Autonomous Region, while the other three are playwrights working in army units. Fu To's dramatic works include *Breaking Through the Darkness Before Dawn* and *The Battle at Pinghsingkuan Pass*; Ma Yung is the author of the film script *The Hui Detachment*. Reprinted from *Chinese Literature*, No. 3 (1966), pp. 3–64.

COLONEL KENT, American "adviser" to the puppet government.
KIM, head of special agents in the "Ministry of Civil Affairs."
NHAN, police commissioner in the city.

A news-boy, four members of the people's militia, residents of the "strategic hamlet," a waiter in the cafe, a customer, a captain in the puppet army, a young puppet soldier, three policemen, a special agent in the "Ministry of Civil Affairs," two American soldiers, several puppet soldiers, and a young woman secretary.

PROLOGUE

[_The curtain rises to the militant tune of "Liberate the South." On a background screen thick smoke is seen curling and flames leaping. Then the title of the play appears: "Letters from the South." Gradually, the title fades and a spot light focuses on HA._]

HA [_reading a letter_]: Dear Father: We've had no news from you since you went north in 1954. The Hien Luong River which separates the north and south is only one _li_ wide, but to get a letter across is harder than communicating with the moon. The vicious American imperialists are preventing our country's unification and separating us from our families. During the past ten years the U.S.-puppet reactionaries have butchered thousands of our people here in the south. But when one falls, ten thousand rise to take his place. No one is willing to live like a slave. Father, under the leadership of the south Vietnam National Front for Liberation we are fighting the enemy tooth and nail. Today the situation is much better. The Liberation Army wins battles every day. "Strategic hamlets"[1] are being destroyed one after the next. We are inflicting heavy losses on the enemy. But they won't give in. The nearer they are to destruction the more desperately they struggle. Last night the Yanks and puppets suddenly came to our village and searched every house. They arrested more than twenty villagers, including Brother Xuan. We are trying to force the enemy to release them. Father, we know that the nearer we come to victory, the crueller the struggle will be. Only by conquering the darkness will we see the morning light.

[_The light slowly dims._]

280

SCENE 1

[*Twilight in a "strategic hamlet" in south Vietnam in 1964. To the right, a corner of* HA's *home. The palm frond roof is supported by bamboo pillars. In several places the roof has been rotted by rain, but it obviously hasn't been repaired in a long time. To the rear, walls topped by barbed wire, and sentry towers can be seen further off.*

As the curtain rises, melancholy singing can be heard. The peasants are waiting anxiously for news.]

GRANDPA: Those dirty Americans, dragging our people away. [*Sighs.*] How are we going to live?

TRAN [*unhappily*]: My pa . . . .

HA'S MOTHER: Don't cry, Tran.

TRAN: Will he be able to come home?

HA'S MOTHER: Don't worry, child. Wait and see. Maybe he will. [*Sighs.*] What a world! We haven't had a day's peace since they moved us into this "strategic hamlet."

CHIN: If only the Liberation Army or our guerrillas² would come. [*Nam's wife enters, carrying a bucket of water.*]

NAM'S WIFE: Those men they've taken away—have they let any of them come back, Ha's mother?

[HA'S MOTHER *shakes her head.*]

NAM'S WIFE: Where's your daughter-in-law Ngoc?

HA'S MOTHER: She went to the city early this morning to try and find out about Xuan. She still hasn't returned.

NAM'S WIFE: Your son Xuan is a fine boy. Always helping people. What crime has he committed that they should arrest him? How will your family manage if anything should happen to him?

HA'S MOTHER: Quiet. Here comes a policeman.

[POLICEMAN A *enters.*]

POLICEMAN A: What are you all standing around here for? Four or five people together are a crowd, and crowds are against the law. Don't you know that? Break it up. Are you trying to defy the government? Break it up, I say.

GRANDPA: We're waiting for those relatives you arrested.

POLICEMAN A: Don't waste your time. They're all Vietcong, all guerrillas. None of them will be coming back. Break it up. [*Forces the peasants to disperse.*]

281

HA'S MOTHER: They've taken your father away, Tran. Stay at my place. [*Exit with the girl.*]

NAM'S WIFE: Dog in man's clothing!

POLICEMAN A: What did you say?

NAM'S WIFE: I said dog in man's clothing!

POLICEMAN A: You dare. . . . [NAM'S WIFE *picks up the bucket of water and stands threateningly.*] All right, all right.

[*She departs with the bucket.*]

POLICEMAN A [*calls towards* HA'S *house*]: You've got a visitor. [*Turns and beckons.*] Come on.

[VAN AN *enters, carrying a package.* HA'S MOTHER *comes out.*]

VAN AN: Aunt!

HA'S MOTHER: Van An!

VAN AN: How are you, Aunt?

HA'S MOTHER: We haven't seen you in a long time, son. How did you find time to visit us? Are you busy at school?

VAN AN: Today is Sunday. I thought a stroll in the country would do me good—at the same time I could call on you.

HA'S MOTHER: It's hot in the house. Let's sit out here for a while. I'll get you a drink. [*Goes into the house.*]

POLICEMAN A: Hey, mister. [*Holds out his hand.*] Be quick.

VAN AN: What do you want?

POLICEMAN A: Money.

VAN AN: Didn't I pay when I came into the village?

POLICEMAN A: That was to the security company. I'm from the police station. The army and the police are two different things. They let you into the village; I let you meet your friends. Fork over.

[VAN AN *helplessly gives him a few notes.* POLICEMAN A *Exit.* HA'S MOTHER *comes out with a coconut.*]

HA'S MOTHER: Have some coconut milk.

VAN AN [*taking the coconut*]: Thank you, Aunt.

HA'S MOTHER: What brings you from the city?

VAN AN: I wanted to ask Xuan and Ha to help me with something.

HA'S MOTHER [*sighs*]: Xuan has been taken away by the enemy.

VAN AN: What? How did it happen?

HA'S MOTHER: Yesterday the American adviser came to inspect, and they arrested over twenty people. Said they had dealings with the guerrillas, that they were "dangerous elements." Our villagers sent Ngoc into the city at dawn today to try and get some news, but till now she hasn't returned.

282

VAN AN [*furious*]: Those Americans bring disaster wherever they go. They're a pack of beasts.

HA'S MOTHER: We're being pressed so hard, we can't live. When Xuan and Ha were fired from the textile mill for taking part in the strike, we moved out here to the country. Then the Americans and their puppet reactionaries forced us into this cursed "strategic hamlet." They robbed us of our belongings, and what they didn't rob, they burned. Our grain was put in their storage bin. We have to draw grain for each meal separately. Our life is worse than a dog's.

VAN AN: North and South are being prevented from uniting; our countrymen are constantly humiliated, murdered. How can we go on like this?

[HA *enters.*]

HA: Cousin Van An!

VAN AN: Your mother says Xuan has been arrested. Can anything be done?

HA: We're trying to think of something. What are you doing here, Cousin?

VAN AN: I bought that medicine you asked me to get. I've had it for some time. You didn't come for it, so I've brought it to you. [*Hands her the package.*]

HA: Thank you, Cousin. [*Gives package to her mother.*] Hide this in a good place, Ma.

HA'S MOTHER: Right. [*Takes package into the house.*]

VAN AN: I'd like to ask you a favor, Ha.

HA: What is it?

VAN AN: I'll speak frankly. I've come to ask you to help me find a way out.

HA: Aren't you teaching in the normal school in the city?

VAN AN: I can't keep betraying my conscience. I'm poisoning our next generation with American "culture." The Americans have taken over the city. They're behaving like pigs. I just can't stand it. Have you any connections that can get me into the liberated area?

HA: So that's what it is. Let's talk inside. [*Starts to go into the house.*]

[POLICEMAN A *enters.*]

POLICEMAN A: Time's up, mister.

VAN AN: But I haven't finished my business here.

Policeman A: No back talk. Get going. That's the rule. [*Pushes him.*]

Van An: I'll come again, Ha.

Policeman A [*angry*]: Beat it. [*Drives* Van An *away.*]

Ha's mother [*emerges from house and calls*]: Come again soon, Van An.

Policeman A: What did your daughter-in-law Ngoc go to the city for, old woman?

Ha's mother: To inquire about Xuan.

Policeman A: Our commissioner just phoned. He says we're not to let you people go to the city and make trouble any more. [*Exit.*]

Ha's mother: Where have you been, Ha? I haven't seen you all day.

Ha: Don't worry about me, Ma. I had something to do.

Ha's mother: Times are so troubled, Ha. You must be very careful when you're away from home. I'm always afraid you'll . . . .

Ha: It's all right, Ma. You know what Brother says: "It takes guts to be a revolutionary." You mustn't let the enemy scare you; no matter how tough things get, you have to fight to the end. The enemy has taken off a lot of comrades. We've got to shoulder the burdens they've left behind. I can tell you this, Ma: We've just had a meeting. We've decided to fight it out.

Ha's mother: Good. If there's anything I can do, let me know.

Ha: Fine.

[Ngoc *enters.*]

Ngoc: Ma!

Ha: Ngoc!

Ha's mother: You're back, Ngoc. Did you see Xuan?

Ngoc: I pleaded at the police bureau for hours. Not only wouldn't they let me in, they set their dogs on me.

Ha's mother: Filthy brutes!

Ha: Rest a while, Ngoc. We'll gradually figure out some way to save them. [*Escorts her mother and sister-in-law into the house.*] [Nam *enters, and bumps into his wife, who is returning with another bucket of water.*]

Nam's wife: You've only just come home, where are you off to again? Why aren't you looking after our sick child?

Nam: I . . . I . . . . [*Shoves some notes into his pocket.*]

Nam's wife: What are you hiding? What's that in your pocket? [*She pulls out the money.*] Fine. You take the money for our child's medicine and go out to buy drink. Have you no heart?

284

NAM: Who wants to drink? Today our captain's first-born son is a month old.

NAM'S WIFE: What's that got to do with you?

NAM: I have to give the little darling a present.

NAM'S WIFE: Better to buy his father some burial clothes!

NAM: Give me that money. If the captain gets mad, our whole family will be out of luck.

NAM'S WIFE: How much more out of luck can we be? Today his son is a month old; tomorrow it will be his wife's birthday. If that isn't pure blackmail, what is?

NAM [*sighs*]: Only they use another name for it. Give me the money.

NAM'S WIFE: I will not! I'm not going to let our child die so that you can give the money to your captain's baby.
[HA *enters.*]

HA: Let him have the money. The neighbors and I will find a way to buy your child some medicine.

NAM: Thank you, Ha. I'll remember your kindness all my life.

HA: You don't have to thank me. Just be a little more considerate of your neighbors in the future, that will be enough. Don't forget you're a Vietnamese, Nam. The enemy won't last long. Sooner or later the "strategic hamlets" will be destroyed. We're sure to drive out the Yankees. You ought to take a long-range view, leave yourself a way out.

NAM: Don't worry, Ha. I'll never do anything to harm our neighbors. It's true I'm wearing this uniform, but I have a lot of troubles I can't talk about. If it weren't for having a wife and child, I would have quit long ago. [*Sighs. To his wife.*] Give it to me.

NAM'S WIFE: Here. [*Hands him the money.*] Let your captain buy coffins for his whole family with it!
[NAM *exits.*]

HA: Don't be too downhearted, sister.

NAM'S WIFE: I've got a belly full of rage. Taking our child's medicine money. They're a pack of thieves. The day will come when I'll cut them to pieces.

HA: Go home and look after your child.
[*They walk off together. Dogs bark in the distance. Tu, bruised and bleeding, runs on.*]

TU [*calls*]: Ha. Ha.
[HA *responds and enters, followed by her mother.*]

HA: Uncle Tu, how did you get away?

HA'S MOTHER: Tu, you . . . .

[TRAN enters.]

TRAN: Pa! [Throws her arms around him and weeps.] Pa . . . .

TU: Don't cry, Tran. Keep a lookout for us over there. Let me know if anyone comes.

TRAN: Yes, pa. [Exit.]

TU [gazes around cautiously]: Please give me a drink, Ha's mother.

HA'S MOTHER [gets him an opened coconut from the house]: How did you escape?

[NGOC comes out on hearing his voice.]

TU: Last night the enemy took us from here to Lam Lake to kill us. I jumped into the water and got away in the dark. I hid in the rice paddies all night.

HA: Why have you come back? The enemy are sure to search for you here.

TU: I've something important to tell you.

NGOC: What happened to Xuan and the others?

TU [sadly]: Ngoc, Ha's mother, you must be brave. . . .

NGOC [fearfully]: Was Xuan . . . .

TU: Last night the Yanks and the police took us to the edge of the lake. They tried to force us to tell them who were members of the People's Revolutionary Party. Of course, none of us spoke. The Yanks got frantic. They had the police whip us. Still no one said a word. They began gouging out eyes with their bayonets. When one man was blinded, two more stepped forward. When two were blinded, a dozen stepped forward. The police poured gasoline over several of our people and set them afire. One was a pregnant woman. A Yankee soldier kicked her in the belly after pushing her around. Then the savages laughed! One of our men struggled to his feet and cursed them. "You'll pay for this in blood, you butchers," he shouted. A Yankee shot him three times. His last words were: "Down with U.S. imperialism! Wipe out the reactionaries! Long live the south Vietnam National Front for Liberation! Long live the People's Revolutionary Party!" Ha's mother, Ngoc, that man was your Xuan. . . .

NGOC: Xuan? [Staggers. HA'S MOTHER helps her into the house.]

HA: And then, Uncle Tu?

TU: The enemy put Xuan and the other murdered comrades into weighted gunny sacks and threw them into the lake. The remaining prisoners were taken to the city.

HA: We mustn't allow the blood of our martyred comrades to have been shed in vain.

TU: Certainly not. That's why I've come back. Xuan was the secretary of our Party branch. Now that he's dead, we must strengthen our organization and continue the fight.

HA: Our branch has already met, Uncle Tu. It was decided to send me to contact the district party committee tonight for guidance about our work.

TU: I've already been to the district committee. They've instructed you to take over the post of branch secretary. They want us to make contact with the guerrillas immediately.

[*A car is heard approaching.* TRAN *runs on.*]

TRAN: The enemy are coming, Pa!

HA: Tran, you and your father hide in Chin's place. We've just dug a shelter there. It's comparatively safe.

TU: Good. [*Exit with* TRAN.]

[HA *starts for the house.* NAM *enters.*]

NAM: Get into the house, quick. The American adviser and a captain have come to search the village.

HA: What's up?

NAM: They say Tu has come back.

[HA *exits.* PUPPET SOLDIER A *hastily enters.*]

SOLDIER A: Search quickly, Nam. [*Exit with* NAM.]

[*Puppet captain,* COLONEL KENT, *American soldiers, and Vietnamese puppet soldiers enter.*]

KENT: You say you didn't know the escaped prisoner came into this "strategic hamlet," Captain. That's very careless. You weren't doing your duty.

CAPTAIN: I've checked with every sentry post, Colonel. Not one of them saw the prisoner pass.

KENT: Don't get tricky with me. Couldn't he have climbed the fence? Crawled under the barbed wire?

[SOLDIER A *enters.*]

SOLDIER A: We can't find him, Captain.

CAPTAIN: He couldn't have sprouted wings and flown. Round up all the villagers and bring them here.

[SOLDIER A *assents. Exit.*]

KENT: I'm reminding you again—you've got to tighten control. There's bound to be more uneasiness here now that we've taken those political prisoners.

CAPTAIN: Yes, sir.

KENT: Advance the curfew two hours, starting today. Double the patrols at night. Every family must keep a light burning in front of its door all night, or they will be regarded as making contact with the guerrillas.

CAPTAIN: Yes, sir.

[SOLDIER A *enters.*]

SOLDIER A: We've got the villagers, Captain.

CAPTAIN: Bring them here.

[*Villagers are pushed forward from all sides.*]

CAPTAIN [*looks them over*]: Where's Tu's daughter? Get her, quick. [SOLDIER A *runs off.*]

CAPTAIN: Attention, villagers. [*Steps up on a mound.*] Tu, that Viet Cong, has come back to your "strategic hamlet." Whoever is hiding him, speak up. We're going to get rough if you don't.

KENT [*restrains him*]: You're too crude. You should speak kindly and respectfully to peasants. [*Hypocritically.*] How are you, dear neighbors?

VILLAGERS: Bah! Stop pretending.

KENT: Calm yourselves, friends. Your government has set up "strategic hamlets" so that you can live in peace, and have freedom and democracy. It is now preparing to build schools, hospitals, and libraries. It will also provide all welfare facilities . . . .

GRANDPA: We don't even have enough to eat. What do we need with that stuff?

KENT: This old gentleman is absolutely right. Your life today is far from ideal. You're forced to live surrounded by barbed wire. But whose fault is that? The Viet Cong's. Once we eliminate the Viet Cong, you'll be able to enjoy the same prosperity as Americans. Tu is a Viet Cong, our common enemy. Whoever is concealing him should turn him over.

[*The people remain silent.* HA *is secretly signalling to them.*]

VILLAGER A: Give us back our relatives.

[*Villagers move forward threateningly.*]

KENT [*shrinks back*]: No violence, now . . . .

[PUPPET CAPTAIN *fires into the air.*]

KENT [*to the captain*]: Tu must be arrested before dawn and brought into the city. [*Exit hastily.*]

VILLAGERS: Stop him. Don't let him go. [*Surge forward.*]

CAPTAIN [*fires another shot into the air*]: Rioters! Who's hiding Tu? Bring him out, or I'll nab some of you.

[SOLDIER A *enters, pulling* TRAN.]

SOLDIER A: Here's Tu's daughter, Captain.

CAPTAIN: Good. Where's your father, little girl? Tell the truth and I'll let you live.

TRAN: He hasn't come home. Give me back my father. [*Slaps his face, hard.*]

CAPTAIN: You're lying. He has come back. Speak up or I'll slaughter you. [*Pulls out a dagger and advances towards her menacingly.*]

HA: Stop. Why do you want to kill that child?

CAPTAIN: Her father has come back home.

HA: What proof have you?

CAPTAIN: None of your business.

HA: We're not going to let you fellows kill anyone you please.

CAPTAIN: Who are you?

HA: A resident of this village.

HA'S MOTHER: Captain, you drove that child's mother into the grave, you arrested her father. Now you want to murder her, too. How can you people be so vicious?

HA: Didn't the American colonel just say you built this "strategic hamlet" so that we could enjoy freedom and democracy? But you arrest and murder at will. What kind of freedom and democracy is that?

CAPTAIN [*laughs*]: Freedom and democracy? That's a line for American colonels to hand out. I can't play that game. [*Tries to grab* TRAN, *but villagers mass around her.*]

CAPTAIN: Get out of the way or I'll shoot.

VILLAGERS: Go ahead!

[SOLDIER A *whispers into captain's ear.*]

CAPTAIN [*to his troops*]: Arrest that old man.

GRANDPA: What do you want with me?

CAPTAIN: You're Tu's guarantor. You won't turn over Tu, so I'll arrest you instead. Take him away.

[*Soldiers seize* GRANDPA *and start to drag him away.* TRAN *throws herself on the captain, biting and clawing.* CAPTAIN *shoots her and she falls. In the confusion, soldiers drag off the old man. Villagers surround the girl.*]

VILLAGERS: Tran . . . Tran . . . .

TRAN [*weakly*]: Sister Ha . . . avenge me. . . . [*Dies.*]

CHIN: They won't let us live. Let's have it out with them!

VILLAGERS: Let's go. We'll have it out with them!

HA: Wait, Chin. We'll suffer if we go after them empty-handed.

CHIN: Is it better to stand with our necks out, waiting for the axe? I may go down, but at least I'll take one or two of them with me.

HA: No, Chin. What we want is for one man to be able to destroy ten of them, a hundred, a thousand. But now is not the time. We must rely on the south Vietnam National Front for Liberation, on the Liberation Army, on our guerrillas. Go home, everybody. We'll figure out how to cope with this.

[The villagers slowly leave. CHIN picks up TRAN in his arms. TU rushes on stage. When he sees his daughter's body, he bursts into tears, but he does not speak. After a moment, he waves his hand for CHIN to carry the child away.]

HA: Our neighbors can't bear it any longer, Tu. They want to fight now.

TU: I'll go and find our guerrillas. I'll ask them to destroy this "strategic hamlet."

HA: No. The enemy is looking for you. It would be dangerous for you to leave the village. I'll go. I know this region well. At the same time, I can deliver the medicine. Tell me the passwords.

TU: Maybe that would be better. You say: "Are there any tigers here, neighbor?" The answer is: "Plenty. Are you afraid?"

HA: Then what do I say?

TU: You say: "I've been thinking of killing a couple to rid the people of their torment. Does that sound as if I'm afraid?"

HA [repeats]: "I've been thinking of killing a couple to rid the people of their torment. Does that sound as if I'm afraid? . . ." You take over the work in the village, Tu. Be sure to keep yourself well hiddden.

TU: I will. Here's a letter to the leader of the guerrillas from the district party committee. [Hands the letter to HA.]

Curtain

SCENE 2

[Before dawn. A camp of the south Vietnam People's Militia. As the curtain rises, militiamen are resting in crude forest shelters. Some are cleaning their weapons, one is repairing a radio, a few are softly singing a battle air. . . .]

290

MILITIAMAN A: Why should that meeting at headquarters be taking so long? Our commander still hasn't returned.

MILITIAMAN B: It must be important.

MILITIAMAN C: Yes. The commander left in an awful hurry. If you ask me, a new battle assignment is coming up for us.

MILITIAMAN A: Great. Why don't we two compete to see who can capture the most enemy weapons?

MILITIAMAN C: Count me in on that too. And let's also have a prisoner-capturing competition.

DA [mutters in his sleep]: Uncle Ho. Uncle Ho.³

MILITIAMEN: Wake up, Da. What's wrong?

DA: I had a wonderful dream, comrades; I dreamt I saw Uncle Ho.

MILITIAMEN: You did?

DA: Yes. He was wearing a cotton uniform. He took my hand and smiled at me in his kindly way and said: I'm sure you're very brave in battle, young fellow. How many of the enemy have you killed?

MILITIAMAN C: What did you answer?

DA: I was full of things I wanted to say. But I was so excited, I couldn't get a word out.

MILITIAMEN [groan]: Oh!

DA: If I could see Uncle Ho, wouldn't that be fine? Too bad it was just a dream.

MILITIAMAN A: It's not just a dream, Da. Winter passes and spring follows. Before long our whole country will be united. We'll be sure to see Uncle Ho then.

MILITIAMEN: Right. We're sure to see him.

MILITIAMAN D: Listen, comrades, the news from Hanoi!

[They crowd round the radio. The announcer says: "The American imperialists are getting one drubbing after another from the people of south Vietnam. But the aggressors haven't given up. They are now strafing and bombing the coastal area of the Democratic Republic of Vietnam daily with hordes of planes, criminally murdering our peaceful civilians. . . ."]

MILITIAMAN A: What? American planes bombing our brothers in the north?

MILITIAMAN D: Listen! Listen!

[The announcer continues: ". . . Today withering fire from the Vietnamese People's Army brought down eleven planes and damaged many others. One American pilot was captured. . . ."]

291

MILITIAMAN A: Good shooting, beautiful shooting!
[*Announcer: "This wanton aggression by the U. S. imperialists is a serious violation of the Geneva Agreements. . . ."*]

DA [*angrily*]: Disgraceful! The Americans not only occupy the south, now they spread the flames of war to the north. Well, they're not going to have things their way. For every blow they strike at the north, we southerners will hit them four times as hard.

MILITIAMEN: Right.

MILITIAMAN A: Lam into them. We won't let them get away with it. [*Very agitated, starts to sing: "Liberate the South."*]
[COMMANDER LE *enters quickly.*]

LE: Comrades.

MILITIAMEN [*crowd around him*]: You're back, Commander.

LE: The Americans are expanding their aggression. They're bombing our north.

MILITIAMEN: We know.

DA: We want to go into action at once, Commander, and hit back.

LE: Comrades, to defend the north, liberate the south, and unite the whole country, headquarters has already decided: We're going to hit the enemy hard. We'll soon be taking the offensive.

MILITIAMEN: Good. When?

LE: Get ready and wait for orders. In this battle, in coordination with our main force, we're going to destroy many "strategic hamlets," expand our liberated areas and join the liberated villages and areas into one. We'll meet and smash any kind of attack the American imperialists make, no matter how many men they throw in. Every American soldier must be driven from our land even if it takes us twenty years to do it. We're sure to win in the end.

MILITIAMEN: Right!

LOOKOUT: Enemy planes. To your places. [*Fires a warning shot.*]
[*Enemy planes approach, strafing.*]

LE: Take up your weapons, comrades. Don't let the vultures get away.

MILITIAMEN: Let's go.
[*Exeunt. Sound of firing.*]
[THANH *enters, guarding* HA, *who is wearing the uniform of a puppet soldier.*]

THANH: March. No looking around. That package of yours must contain poison. You can't bring it in here. [*Takes the package from her and puts it aside.*] Sit down. You sit there quietly, young woman—that's an order. Do you hear me? If you disobey me again, things will go badly for you. Do you hear?

[HA *nods helplessly. She sits down on the ground.*]

THANH: Now answer my questions. Wait a minute. [*Pulls out a small notebook and says as he writes.*] Today, another prisoner captured . . . .

HA: Old grandpa, you're making a mistake.

THANH: What? A prisoner dares to contradict me in broad daylight? Let me ask you: Where are you from?

HA: From a "strategic hamlet." I'm looking for—

THANH: Who are you looking for?

HA: If you don't mind telling me who you are, Old Grandpa . . . .

THANH: I'm asking the questions, not you. . . . All right, I'll tell you. [*Proudly.*] A soldier in the People's Militia of the south Vietnam National Front for Liberation. Got that?

HA: You're just the ones I'm looking for. We're on the same side, Old Grandpa.

THANH: Nonsense!

HA: I want to see your leader. It's important.

THANH: I'm the leader.

HA [*tries him*]: Are there any tigers here, neighbor?

THANH: How could there be? This place is full of Liberation Army men and guerrillas.

HA: Old Grandpa, I must see your leader about something important.

THANH: He's very busy. Didn't you hear? We're shooting planes.

[*Sound of firing offstage.*]

HA [*eagerly*]: Did we hit any?

THANH: Naturally. Hope they'll get away, do you?

HA: No, Old Grandpa. I hope you shoot them all down.

THANH: Of course, that's what you'd say. You probably came to signal the planes.

HA [*laughs wryly*]: Old Grandpa, you certainly are—

THANH: Can't be too careful with birds like you.

[*Another intense burst of firing. An enemy plane, in flames, falls to earth.*]

HA [*delighted*]: We've hit it! We've hit it! Did you see that, Old Grandpa?

THANH: Stay where you are. If you think this is your chance to escape, you're mistaken.

HA [*stamps her foot in frustration*]: Old Grandpa!

THANH: Quit hopping around. Sit down.

[*She has no choice but to comply.*]

HA: Could you give me a little water? I'm dying of thirst.

THANH: That's a request I can grant. [*Hands her a cup of water.*] Drink slowly.

HA: My wrists hurt. Could you—

THANH: Untie you? Nothing doing. It's a matter of principle.

HA: I can't run away. Why worry?

THANH: You're a glib talker. I untie you. Then, when I'm off my guard, you slug me and sprint like a runner in an American track meet. Right? What are you laughing about?

HA: I know my uniform makes you suspicious. But it's only a disguise. I put it on so that I could come here more easily. My work required it.

THANH [*sarcastically*]: And because my work required it, I captured you.

HA: You can't capture one of your own people.

THANH: Stow the gab. You're my prisoner now.

HA: Does your outfit belong to the BV district, Grandpa?

THANH: Crafty, aren't you? Well, you'll never get any military secrets out of me. [*Gags HA with a handkerchief.*] That'll keep you quiet. I'm warning you—tell the truth when you're questioned. Lying will only make things worse for you.

[*Militiamen enter with battle trophies.*]

MILITIAMAN A: We just fought a pretty battle, Grandpa. The planes went down in flames, the pilots were killed. Look—parachutes, pistols.

MILITIAMAN B: And biscuits, and canned goods.

MILITIAMAN C [*holding up transistor radio*]: And look at this.

DA: Jealous, Grandpa?

THANH: Not me. You didn't capture any of the enemy alive.

DA: How could we? The pilots were killed.

THANH: Well, see that? [*Points at HA.*] I've caught another one.

MILITIAMEN: Nice work, Grandpa.

[COMMANDER LE *enters.*]

LE: You fought very well, comrades. You were quick and courageous. Two enemy planes were destroyed.

THANH: Reporting to the commander. Scout Thanh has taken another prisoner. [*Points at HA.*]

LE: Where did you catch her?

294

THANH: In an enemy-patrolled zone.

LE: Let me have your little notebook. I'll enter it for you.

THANH: I . . . I've already entered it.

LE [*looks at the book*]: You've killed or captured a total of twenty-seven of the enemy! You're quite remarkable, old comrade. I'm going to recommend to headquarters that you be given a citation. Is there anything else you have to report?

THANH: Twenty-five enemy trucks passed on Route 18 this afternoon. I think they're delivering military supplies to the "strategic hamlets."

LE: Right. [*Indicating* HA.] Untie the prisoner.

THANH: Be careful, Commander. She's very crafty.

HA [*very agitated*]: Comrade Commander.

MILITIAMAN B: Stand where you are.

LE [*to* HA]: Where are you from?

HA: Are there any tigers here, neighbor?

LE: Plenty. Are you afraid?

HA: I've been thinking of killing a couple to rid the people of their torments. Does that sound as if I'm afraid?

LE [*grasps* HA's *hand*]: Comrade.

HA [*producing the letter*]: This is a letter to you from the district Party committee.

LE: What's your name, comrade?

HA: I'm called Ha.

LE: So you're Comrade Ha. I've heard a lot about you. Comrades, she's one of us.

[*The militiamen crowd around and hug her, shake her hand.*]

LE: Quick, comrades, bring Comrade Ha something to eat.

DA: Have some American biscuits.

THANH: This is a can of American beef. I'm awfully sorry, Comrade Ha. Enemy spies use all kinds of tricks to get information about us. I was afraid you might be one of them. Just now I was pretty rough on you. I hope you'll excuse me.

HA: You were absolutely right, Old Grandpa. We have to be cautious.

LE: Do have something to eat, Comrade Ha.

MILITIAMEN: Eat. Eat.

[HA *looks at the food they forced upon her. Tears roll from her eyes.*]

LE: When you come to one of our detachments, Comrade Ha, it's

295

like coming to your own home. We're all brothers and sisters. Go ahead and eat.

HA [*puts a biscuit to her lips, then lowers it and shakes her head*]: I don't know what's the matter with me. In the face of the enemy, I've never shed a single tear. But here with you dear brothers I .... [*Wipes her eyes.*] Comrades, the people in the "strategic hamlet" where I live can't bear it any longer. As soon as the autumn grain was harvested, the enemy took it away. Every day, they press us for taxes and levies. One old grandpa couldn't pay a levy of fifty bamboos, so they hung him all night by his hands from a tree. The next day they rounded up everybody to watch, and the captain of the puppet company questioned him personally. "Why haven't you handed in the bamboos?" the captain asked. "Your gang has plundered me of everything. Where would I get money to buy bamboos?" the old grandpa replied. "And even if I had any bamboos, I'd give them to the Liberation Army and our guerrillas, the better for them to kill you crooks with." The captain was so furious, he beat him to death. He had his soldiers drag the body through the hamlet. The streets were dyed with that old grandpa's blood.

MILITIAMAN A: Those sons of bitches are getting worse and worse.

HA: Only a few days later, three peasants came back after curfew because they were trying to get all their planting done in a hurry. The enemy said they were in league with the guerrillas and chopped off their hands and feet. Then they threw them into the paddy field and made the water buffalo pull a plough back and forth across them. All the water in the field turned red. But those three peasants never gave in. They shouted: "Don't cry, neighbors. Don't be afraid. Fight them to the end."

DA: Right. Rather death than surrender.

HA: We weren't cowed by the enemy's bloody methods. Our Party branch led us in the fight. We refused to pay taxes or levies; we broke the walls, ditches, and barbed wire and bamboo fences around the hamlet. The enemy couldn't do anything with us. The night before last they seized over twenty of our comrades and dragged them to Lam Lake, where they tortured them, trying to force them to tell who our Party leaders are. They burned their faces with fire, they pierced their eyeballs with bayonets, but our comrades only shouted slogans and swore that they would be avenged.

296

MILITIAMEN: Right. Blood debts will be paid in blood.

LE: Then what happened?

HA: Several of our men were killed. To conceal the crime, the enemy weighted their bodies and threw them in the lake. . . . Our people are longing for you comrades to come and destroy our "strategic hamlets." We're all prepared. When you attack, we'll strike from within. The sooner you come, the sooner there'll be an end to our misery.

LE: Comrades, our people are suffering the torments of hell in that "'strategic hamlet." Remember these blood debts and strike the enemy with the full force of our rage. We must make them pay a hundredfold for their crimes.

THANH: Let's go right now. Destroy the "strategic hamlet" and rescue our neighbors.

MILITIAMEN: How soon can we go into action, commander?

LE: We definitely will destroy the hamlets; we definitely will rescue the arrested comrades. Headquarters has already ordered us to go into action; we'll soon liberate our brothers in the "strategic hamlets." Comrade Ha, you rest a while. I must report what you've just told me to my superiors.

MILITIAMEN: Have a seat, Comrade Ha.

HA: I've brought you the quinine and other medicines you need, comrades. They're in a package—Old Grandpa said it had poison in it, and nearly threw it into the ditch.

THANH: I certainly am an old muddle-head. [*Gets the package.*] We thank you and your neighbors, Comrade Ha. Life is hard in that "strategic hamlet," yet you still think of us. [*To* MILITIAMAN C.] It wasn't easy to bring this medicine here, comrade medical orderly. Take good care of it. It's not just medicine—it's the people's hearts.

HA: The enemy are doing everything in their power to cut us off from our guerrillas. But that's impossible. Barbed wire and bamboo fences may separate us physically for a time, but our hearts are always with you. No matter how hard life may be, we can grit our teeth and carry on. No matter how savagely the enemy may act, we'll struggle against them as usual. However hard they press us, we give them nothing, but you comrades have only to ask and we'll give you anything you need. Isn't that so, Old Grandpa?

THANH: Right, right. By the way, Comrade Ha, my name is Thanh. Hereafter, you can call me Old Comrade Thanh.

HA: I'd rather call you Old Grandpa.

THANH: Or Old Soldier will be all right.

HA: I still insist on Old Grandpa.

THANH: All right. I'll make a special exception in your case. But please call me that only when no one else is around. . . .

HA: [softly]: Yes, Old Grandpa.

[Everyone laughs.]

THANH: What's so funny? Aren't I old enough to be her grandpa?

DA: That score in your notebook, Comrade Thanh—

MILITIAMEN: Naturally you'll erase this prisoner out.

THANH: No, I'll catch a real enemy in the next encounter to make up for it.

[COMMANDER LE enters.]

LE: Go and get some rest, comrades.

[Exeunt militiamen.]

LE: You've come exactly at the right moment, Comrade Ha. Headquarters feels that what you've just told us can be extremely useful to us in the fight to liberate the "strategic hamlets." We want to advance the time of our attack. If the atrocity at Lam Lake is used to arouse the people and they carry the bodies of the victims into the city in a mass demonstration . . . .

HA: A mass demonstration?

LE: Yes. That will expose the shocking crimes of the American imperialists and their running dogs to the Vietnamese people and to the people of the whole world. Even more important, it will tie up the enemy troops in the city while we're fighting in the outskirts. What do you say? Can you do it?

HA: Definitely.

LE: Headquarters has notified the city underground organization to call the workers, students, and ordinary citizens out to coordinate with your demonstration.

HA: Wonderful!

LE: With our military and political actions coordinated, with the struggles in town and countryside coordinated, we'll be much surer of victory. You can work out the details of the demonstration with Comrade Pham. He's a mechanic in the garage in the city. He'll meet you at the CC Cafe in Central Park at seven p.m. sharp the day after tomorrow.

HA: How do we make contact?

LE: Look for a man who's winding his watch, then ask him: "Could you tell me the time, please?" He'll say: "I'm sorry, my watch has stopped." Then you say: "You look very familiar."

HA: What will he reply?

LE: He'll tap his forehead three times and say: "Aren't you Ha?" That's all there is to it.

HA: Good, I've got it. I'll leave immediately.

LE [*calls*]: Comrade Thanh, see Comrade Ha through the enemy-patrolled zone.

THANH: Right.

LE: Comrade Ha is going, comrades.

[*Militiamen enter.*]

HA [*shakes hands with them*]: Goodbye.

LE: You've an important task, Comrade Ha. Be especially careful.

HA [*stimulated*]: Don't worry, Commander. Goodbye. [*To the militiamen.*] I'll be seeing you at the razing of the "strategic hamlet," comrades.

All [*in high spirits*]: We'll be seeing you.

Curtain

SCENE 3

[*The evening before the demonstration, in front of the CC Cafe in a corner of the park. There are a few tables on the lawn. A kiosk stands to the left. Rows of trees and flowering shrubs to the rear. Behind them, in the distance, the outlines of the city can be seen.*

As the curtain rises, people stroll by in two's and three's. Only a few customers sit at the tables. A newsboy calls in a gloomy voice: "Evening paper, get your evening paper." A drunken American soldier staggers on, makes rude gestures at the passers-by, picks up a customer's glass from the table and drains it. Suddenly a police whistle shrills, shots ring out. Everything is thrown into confusion. The American soldier runs off.]

CUSTOMER [*irritably*]: Police whistles and shooting from morning till night. A fine freedom and democracy! [*Raises his glass to drink and finds that it is empty.*] A hell of a society this is!

[*HA enters. Sits down and orders a cup of coffee. Notices the customer winding his watch. Walks over.*]

HA: Could you tell me the time, please?

CUSTOMER: Ten to seven.

HA: Oh. Thank you.

CUSTOMER: Not at all. [*Gets up and leaves.*]

[HA *looks around, slowly drinks her coffee.* VAN AN *enters.*]

VAN AN: What brings you to town, Ha?

HA: I have a little business here. How come you've got time to wander around the park, Cousin?

VAN AN: I've lost my job.

HA: What happened?

VAN AN: When I came back from your place, I told my students in class the next day everything I had seen and heard. The principal said I was agitating them to oppose the government. He dismissed me.

HA: Disgraceful.

VAN AN: As a matter of fact, I was very pleased. I felt it was an honor, my first step toward joining the struggle.

HA: You're right, Cousin. The American invaders have turned our beautiful land into a charnel house. Now they've begun to bomb our north. But we're going to make the enemy pay every one of these bloody debts.

VAN AN: It's a pity I have no arms. If I had a gun or a grenade, I could rush into the American "adviser's" headquarters and shoot them all dead—blow them to bits.

HA: Not so loud.

VAN AN: Did you do what I asked you that day, Ha? I'm burning with impatience. I wish I could fly to the liberated area. I want to take up a weapon, put on a uniform, and become a member of our glorious partisans.

HA: I'll definitely satisfy your request.

VAN AN: How much longer do I have to wait?

HA: Only a few days more. I'll send you word.

VAN AN: That's marvellous. How can I thank you? My heart is leaping for joy. I knew long ago that you were no ordinary person, Ha. There's something else I want to ask you.

HA: What is it?

VAN AN: I've just picked up a leaflet. It says the government killed a lot of our compatriots at Lam Lake. Are the people going to take any action about this? Will they protest to the government?

HA: What do you think?

VAN AN: If we stand for this savagery, we won't deserve to be called decent human beings.

HA: You're quite right, Van An. When the people take action, we should join them wholeheartedly. Even if we run into serious trouble, it's up to us to see it through to the end. To contribute to the liberation of your homeland is an honor, even if it means losing your life.

VAN AN: Of course. I'm going to do my very utmost; I'm going to stand in the forefront of the struggle. [*Sees* HA *looking at her watch.*] You have an appointment?

HA: Yes. I'm waiting for a friend.

VAN AN: Ah. Is there anything I can do for you?

HA: No, thanks.

VAN AN: Then I'll be running along. Goodbye. I'll be waiting to hear from you. [*Exit.*]

[*People continue to stroll by.* PHAM *enters and sits down at a table opposite* HA.]

PHAM [*calls towards cafe*]: Boy, bring me a coffee. [*Removes his wristwatch and starts to wind it.*]

HA: Could you tell me the time, please?

PHAM: I'm sorry, my watch has stopped.

HA: You look very familiar.

PHAM [*taps his forehead three times*]: Aren't you Ha?

HA: Yes!

PHAM: Comrade Ha! [*Warmly shakes her hand.*]

HA: Comrade Pham!

PHAM [*in an undertone*]: Have you roused the people in the "strategic hamlets?"

HA: Six "strategic hamlets" will be marching with us; there'll be a total of over two thousand people.

PHAM: Excellent. Five or six thousand in the city will join your demonstration. It will be the biggest turnout our province has ever had. [*Waiter brings coffee.* PHAM *pretends to be reading the newspaper.*] Another ammunition dump blown up. There's trouble every day. [*Exit Waiter.*] We think the demonstration should be tomorrow morning at six, Comrade Ha. Can you manage it?

HA: Yes.

PHAM: Will your people have any difficulty in leaving the hamlets?

HA: That part will be easy. They're allowed out to go to the fields every morning. But the government guards may stop us from entering the city.

PHAM [*thinks a moment*]: Come along Highway 7. We'll send men

301

to meet you. Drive your water buffaloes into the city ahead of you. We can use them to block traffic.

HA: Right. That's how we'll do it.

PHAM: We're planning a few things to keep the enemy busy. While you're demonstrating, we're going to blow up their ammunition dump outside the city. They'll have to rush part of their soldiers and police there, which will ease their pressure on the marchers.

HA: Very good.

PHAM: Tomorrow's demonstration will not only expose the enemy's crimes. It will help our brothers and sisters in the "strategic hamlets" see the light of day once more. Our Party leaders have instructed us to keep the demonstration going, come what may, until nightfall when the fighting in the outskirts will be over.

HA: Right, we won't stop demonstrating before dark.

PHAM: Any other problems?

HA: It would be better if you got the banners ready that we're going to carry, so the enemy won't see us bringing them into the city.

PHAM: We'll do that. Anything else?

HA: No, that's all.

PHAM: Good. You'd better go back.

HA: I'll be seeing you. [*Exit.*]

[PHAM *waits till she is out of sight, then he also leaves.* VAN AN *enters hurriedly.*]

VAN AN [*looks about anxiously. Just then* HA *comes running back. He walks quickly forward to meet her*]: Ha!

HA [*doesn't want to stop. Gives him a significant look*]: Van An.

VAN AN [*grasps her arm*]: Don't go that way. I just saw a couple of enemy agents over there.

HA [*halts*]: There are men following me, Cousin. Cover up for me. [*Gives him her red scarf, which he conceals. Takes a white scarf from her purse and puts it around her neck. Puts her arm through his, and they start strolling back in the direction from which she came.*]

[ENEMY AGENT A *enters.*]

HA: What time is our film, Cousin?

VAN AN: Eight-thirty.

HA: It's still early. Let's have some coffee.

VAN AN: All right.

HA: Boy! Two coffees.

[*She and* VAN AN *sit down at a table. The agent watches her.* WAITER *serves the coffee and goes up to agent.*]

WAITER: What will you have, sir? Milk, coffee, brandy?

AGENT A: Beat it. [*Pushes waiter away. His eyes never leave* HA.]

[WAITER *exits. Newsboy enters.*]

NEWSBOY: Evening paper, get your evening paper. [*To agent.*] Evening paper, sir?

AGENT A: Beat it. [*Knocks paper away.*]

[*Exit newsboy.*]

[*A girl dressed nearly the same as* HA, *and wearing a red scarf, passes. Agent hestitates a moment, then gets up and follows.*]

VAN AN [*with an eye on the disappearing agent*]: Get out of here, Ha, fast.

HA: Goodbye, Cousin.

VAN AN: I'll go with you part of the way.

[KIM *suddenly enters and stands behind them.*]

HA: No need. [*Exit.*]

[KIM *starts to follow.*]

VAN AN [*sees him*]: Kim?

[KIM *turns around.*]

VAN AN: Don't you know your old classmate, Kim?

KIM: Why, hello, Van An. I'm busy at the moment. We'll talk some other time. [*Tries to leave.*]

VAN AN [*steps in his path and blocks his view of the retreating* HA]: But we haven't seen each other in years. Have you made money, or become an official, that you're too high and mighty to chat with me?

KIM: It's not that. I'm just busy.

VAN AN: Busy? Strolling around the park? Nonsense. Sit down. It isn't every day old classmates meet. You're my guest. Boy! Champagne.

KIM [*hopelessly*]: Oh, well . . . .

VAN AN: Sit down. You've no idea how I've missed you. It's only been a few years, but you've changed tremendously. Where are you working?

KIM [*his mind still elsewhere*]: That girl who was with you . . . .

VAN AN: A relative of mine.

KIM: Ah, a relative.

VAN AN: Please sit down.

[*Waiter brings glasses and a bottle of champagne and opens it. Exit.*]

VAN AN: Here, let's drink to our reunion and your good health.

[KIM *takes glass and drinks.*]

303

VAN AN: Where are you working?

KIM: I was in Saigon. Now I'm helping out in my father's company here.

VAN AN: I teach in the normal school.

KIM: Are you satisfied with your job?

VAN AN: Very. You know I've always been interested in education. I'm quite pleased.

KIM: I've just come to this city. Has anything been happening around here lately?

VAN AN: I've no idea. I'm only interested in my teaching.

KIM: Not even national affairs?

VAN AN: Teaching keeps me fully occupied.

[KIM sighs.]

VAN AN: What's the matter?

KIM: Well, I'm not satisfied. Dark things are happening in our society today. The government is very cruel.

VAN AN: What do you mean?

KIM: Look at this leaflet I just picked up. Another government massacre, this time at Lam Lake. You'd never think we were living in the middle of the twentieth century. They're absolute barbarians.

VAN AN: Let me see it. [Reads the leaflet.] This has nothing to do with us, Kim. You do your job and I'll do mine. No use in getting mixed up in things that are none of our business.

KIM: In this political turmoil all around us, can your mind really be like a stagnant pool, without a ripple?

VAN AN: I'm a law-abiding citizen. I've never meddled in politics. But enough of that. Let's drink. Bottoms up.

[AGENT A enters.]

AGENT A [whispers to KIM]: The girl has disappeared.

KIM [also whispers]: Where's she gone?

AGENT A: I don't know. She was just sitting with this gentleman here.

KIM: With him? [Points surreptitiously at VAN AN.]

AGENT A: Yes.

[KIM realizes he's been hoaxed. Signals for agent to leave.]

VAN AN: You seem busy. I won't keep you any longer. [Rises.]

KIM: No, no. That was only a clerk from the company. Nothing important.

VAN AN: I must be going anyway. I've got to prepare tomorrow's lessons.

304

KIM: As you say, we haven't seen each other in years. Why not talk a while longer?

VAN AN: There'll be other opportunities. I'll be seeing you.

KIM [*stops him*]: Now it's my turn to detain you. I can't bear to part with you, old friend. Bottoms up. [*Drinks.*] You're not as simple as you pretend, Van An, eh? [*Laughs.*]

VAN AN: What do you mean?

KIM: That's quite an act you put on. Nearly had me fooled.

VAN AN: You're drunk. Goodbye. [*Gets up.*]

KIM: Not so fast. I'm afraid I'll have to trouble you about something.

VAN AN: What?

KIM: Take me to that relative of yours.

VAN AN: Forgive me. I don't know where she lives. [*Tries to leave.*]

KIM [*prevents him*]: You're not a very good liar. Don't even know the address of your own relative? [*Takes his arm.*] You shouldn't fool me, old classmate.

VAN AN [*flings him off*]: We used to be classmates, that's true. But old classmates have gone many different ways. Some have been falsely accused of crimes and thrown into jail. Some have given their lives for liberation of our homeland. And some have betrayed our homeland, become traitors, the scum of our nation.

KIM: Shut your mouth. [*Seizes him roughly.*]

VAN AN: What's the meaning of this?

KIM: I must ask you to come with me.

VAN AN: Take your hands off me.

KIM: Don't get excited, Mr. Van An. Just come along quietly.

VAN AN: Where to?

KIM: The Bureau of Police.

VAN AN: Very well. [*Throws the contents of his champagne glass in KIM's face and starts to run.*]

KIM [*pulls out a pistol*]: Grab him.

[AGENTS A and B pounce upon VAN AN.]

KIM: Trying to pull that trick on me. A fat chance.

VAN AN [*swings a punch, but is dragged back*]: Dirty police spy.

KIM: Take him away.

Curtain

SCENE 4

[*Early the next morning. The office of the city police bureau of the puppet government. In the rear, direct center, is a set of doors with glass panes opening on to a balcony. An American flag and a flag of the puppet government hang on the walls on either side. On the left side of the stage stand a large desk and a swivel chair. Several telephones are on the desk. Near the wall are a radio transmitter and a microphone. Two upholstered chairs are on the right side of the stage.* NHAN, *the police commissioner, is speaking on the telephone as the curtain rises.*]

NHAN: What? The demonstrators from the "strategic hamlets" have entered the city? They're carrying bodies and driving water buffaloes before them? Why didn't you keep them out? They're unarmed and you've got guns. Get your men there on the double and stop them from coming any farther. [*Hangs up. Another phone rings. He answers it.*] Hello. What? More demonstrators outside the east gate? Who are they? Workers! Use tear gas, turn the fire hoses on them. [*Another phone rings urgently.*] The students inside the south gate and citizens are demonstrating, too? Well, what are you waiting for? Get the vans and mounted police out. [*Hangs up.*] Stupid fools. [*Dials a number.*] Plainclothes department? What about that girl you were tailing in the park yesterday? Still no sign of her? Send some of your men to mingle with the demonstrators. She must be found. I'm warning you: if you don't come through, you'll answer for this with your head. Nitwit! [*Paces the floor, pondering. The phone rings again. He ignores it. The ringing persists. He snatches it up in a rage.*] What the hell do you want! [*Hearing the response, he immediately lowers his voice.*] Yes, this is Nhan, Colonel Kent. . . . We've got everything under control, sir. Don't worry. I guarantee we'll find the girl and put down the demonstration. . . . Believe me, sir, I've had plenty of experience. [*Hangs up. Shouts.*] Bring in Van An.

[*Two policemen drag in* VAN AN *who has been tortured.*]

NHAN: Not very pleasant, eh, Mr. Van An? [*Walks up to him.*] Be sensible. We can play much rougher. I hope you'll make things easy for yourself. You've already lost your job for instigating the students against the government. It would be a pity if you lost your life as well just because you were momentarily deluded by the terrorists. I've already told you, Mr. Van An. All you have to do is give us the address of your relative, and you're free to go. What do you say?

VAN AN: And I've already told you: I don't know anything. I won't say a single word. My soul is not for sale.

NHAN [*laughs*]: That's no way to talk, Mr. Van An. You're an educated man; you ought to understand. In this time of national turmoil, every citizen has the duty to cooperate with his government and help restore order. Turning a suspect over to the government is a meritorious act. What has that to do with selling souls?

VAN AN: To you and your kind betrayal of country and conscience isn't shameful; it's glorious. That's your philosophy.

NHAN [*his face hardens*]: Don't forget who you're talking to, Van An. You may not know that I was police commissioner of this city when the French were here. When I tell you to talk, you'd better talk. If you do what I say, you'll go free, get your job back, be given a raise in pay. If you don't—

VAN AN: Then I'll be killed, is that it? Well, let's get it over with.

NHAN [*viciously*]: It's not that simple. First, we'll feed you with pepper and soapy water; then one of our big fellows will dance on your belly with his hobnailed boots. If that doesn't satisfy you, we'll run hooks through your heel tendons and hang you head down from a rafter and let you swing. Then you can taste our electric torture. How does that sound to you, Mr. Van An?

VAN AN: You're dreaming. I won't talk, no matter what you do.

NHAN: Mr. Van An, you'll be sorry.

VAN AN: I'm sorry now—that I won't be there to see you traitorous dogs being tried by the people. I'm sorry that I haven't a gun in my hands this minute—

NHAN [*in a rage*]: Take him to the torture chamber! [VAN AN *is pulled out.* NHAN *lights a cigarette and waits confidently.*]
[*Shouts of torturers can be heard offstage.*]

NHAN [*calls*]: Has he confessed?
[*Voice backstage:* "Not yet."]

NHAN: That bastard. Give him the electric treatment.
[NHAN'S SECRETARY, *a young woman, enters hurriedly.*]

SECRETARY: Mr. Kim of the Ministry of Civil Affairs has sent us a girl they've caught.

NHAN: Where did they pick her up?

SECRETARY: Among the demonstrators. She's the one who was at the CC Cafe yesterday. Mr. Kim thinks she's one of the leaders.

NHAN: Good. Bring her in.

SECRETARY: Yes, sir. [*Exits.*]

[*A policeman enters with* HA.]

POLICEMAN: Here is the prisoner, Commissioner.

NHAN [*with feigned anger*]: Idiot. What do you mean—prisoner? She's a guest. Get out.

[*Exit* POLICEMAN.]

NHAN: Please be seated. Secretary, some tea for our guest.

HA: I don't need your courtesies.

[SECRETARY *gives her a furious glance.*]

NHAN: What's your name, miss? [*Waits, but there is no response from* HA.] Your face is very familiar. [*Whispers a few words in secretary's ear.*] Be quick.

[*Exit* SECRETARY.]

NHAN: If I remember correctly, you were one of the leaders of the strike at the textile mill last year, and your name is Ha. Right?

HA: You're wrong, Commissioner. I live in the country.

NHAN: My memory has never failed me yet.

[SECRETARY *enters, hands him a dossier. Exits.*]

NHAN: I have your record right here, miss. Denials are no use. What good did the strike do you? You lost your job. Haven't you had enough hardship? Why must you engage in conspiracies against the government?

HA: Make yourself plain, Commissioner. What do you mean by that?

[NHAN *pushes open the balcony doors. Voices are shouting slogans.*]

NHAN: Listen. What are those people doing in the street? Why have you instigated them to demonstrate and disturb social order?

HA: Don't pretend, Commissioner. Surely you haven't forgotten the frightful crime you and your men have committed?

NHAN [*with a wave of the hand*]: I don't know what you're talking about.

HA: Lam Lake. Why did you murder those peasants from the "strategic hamlet?"

NHAN: Why, that's a lie, miss, invented by troublemakers.

HA: You think because you do things secretly they won't be found out. Let me tell you this—we've a mountain of proof. You can't get away with it.

NHAN: Proof? What proof?

HA: The bodies of the victims.

308

NHAN [*pretends to be shocked*]: Can such a terrible thing really have happened? I'm going to order a full investigation. Killing innocent peasants! Not one of the murderers will escape the law.

HA: You can quit acting, Commissioner. What exactly do you want with me?

NHAN: Nothing very special. Only to say a few words to the demonstrators through the microphone.

HA: What good will that do?

NHAN: Since you're one of the leaders—

HA: Have you any proof of that?

NHAN: Someone has exposed you.

HA: Who?

NHAN: Van An.

HA: Van An?

NHAN: We've arrested him.

HA: Can I see him?

NHAN: That's not necessary. Besides, after he confessed, we let him go.

[POLICEMAN B *enters.*]

POLICEMAN B: Van An has fainted, Commissioner. But he hasn't said a word.

NHAN [*angrily*]: Get out, get out. . . .

[POLICEMAN B *exits.*]

NHAN: I think you know, miss, this place of ours is easy to come to but hard to leave. But we'll make an exception in your case. If you speak to the demonstrators, we'll release you immediately.

HA: What do you want me to say?

NHAN: Just say the government is investigating the Lam Lake incident. As soon as we've got the facts, we'll deal with the matter justly. This is the busy season on the farms. Everyone should go home and tend their fields.

HA: You're not very clever, are you, Commissioner? You think all I have to do is say a few words and the demonstrators will leave? Unless the murderers are punished, the people will fight you to the end.

[POLICEMAN C *enters, running.*]

POLICEMAN C: The demonstrators are gathering in the square, Commissioner.

NHAN: Drive them out.

POLICEMAN C: They've poured gasoline all around the sides and set fire to it. We can't get in.

NHAN: Call the armoured cars. Get ready to charge.

POLICEMAN C: Yes, sir. [*Exit.*]

NHAN: I'm not going to be polite to those demonstrators any longer. Of course, we have only to fire one shot, and they'll scatter.

HA: Since it's so easy, why ask me to talk to them?

NHAN: Only because of my love for the people. I don't want the streets of our beautiful city stained with blood. Besides, I want to give you a chance to do a good deed and expiate your crime.

HA: I haven't done anything wrong. It's you who are the criminals. How many people have you driven with tears in their eyes into "strategic hamlets?" How many are wandering the streets because you won't let anyone employ them? How many have been slaughtered by your American masters? There's no end to your crimes.

NHAN: Don't be obstinate, miss. A single bullet can end your life. Why risk it? You only live once.

HA: True enough, you only live once. You fellows will do anything in order to live—even let the Americans kick you around like dogs. A revolutionary's life may be short, but it shines like a gem. Countless revolutionaries have given their lives for liberation of our country, and their dauntless integrity has inspired many more people to rise up and continue the fight.

NHAN: [*in frustrated rage and hatred*]: Shut your mouth.

[POLICEMAN C *runs on in panic.*]

POLICEMAN C: The demonstrators are coming this way.

NHAN: Son of a bitch. I'll deal with them myself. Hey, guard.

[POLICEMAN B *enters.*]

NHAN: Lock her up. [*Rushes out.*]

POLICEMAN B: Come on. [*Takes* HA *off.*]

[*Telephone rings.* SECRETARY *enters and picks up the phone.*]

SECRETARY: Hello, the Municipal Bureau of Police. Oh, Colonel Kent. Mr. Kim hasn't arrived yet. That girl he sent over? No, she hasn't admitted anything. The Commissioner has gone to put down the demonstration. Yes, I'll remember. Right, right. O.K. [*Hangs up.*]

[NHAN *returns looking very disgruntled. His hair is tousled, his clothes are torn. He snatches up a phone.*]

NHAN: Hello, General? I can't cope with the demonstrators. There are too many of them. Give me a hand, will you, brother? Not enough troops? Pull a few back from the "strategic hamlets." I'm in a tight spot, brother, the flames are burning the seat of my

310

pants. Hello . . . hello . . . . [*The phone has gone dead. He puts down the receiver.*]

SECRETARY: The American adviser just called, Commissioner. He says you must take strong measures and break up the demonstration. [*Hands him a memorandum of her telephone conversation.*] [POLICEMAN C enters.]

POLICEMAN C: Mr. Kim of the Ministry of Civil Affairs is here.

NHAN: Ask him in.

[POLICEMAN *and* SECRETARY *exit.* KIM *enters a moment later.*]

KIM: The demonstration is growing larger and more dangerous by the minute, Commissioner. You've got to do something, quickly. Colonel Kent is very angry.

NHAN: It's a difficult situation; it's hard to handle.

KIM: What's so hard about it? Use that girl.

NHAN: It's not so simple. She's no ordinary girl. She's a Viet Cong.

KIM: Just because she's a Viet Cong you can't handle her?

NHAN: I can handle her all right, but it will take time.

KIM: You don't have any time, Commissioner.

NHAN: What can I do?

KIM: Don't forget who you are. Saigon already knows about this disturbance. If it's permitted to go on, your office will have to bear full responsibility.

NHAN: You're joking, Mr. Kim. How can my little police bureau cope with such a big problem?

KIM: What do you propose to do?

NHAN: I don't know what to do. The demonstration is so large. But I can't get troops to help. I can't scatter the demonstrators, or drive them out, or stop them from spreading, or shoot them—

KIM: Why not?

NHAN: It might make things worse.

KIM: You've got to put down the demonstration quickly. I hear you were police commissioner here under the French, and then under the Japanese. Now you're serving Saigon. [*Sneers.*] For a man with so much experience, you don't show much ability.

NHAN: Let's see you do the job if you're so stinking clever.

KIM: If I have to do it, what will we need a Commissioner of Police for? I'm warning you—Colonel Kent says if this thing isn't stopped, fast, he's going to have you fired. [*Exit.*]

NHAN: Bastard. Who the hell do you think you are? [*Shouts.*] Bring Ha here.

POLICEMAN B *comes in with* HA. *She smiles at* NHAN's *ruffled appearance.*]

NHAN: Well, miss, have you thought it over? If you say a few words to the demonstrators, I'll let you go home. And you won't go empty-handed, either, but with a big roll of U.S. dollars. How about it?

HA: I'll speak to them, but on certain conditions.

NHAN: Good. What are they?

HA: First, pay damages to the families of the victims.

NHAN: Agreed. Second?

HA: Release those arrested.

NHAN: I can do that, too. Third?

HA: Punish the murderers.

NHAN: Anything else?

HA: Demolish the "strategic hamlets."

NHAN: Shut your mouth.

HA: And also—

NHAN: Enough. You're deliberately opposing the government.

[POLICEMAN C *rushes on.*]

POLICEMAN C: The demonstrators are at the gates of the police bureau.

NHAN [*startled, but pretends to be calm*]: Notify the men to get ready to shoot. [*To* Ha.] I have only to give the order, miss, and your comrades and neighbors will go down in pools of blood. Maybe you're not afraid to die, but think of those peasants. I give you one minute to decide whether you're willing to speak.

[HA *stands motionless.* NHAN *shouts hysterically to* POLICEMAN C.] Tell them to shoot.

POLICEMAN C: Yes, sir.

HA: Wait. I'll speak.

NHAN [*very relieved*]: That's fine. [*To policeman.*] Turn on the microphone. [*Picks it up.*] Quiet down, citizens. [*Stones and rotten fruit fly in through window and hit him.*] We have asked Miss Ha of the "strategic hamlet" to say a few words to you. All right, miss, if you please.

HA: Neighbors, listen to me, neighbors. The Commissioner of Police has promised to investigate the Lam Lake massacre. He wants you all to go home.

NHAN: Right. Go on, miss, go on.

HA: But it's a trick, neighbors. They're the ones who committed the massacre. The murderers are the Bureau of Police and their

312

master—the American imperialists. We're not going to fall for it, neighbors. We won't be fooled by honeyed words, we won't be frightened by bloody measures. Unless they release our neighbors, punish the murderers, demolish the "strategic hamlets," pay damages to the victims' families; unless the Americans get out of our beautiful land and the people of south Vietnam attain their full freedom, we'll go on fighting.

[*A huge cheer goes up from the demonstrators.*]

NHAN: Turn that microphone off, turn it off. You certainly have got your nerve. How dare you be so rash?

HA: It's the U. S. imperialists and you—their running dogs—who've made me that way. You murdered my neighbors at Lam Lake and sank their bodies. Now you tremble for fear that your crime will be exposed.

NHAN: Shut up. Take her to the torture room.

HA: I've already had a taste of your fascist methods. You eat people's livers, drink their blood, rape, burn, murder—there's nothing you won't do. You've turned south Vietnam into a living hell. But the people haven't given in. Be careful of your head, Commissioner. Don't forget the people's stones and sharpened bamboo stakes.

NHAN: You're still young. Would you have no regrets if you lost your life?

HA: My only regret would be that I hadn't killed a few Americans first with my own hands to revenge my massacred neighbors.

NHAN: Take her away. Put her to the torture.

[*Policemen close in on her.*]

HA: Don't touch me. [*Walks off, head high.*]

[*Slogans are shouted in the street.*]

NHAN: Secretary.

[SECRETARY *enters.*]

NHAN: Notify our men. They can open fire.

SECRETARY: Yes, sir.

[*An explosion shakes the room.* NHAN *plunges, terrified, under the table. Smoke can be seen billowing up outside the window. Police car sirens wail in the street. There is great confusion.*]

NHAN: Secretary, secretary, what's happened?

SECRETARY: I don't know. It sounded like a bomb.

NHAN [*prostrate under the table*]: Find out what it was, quick.

[SECRETARY *picks up phone.* KENT *and* KIM *their faces bleeding, enter.* SECRETARY *slips off.*]

313

KENT: What kind of police commissioner are you? Can't even deal with unarmed peasants. The ammunition dump has been blown up, do you know that? And the streets are jammed with people and water buffaloes. My car has been smashed. Can you or can you not get this situation under control?

NHAN: I've got my entire complement out, Colonel. I've even been out there myself, but . . . .

KENT: Why don't you fire on the demonstrators?

NHAN: I'm afraid that would cause them to get out of hand altogether.

KENT: Coward. [*Picks up phone and dials a number.*] General? Call your troops out and quell this riot. What? Your troops are where? Outside the city fighting the fire in the ammunition dump? Then get soldiers from the "strategic hamlets." Quick.

[SECRETARY *enters.*]

SECRETARY: The demonstrators have forced their way to the main gate of our police bureau, Commissioner. They're demanding that we release Ha, and they want to see you.

KENT: Quell them by force, immediately.

NHAN: Yes, sir.

KENT: Wait a minute. This place of yours isn't safe. I'll take the prisoner with me. Otherwise, the crowd might break in here and grab her from us. That would ruin my entire plan.

[*To* KIM.] Take the prisoner away.

KIM: Yes, sir. But where shall I take her to?

KENT: Office of the American advisory group.

[KIM *assents. Exit.*]

SECRETARY: The demonstrators are breaking in.

[*All are thrown into a panic.*]

KENT: How do you get out of here?

NHAN: There's a street tunnel downstairs.

KENT: Take me there quick.

[*As* KENT *starts to run, a round black object sails in through the window and lands at his feet. He clutches his head and collapses in terror.*]

KENT: A bomb.

[*The others frantically throw themselves to the floor. A long pause.*]

NHAN [*cautiously raises his head and peers at the round object*]: I don't think it's a bomb, Colonel. It looks more like a coconut.

Curtain

314

SCENE 5

[*Dusk. H*A'*s home. It is very simply furnished, with a small door leading to an inner room. Outside, on the right, is a lane connecting with the street. On either side of the lane stand two old phoenix trees. In the distance can be seen the barricades, barbed wire and watchtowers which surround the "strategic hamlet." H*A'*s* MOTHER *and N*GOC *are sharpening bamboo stakes for pit traps as the curtain rises. Raucous laughter of puppet soldiers and the barking of dogs break the silence from time to time.*]

HA'S MOTHER [*sighs*]: Ai.

NGOC: You've been sharpening all day. Rest a while.

HA'S MOTHER: I'm not tired. They've killed Xuan, and now today, during the demonstration, they've arrested Ha. I hate them so, I can't bear it.

NGOC: Hasn't Uncle Tu said that the Liberation Army and guerrillas are coming tonight to demolish this "strategic hamlet"? Let's put good points on our stakes and sharpen our knives. When the fighting starts we can join in and kill a few of the dirty wretches.

[*The voice of a sentry carries clearly from outside the hamlet: "Attention, someone is coming from the east. Stand where you are." There is a shot. Dogs set up a clamor of barking. A searchlight beam sweeps across from a watchtower.*]

HA'S MOTHER: Why are those puppet troops so jumpy, Ngoc? Surely they can't know that the hamlet will be demolished tonight?

NGOC: They feel guilty and scared. The demonstration is still going on in the town. They're putting up a big front to give themselves courage.

[CHIN *enters, beating a watchman's bamboo segment, followed stealthily by T*U.]

TU: Go out and make contact with the guerrillas, Chin. Tell them that we're prepared. Find out what time they're going to attack and what the signal will be. Be sure to get it all straight. Then hurry back and let me know.

CHIN: Right. [*Exits.*]

[T*U raps softly on the door of H*A'*s house.*]

HA'S MOTHER [*opens the door*]: Tu. Come in, quick.

[N*GOC keeps watch outside.*]

HA'S MOTHER: The enemy are still looking for you. Why haven't you remained in hiding?

TU: It doesn't matter.

HA'S MOTHER: Doesn't matter? If anything should happen to you, who would we have to rely on?

TU: Tonight, with our Liberation Army and guerrillas striking from without and us striking from within, we're going to destroy this "strategic hamlet." I've a million things to do. I can't stay holed up for ever. Have the knives been whetted?

HA'S MOTHER: They're nice and keen.

TU: Have you sharpened the bamboo stakes?

HA'S MOTHER: We certainly have.

TU: Give them to me.

[HA'S MOTHER goes to get them. NGOC swiftly enters.]

NGOC: The enemy are coming, Tu. Get out of sight.

[The two women push him into the next room. A puppet policeman steals up to the house and listens outside the window. Puppet army captain and a puppet soldier approach.]

CAPTAIN: Who's there?

POLICEMAN: It's me, Captain.

CAPTAIN: What are you doing?

POLICEMAN: I'm searching for Tu.

CAPTAIN: Any trace of him?

POLICEMAN: No.

CAPTAIN: You useless clod. He's been on the loose for days and you can't even find his shadow. Tu is a Viet Cong. Hidden in this hamlet, he's like a time bomb. Can't you understand that? He must be behind our villagers going to the city and demonstrating today. The American adviser has been mad enough about your not recapturing Tu. Now the peasants demonstrate in the city and the ammunition dump in the outskirts gets blown up. I'm warning you. The American advisor just telephoned. He says if we don't catch Tu tonight and anything else goes wrong with this hamlet, you and I are liable to lose our heads.

POLICEMAN: Don't worry, Captain. I'll catch him for sure. [Starts to leave.]

CAPTAIN: Why haven't the house lamps been lit?

POLICEMAN: It isn't time yet.

CAPTAIN: Do it earlier tonight.

POLICEMAN: Yes, sir. [Shouts.] Light the door lamps. . . . [Exits.]

CAPTAIN [to the soldier]: Sergeant, tell the lieutenant on duty—the city wants us to send them a platoon immediately. Double the

316

guard at both the east and west entrances to the village. The patrols must keep moving all night. Strictly enforce the curfew. If the guerrillas catch us napping while we're so shorthanded, we'll be finished.

SOLDIER: Yes, sir.

CAPTAIN: Get going.

[*Soldier exits with captain. NAM and his wife enter. NGOC lights the door lamp.*]

NAM'S WIFE: You mustn't go. That Con Lon Island[4] is a living hell.

NAM: I'm not being sent to Con Lon Island. It's just that my platoon has to take Ha and some of the other political prisoners there under guard.

NAM'S WIFE: Take Ha to Con Lon? You mustn't do a terrible thing like that. I'm not letting you go, no matter what you say.

NAM: What else can I do? All the troops in the city are tied down by the demonstration, so this dirty job has been given to us. I must go now. Be sure and tell Ha's mother.

CAPTAIN [*entering*]: Your platoon is leaving immediately, Nam. Why aren't you with it?

NAM'S WIFE: I beg you, Captain. Don't make him go to Con Lon Island.

CAPTAIN [*slaps her face*]: What do you know about it, you slut?

NAM [*protestingly*]: Captain . . . .

CAPTAIN: You listen to orders or I'll have you shot. Now get out of here. [*Drives NAM away.*]

NAM'S WIFE [*throws herself on captain, begs*]: You mustn't force him to go.

[CAPTAIN *pushes her away and kicks her to the ground. Exit.*]

NAM'S WIFE [*bitterly*]: Filthy dog. Sooner or later the guerrillas will come and finish you off. [*Crawls to her feet and runs to the window of HA's house.*] Ha's mother, Ha's mother. [HA's MOTHER *comes out.*] Your Ha is being sent to Con Lon. You've got to find a way to rescue her, fast.

HA'S MOTHER: Thank you.

NAM'S WIFE: No need for thanks. I must tell Nam to look after her on the road. . . . Nam . . . . [*Runs off.*]

HA'S MOTHER [*goes back into house*]: Tu, just now—

TU: I heard everything. We've got to let the guerrillas know, so they can save Ha and the others.

NGOC: I'll go, Tu.

Tu: No, I will. [*Starts for the door.*]

[CHIN *enters, running.* HA's MOTHER *goes outside to keep watch.*]

Tu: Did you find our guerrillas?

CHIN: I couldn't get out of the village. There are guards posted all over the place.

Tu: What about our old spot?

CHIN: That's guarded, too.

Tu: What are we going to do? There's been a new development. The enemy are getting ready to send Ha and some others to Con Lon. We must let our guerrillas know. They not only have to demolish the hamlet tonight, they've also got to save Ha and the others.

CHIN: What can we do?

Tu: Isn't there any other way to get out of the hamlet?

CHIN: I'll try again. [*Starts to leave.* HA's MOTHER *enters the house.*]

HA's MOTHER: A policeman is coming.

[Tu *and* CHIN *hide in the next room.* POLICEMAN *enters. Blows out lamp over door.*]

POLICEMAN: Ngoc, come out here. [NGOC *goes to door.*] Why haven't you lit your lamp?

NGOC: We did.

POLICEMAN: Look. Is it burning?

NGOC: The wind must have blown it out.

POLICEMAN: Nonsense. There's not a breath of wind tonight.

NGOC: I'll light it again at once.

POLICEMAN: Too late for that. You've got to pay a fine of fifty *dong* for not lighting your lamp. That's a village regulation. Fork over.

NGOC: We haven't any money.

POLICEMAN: Then you'll have to go to jail. [*Starts to haul her away.*]

HA's MOTHER [*comes out*]: Stop. Have you fellows no shame at all?

POLICEMAN: Why isn't your door lamp burning?

HA's MOTHER: Obviously you blew it out.

POLICEMAN: Insulting a government functionary, eh? That's another violation. Your fine is now one hundred *dong*. Let's have it.

HA's MOTHER: We don't have a single *dong*.

POLICEMAN: No money? Then I'll confiscate some of your property. [*Tries to enter the house.* HA's MOTHER *blocks his way.* NGOC *quickly goes inside.*]

HA's MOTHER: You've long since robbed us clean. There's nothing left.

[POLICEMAN *kicks her aside. Enters house.*]

318

POLICEMAN [*shakes his finger at* NGOC]: Well, what are you giving—
money or goods?

TU [*emerges from inner room and stabs his gun in policeman's back*]:
How about a bullet?

POLICEMAN [*whirls around, see* TU]: Tu!

TU: Keep your voice down. [POLICEMAN *drops to his knees beseechingly.*] Take off that uniform. [POLICEMAN *starts to comply.*] Be
quick.

POLICEMAN: My hands are trembling.

TU: Put it on, Chin, and leave the hamlet.

[CHIN *changes clothes and runs off.*]

NGOC: Kill him, Tu.

TU: No. Let him live.

NGOC: What for? A dog like that.

TU: He may still be useful. Tie him up and put him in the hole in
the inner room.

[NGOC *binds the policeman and shoves him into the inner room.*]

HA'S MOTHER [*enters*]: Are you sure it's all right, Tu?

TU: Yes. The hamlet will be liberated soon. Call the group leaders
here. I want to give them their battle assignments.

[*Exit* HA'S MOTHER.]

TU: Get the bamboo stakes, Ngoc, and hand them out to our neighbors.

[NGOC *picks up a big armful.*]

NGOC: Here they are.

TU: What a lot. You two must be worn out.

NGOC: When we heard that this hamlet would be demolished
tonight, and remembered Xuan and Tran and all the other dear
ones who have been murdered, we felt so strong we could have
sharpened every bamboo in south Vietnam.

TU: It's true. The U.S. imperialists and their running dogs have
committed no end of atrocities. Even when all our bamboo stakes
pierce their chests, it still won't ease our hatred completely.

[*Leaders of the various groups slip into the house.* HA'S MOTHER,
who has been following, stands outside the door to keep watch.]

TU: Gather close, neighbors. We've suffered enough. Tonight this
hamlet is going to be liberated. This will be an important battle,
for not only this one but all hamlets around the city will be
demolished. The city will then be surrounded by our armed forces
like a lone island in the sea.

VILLAGER A: Why don't we finish off the whole lot, inside the city and out, and be done with it?

TU: Don't worry. We shall liberate the cities after we destroy the "strategic hamlets." We're going to liberate all of the south and unite the entire country. We're going to drive the Yankees out of Vietnam. [*Excitedly.*] The situation is good. Our liberated areas are growing steadily, our armed forces are getting stronger every day. We're winning victories everywhere—in the air and on land, in the countryside and in the towns, in the south and in the north. [*Humorously.*] We even won a victory right here in this room a few minutes ago.

VILLAGERS [*animated*]: What do you mean?

TU: We tied up a policeman.

VILLAGER: Where is he?

TU: You'll see him soon. Let's assign our duties for tonight's battle.

VILLAGERS: Good.

TU [*to group leaders in turn*]: Your group will take over the sentry posts at the east and west ends of the hamlet. Don't let any of the enemy leave. Your group will cut the barbed wire and knock down the bamboo barricade at the northeast corner and build a ramp over it so that our forces can come in. The rest of you join them when they attack the central tower. Does everybody understand?

VILLAGERS: Yes. We guarantee to do our jobs.

VILLAGER A: When does it start?

TU: We'll know when Chin gets back. Everyone hurry now and prepare. Tell our neighbors that tonight they can get their revenge.

VILLAGERS: Right.

TU: Take the stakes with you.

[*Each man exits with a bundle.*]

TU: You and Mother arm yourselves with knives and stakes, Ngoc. When the fighting starts, you can take part.

NGOC: Good.

[*Outside there are shots and the barking of dogs. CHIN enters with THANH.*]

TU: You're back, Chin. Did you find our guerrillas?

CHIN: I did. They've sent this comrade Thanh. [*Introduces the others to THANH.*] This is Tu, Ha's mother, Ngoc . . . .

[*They greet each other warmly.*]

THANH: Are you all ready here, Comrade Tu?

320

Tu: All ready. The assignments have been given out. We're just waiting for the attack to begin. There's a new development, Comrade Thanh. The enemy wants to take Ha and the others—

THANH: That's why I've come. Our underground organization in the city has already reported it to headquarters. It's for that reason that headquarters is advancing the time of the attack. The moment the battle is over we're going directly to the harbor to rescue our comrades.

Tu: Excellent.

THANH: There are a lot of enemy troops in this village, and they have strong fortifications. Headquarters wants us to capture the captain before the attack starts. We'll be able to wipe out the enemy more quickly if they have no leader.

Tu [*thoughtfully*]: Capture the captain, eh?

THANH: Got any ideas, Comrade Tu?

Tu: He lives in the guntower. But he's a crafty dog. It might be hard to get him out of there.

HA'S MOTHER: Any time the door lamps aren't lit, he dashes out to check personally. If we extinguish a whole row of them he'll come running, never fear.

THANH: But suppose he doesn't?

HA'S MOTHER: I'll send him a false report that Tu is in my house.

Tu: No. I've got a better idea. [*Whispers in their ears.*] How about it?

ALL: Fine.

Tu: Comrade Thanh, go back and tell your leaders that we will definitely carry out our tasks.

THANH: My leaders have instructed me to stay here and help you capture the captain. As soon as that's done, we strike three quick raps on the bamboo segment, then three slow ones. When our scouts outside hear that, they'll fire two red flares into the sky as the signal for the attack to begin.

Tu: Good. We'll get to work immediately. Chin, you go with Comrade Thanh and round up some of our young men. Then hide in the shadows and wait for the captain.

CHIN: Right. Come with me, Comrade Thanh. [*Exeunt* CHIN *and* THANH.]

Tu: You can get started, Ha's mother. [*Conceals himself.*]

HA'S MOTHER: Come on, Ngoc. [*They go into the inner room and pull out policeman.*] Walk. We're moving you to another place. [*They go outside.*]

321

POLICEMAN: Don't, old mother. You mustn't kill me.

HA'S MOTHER: We're not going to kill you. We're only taking you to another place. But if you don't behave yourself on the way, I'll give you a taste of this knife. March.

NGOC: The enemy can see that lane, Ma. Take the other one.

HA'S MOTHER: Walk down a distance and see if there are any enemy around.

NGOC: All right, Ma. Watch him carefully. Don't let him get away. [*Exit.*]

[*HA'S MOTHER pretends to be looking around. Policeman kicks her to the ground and runs.*]

HA'S MOTHER [*calls*]: Oh, Ngoc, he's escaped. It's terrible, he's escaped.

[*NGOC returns. The two women look in the direction which the policeman has run. They smile at each other.*]

HA'S MOTHER: Good. He's gone back to the tower. [*Tu enters.*]

TU: Gone, eh? Fine. I'll get our men in position. When the captain comes, keep him busy for a few minutes. [*Runs off.*]

HA'S MOTHER: Sit down, Ngoc. We'll wait.

NGOC: My heart's beating like anything, Ma. Will the captain fall into our trap?

HA'S MOTHER: He will. Just wait.

[*Dogs begin to bark outside, men are heard shouting.*]

HA'S MOTHER: He's coming, he's coming.

[*They go back inside. Policeman and captain enter, with several soldiers. They creep up to house.*]

CAPTAIN: Are you telling me the truth?

POLICEMAN: They took my uniform, didn't they? You can see that.

CAPTAIN: Go in.

POLICEMAN [*enters house with a puppet soldier*]: Don't move. Get outside. [*HA'S MOTHER and NGOC emerge. Policeman and soldier search for TU, fire a few shots into concealment hole in the inner room.*] Damn. Tu's gone. [*Comes out of house and reports to captain.*] Tu's got away.

CAPTAIN [*slaps his face*]: Donkey. Why didn't you nab him when you had the chance? [*To a soldier.*] Alert all the guard posts to keep a sharp watch. Don't let Tu leave the village. Tie up Ngoc.

HA'S MOTHER [*bars their way*]: Tie me instead.

CAPTAIN [*kicks her*]: You're not going to live either. [*To NGOC.*] Where has Tu gone?

322

NGOC: Tu? I haven't seen him.

POLICEMAN: What do you mean, you haven't? You and he took my
  uniform and my gun, tied me up—

NGOC: Don't try to blame it on me. Just because you got drunk and
  left your gun and uniform somewhere, you come here and invent
  a story—

CAPTAIN: Quit lying. This family is a nest of Viet Cong. Every one
  of you deserves to be killed. Tu has been hiding in this village for
  days and you've known all about it, but none of you reported him.
  Just now you tied up a policeman and helped a criminal to escape.
  You're all rebels. Hand over Tu, and be quick about it. Otherwise, I'll tie you to a tree and light you up for a torch. [NGOC *does
  not respond.*] I'm asking you for the last time, Ngoc. If you tell
  the truth, I'll let you live. But if you dare to say you don't know,
  you'll leave this world in flames. Where is Tu?

NGOC: I don't know.

CAPTAIN: Where is he hiding?

NGOC: I don't know.

CAPTAIN: This is your last chance.

NGOC: I don't know. I don't know.

CAPTAIN: Tie her to the tree. Burn her.

  [*Soldiers tie* NGOC *to the tree, heap branches at her feet and soak
  them with gasoline. Just as they are about to light them,* THANH,
  TU, CHIN, *and a band of young men rush out and fight. They seize
  the captain, the policeman, and the soldiers. Villagers—men and
  women—quickly gather, armed with knives, bamboo stakes, bows
  and arrows.*]

THANH: Sound the signal, Comrade Tu. Three quick, three slow.
  [*The signal is rapped out on the bamboo segment.*] Look, there
  go the red flares. The attack is starting. We're going to change
  the "strategic hamlets" into villages armed against the enemy.
  [*Red signal flares arch across the night sky. Intense firing commences. Smoke spreads through the village.*]

THANH: Neighbors, the time to collect your debts of blood from the
  enemy has come. Charge.

  [*The peasants rush off, brandishing their arms.*]

Curtain

SCENE 6

[*Shortly before dawn. On the deck of the freighter "Liberty," which is moored to a dock. A gale is driving waves against the shore. Lights around the bay reflect on the turbulent water.* NAM *and a young puppet soldier are standing listlessly on guard.*]

YOUNG SOLDIER: Will we be able to sail with the wind so strong?

NAM: The sailors say it will probably die down in about half an hour.

YOUNG SOLDIER: I'm afraid.

NAM: Afraid of what?

YOUNG SOLDIER: I'm afraid that when we get to Con Lon Island, they won't let me come back. My old mother at home is very ill.

NAM: It's all in the hands of fate. Who told you to take such a dirty job?

YOUNG SOLDIER: I was conscripted. I cried when they put this made-in-America uniform on me. [*Sobs.*]

NAM [*concerned*]: Don't cry. If the Yanks hear you, you'll be beaten.
[*An American soldier saunters by.*]

AMERICAN SOLDIER: Look sharp. The prisoners are coming aboard.
[*Exit.*]
[*Shackles clank, whips snap, shots are fired.* YOUNG SOLDIER *stares at prisoners mounting gangplank.*]

YOUNG SOLDIER [*shocked*]: Isn't that girl Ha, from your village?
[NAM *also stares.*] What a state they've been beaten into. Those government men are really savages.
[KIM *enters.*]

KIM [*walks up to young soldier*]: What did you say?

NAM: He didn't say anything.

KIM [*slaps the young soldier's face*]: So you're sorry for the Viet Congs.
[KENT *enters.*]

KENT: What's the matter?

KIM: He's a Viet Cong sympathizer.
[KENT *waves his hand. Two American soldiers enter.*]

KENT: Throw him into the sea.

NAM: You can't, sir, you mustn't. . . . [KIM *kicks him away. The GI's grab the young soldier.*]

YOUNG SOLDIER: What are you doing? What are you trying to do? Down with the Yankees. . . .
[*He is thrown into the sea.* KIM *fires several shots at him.*]

324

KIM: The prisoners are all on board, Colonel. Shall we set sail?

KENT: Wait a while. I just got an urgent phone call from Saigon saying we've got to get the names of the people in the Viet Cong underground organization out of Ha. Bring her up on deck. I'll question her myself.

KIM: Yes, sir. [Shouts.] Bring Ha.

[HA has been bruised and battered from head to toe, but her eyes still burn fearlessly. She advances slowly but firmly.]

KIM: Saigon has just phoned, Ha. They say we should execute you.

HA: Shoot, then.

KENT: I hate to do it, miss. Look around. The blue sea, the lights of the harbor, the beauty of the night—aren't you sorry to leave all this?

HA: Our bays, our land are beautiful indeed. But with you savage brutes roaming all over them, looking at them makes me feel humiliated.

KENT: You're only twenty-four. You could easily live twice that number of years more.

HA: If I were free, I wouldn't mind living to be a thousand, ten thousand. But today, my only regret is that I can't strangle all you Yankees with my own hands, that I can't build up the southern part of our country with my own hands into a still more beautiful place.

KENT: Don't forget your old mother. You're her sole support. She's standing at the door under the phoenix tree right now waiting for your return.

HA: She's waiting for the return of a daughter who is of use to the people, not a despicable turncoat.

KENT: Oh, come now, it's not all that serious. Let's talk calmly. Take off her shackles. [American soldiers comply.] I'm a humanitarian, miss, and a devout Christian. The Lord prohibits me from interfering in the least with the happiness of others. Though Saigon has ordered me to execute you, I want you to live—and live very well, too. However, we all have to earn our happiness. Tell me who led the demonstration, and you'll be completely free.

HA: Anything else you want?

KENT: Naturally. If you're willing to go with me a step further, and give me the names of the members of the secret Viet Cong organization in the city, not only will you be free, but we'll send you to America to study. Or you can have your pick of jobs in glittering

325

New York, or in picturesque San Francisco. My government will give you a medal if you cooperate well. When your picture with the medal on your chest is published in the U. S. newspapers, you—a simple Vietnamese girl—will be the idol of the free world. [*Produces two glasses of wine and offers her one.*] Come on, let's drink to our friendship and cooperation.

HA [*dashes the proffered glass from his hand*]: You dirty butcher. Do you really expect me to betray my homeland, sell out my comrades? You're mad. I'd rather die on my feet than live on my knees.

KIM [*threatening*]: I'll have you shot.

HA: Scum. And you call yourself a Vietnamese. [*Slaps his face.*]

KENT: This is no insult, miss. I'm offering you our friendship.

HA: Friendship? Let me ask you: why do you send your bombers into our sky to slaughter our people? Why do you burn our coconut groves and rice fields with napalm? Why do you poison our wells and murder our peasants by the thousands? Why do you make mothers lose their sons, young brides their husbands, turn babies who have just learned how to say papa and mama into orphans? Is that your friendship for the Vietnamese people, for the people of Asia?

KENT: You Vietnamese are too wild.

HA: It's not we who are wild, it's you. It's you who burn, kill and pillage. You're spreading the flames of war to Laos, you're occupying Taiwan—part of the sacred soil of the People's Republic of China. You refuse to get out of south Korea and Japan. Everywhere you've set up military bases. You want to rule the whole world. But let me tell you—you American barbarians and Vietnamese traitors—the oppressed people everywhere have awakened, we're no longer going to let you murder at will. We've taken up arms, we're fighting. Our country will be united, as surely as the sun rises in the east.

[KENT *fires at her.* HA *falls, wounded. Before he can fire again,* NAM *shoots the gun out of his hand.*]

KIM: Nam. You dare . . . . [*Pulls out his pistol.*]

KENT: Grab him.

[NAM *runs off,* KIM *starts after him. An American soldier rushes on in panic.*]

AMERICAN SOLDIER [*shouting*]: The guerrillas! The guerrillas!

[*Intense shooting breaks out.*]

326

KENT: Concentrate all your fire on them, Kim. Annihilate them.

[*KIM runs toward the scene of the fray. KENT flees in the opposite direction. NAM returns. Sees HA, lying on deck.*]

NAM [*goes to her*]: Ha.

[*HA struggles to her feet, picking up KENT's pistol. KIM comes running back, defeated. Rushes to rail to jump into sea. HA and NAM shoot him dead. COMMANDER LE, guerrillas, peasants, swarm aboard.*]

LE: Finish off the enemy quickly. Open the hatch and release our captured comrades.

HA [*excitedly*]: Commander Le.

LE [*rushes over to her*]: Comrade Ha. Sorry we couldn't get here sooner. [*They warmly shake hands.*]

[*KENT, trying to escape, runs on. Throws one leg over rail. Is killed by a volley of shots from THANH and militiamen. His body tumbles into the sea. Rescued comrades, their shackles broken, surge out of hatch. Ardently shake hands with militiamen and embrace them.*]

HA: Neighbors, comrades, we've won. We must write letters about this to our loved ones in the north. We must tell Uncle Ho, we must tell all the peace-loving people of the world, that we definitely will liberate the south, defend the north, and fight until our entire country is united.

[*Everyone cheers and shouts: "Victory will be ours."*]

Curtain

NOTES

1. Villages set up in south Vietnam by the U.S. imperialists and surrounded by fences, barbed wire, and guntowers. The people are forced to move in so as to be cut off from contact with their armed fighters. [Communist China does not recognize two Vietnamese republics. Eds.]

2. Referring to the South Vietnam People's Militia.

3. President Ho Chi Minh of the Democratic Republic of Vietnam.

4. A concentration camp of the U.S. imperialists and south Vietnam puppet regime where many people are imprisoned and killed.

THE RED LANTERN*
(A Peking Opera)

Adapted by Wong Ou-hung and Ah Chia
from the Shanghai opera version

Translated by Yang Hsien-yi and Gladys Yang

CHARACTERS

LI YU-HO, a switchman.

TIEH-MEI, his daughter.

GRANNY, TIEH-MEI's grandmother.

OLD CHOU, a worker.

AUNT LIU, LI's neighbor.

KUEI-LAN, her daughter.

THE LIAISON MAN.

THE KNIFE-GRINDER.

GUERRILLA COMMANDER LIU.

THE GRUEL-WOMAN.

THE CIGARETTE-VENDOR.

HATOYAMA, chief of the Japanese military police.

HOU HSIEN-PU, his Chinese lieutenant.

A JAPANESE SERGEANT.

INSPECTOR WANG, underground agent for the guerrillas.

THE PEDDLER, a spy for the Japanese.

THE COBBLER, a spy for the Japanese.

JAPANESE GENDARMES, THUGS, TOWNSPEOPLE, GUERRILLAS, ETC.

*Reprinted from *Chinese Literature* (May, 1965), pp. 3–48.

SCENE 1

THE LIAISON MAN IS RESCUED

[*A late autumn night during the War of Resistance Against Japan. A siding near Lungtan Station in northeast China. It is dark and the wind is howling. Four Japanese gendarmes march past on a tour of inspection. There is a slope near by, with hills in the distance. A train passes on the other side of the slope.*]

[*Enter* LI YU-HO, *quietly, with a signal lantern.*]

LI:

> Red lantern in hand, I look round;
> The Party is sending a man here from the north;
> The time fixed is half past ten. [*Looks at his watch.*]
> The next train should bring him.

[*Enter* TIEH-MEI *with a basket.*]

TIEH-MEI: Dad!

LI: Well, Tieh-mei, how was business today?

TIEH-MEI [*angrily*]: The gendarmes and their thugs kept searching people and made them too jittery to buy anything.

LI: Those gangsters!

TIEH-MEI: Do be careful, Dad.

LI: Don't worry. Go home and tell Granny that an uncle is coming. Ask her to have a meal ready.

TIEH-MEI: Right.

LI: Come over here. [*Wraps his scarf round her neck.*]

TIEH-MEI: Dad, I'm not cold.

LI: No, you have it.

TIEH-MEI: Where's he from, this uncle?

LI [*kindly*]: Children shouldn't bother their heads about such things.

TIEH-MEI [*to herself*]: I'll go and ask Granny. Take good care of yourself, Dad. I'm off now. [*Exit.*]

LI: Our girl is doing all right.

> She can peddle goods, collect cinders,
> Carry water and chop wood.
> A poor man's child soon learns to cope
> With all tasks at home and outside.
> Different trees bear different fruit,
> Different seeds grow different flowers.

[*Enter* INSPECTOR WANG.]

329

WANG: Who's that?

LI: It's Li.

WANG: The Japanese are keeping a close watch today, Old Li. They must be up to something.

[Enter two Japanese soldiers. WANG and LI step apart. Exeunt the Japanese.]

WANG [taking out a cigarette]: Got a light?

LI: Here. [He goes over to light his cigarette, bending close to WANG.] Things are tense, Old Wang. We must take special care. Let's get in touch once every ten days from now on. I'll let you know where to meet.

WANG: Right.

[A whistle sounds in the distance and a train roars past. When it nears the station the LIAISON MAN jumps off. The Japanese police on the train fire two shots. LI and WANG step back.]

[The LIAISON MAN, wounded in the chest, staggers in and falls by the track. LI and WANG rush over to him.]

LI [helping him up]: Well, mate.

LIAISON [regaining consciousness, looks around]: What's this place?

LI: The fifty-first siding, Lungtan Station. You . . . .

[With an effort the LIAISON MAN puts a blue glove on his left hand and raises this. Then he faints.]

LI: [to himself]: The left hand gloved. [To WANG] He's our man. [Not far off Japanese yell and whistles are blown.]

WANG: Get him away, quick. I'll cover you.

LI [carrying off the man on his back]: Be careful, Old Wang. [Exit.] [The shouts and whistles come nearer.]

[WANG draws his pistol and fires two shots in the direction opposite to that taken by LI. Pounding footsteps can be heard and angry yells. To fox the enemy, WANG clenches his teeth and shoots himself in the arm. As he falls to the ground in come the Japanese sergeant, HOU HSIEN-PU and several gendarmes.]

SERGEANT [to WANG]: Where's the man from that train?

WANG [pointing towards the opposite direction and groaning]: Over there.

SERGEANT [in alarm]: Down! [All the Japanese flop to the ground.]

SCENE 2

THE SECRET CODE

[*The same evening. The road where Li's house stands. The house, in the center of the stage, has a door on the right and by the door a window. In the middle of the room is a square table with a lamp on it. Behind is a kang. The north wind howls. The room is dark.* GRANNY *strikes a match and lights the lamp. Wind rustles the window paper.*]

GRANNY:

> Fishermen brave the wind and waves,
> Hunters fear neither tigers nor wolves;
> The darkest night must end at last
> In the bright blaze of revolution.

GRANNY *draws back the curtain and looks out. Shaking her head she mutters, "Still not back." She goes to the table and takes up her needlework. Enter* TIEH-MEI *with a basket.*]

TIEH-MEI: Granny.

GRANNY: You must be cold, child.

TIEH-MEI: I'm not. Granny, Dad told me to let you know there's an uncle coming. He wants you to get a meal ready. [*Puts down the basket.*]

GRANNY: Oh, just coming, are they? I've rice and dishes ready.

TIEH-MEI: Why do I have so many uncles, Granny?

GRANNY: Your father has so many sisters, of course you have lots of uncles.

TIEH-MEI: Which one is this coming today?

GRANNY: Why ask? You'll know when he arrives.

TIEH-MEI: Even if you won't tell me, Granny, I know.

GRANNY: What do you know?

TIEH-MEI: Listen.

> I've more uncles than I can count;
> They only come when there's important business.
> Though we call them relatives we have never met,
> Yet they're closer to us than our own family.
> Both you and Dad call them your own folk;
> Well, I can guess the secret—
> They're all men like my dad,
> Men with fine, loyal hearts.

331

GRANNY [*smiling*]: You smart girl.

[*Sound of a police siren. Enter* LI *with the wounded man on his back. He pushes open the door and staggers in.* GRANNY *and* TIEH-MEI *hurry to help the* LIAISON MAN *to a chair.*]

TIEH-MEI [*frightened*]: Oh!

LI [*to* TIEH-MEI]: Watch the street.

[*With a sigh the girl goes to the window.* GRANNY *brings a towel.* LI *cleans the man's wound and gives him a drink of water.*]

LIAISON: Can you tell me if there's a switchman here named LI?

LI: That's me.

[THE LIAISON MAN's *eye lights on* GRANNY *and he hesitates.*]

LI: It's all right. You can speak.

LIAISON [*using the password*]: I sell wooden combs.

LI: Any made of peach-wood?

LIAISON [*eagerly*]: Yes, for cash down.

LI [*with a pleased glance at* GRANNY]: Fine.

[GRANNY *lights the small square lantern to show the* LIAISON MAN *that one side is pasted with red paper.*]

LIAISON [*not seeing the right lantern, struggles to get up*]: I must . . . go.

LI [*holding high the other lantern*]: Look, comrade!

LIAISON [*grasping* LI's *hand*]: Comrade, I've found you at last.

[*He faints away.*]

[TIEH-MEI *is puzzled by this business with the lantern.*]

LI: Comrade. . . .

GRANNY: Comrade, comrade. . . .

[THE LIAISON MAN *comes to.*]

LIAISON: Comrade Li, I'm . . . the liaison man . . . sent . . . from the north. [*With difficulty he tears open the lining of his padded jacket, produces the code and hands it to* LI.] This is . . . a secret code. [*Panting.*] Send it . . . quickly . . . to the guerrillas in the north hills. [*Gasping for breath.*] Tomorrow afternoon, the gruel stall in the junk market . . . .

LI: Yes, comrade. What about the junk market?

LIAISON: A knife-grinder will get in touch with you there.

LI: So a knife-grinder will get in touch with me.

LIAISON: Same password as before.

LI: The same, yes.

LIAISON: The task must be carried out. . . . [*He dies.*]

[TIEH-MEI *cries.* GRANNY *quickly stops her.* LI *takes off his cap* and looks at the code in his hand. All three bow their heads before the dead man.]

LI: I swear to carry out the task.

[The siren of the police car wails. GRANNY hastily blows out the light.]

SCENE 3

A COMMOTION AT THE GRUEL STALL

[The next afternoon. The gruel stall in the junk market. To the right of the shabby booth is a rickety table at which three men, A, B, and C are eating gruel. At the foot of the pillar on the left squats a woman selling cigarettes. As the curtain rises the market hums with noise.]

[Enter LI with his lantern in one hand and a canteen in the other.]

LI:

Come to find our man in the junk market
I have hidden the code in my canteen;
No obstacles can stop me,
I must send it up to the hills.

[He enters the booth and greets the people there.] A bowl of gruel, please, mum. [Hangs his lantern on the right-hand pillar.] How is business?

GRUEL-WOMAN: So-so [She serves him.]

[C finishes his gruel and pays for it.]

GRUEL-WOMAN: Another bowl, brother?

C: No more, thanks.

GRUEL-WOMAN: Is one bowl enough for you?

C: Enough? It's all I can afford. We work all day but don't earn enough to buy gruel. It's a hell of a life. [Exit.]

[Enter another man, D.]

D: A bowl of gruel, please.

[The woman serves him.]

D [stirring the gruel with his chopsticks]: This is thin, watery stuff.

A: It's government rice. What can we do?

[With a sigh D takes the bowl to the left pillar to drink. He then squats down and buys a cigarette.]

B: Hey, what's this in the gruel? Nearly broke one of my teeth.

A: It's full of stones.

GRÜEL-WOMAN: You'd better put up with it.

B: The swine just don't treat us as human.

A: Keep quiet, or you'll find yourself in trouble.

B [*sighing*]: How are we to live?

LI: Let's have another bowl, mum.

> Our people are fuming with discontent,
> Trampled by iron hoofs they seethe with fury
> And wait for the first rumble of spring thunder.
> China's brave sons will never bow their heads;
> May our guerillas come soon from the north hills!

[*Enter the* KNIFE-GRINDER *with a carrying-pole.*]

KNIFE-GRINDER:

> Glancing around in search of my man,
> I see the red lantern hanging high to greet me. [*Raising his
> gloved left hand to his ear he cries.*]
> Any knives or scissors to grind?

LI:

> The knife-grinder has his eye on my red lantern
> And he raised his hand to accost me.
> I shall casually give him the password.

[*Before* LI *can speak the siren wails and Japanese gendarmes
charge in.*]

GENDARMES: Don't move. This is a search.

[THE KNIFE-GRINDER *deliberately drops his tools to divert the
attention of the Japanese.*]

LI: Good man.

> He draws their fire in order to cover me.

[*He empties his bowl of gruel into his canteen and asks for
another helping. The gendarmes finish searching the* KNIFE-
GRINDER, *wave him angrily away and turn towards* LI. *He offers
them his canteen and lantern but they push them aside.* LI *puts
them on the table and lets himself be searched.*]

GENDARME A [*having searched him*]: Clear out.

[LI *picks up his canteen and lantern and goes out.*]

SCENE 4

WANG TURNS RENEGADE

[*The following afternoon.* HATOYAMA's *office. On his desk are a medal, a medical report and a telephone. Beside the desk stands a screen.*]

[*Enter* HOU HSIEN-PU *with Wang's file.*]

HOU:

> The man from the train fired a shot
> And wounded Inspector Wang's arm;
> The damage done is not serious
> But Hatoyama is making much of it.
> No doubt he has his reasons.

[*The telephone rings.* HOU *takes the call.*]

HOU: Yes? [*Standing to attention.*] Yes, sir. [*He puts the receiver down.*] A call for you, Captain Hatoyama.

[*Enter* HATOYAMA *from behind the screen.*]

HATOYAMA: Where from?

HOU: From the commander.

HATOYAMA: You should have said so. [*Takes the phone.*] Hatoyama speaking. What? Got away? Eh? Hmm. . . . . Don't worry, sir, I promise to get the code. Yes, sir. What? An order from the Kwantung Army Headquarters. [*He stands to attention.*] The deadline for clearing this up . . . Yes, sir. [*Rings off, muttering to himself.*] Those Reds are the devil. Headquarters discovered some clues in the north, but now they've covered their tracks again. The Communists are the very devil.

HOU: Report! Here is the dossier on Inspector Wang. [*Presents the file.*]

HATOYAMA: Good. [*He takes it and looks through it casually.*]

SERGEANT [*off*]: Report!

HATOYAMA: Come in.

[*Enter the sergeant.*]

HATOYAMA: Find him?

SERGEANT: We searched all the hotels, bath-houses, theaters and gambling dens but found no trace of the man from the train. We arrested a few suspects. Would you like to see them, sir?

HATOYAMA: What's the use of arresting suspects? This is urgent. Headquarters have just notified us that this man from the train is a liaison officer for the Communists in the north. He has a very important secret code with him.

HOU and SERGEANT [*standing at attention*]: Yes, sir.

HATOYAMA: This code has been sent from the Reds' headquarters
    in the north to the guerrillas in the northern hills, who are wait-
    ing for this to get in touch with them. If this code reaches the
    guerrillas it will be like fitting several thousand tigers with wings,
    and that would be most detrimental to our empire.

HOU and SERGEANT [*standing at attention*]: Most detrimental. Yes,
    sir.

HATOYAMA: How could you let such an important Red slip through
    your fingers?

[*The sergeant and Hou look at each other.*]

HATOYAMA: Fools!

HOU and SERGEANT: Yes, sir.

HATOYAMA: How about Inspector Wang?

HOU: He was shot in the left arm, but the bone . . . .

HATOYAMA: That's not what I was asking. Tell me his background.

HOU: Very good, sir. His name is Wang Hung-chang, otherwise
    known as Wang Lien-chu. His grandfather used to sell opium, his
    father kept a tavern, and he was one of the first graduates from
    the Manchukuo police school. He has one wife, one son, and one
    father.

HATOYAMA: So he comes from a good family. This time he did his
    best. Bring him here.

HOU: Yes, sir. [*Calling.*] Inspector Wang.

[*Enter WANG with one arm in a sling. He salutes HATOYAMA.*]

WANG: Captain.

HATOYAMA: Well, young man.

> You have paid for your courage, young fellow,
> Stopping the enemy's bullet with your body
> And fearlessly defending our great empire.
> On behalf of headquarters I give you this medal, third class.

WANG [*surprised and pleased*]: Ah!

> My ill luck has changed to good,
> Hatoyama does not suspect me.
> Thank you, sir, for your goodness,
> This is too great an honor.

HATOYAMA: Young man,

> Provided you serve the empire loyally
> You have every chance to rise high;

> One who repents can leave the sea of troubles,
> The choice is up to you.

WANG: I don't follow you, sir.

HATOYAMA: You should understand. You are not an actor, so why try to fool me? I'm afraid I can't compliment you on your performance.

WANG: Sir . . . .

HATOYAMA: I don't suppose you have followed my career. Let me tell you that when you were still a baby I was already a surgeon of some reputation. Though you fired that shot accurately enough, you forgot one thing. How could the man from the train get within three centimeters of your arm to fire?

WANG: I'm sorry you should think such a thing, sir.

HATOYAMA [chuckling]: Sorry. I'm sure you are. Sorry that I wasn't taken in by your trick. You can't fox me so easily, young fellow. So now, out with the truth. Who was your accomplice?

WANG: Accomplice?

HATOYAMA: Does that word surprise you? It's obvious enough. That man who jumped off the train was badly wounded. Without an accomplice to help him and another to cover their escape, could he have grown wings and flown away?

WANG: Sir, you can investigate what happened. I was shot and fell to the ground. How could I know where that man went?

HATOYAMA: You knew all right. Why else should you shoot yourself? Don't try to outsmart me, young fellow. Tell me the truth. Who's in the underground Communist Party? Who were your accomplices? Where is the liaison man hiding? Who's got the secret code now? Make a clean breast of things and I have ready plenty of medals and rewards.

WANG: You're making my brain whirl, sir.

HATOYAMA [laughing derisively]: In that case we shall have to sober you up. Hou Hsien-pu!

HOU: Yes, sir.

HATOYAMA: Take this young man out and help to sober him.

HOU: Very good, sir. Guards!

[Enter two gendarmes.]

WANG: I've done nothing, sir. Nothing wrong.

HATOYAMA: Take him away.

WANG: Don't punish an innocent man, sir.

[Hatoyama jerks his head in dismissal.]

337

Hou: Come on.

[*The guards march* Wang *out, followed by* Hou.]

Hatoyama [*smiling cynically after them*]:

> Iron hoofs trample the whole northeast,
> Human skulls are used for goblets;
> The crack of whips, the sound of sobs
> And drumming on bones make music.
> No matter how tough the fellow,

[*His singing is punctuated by the sound of blows and cries.*]

> He must break down under torture.

[*Enter* Hou.]

Hou: If you please, sir, he has confessed.

Hatoyama: Who was his accomplice?

Hou: Li Yu-ho, the switchman of the No. 51 Siding.

Hatoyama: Li Yu-ho! [*He takes off his glasses.*] Well, well . . . .

SCENE 5

THE FAMILY'S REVOLUTIONARY HISTORY

[*The next afternoon.* Li's *house.* Granny *is sewing and worrying about* Li.]

Granny:

> Already dusk, but my son is still not back.

[*In the distance sound shouts and the wail of the siren.* Tieh-mei *rushes fearfully in with her basket and locks the door.*]

Tieh-mei: It looks bad, Granny.

Granny: What's happening?

Tieh-mei: Granny,

> The streets are in confusion
> With sentries at every crossroad;
> They are searching and arresting men right and left,
> It's even worse at the station.
> I ran home because I'm worried about Dad.

Granny: Don't worry, child.

> Your dad is brave and wary,
> He knows the way to deal with the Japanese.

[*She tries to calm herself.*]

TIEH-MEI: Yes, of course, Granny.

[*Enter* LI *with the red lantern and canteen.*]

LI [*knocking at the door*]: Mother.

TIEH-MEI: It's Dad. [*She quickly opens the door.*] At last you're back, Dad.

LI: Yes. . . . Mother.

GRANNY: So you're back, son. You had me really worried.

LI: It was a near thing, Mother. [*He walks toward the pillar by the bed and signs to her to take the canteen.*] Let me have the thing in that, quick.

GRANNY [*signing to* TIEH-MEI *to watch the street while she opens the canteen*]: There's nothing here but gruel.

LI: It's underneath, Mother.

[*She empties out the gruel, produces the code which is wrapped in cellophane and hands it to* LI.]

GRANNY: What is this?

[TIEH-MEI, *standing guard by the window, keeps an eye on her father.*]

LI [*hiding the code in a crack in the pillar by the bed*]: Mother,

> I'd just met the knife-grinder by the gruel stall
> When a police car came and the Japanese started a search;
> They didn't find the code hidden under the gruel,
> I smiled calmly while they searched.

TIEH-MEI: Trust you, Dad. But what are we to do with this?

LI: Don't worry. We'll think of some way to send it, Tieh-mei. [*He makes her sit down opposite him and speaks gravely.*] You've seen everything. I can't keep this from you any longer. This is something more important than our own lives. We must keep it a secret even if it costs us our heads.

[GRANNY *lights the paraffin lamp.*]

TIEH-MEI [*naïvely yet earnestly*]: I understand.

LI: Hah, I suppose you think you're the smartest girl in the world.

TIEH-MEI [*pouting*]: Dad!

GRANNY: Look at you both.

TIEH-MEI: Granny.

LI [*consulting his watch*]: It's getting late. I must go out.

TIEH-MEI: Wait till you've had supper, Dad.

LI: I'll eat when I come back.

GRANNY: Don't be too late.

LI: I won't. [*He gets up to go.*]

339

TIEH-MEI [*giving him the scarf*]: Take this, Dad. [*She wraps the scarf round his neck.*] Come back early.

LI: I will. [*Exit.*]

[*Granny polishes the lantern with care.*]

TIEH-MEI [*struck by an idea*]: Polishing the red lantern again, Granny?

GRANNY [*deciding to satisfy her curiosity*]: Tieh-mei, the time has come to tell you something. Sit down and listen to the story of the red lantern.

TIEH-MEI: Yes.

GRANNY: We've had this lantern for thirty years. For thirty years it has lighted the way for us poor people, for workers. Your grandad carried this lantern, and now your dad carries it. It's bound up with all that happened last night and today, which you saw for yourself. I tell you, the red lantern is our family treasure.

TIEH-MEI: Ah, the red lantern is our family treasure. I'll remember that.

GRANNY: It's dark, time to get supper. [*She puts the lantern carefully down and goes to the kitchen.*]

[*TIEH-MEI picks up the lantern to examine it carefully and then puts it gently down. She pensively turns up the paraffin lamp.*]

TIEH-MEI:

> Granny has told me the story of the red lantern,
> Only a few words, yet how much it means.
> I have seen my father's courage,
> My uncles' willingness to die for it.
> What are they working for?
> To save China, save the poor and defeat the Japanese invaders.
> I know they are in the right,
> They are examples for the rest of us.
> You are seventeen, Tieh-mei, no longer a child,
> You should lend your father a hand.
> If his load weighs a thousand pounds,
> You should carry eight hundred.

[*Enter GRANNY. She calls TIEH-MEI, who does not hear.*]

GRANNY: What were you thinking about, child?

TIEH-MEI: Nothing.

GRANNY: The food will soon be ready. When your dad comes, we'll start.

340

TIEH-MEI: Right.

[*The child next door cries.*]

GRANNY: Listen, is that Lung-erh crying next door?

TIEH-MEI [*looking towards the curtain behind the kang*]: Yes, it is.

GRANNY: Poor child, he's hungry I'll be bound. Have we any of that acorn flour[1] left?

TIEH-MEI: Not much.

[*The child cries again.*]

TIEH-MEI [*eager to help*]: There's a little, Granny. Shall I take them a bowl? [*She gets the flour.*]

GRANNY: Yes, do.

[*Enter KUEI-LAN.*]

KUEI-LAN [*knocking at the door*]: Aunty Li.

TIEH-MEI: It's Sister Kuei-lan. [*Opens the door.*] I was just going to call on you, sister.

GRANNY: Is Lung-erh any better?

KUEI-LAN: Yes, but . . . we've nothing at home to eat.

TIEH-MEI: Sister Kuei-lan, this is for you. [*Gives her the bowl of flour.*]

KUEI-LAN [*hesitating to accept it*]: Well . . .

GRANNY: Take it. I heard Lung-erh crying and thought you probably had nothing he could eat. Tieh-mei was just going to take this over.

TIEH-MEI [*to KUEI-LAN*]: Go on, take it.

KUEI-LAN [*accepting the bowl*]: I don't know what to say, Aunty. You're too good to us.

GRANNY: Well, with the wall between us we're two families. If we pulled the wall down we'd be one family, wouldn't we?

TIEH-MEI: We are one family even with the wall.

GRANNY: That's true.

[*The child next door cries again.*]

[*Enter Aunt Liu and she opens the door.*]

AUNT LIU: Kuei-lan, the child is crying. [*Sees the bowl in her hand.*] Aunty, Tieh-mei, you . . . . How can we accept it? You haven't got much yourselves.

GRANNY: Never mind. In times like these we must help each other and make do as best we can. You'd better go and fix a meal for the child.

AUNT LIU: I don't know how to thank you. [*She starts out with KUEI-LAN.*]

341

GRANNY: It's nothing. [*She sees them to the door.*]

TIEH-MEI [*closing the door*]: Granny, look at Kuei-lan's family. Her husband out of work and the little boy ill. How are they going to manage?

GRANNY: We'll do our best to help them.

TIEH-MEI: Yes.

[*An enemy agent posing as a peddler comes to the door and knocks lightly three times.*]

PEDDLER: Is Old Li in?

TIEH-MEI: Someone wants Dad.

GRANNY: Open the door.

TIEH-MEI: Right. [*Opens the door.*]

GRANNY: You want . . . .

[*Enter the* PEDDLER. *He looks around and closes the door behind him.*]

PEDDLER [*raising his gloved left hand*]: I sell wooden combs.

GRANNY [*observing him carefully*]: Have you any peach-wood combs?

PEDDLER: Yes, for cash down.

TIEH-MEI [*eagerly*]: Wait! [*She turns to pick up the red lantern.*] [GRANNY *coughs.* TIEH-MEI *stops.* GRANNY *strikes a match and lights the small square lantern while* TIEH-MEI, *understanding, catches her breath.*]

PEDDLER [*raises the curtain and looks out as if on his guard. Then he eyes the small lantern*]: Thank goodness, I've found you at last.

TIEH-MI [*realizing that this is a trick, angrily*]: You . . . .

GRANNY [*throwing her a warning glance*]: Well, let me see your combs.

PEDDLER [*pretending to be in earnest*]: This is no time for jokes, old lady. I've come for the code. That's important to the communist cause. The revolution depends on it. Every minute is more precious than gold to the revolution. Give it me quickly, without any more delay.

TIEH-MEI [*vehemently*]: What nonsense are you talking? Get out.

PEDDLER: Now then . . . .

TIEH-MEI: Are you going? [*She pushes him.*]

GRANNY: Tieh-mei, call the police.

TIEH-MEI: If you won't go, I'll call the police.

PEDDLER: Don't do that. I'll go, I'll go.

TIEH-MEI: Get out quickly.

[*The spy gives her a dirty look and shuffles out.* TIEH-MEI *closes the* door with a bang. *Two plainclothes men enter, making signs to each other, and stand outside the door.*]

TIEH-MEI: He nearly fooled me, Granny. Where did that mangy dog come from?

GRANNY: Child, this is a bad business.

> *Never mind that mangy dog,*
> *A poisonous snake will be following behind;*
> *It's clear that someone*
> *Has talked.*

TIEH-MEI: We must send the secret code away at once.

GRANNY: It's too late. They'll have laid a trap.

TIEH-MEI: Ah! [*Runs to the window and looks out.*] Granny. [*She comes back to her.*] There's a man by the telegraph pole watching our door.

GRANNY: You see? Hurry up and paste the sign on the window.

TIEH-MEI: What sign?

GRANNY: The paper butterfly² I told you to cut out.

TIEH-MEI: It's in the box of patterns.

GRANNY: Get it out then.

TIEH-MEI: Right. [*Hurries behind the bed-curtain and fetches the paper.*] How shall I paste it, Granny?

GRANNY: Open the door to keep the window dark before you start. I'll sweep the ground outside so that they can't see you.

[*TIEH-MEI opens the door and GRANNY gets a broom. Before she can go out LI enters and walks in.*]

TIEH-MEI [*startled*]: Why, Dad. [*The paper butterfly falls to the ground. The old woman drops her broom.*]

LI [*seeing the paper butterfly on the ground*]: Has something happened, Mother? [*Closes the door.*]

GRANNY: There are agents outside.

[*They fall silent. GRANNY is thinking hard. TIEH-MEI waits for her father to speak. LI paces thoughtfully up and down.*]

[*Enter HOU HSIEN-PU and he knocks at the door.*]

LI: Mother, they may be coming to arrest me. I went to look for Old Chou just now but couldn't find him. If you need any help, get in touch with Old Chou at No. 36 West Bank. You must be careful.

GRANNY: I know. Don't worry.

LI: Tieh-mei, open the door.

[*LI calmly sits down. HOU enters the room beaming. GRANNY*

makes a show of sweeping the floor. TIEH-MEI *takes this chance to paste up the paper sign.*]

HOU: Are you Mr. Li?

LI: Yes, sir. Take a seat.

HOU [*with an awkward laugh presenting an invitation card*]: Mr. Li, Mr. Hatoyama is celebrating his birthday today. He wants you to go and have a cup of wine with him.

[GRANNY *and* TIEH-MEI *are startled.*]

LI [*calmly*]: What, is Mr. Hatoyama inviting me to a feast?

HOU: Just to be friendly.

LI: He wants to make friends with me?

HOU: You'll understand when you see him. Come along.

LI: All right. Mother, [*gravely*] I'm going now.

GRANNY: Wait. Tieh-mei, bring some wine.

TIEH-MEI: Yes. [*She fetches wine from the table.*]

HOU: There'll be plenty for him to drink at the feast, old lady.

GRANNY [*with a contemptuous glance*]: Pah.

> The poor prefer their own wine,
> Each drop of it warms the heart.

You like wine, son, but I don't usually encourage you to drink. Today I want you to drink up this bowl. [*She passes him the wine.*]

LI [*taking the bowl*]: Right. With this to put heart into me I can cope with whatever's coming. Watch me drink, Mother.

GRANNY: I'm watching you.

LI [*looking at her as if to reassure her with his strength. He grasps the bowl hard and drains it in one breath. His cheeks are flushed, his eyes gleam*]: Thank you, Mother.

GRANNY [*proudly*]: That's my fine son.

LI: Mother,

> I drink your wine at parting
> And it fills me with courage and strength.
> The Japanese is offering me a feast,
> Well, I can manage even a thousand cups.
> This is stormy, treacherous weather,
> Be ready for squalls.

TIEH-MEI: Dad. [*Clasps him and sobs.*]

LI: Tieh-mei.

> Keep your weather eye open outside,
> Don't forget our unsettled accounts;
> Keep watch for wild dogs at the door,

344

> And listen for the magpie's lucky cry.[3]
> You must help at home
> And share your granny's troubles.

TIEH-MEI: Dad. [*Clasps him and sobs.*]

GRANNY: Don't cry, Tieh-mei. Our family has this rule: when one of us leaves, nobody must cry.

LI: Always do as Granny says, Tieh-mei. Don't cry.

TIEH MEI [*wiping her tears*]: I won't.

GRANNY: Open the door, child, and let your father go to the feast.

LI: Mother, look after yourself.

[*Grasping* LI's *hands,* GRANNY *gazes at him while* TIEH-MEI *opens the door. A gust of wind.* LI *strides out into the wind. Huddled up in his coat* HOU *follows.* TIEH-MEI *runs after them with the scarf.*]

TIEH-MEI: Dad!

[*Four enemy thugs bar her way.*]

THUG A: Go back. [*He forces her back through the door. Then he enters and tells* GRANNY.] We're making a search.

[*The thugs give the place a professional going over.* TIEH-MEI *nestles up to* GRANNY *as they turn everything upside down. They discover an almanac and toss it away but fail to find anything incriminating.*]

THUG A: Come on. [*He signs to the others to leave. Exeunt.*]

TIEH-MEI: [*closes the door, draws the curtain and looks at the chaos in the room*]: Granny! [*She falls into her arms and sobs.*]

GRANNY [*weeping despite herself*]: All right, cry, child. Have a good cry.

TIEH-MEI: Granny, will Dad ever come back?

GRANNY [*restraining her own tears. She knows there is little hope of his returning but does not want to say so. She takes up* LI's *scarf and strokes it*]: Tears won't help him, child. [*Looks at her.*] Tieh-mei, the time has come to tell you about our family.

TIEH-MEI: Yes, Granny?

GRANNY: Sit down. I'll tell you.

TIEH-MEI: Yes. [*Sits down on a stool.*]

GRANNY: Tell me: Is your dad good?

TIEH-MEI: There's no one better in the whole wide world.

GRANNY: Well . . . he's not your real father.

TIEH-MEI [*incredulously*]: Ah! What do you mean, Granny?

GRANNY: Neither am I your real granny.

TIEH-MEI [startled]: What's come over you, Granny? Have you taken leave of your senses?

GRANNY: No, child. We don't belong to one family. Your surname is Chen, mine is Li and your dad's is Chang.

TIEH-MEI [blankly]: Oh.

GRANNY:

> For seventeen storm-tossed years I held my peace,
> Eager to speak but afraid you were not ready for the truth.

TIEH-MEI: You can tell me, Granny. I won't cry.

GRANNY:

> Your father can hardly escape
> And they may imprison me too;
> Then the work for the revolution will fall to you.
> When I tell you the truth, Tieh-mei,
> Don't break down but take it bravely,
> Like a girl of iron.

TIEH-MEI: Tell me. I won't cry.

GRANNY: It's a long story. When the railway was seized by the Japanese at the end of the Ching dynasty, my husband fled to the south and became a maintenance man in Kiangan. He had two apprentices. One was your real father, Chen Chih-hsing.

TIEH-MEI: My father, Chen Chih-hsing.

GRANNY: The other was your present dad, Chang Yu-ho.

TIEH-MEI: Chang Yu-ho.

GRANNY [standing up]: The country was torn by the fighting between warlords. But then the Chinese Communist Party was born to lead the Chinese people's revolution. In February, 1923, workers of the Peking-Hankow Railway set up a trade union in Chengchow. One of the warlords, Wu Pei-fu, was a stooge of the foreign invaders. When he tried to suppress the union, it called on all the workers on the line to strike. More than ten thousand men in Kiangan demonstrated. That was another cold, dark night. I was so worried about your grandfather that I couldn't rest or sleep. I was mending clothes by the lamp when I heard someone knocking at the door, calling, "Aunty, Aunty, quickly open the door." I opened the door, and he came in.

TIEH-MEI: Who was it?

GRANNY: Your dad.

TIEH-MEI [surprised]: My dad?

346

GRANNY: Yes, your present dad. Dripping with blood and all gashed with wounds, in his left hand he held this red lantern. . . .

TIEH-MEI: Ah, the red lantern.

GRANNY: In his right arm he held a baby.

TIEH-MEI: A baby?

GRANNY: A mite less than one year old.

TIEH-MEI: That baby . . . .

GRANNY: That baby was none other . . . .

TIEH-MEI: Than who?

GRANNY: Than you.

TIEH-MEI: Me . . . .

GRANNY [quickly]: Hugging you tight to his chest, with tears in his eyes your dad stood before me and said, "Aunty, Aunty . . . ." [TIEH-MEI gazes expectantly at her.]

GRANNY: For some minutes he just stared at me and couldn't go on. In a panic, I begged him to speak. He said, "They've murdered . . . my master and brother. This is Brother Chen's child, a child of the revolution. I must bring her up to carry on our work." He said, "Aunty, from now on I am your son and this child is your granddaughter." Then I took you in my arms.

TIEH-MEI: Granny! [She buries her head in the old woman's lap.] [GRANNY holds and comforts her.]

GRANNY: Ah! You mustn't cry. Take a grip on yourself and listen.

> In the strike those devils murdered your father and mother,
> Li Yu-ho went east and west for the revolution;
> He swore to tread in their steps, keep the red lantern burning;
> He staunched his wounds, buried the dead, and went back to
>   the fight.
> Now the Japanese brigands are burning, killing, and looting,
> Before our eyes your dad was taken away;
> Remember this debt of blood and tears,
> Be brave and make up your mind to settle scores,
> A debt of blood must be paid for with enemy blood.

TIEH-MEI:

> Granny tells a stirring tale of the revolution,
> They brought me up in wind and rain and storm,
> How much I owe you, Granny, for all these years!
> My mind is made up now, I see my way clear;
> Blood must be shed for our blood,
> I must carry on the task my father began.

347

Here I raise the red lantern, let its light shine far.
My father is as dauntless as the pine,
The Communist Party fears nothing under the sun,
I shall follow it and never, never waver.
The red lantern's light
Shines on my father fighting those wild beasts.
Generation shall fight on after generation,
Never leaving the field until the victory is won.

[GRANNY and TIEH-MEI hold high the red lantern.]

SCENE 6

HATOYAMA IS DEFIED

[That evening. Hatoyama's house. A sumptuous feast is spread.
Through the lattice windows glittering lights can be seen. Jazz
sounds and girls dance past the window.]

[Enter Hou with LI YU-HO.]

HOU: Please wait a minute. [He starts off to report LI's attitude to
 HATOYAMA.]

LI: As you like. [He stands there looking round, puffing his cigarette,
 disgusted by the surroundings.]

HOU [off]: Captain Hatoyama.

HATOYAMA [hurrying in]: Ah, my old friend, it's good to see you
 again. Have you been keeping well?

LI: How are you, Mr. Hatoyama?

HATOYAMA: So we meet again after all this time. Do you remember when we were both working on the railway in Harbin?

LI [drily]: You were a celebrated Japanese doctor while I was a
 poor Chinese worker. We were like two trains running on different tracks, not traveling the same road.

HATOYAMA: Well, brother, there's not all that difference between
 a surgeon and a worker. We're old friends, not strangers, right?

LI: In that case can I hope for good treatment from you?

HATOYAMA: That's why I asked you over for a chat. Do sit down,
 please. [They sit down.] Today is my birthday, friend, a time
 to celebrate. Suppose we just talk of friendship and leave politics
 out of it?

348

LI: I'm a switchman. I don't understand politics. You can say whatever you like.

HATOYAMA: Fine, I like your frankness. Come on. [*Pours wine.*]
Just a cup of wine for friendship's sake. Now, drink up. [*Raises
the cup.*]

LI: You are too polite, Mr. Hatoyama. Sorry, but I've given up
drinking. [*He pushes the cup away.*]

HATOYAMA: Well, friend. [*Taking up his own cup.*] If you won't
oblige me, I can't force you. [*He drinks and then starts his offensive.*] Why take things so seriously? There's an old Chinese
saying, "Life is over in a flash like a dream. We should drink and
sing, for who knows how soon life will end?"

LI: Yes, listening to songs and watching dances is living like an
immortal. I wish you long life, Mr. Hatoyama, and all prosperity.

HATOYAMA [*frustrated, lamely*]: Thank you, thank you.

LI [*eyeing him contemptuously*]: You are too ceremonious. [*He
laughs.*]

HATOYAMA [*with a hollow laugh*]: My friend, I am a believer in
Buddhism. A Buddhist sutra tells us, "Boundless the sea of sorrow, yet a man who will turn back can reach the shore."

LI [*jokingly*]: For myself, I don't believe in Buddhism but I've
heard the saying, "A butcher who lays down his knife can become
a Buddha, too."

HATOYAMA: Good. [*On the defensive.*] Well said. But both add up
to the same thing. In fact we can sum up all human beliefs in
two words.

LI: What are they?

HATOYAMA: "For me."

LI: "For you," eh?

HATOYAMA: No. "Each for himself."

LI: "Each for himself." [*He laughs.*]

HATOYAMA [*earnestly*]: Old friend, you know the saying, "Heaven
destroys men who won't look out for themselves."

LI: Oh? Heaven destroys men who won't look out for themselves?

HATOYAMA: That's the secret of life.

LI: So life has a secret. I'm afraid it's too difficult for a blockhead
like me to grasp. [*He laughs.*]

HATOYAMA [*to himself*]: What a stubborn fool!

> *His heart is hard to fathom;*
> *He parries my thrusts*

> With no thought of his own safety,
> Impervious to both praise and flattery.
> I must be patient.
> With my experience and tact
> I'll get hold of that secret code.

Let's stop this shadow-boxing, friend. I want your help.

LI [*with an air of surprise*]: What do you mean? How can a poor switchman help you?

HATOYAMA [*unable to keep his temper*]: Quit joking. Hand it over.

LI: What is it you want?

HATOYAMA [*coldly and distinctly*]: The secret code.

LI: What's that? All I can do is work switches. I've never used any such thing as a code.

HATOYAMA [*rising abruptly*]: If you choose to do things the hard way instead of the easy way, friend, don't blame me if we get rough.

LI: Do as you like.

HATOYAMA: All right. [*Beats his plate with a chopstick.*]

[*Enter INSPECTOR WANG in army uniform wearing his medal.*]

HATOYAMA: My old friend, look, who is this?

LI [*shocked by the sight of WANG*]: Ah!

WANG: Take my advice, brother . . . .

LI: You shameless renegade!

> Only a coward would bend his knees in surrender,
> A cur afraid of death and clinging to life.
> How often did I warn you
> Against enemy threats and bribes?
> You swore you would gladly die for the revolution;
> How could you sell out and help the Japanese?
> They are treating you like a dog,
> Yet you count disgrace an honor.
> Come here and look me in the eyes,
> Shame on you, you sneaking slave.

[*HATOYAMA waves WANG away and he slinks out.*]

HATOYAMA: Steady on, my friend. I didn't want to play my trump card but you forced me to.

LI [*laughing derisively*]: I expected as much. Your trump card is nothing but a mangy dog with a broken back. You'll get no satisfaction out of me.

HATOYAMA: I can give you some satisfaction. Let's hear your terms.

350

Lı: Terms?

HATOYAMA: Here's your chance to strike a good bargain.

Lı: Bargain?

HATOYAMA: Yes, bargain. I understand you Communists very well; you have your beliefs. But beliefs can be bought or sold. The main thing is to make a profit.

Lı: That's frank enough. It follows that there's nothing you wouldn't sell if you could make a profit. [He laughs.]

HATOYAMA: [furious]: You . . . . [Fuming.] You go too far, friend. You must know my job. I'm the one who issues passes to Hell.

Lı: You don't seem to know my job. I'm the one who takes your pass and destroys your Hell.

HATOYAMA: You know, my leg-screws are hungry for human flesh.

Lı: I tried out that silly gadget of yours long ago.

HATOYAMA [impressed by Lı's spirit, makes a show of sympathy]: Take my advice and recant before your bones are broken.

Lı: I'd sooner have my bones broken than recant.

HATOYAMA: Our police are rough. They think nothing of killing people.

Lı: We Communists are tough. We look on death as nothing.

HATOYAMA: Even if you are made of iron, I'll force you to speak.

Lı: Even if you have hills of swords and a forest of knives, you'll get nothing out of me, Hatoyama.

> The Japanese militarists are wolves
> Hiding their savagery under a smile;
> You kill our people and invade our land
> In the name of "Co-prosperity in East Asia."
> The Communists lead the people's revolution;
> We have hundreds of millions of heroes in the resistance;
> For you to rely on renegades
> Is like fishing for the moon in the lake.

HATOYAMA:

> I'll let you taste the leg-screws.
> [Enter the sergeant and two gendarmes.]

Lı:

> I need to take the weight off my feet.

SERGEANT: Get moving.

> [The gendarmes grasp Lı's arms.]

Lı: I can do without your help. [He throws them off and calmly

*picks up his cap, blows the dust off it, shakes it, and walks out
with dignity.*]

[*The sergeant and gendarmes follow* Li *out.*]

HATOYAMA [*pacing to and fro, very put out, scratches his head and
mutters*]: Quite mad, these Reds.

> My eyes are dim, my head is ready to burst;
> My blood pressure has risen, my hands are cold;
> The Reds are flesh and blood like us,
> What makes them tougher than steel?
> He refuses to say where the code is hidden, curse him!
> What shall I do if I can't get hold of it?

[*The telephone rings.*]

HATOYAMA [*taking the call*]: Hatoyama here. Yes, sir, we are still
searching for the code. Quite so, sir. Certainly, certainly. Yes, sir.
I'll stake my life on it. [*He replaces the receiver and shouts.*] Here.
How are you doing?

[*Enter the sergeant.*]

SERGEANT: We have tried all the tortures, but Li Yu-ho would
rather die than speak.

HATOYAMA: Rather die than speak?

SERGEANT: Let me take some men to search his house, sir.

HATOYAMA: That's no use. Judging by my experience, ten thousand
men can't find something which a Communist has hidden. Fetch
him in.

SERGEANT: Bring Li Yu-ho here!

[*Two gendarmes push* Li *in. Blood-stained and battered, he stands
there defiantly.*]

Li:

> You cur with the heart of a wolf.

HATOYAMA: The code! Give me the code!

Li: Hatoyama!

> You have tried every torture to break me;
> Though my body is mangled I clench my teeth,
> I shall never bow my head. [*He laughs.*]

352

SCENE 7

THE CODE FINDS A NEW HIDING-PLACE

[*One morning several days later. Li's house. By the telegraph pole not far from the door is an enemy agent disguised as a cobbler. While pretending to mend shoes he watches the house.*]

TIEH-MEI [*just out of bed and emerging from behind the curtain*]: Why isn't Dad back yet, Granny?

> *Ever since Dad was arrested—*

GRANNY:

> We've been worrying and cannot rest.
>
> [The KNIFE-GRINDER *offstage cries*, "Any knives or scissors to grind?"]

TIEH-MEI: Granny, listen.

> [*Enter the* KNIFE-GRINDER.]

KNIFE-GRINDER: Any knives or scissors to grind?

> [GRANNY *pulls* TIEH-MEI *to the window and they look out.*]
>
> [*The* KNIFE-GRINDER *comes up to the window and sees the butterfly sign. He hesitates, then nods and starts shouting again.*]

COBBLER: There's no business for you in this poor part of town. Why do your caterwauling here?

KNIFE-GRINDER [*in a loud, friendly voice*]: You stick to your business, friend, and I'll stick to mine. We knife-grinders have to call out. If you make me keep quiet, how am I to find customers?

COBBLER: You clear out if you don't want to run into trouble.

KNIFE-GRINDER: All right, all right. I get it. I'll try my luck somewhere else. [*As he leaves he raises his left hand to his ear and yells.*] Any knives or scissors to grind? [*Exit.*]

COBBLER: Still caterwauling, blast him.

GRANNY [*pulling* TIEH-MEI *close*]: Did you hear that, child?

TIEH-MEI: What?

GRANNY: That knife-grinder probably came to make contact with us. He went away after seeing the sign on the window. Run after him quickly with the code and lantern and see whether he's our man or not. I'll get the code.

TIEH-MEI: All right. [*Goes to the window.*]

GRANNY: It won't do, child, not with those agents outside. You can't go.

TIEH-MEI: What shall we do, then?

> I want to run after the knife-grinder,
> But I can't leave the house and am worried.
> I wish I could grow wings and fly like a bird.

[The child next door cries.]

TIEH-MEI: Granny, I have an idea.

GRANNY: What is it?

TIEH-MEI: Granny.

> I know a way out.

Look. [Points to the kang.] There's only a wall between this and the Liu's kang. I can make a hole and slip through.

GRANNY [pleased]: That's a good idea. Go ahead.

[TIEH-MEI disappears behind the curtain. GRANNY starts chopping cabbage to hide the noise she makes.]

TIEH-MEI [coming back]: It's done, Granny.

GRANNY [takes the code from the crack in the pillar and gives it to her with the red lantern. Solemnly]: Make sure he's the right man, Tieh-mei. He must get the password correct. Be very careful.

TIEH-MEI: I will. [She disappears behind the curtain.]

COBBLER [calling outside]: Open the door.

GRANNY: Who's that?

COBBLER: It's me. The cobbler.

GRANNY: Wait, I'll open the door. [Opens the door.]

COBBLER [sees the knife in her hand]: What are you doing?

GRANNY: Tomorrow is my son's birthday. We are going to have some vegetable rolls.

COBBLER: Ah, vegetable rolls.

GRANNY: What do you want?

COBBLER: I want to borrow a light.

GRANNY [indicating the match-box on the table]: Help yourself.

COBBLER: How many of you are there, old lady?

GRANNY: You've been squatting outside our door the last few days; you should know all about us. One has gone, there are two of us left.

COBBLER: Where's the girl?

GRANNY: She's not well.

COBBLER: Not well? Where is she?

GRANNY: She's lying down in bed.

COBBLER: Lying down, eh? [He walks towards the kang.]

GRANNY [stopping him]: Keep away. Don't frighten the child.

COBBLER [*sniggering*]: If she's ill, old lady, why isn't she whimpering?

GRANNY: My granddaughter never whimpers when she's ill.

COBBLER: That means she isn't ill. But perhaps you feel sick at heart?

GRANNY: Seems to me you're the one who is sick.

COBBLER: Me sick? How?

GRANNY: There's a canker gnawing at your bones—they're moldering.

COBBLER: That's nothing that a little sun won't cure.

GRANNY: You're too rotten to face the sun.

COBBLER: Never mind. Men's bones have got to rot some day, so let them be rotten. Tell your girl to sit up for a bit, old lady. It's no good lying down all the time. [*He tries to lift the curtain.*]

GRANNY: What d'you think you're doing? Asking all these foolish questions, throwing your weight about in other people's houses, and insulting women. What's the idea? Clear off. Get out!

COBBLER: All right, just wait. [*Enter two enemy agents. They whisper together and the agents open the door.*]

GRANNY: Who are you?

AGENTS: We are checking up. How many people live here?

GRANNY: Three.

AGENTS: Where are the other two?

GRANNY: You should know where my son is now.

AGENTS: Where's your granddaughter?

GRANNY: She's ill.

AGENTS: Where is she? Where is she? [*Goes to lift the curtain.*] [*Voice from behind the curtain: "Granny. Who's there?"*]

GRANNY: Police checking up. [*The agents grunt, shrug and go out.* GRANNY *closes the door behind them.*]

AGENTS [*to the* COBBLER]: What a fuss over nothing. She was on the kang all the time. She didn't go out.

COBBLER: All right. That old bitch tried to make a fool of me. [*Exeunt.*]

GRANNY: What a near thing! When did you come back, Tieh-mei? [*She lifts the curtain and* KUEI-LAN *sits up.*]

GRANNY: So it's you, Kuei-lan.

KUEI-LAN [*getting off the kang to catch hold of* GRANNY]: Granny Li.

> After Tieh-mei slipped away from our house
> My mother sent me to tell you.
> When I heard those spies questioning you

I pretended to be Tieh-mei lying ill in bed.
When Tieh-mei comes, she can come through our house,
With me helping, you don't have to worry.

GRANNY: You've saved us. We shall never forget what you've done.
TIEH-MEI [*emerging from behind the curtain*]: Granny. Sister Kuei-lan.
GRANNY: So you're back at last.
KUEI-LAN: Your granny was worried about you.
GRANNY: My heart nearly jumped out of my mouth. If not for Kuei-lan we'd have been in serious trouble.
TIEH-MEI: Thank you, Sister Kuei-lan. What would we have done without you?
KUEI-LAN: It was nothing. Why thank me for such a little thing? It's good that you're back. I must be going now.
TIEH-MEI: Won't you stay a while?
GRANNY: You go and tidy up the kang.
TIEH-MEI: Yes.
[*Kuei-lan points at the door and they understand. She steps behind the curtain and leaves. Tieh-mei straightens the bedding and pulls the curtain back.*]
GRANNY: Did you find the knife-grinder?
TIEH-MEI [*in a low voice*]: I searched several streets but couldn't find him. Then I looked for Uncle Chou but he wasn't at home. So I hurried back for fear those spies might discover that I was out.
GRANNY: Where is the code?
TIEH-MEI: I left it outside.
GRANNY [*disturbed*]: But why?
TIEH-MEI: I thought it would be safer outside, so I hid it under a pier of Short Bridge.
GRANNY [*relieved*]: Ah, you made me break into a cold sweat, child. You've done right. I shan't worry provided the code's in a safe place.
[*Enter HATOYAMA in a Chinese gown and hat with a walking stick. He is followed by HOU carrying two boxes of cakes. They knock at the door.*]
GRANNY: Who's there?
HOU: Captain Hatoyama is paying you a visit.
GRANNY [*grasping TIEH-MEI*]: Child, if your granny is arrested now, you must find Uncle Chou and give him the code, then go to the north hills.

356

TIEH-MEI: Granny! [*She cries.*]

GRANNY: Don't cry. Go and open the door.

[TIEH-MEI *opens the door.*]

HATOYAMA [*entering with a show of sympathy*]: How are you, madam? I am Li Yu-ho's old friend, but I have been too busy to call before. [*Signs to* HOU *to leave after he has put the cakes on the table.*] This is a trifling present.

GRANNY: So you are Mr. Hatoyama?

HATOYAMA: Yes. I'm Hatoyama, Hatoyama.

GRANNY: Will you let me tidy up a bit before I come with you?

HATOYAMA: Don't misunderstand. That's not what I came for. Please sit down.

[GRANNY *ignores him.* HATOYAMA *takes a seat.*]

HATOYAMA: You must be longing to see your son, madam.

GRANNY: Of course, a mother naturally thinks of her son.

HATOYAMA: You needn't worry. He'll come back very soon safe and sound.

GRANNY: So much the better.

HATOYAMA: This wasn't our doing. We had orders from above. As a matter of fact we are looking after him very well.

GRANNY: Thank you.

HATOYAMA: We heard from Li, madam, that he left something with you.

GRANNY: Left what?

HATOYAMA [*casually*]: Some code.

GRANNY: I don't know what you mean. [*To* TIEH-MEI.] What does he mean, child?

HATOYAMA: A code. A book.

GRANNY: A book? My son can't read, Mr. Hatoyama. My granddaughter has never been to school and I can't tell one character from another. Our family has never bought books.

HATOYAMA: Since Li Yu-ho has told us about that book, old lady, why try to hide it?

GRANNY: If he told you, why not let him come and find it? Wouldn't that be simpler?

HATOYAMA [*to himself*]: She's a crafty old bitch. [*To* GRANNY.] Don't try to fool me, old lady. Let's make a bargain. You give me that book and I'll send your son straight back. If he wants a job, the railway can make him a vice-section-chief. If he wants money, he can have five thousand dollars.

357

GRANNY: Five thousand dollars and the job of a vice-section-chief? What book can be worth that much?

HATOYAMA: You have to sell to someone who knows its value.

GRANNY: If that book means so much to you, I'll have a look for it. Wait a minute. Tieh-mei, help me find it.

HATOYAMA: Take your time. There's no hurry.

[GRANNY takes TIEH-MEI behind the curtain.]

HATOYAMA [waiting expectantly, to himself]: So after all money can work miracles.

[GRANNY comes back with TIEH-MEI carrying a bundle.]

HATOYAMA [very pleased]: You've found it, madam?

GRANNY: Yes. This is what my son brought back.

HATOYAMA: Right, that must be it. That's it.

GRANNY: You can have it. [Gives him an almanac.]

HATOYAMA [furiously]: Bah, an almanac. [He wants to throw it away but thinks better of it, fuming.] I'll take it back anyway. Ah . . . . You must be worried about your son. Suppose I take you to see him and find out about the book. We are bound to find it. There's no hurry.

GRANNY: That's very good of you. Thank you. [To TIEH-MEI.] Look after the house, child.

HATOYAMA: She had better come as well to see her father.

GRANNY [startled]: But she's only a child.

HATOYAMA [beckoning]: Come along.

TIEH-MEI: All right. I want to see my dad.

HATOYAMA: You'd like to help your father, wouldn't you?

TIEH-MEI: Yes.

HATOYAMA: Fine. Come on.

[Enter HOU with several gendarmes.]

HATOYAMA: Look after them well. [He strides out. To the agents.] Keep an eye on the house. [Exit.]

HOU [to GRANNY and TIEH-MEI with a sinister smile]: Come on, old lady. Come on, miss.

[They leave the house together. The agents seal up the door.]

TIEH-MEI [upset to see the door sealed]: Granny!

GRANNY [putting one hand through TIEH-MEI's arm and wrapping the scarf round her neck]: Come on.

[A gust of wind.]

358

SCENE 8

THE EXECUTION GROUNDS

[*Night. The Japanese police headquarters outside the prison. Enter* HATOYAMA, HOU HSIEN-PU *and the sergeant.*]

HATOYAMA: It doesn't look as if we shall get anywhere with our interrogation. Hurry up and get the tape recorder ready. We'll hear what the old woman says when she meets her son. We may find out something.

HOU and SERGEANT: Yes, sir.

HATOYAMA: Bring the old woman in.

HOU: Yes, sir. Fetch the old woman.

[*Two Japanese gendarmes bring* GRANNY *in.*]

HATOYAMA: Do you know this place, madam?

GRANNY: It's the police headquarters.

HATOYAMA [*pointing*]: And over there?

[GRANNY *glances in that direction.*]

HATOYAMA [*with a menacing smile*]: That's the gate to paradise, where your son will mount to heaven.

[GRANNY *shivers.*]

HATOYAMA: When a man has committed a crime, madam, and his mother refuses to save his life, don't you think she is rather cruel?

GRANNY: What do you mean, Mr. Hatoyama? You've arrested my son for no reason and thrown him into prison. Now you want to kill him. You are the ones that are committing a crime, you are the ones that are cruel. How can you shift the blame for his murder on to me?

HATOYAMA: Have you thought what will come of talking like that, old lady?

GRANNY: The lives of our family are in your hands. You can do whatever you like.

HATOYAMA [*controlling himself*]: All right, go and see your son. [GRANNY *starts off.*] This is his last chance, old lady. I hope you will all decide to steer clear of trouble and be reunited as one family.

GRANNY: I know what's right.

HATOYAMA: Take her away.

[*Exit* HOU *with* GRANNY.]

HATOYAMA: Here. Take Li to the execution grounds.

359

SERGEANT: Bring Li Yu-ho.

[*The scene changes. On the left is the path to the prison. In the center is a stone. In the rear on the left a slope leading to the execution grounds is backed by a high wall covered with barbed wire. It is dark. Offstage the Japanese gendarmes yell: "Fetch Li Yu-ho!" Chains clank.*]

[*Enter* LI.]

LI:

> At the jailers' blood-thirsty cry I leave my cell;
> Though my hands and feet are manacled and fettered
> They cannot chain my soaring spirit.
> Hatoyama has tortured me to get the code;
> My bones are broken, my flesh torn, but firm my will.
> Walking boldly to the execution grounds
> I look up and see the red flag of revolution,
> The flames of the resistance.
> Not for long will these invaders lord it over us,
> And once the storm is past fresh flowers will bloom;
> New China will shine like the morning sun,
> Red flags will flutter over all the country—
> I smile through tears of joy at the thought of it.
> I have done very little for the Party,
> Worst of all, I failed to send the code to the hills;
> That renegade Wang's only contact was with me,
> The wretch can betray no one else;
> And my mother and daughter are as staunch as steel,
> So Hatoyama may search heaven and earth,
> But he will never find the secret code.

[*Enter* GRANNY *and she looks round.*]

GRANNY [*seeing* LI, *cries*]: Yu-ho!

LI [*startled*]: Mother!

GRANNY: My son.

LI: Mother.

[GRANNY *runs over to put her arms around him.*]

> Again I live through that day seventeen years ago,
> And burn with hate for the foe of my class and country.
> The cruel Japanese devils
> Have beaten and tortured you, my son, my son!

LI: Don't grieve for me, mother.

360

GRANNY:

> I shouldn't grieve to have such a fine son.

LI:

> Brought up in a hard school
> I'll fight and never give ground;
> Though they break every bone in my body,
> Though they lock me up until I wear through my chains.
> As long as our country is ravaged my heart must bleed;
> As long as the war lasts my family is in danger;
> However hard the road to revolution,
> We must press on in the steps of the glorious dead.
> My one regret if I die today
> Is the debt I have left unpaid.
> I long to soar like an eagle through the sky,
> Borne on the wind above the mountain passes
> To rescue our millions of suffering countrymen—
> Then how gladly would I die for the revolution!

GRANNY:

> That unpaid debt is in good hands,
> Cost what it may, we shall pay it.

[Enter Hou with the guards.]

HOU: I'll say this for you: You certainly know how to keep your mouths shut and not give anything away. Come on, old woman. Captain Hatoyama wants you.

LI: Mother . . . .

GRANNY: Don't worry, son. I know what he wants. [She goes out fearlessly, followed by the guards.]

HOU: Bring Tieh-mei here! [Exit.]

LI [calling]: Tieh-mei!

TIEH-MEI [running in]: Dad!

LI: Tieh-mei.

TIEH-MEI: Dad.

> I hoped day and night to see my dad again,
> Yet I hardly know you, so battered and drenched with blood
> I wish I could break your chains,
> Dear father. . . .

LI [smiling]: Silly child.

TIEH-MEI [sobbing]: If you have anything to say to me, Dad, tell me quickly.

LI: Child,
>One thing I have wanted many times to tell you,
>It's been hidden in my heart for seventeen years. . . .

TIEH-MEI [quickly stopping him]: Don't say it. You are my own
true father.
>Don't say it, Father,
>I know the bitter tale of these seventeen years.
>You are so good, our country needs you;
>Why can't I die in your stead?
>Ah, Dad. [She kneels and clasps LI's knees, sobbing.]

LI:
>Nurse your hatred in your heart.
>Men say that family love outweighs all else,
>But class love is greater yet.
>Listen, child, your dad is a poor man,
>With no money at home to leave you;
>All I have is a red lantern,
>I entrust it to your safe keeping.

TIEH-MEI:
>You have left me a priceless treasure,
>How can you speak of money?
>You have left me your integrity
>To help me stand firm as a rock;
>You have left me your wisdom
>To help me see clearly through the enemy's wiles;
>You have left me your courage
>To help me fight those brutes;
>This red lantern is our heirloom,
>A treasure so great
>That a thousand carts and boats
>Could not hold it all.
>I give you my word I shall keep the lantern safe.

LI:
>As wave follows wave in the great Yangtse River,
>Our red lantern will be passed from hand to hand.
>If they let you go home,
>Find friends to help settle that debt and I'll be content.

TIEH-MEI: I will, father.
LI: Good child.
   [Enter HOU.]

Hou [to Tieh-mei]: What about the secret code, girl?

[She ignores him.]

Hou: Why don't you speak?

Tieh-mei: My dad and my grandmother have said all there is to say. I've nothing to add.

Hou: Even this child is so pig-headed, confound her! Here. Bring that old woman back.

[Two guards bring in Granny.]

Hou: Now your whole family is here. Think well. If you don't give us the code, not one of you will leave this place alive. [Exit.]

[Li and Tieh-mei help Granny to the stone.]

Li: They've tortured you, mother. The swine!

Granny: It doesn't matter if my old bones ache a little, my heart is still sound.

[Tieh-mei sobs with her head on Granny's lap. Enter the sergeant. Tieh-mei looks up.]

Sergeant: Captain Hatoyama gives you five more minutes to think it over. It you still won't give up the secret code, you will all be shot.

Granny [indignantly]: You brutes, won't you even let the child go?

Sergeant: We'll spare no one.

[Li and Granny look at Tieh-mei, who meets their eyes and straightens up.]

Sergeant [dragging Tieh-mei away]: Only five minutes left, girl. Give up the code and save your whole family. Speak!

[Tieh-mei shakes off his hand and walks back to stand between Granny and Li.]

Sergeant: Where is the code?

Tieh-mei: I don't know.

Sergeant [looking at his watch]: Firing squad!

Li: There's no need for such a commotion. This is nothing much.

Granny: That's right, child, let's go together, the three of us.

Li: Tieh-mei, take Granny's other arm.

Tieh-mei: Right.

Li: Tieh-mei, mother, I'll lead the way. [He holds himself proudly.]

[They walk up the slope. Enter Hatoyama.]

Hatoyama: Wait! I want to give you every chance. You can have another minute to think it over.

Li: Hatoyama, you can never kill all the Chinese people or Chinese Communists. I advise you to think that over.

HATOYAMA [frustratedly to himself]: These Reds are the very devil. Carry out your orders. [Exit.]

SERGEANT: Shoot them!

[The three disappear from the slope followed by the sergeant and guards.]

LI [off]: Down with Japanese imperialism! Long live the Chinese Communist Party!

[Two shots are heard. Then two guards push TIEH-MEI back.]

TIEH-MEI [walking down the slope in a daze, turns to call]: Dad! Granny!

HATOYAMA [entering behind her, followed by HOU]: Where is the code book? Tell me quick.

[TIEH-MEI says nothing but stares at him with loathing.]

HATOYAMA: Here. Let her go.

HOU: What? Let her go? [He looks at HATOYAMA in surprise.]

HATOYAMA: Yes, let her go.

HOU: Very good, sir. [He grabs TIEH-MEI.] Get out, get out. [He pushes her away. Exit TIEH-MEI.] Why are you letting her off, sir?

HATOYAMA [smiling coldly]: If I kill them all, how can I find the code? This is called using a long line to catch a big fish.

SCENE 9

THE NEIGHBORS HELP

[Immediately after the last scene. LI's house. The door is sealed. The room is unchanged but wears an air of desolation.]

[TIEH-MEI walks slowly in. She stares at the house, quickens her steps and pushing the door open steps inside. She looks around, crying "Dad! Granny!" then rests her head on the table and sobs. Slowly rising, she sees the red lantern and picks it up.]

TIEH-MEI: Ah, red lantern, I've found you again but I shall never see Granny or Dad again. Granny, Dad, I know what you died for. I shall carry on your work. I've inherited the red lantern. That scoundrel Hatoyama has only let me go in the hope that I will lead them to the code. [Pause.] Never mind whether you arrest me or release me, you'll never get the code. [*She puts down the red lantern and smooths her hair.*]

> My heart is bursting with anger,
> I grind my teeth with rage;
> Hatoyama has tried every trick to get the code,
> He has killed my granny and dad.
> In desperation he threatened me,
> But I defy his threats,
> Nursing hatred in my heart;
> No cry shall escape me,
> No tears wet my cheeks,
> But the sparks of my smoldering fury
> Will blaze up in flames of anger
> To consume this black reign of night.
> Nothing can daunt me now:
> Arrest, release, torture, imprisonment. . . .
> I shall guard the code with my life.
> Wait, Hatoyama! This is Tieh-mei's answer.

[*She polishes the red lantern and rearranges her peddler's basket. Sadly.*] Granny, Dad, I'm leaving now. This isn't our home any more. Only the red lantern will be ours for ever. I promise to take the code to the north hills. I promise to avenge you. Don't you worry. [*She puts on her scarf and picks up the lantern and basket.*]

[Aunt Liu *and* Kuei-lan *have heard* Tieh-mei's *sobbing and slipped in through the hole in the wall.*]

Aunt Liu: Tieh-mei!

Tieh-mei: Aunty. Sister Kuei-lan.

Aunt Liu: Where are your dad and granny?

Tieh-mei: Aunty . . . . [*She leans her head on* Aunt Liu's *shoulder and cries.*]

Aunt Liu: I see. It'll soon be their turn, the devils. There's a spy outside, Tieh-mei, so you mustn't leave by the door. You can slip out again from our house. Hurry up now and change clothes with Kuei-lan.

Kuei-lan: Yes, quick. [*She takes off her jacket.*]

Tieh-mei: No, Aunty, Sister, I mustn't bring you into this.

Aunt Liu [*helping* Tieh-mei *to change*]: Tieh-mei,

> None but the poor will help the poor,
> Two bitter gourds grow on a single vine;

365

We must save you from the tiger's jaws,
And then you can press on.

TIEH-MEI: But what if something happens to you?

AUNT LIU: Tieh-mei, your people were good people. I may not understand much, but that I know. No matter how risky it is, I must see you safely away. [She weeps.]

TIEH-MEI: Aunty. [Kneels.]

[AUNT LIU hastily helps her up.]

KUEI-LAN: Go quickly. [Gives her the red lantern.]

TIEH-MEI: I shall never forget you, sister.

AUNT LIU: Hurry, child. [TIEH-MEI slips behind the curtain.] Be very careful, Kuei-lan. [AUNT LIU in turn leaves from behind the curtain.]

[KUEI-LAN wraps TIEH-MEI's scarf round her head and steps out of the door with the basket. Enemy agent C comes up and follows her. Enter the KNIFE-GRINDER. He is about to call out when he notices the agent trailing a girl who looks like TIEH-MEI. He follows them.]

SCENE 10

THE END OF THE RENEGADE

[Immediately after the last scene. The street.]

[Enter INSPECTOR WANG with two agents. A third agent comes in from the other side.]

THIRD AGENT: Inspector, I've lost Tieh-mei.

WANG: What?

THIRD AGENT: She got away.

WANG: You fool! [Slaps his face.] Well, she must be making for the north hills. Ring up Captain Hatoyama and ask him to send reinforcements to the road to the north hills. The rest of you come with me to catch her. I'll see that you don't escape me, Li Tieh-mei.

[Black-out. The scene changes to the north suburb of Lungtan and the road to the hills. Enter CHOU with three guerrillas.]

[Enter TIEH-MEI with the lantern. She greets the men.]

TIEH-MEI: Uncle Chou!

CHOU: Tieh-mei!

TIEH-MEI: At last I've found you. [*Cries.*] My granny and dad . . .

CHOU: We know. [*Pause.*] Don't give way. Take a grip on yourself. Have you got the code with you?

TIEH-MEI: Yes, I took it from under Short Bridge where I'd hidden it.

CHOU: Good.

[THE KNIFE-GRINDER *hurries in.*]

KNIFE-GRINDER: Old Chou. Ah, Tieh-mei, so you're here. How was it I missed you?

TIEH-MEI: It was thanks to the help of my neighbors, Uncle. Kuei-lan disguised herself as me and led the agent off on the wrong track so that I could get the code and bring it here.

KNIFE-GRINDER: So I was chasing the wrong girl.

CHOU: They'll start suspecting Kuei-lan's family now. [*To one of the guerrillas.*] Old Feng, go and help them move away at once.

FENG: Right. Just leave it to me. [*Exit.*]

[*The police car's siren is heard.*]

CHOU [*to the* KNIFE-GRINDER]: The enemy's coming, Old Chao. You deal with them while I take Tieh-mei to the north hills. [*Exit with* TIEH-MEI.]

KNIFE-GRINDER: Look, comrades, there aren't too many of them. I'll handle their leader. You take care of the rest.

GUERRILLAS: Right.

[*Enter* INSPECTOR WANG *with four enemy agents.*]

WANG: Now, where is Tieh-mei?

[THE KNIFE-GRINDER *kicks the pistol out of* WANG's *hand and they start fighting.* WANG *and the agents are killed. The police siren wails in the distance.*]

SCENE 11

THE TASK IS ACCOMPLISHED

[*The north hills, which rise steep and sheer. The guerrillas have formed a line stretching behind the hills. Halfway up the slope is a big red flag and scouts there are keeping a lookout.*]

[LIU *and other guerrilla officers come up the slope. Enter the* KNIFE-GRINDER. *He salutes* LIU *and points behind him.* CHOU *comes in with* TIEH-MEI. *A bugle blows.* TIEH-MEI *salutes* LIU *and gives him the code.*]

Curtain

NOTES

1. During the Japanese occupation the Chinese population in north-east China lived on acorn flour, a mixture of ground acorns and grain husks.

2. In North China it is customary to decorate windows with colored paper cutouts.

3. In Chinese folklore the magpie is a lucky bird, bringing good news.